WITHDRAWN

HARVARD LIBRARY

WITHDRAWN

EAST AND WEST IN THE CRUSADER STATES
Context — Contacts — Confrontations

III

ORIENTALIA LOVANIENSIA
ANALECTA
———— 125 ————

EAST AND WEST IN THE CRUSADER STATES

CONTEXT — CONTACTS — CONFRONTATIONS

III

Acta of the congress held at Hernen Castle in September 2000

EDITED BY

KRIJNIE CIGGAAR
and HERMAN TEULE

A.A. BREDIUS FOUNDATION

UITGEVERIJ PEETERS
LEUVEN — DUDLEY, MA
2003

Library of Congress Cataloging-in-Publication Data

East and West in the Crusader states: context, contacts, confrontations: acta of the congress held at Hernen Castle in September 2000 / edited by Krijnie Ciggaar and Herman Teule.
   p. cm. -- (Orientalia Lovaniensia analecta ; 125)
   A. A. Bredius Foundation
   ISBN 90-429-1287-1
   1. Latin Orient--Congresses. 2. Civilization, Medieval--Congresses.
3. Crusades--Congresses. 4. Christianity and other religions--Islam--Congresses. I. Ciggaar, Krijna N. II. Teule, Herman G. B.
III. A. A. Bredius Foundation. IV. Series.

D182.E19 2003
956'.014--dc21   2003042881

A.A. Bredius Foundation
Kasteel Hernen
NL-6616 AH Hernen

© Peeters Press
Bondgenotenlaan 153,
B-3000 Leuven (Belgium)

All rights reserved, including the right to translate or to reproduce this book or parts thereof in any form.

D. 2003/0602/45
ISBN 90-429-1287-1 (Peeters, Leuven)

CONTENTS

List of Illustrations VII
List of Contributors IX
Preface XI
Abbreviations XIII

Andrew Jotischky, Ethnographic Attitudes in the Crusader States: The Franks and the Indigenous Orthodox People 1

Krijnie Ciggaar, The Abbey of Prémontré — Royal Contacts, Royal News: The Context of the So-Called *Continuatio Praemonstratensis* 21

Johannes Pahlitzsch, Georgians and Greeks in Jerusalem (1099-1310) 35

Dorothea Weltecke, Contacts between Syriac Orthodox and Latin Military Orders 53

Mane Erna Shirinian, "The Letter of Love and Concord" between Rome and Armenia: A Case of Forgery from the Crusader Period 79

Herman Teule, Saint Louis and the East Syrians, the Dream of a Terrestrial Empire: East Syrian Attitudes to the West . . . 101

Jo Van Steenbergen, The Alexandrian Crusade (1365) and the Mamlūk Sources: Reassessment of the *kitāb al-ilmām* of an-Nuwayrī al-Iskandarānī 123

Rudolf Hiestand, Ein Zimmer mit Blick auf das Meer: Einige wenig beachtete Aspekte der Pilgerreisen ins Hl. Land im 12. und 13. Jahrhundert 139

W.J. Aerts, A Byzantine Traveller to one of the Crusader States . 165

D.M. Metcalf, East Meets West, and Money Changes Hands . . 223

Zuzana Skalova, The Icon of the Virgin *Galaktotrophousa* in the Coptic Monastery of St Antony the Great at the Red Sea, Egypt: A Preliminary Note 235

Mat Immerzeel, Divine Cavalry: Mounted Saints in Middle Eastern Christian Art 265

LIST OF ILLUSTRATIONS

(*Mat Immerzeel*, Divine Cavalry: Mounted Saints in Middle Eastern Christian Art, pp. 265-286)

Fig. 1. Distribution map of wall paintings (author).
Fig. 2. Qalamoun, church of Mar Marina: Saint Demetrius and scenes from the life of Saint Marina (Sader, *Painted Churches*, fig. 123).
Fig. 3. Mosaic from Olynthos: Bellerophon.
Fig. 4. Parchment leaf, Augustinermuseum, Freiburg.
Pl. 1. Qara, church of SS Sergius and Bacchus: Saint Theodore.
Pl. 2. Qara, church of SS Sergius and Bacchus: Saint Sergius.
Pl. 3. Deir Mar Musa al-Habashi: Saint Sergius (after Westphalen, "Wandmalereien"(see n. 2), p. 499).
Pl. 4. Monastery of Our Lady, Kaftoun: Virgin with the Child (*Icônes du Liban* (see n. 19), p. 21).
Pl. 5. Monastery of Our Lady, Kaftoun: Baptism (*Icônes du Liban* (see n. 19), p. 27).
Pl. 6. Monastery of Saint Catherine: SS Sergius and Bacchus.

(*Zuzana Skalova*, The Icon of the Virgin *Galaktotrophousa* in the Coptic Monastery of St Antony the Great at the Red Sea, Egypt: A Preliminary Note, pp. 235-264)

Text fig. 1. Monastery of St Antony, Old Church of St Antony with the chapel of the Four Creatures: ground plan (after P. Grossmann, in van Moorsel, *Les peintures du Monastère de Saint Antoine* (see n. 1), text fig. 13).
Text fig. 2. Monastery of St Antony, apse of the chapel of the Four Creatures: *Deesis* (drawing by P.-H. Laferrière in Van Moorsel, *Les peintures du Monastère de Saint Antoine* (see n. 1), text fig. 36, p. 168 ff.).
Fig. 1. Monastery of St Antony, the chapel of the Four Creatures: sanctuary screen with the Virgin *Galaktotrophousa* guarded by the Archangels Michael, Gabriel, Rafael and Suriel (photo Patric Goddeau, 2001. Courtesy of the American Research Center, Egypt).
Fig. 2a. Monastery of St Antony: the Virgin *Galaktotrophousa* (photo Adriano Luzi, 1999).

VIII LIST OF ILLUSTRATIONS

Fig. 2b. Monastery of St Antony: the Archangels Gabriel and Suriel (photo Adriano Luzi, 1999).

Fig. 2c. Monastery of St Antony: the Archangels Michael and Rafael (photo Adriano Luzi, 1999).

Fig. 3a. The Archangel Michael, New York, Pierpont Morgan Library MS 603 (after J. Leroy, *Les Manuscrits Coptes et Coptes-Arabes Illustrés* (Paris, 1974), fig. 30/2).

Fig. 3b. The *Galaktotrophousa*, tenth-century illumination in the Coptic MS in London, British Library, MS Oriental 6782, fol. 1v and New York, Pierpont Morgan Libr. MS 612, fol. 1v. (Leroy, *Manuscrits Coptes* (Paris, 1974), pl. 31). The scribe and illuminator was the Copt Isaq.

Fig. 4a. St Michael, thirteenth-century (?) mural on the south pillar in the nave of the church of the Virgin Mary, monastery of the Syrians, Wadi Natrun (photo Zuzana Skalova, 1998).

Fig. 4b. The *Galaktotrophousa*, mediaeval mural in the church of the Virgin, monastery of the Syrians, Wadi Natrun, rediscovered by the University of Leiden team, directed by K. Innemee, in the 1990s (photo Zuzana Skalova).

Fig. 5. The Enthroned Virgin holding the Child Christ and the Host, illumination from *Vitae Sanctorum*, Brussels, Bibliothèque Royale, MS II 2544, fol. 2v, inscribed SCA MARIA, dated 1220-1225. See Jeffrey M. Hamburger, *The Rothschild Canticles: Art and Mysticism in Flanders and the Rhineland circa 1300* (New Haven and London, 1990), p. 101, fig. 176.

Fig. 6. The Anastasis, fol. 156v, Syriac Lectionary, 1216-1220, tempera on paper, monastery of Mar Mattai (?) (after Evans and Wixum, *Glory of Byzantium* (see n. 46), cat. no. 254.

Fig. 7. The Nativity, thirteenth-century mural in the church of the Virgin, monastery of the Syrians, Wadi Natrun (photo Zuzana Skalova).

Fig. 8. The Archangels Michael and Gabriel (not yet cleaned and conserved) in the Old Church of the monastery of St Antony.

Fig. 9. St Theodore the Oriental, thirteenth-century mural in the nave of the Old Church of the monastery of St Antony (before cleaning, demonstrating an overpainting) (photo Cees Crena de Jongh/archives Paul van Moorsel Centre).

LIST OF CONTRIBUTORS

V. van Aalst, Curator of the A.A. Bredius Foundation, Hernen, the Netherlands; text-editor of the present volume.

W. Aerts, Emeritus Professor of Byzantine and New Greek Studies in the University of Groningen, the Netherlands.

K. Ciggaar, Dr of Mediaeval Studies, Byzantinist, Leiden, the Netherlands.

R. Hiestand, Emeritus Professor of Mediaeval History in the University of Düsseldorf, Germany.

M. Immerzeel, Director of the Paul van Moorsel Centre for Christian Art and Culture in the Middle East, Leiden, the Netherlands.

A. Jotischky, Lecturer of Mediaeval History, University of Lancaster, England.

D.M. Metcalf, until recently keeper of the Herberden Coin Room in the Ashmolean Museum and Professor of Numismatics in the University of Oxford, England.

J. Pahlitzsch, Dr of Mediaeval Studies, Byzantinist, Arabist, Göttingen, Germany.

E. Shirinian, Head of 'Ancient Armenian Literature' Department Mashtots', Matenadaran Mashtots', Yerevan, Armenia.

J. Van Steenbergen, Aspirant in Arabic Studies in the Catholic University of Leuven, Belgium, Department of Eastern and Slavic Studies.

Z. Skalova, former Director of the Foundation for the Conservation of Icons in the Middle East, Cairo, Egypt.

H. Teule, Director of the Institute of Eastern Christian Studies, Nijmegen; Professor of Eastern Christianity in the University of Nijmegen, the Netherlands.

D. Weltecke, Dr of Mediaeval Studies, wissenschaftliche Mitarbeiterin, Georg-August University, Göttingen, Germany.

PREFACE

The present volume is the third in a series of publications containing the *acta* of symposia on different aspects of the relations between East and West in the Crusader States organised by the A.A. Bredius Foundation and held at Hernen Castle, the Netherlands. The first meeting took place in 1993,[1] the second in 1997[2] and the third in September 2000.

The aim of our symposia is to bring together scholars studying texts, works of art and other material belonging to the different communities (Christian and Muslim, eastern and western) affected by the crusader phenomenon. In the first section — with articles by Andrew Jotischky on the ethnographic attitudes of the Franks towards the Orthodox and Krijnie Ciggaar with a study on the *Continuatio Praemonstratensis*, the chronicle composed by Sigebert of Gembloux —, the reader will find the western, Latin perspective.

More clearly than on previous occasions, in the second section, the floor is taken by the various indigenous Christian communities. It contains articles on the Greeks and Georgians in Jerusalem (Johannes Pahlitzsch), on the contacts between the West Syrians and the Latin military orders (Dorothea Weltecke) on the *apocryphal* Armenian Letter of Love and Concord by Erna Shirinian and on a *genuine* East Syrian Letter of Love and other East-Syrian theological texts by Herman Teule. The Islamic perspective is dealt with by Jo Van Steenbergen in his article about the Mamluk sources on the Alexandrian Crusade.

The next section contains two studies on different travel reports characterized by strong personal and even intimate observations. Rudolf Hiestand concentrates on the day-to-day problems of pilgrims in the Holy Land, whereas Wim Aerts studies the dreams and "guidebook" of the Byzantine scholar, author and metropolitan Konstantinos Manasses who, in his poem *Hodoiporikon*, relates his journey to crusader territory. Aerts also presents the first English translation of this poem.

---

[1] *East and West in the Crusader States: Context-Contacts-Confrontations*, I , ed. Krijnie Ciggaar, Adelbert Davids and Herman Teule, Orientalia Lovaniensia Analecta, 75 (Leuven, 1996).

[2] *East and West in the Crusader States: Context-Contacts-Confrontations*, II, ed. Krijnie Ciggaar and Herman Teule, Orientalia Lovaniensia Analecta, 92 (Leuven, 1999).

As in the previous volumes, the concluding section is devoted to crafts and arts. D.M. Metcalf discusses how East meets West when money changes hands, Suzanna Skalova analyses the different cultural and spiritual influences — including Latin ones – on a Coptic Icon of the Virgin *Galaktotrophousa* in the monastery of Saint Antony, and Mat Immerzeel analyzes the pictures of the mounted saints, of whom St George in particular made a deep impression on the crusaders.

This symposium could not have taken place without the hospitality and the generous financial and practical support of the A.A. Bredius Foundation. Our thanks are therefore particularly due to the Board of the foundation. We would also like to thank Prof. Robert Thomson (Oxford) for his assistence and Mrs Ania Lentz-Michaelis and Mrs Angela Needham for correcting the greater part of the texts.

This symposium on the theme East and West in the Crusader States was certainly not the last. Preparations for the next meeting are under way. It will focuss on Antioch in the period from the Byzantine reconquest in 969 to the fall of the crusader principality, and will take place in May 2003.

December 2002, Victoria van Aalst
Krijnie Ciggaar
Herman Teule

ABBREVIATIONS

CSCO Corpus scriptorum christianorum orientalium.
DOP Dumbarton Oaks Papers.
EI² *The Encyclopedia of Islam*, vols 1- (Leiden and London, 1960² -).
East and West in the Crusader States
I = *East and West in the Crusader States: Context-Contacts-Confrontations*, ed. K. Ciggaar, A. Davids and H. Teule, Orientalia Lovaniensia Analecta, 75 (Leuven, 1996);
II = *East and West in the Crusader States: Context-Contacts-Confrontations*, ed. K. Ciggaar and H. Teule, Orientalia Lovaniensia Analecta, 92 (Leuven, 1999).
Hamilton, *Latin Church*
  Bernard Hamilton, *The Latin Church in the Crusader States: The Secular Church* (London, 1980).
Jacques de Vitry, *Historia orientalis*
  Jacques de Vitry, *Historia orientalis*, ed. F. Moschus (Douai, 1597; reprint Farnborough, 1971).
MGH Monumenta Germaniae historica.
MGH SS Monumenta Germaniae historica: Scriptores, 32 vols (Hanover, 1826-1934).
OCP *Orientalia Christiana Periodica*.
Or. Chr. Oriens Christianus.
PL Patrologiae cursus completus, Series latina, ed. J.-P. Migne, 221 vols (Paris, 1904-).
PO Patrologia orientalis, ed. R. Graffin and F. Nau (Paris, 1904-).
RHC Recueil des historiens des croisades (Paris, 1841-1906).
RHC Occ. RHC: Historiens occidentaux, 5 vols in 8 parts (Paris, 1844-1895).
RHC Or. RHC: Historiens orientaux, 5 vols in 6 parts (Paris, 1872-1906).
William of Tyre, *Chronicon*
  William of Tyre, *Chronicon / Historia rerum in partibus transmarinis gestarum*, ed. R.B.C. Huygens (Turnhout, 1986).

ETHNOGRAPHIC ATTITUDES IN THE CRUSADER STATES

THE FRANKS AND THE INDIGENOUS ORTHODOX PEOPLE*

ANDREW JOTISCHKY

The crusader conquest of the Holy Land created a new ethnic, religious and social balance in the Levant. Exactly what Urban II, the instigator of the crusade, intended for the longer-term future of the peoples whom he wished to liberate, remains uncertain. At any rate, however, he could scarcely have countenanced the scenes of destruction in Jerusalem in July 1099. Probably he intended the Orthodox and other indigenous Christians to retain their positions in the shrines and to maintain their churches as before, with the proviso that they recognise papal authority. This may have been the substance of negotiations conducted between Urban, his legate Adhemar of Le Puy and Symeon II, patriarch of Jerusalem.[1] The death of Adhemar in 1098 and of Symeon, who had been exiled by the Fatimids to Cyprus, and of Urban himself in 1099, forestalled any such arrangement.[2]

After 1099, the Frankish settlers encountered groups of indigenous Christians whose existence had scarcely impinged on western consciousness before the late eleventh century. These Christians must have been incomprehensible to most of the Franks. They resembled in manners, dress and speech the Muslim targets of the crusade, while their beliefs and ritual, though Christian, were Greek Orthodox, or even more exotic.

The place occupied by the indigenous Christians in the new Latin state has been considered by most historians within the wider framework of a long-running debate over colonialism. The prevailing view among Francophile historians of the Crusader States since the nineteenth century, such as Madelin and Grousset, has been that the Franks succeeded in integrating with the indigenous society and in creating a hybrid Frankish/Oriental culture. Exponents of this historiographical tradition have emphasized the tolerance shown to indigenous peoples, Christians

---

* For the abbreviations used in the footnotes see the end of this article.
[1] Hamilton, *Latin Church*, pp. 4-8.
[2] Albert of Aix, *Historia Hierosolymitana*, VI, 39, RHC Occ., IV, p. 489, reports the death of Symeon just before the capture of Jerusalem.

and Muslims alike, in the matter of religious worship.[3] The opposing view is best summarized by Joshua Prawer: "The attitude of the Crusader States is explained by colonial pragmatism, which overruled all other possible approaches and recognized a caste of native inferiors."[4] Prawer identified this colonial pragmatism most explicitly in the laws of the Crusader Kingdom, in which ethnicity, rather than religion, defined one's status. All Franks were classed above natives, whatever their status might have been in the West, and no distinction was made in law between the religious affiliation of the natives.[5] Scholars from other fields, such as the historian of Russia, Charles Halperin, have borrowed from this view to see the Crusader States as a classical example of a "frontier society" in which the fate of the indigenous peoples is determined by the adversarial position of the powers on each side of the frontier.[6]

In part, the question depends on one's perception not simply of what constituted a distinct "society" in the period of the crusades, but of how societies are themselves constructed. Comparisons with other acts of conquest and settlement contemporaneous with the First Crusade, such as the Norman invasions of Sicily and England, can be useful in a general way, if distracting in their particular differences. At a fundamental level, however, what defines the "overlapping networks of social interaction" that sociologists identify as the bases of social power, is the relationship — the "cleavage", in the words of Michael Mann —, between those networks themselves and their environment, both human and physical.[7] If we think of the Crusader States as such overlapping networks,

---

[3] For example, R. Grousset, *Histoire des croisades et du royaume franc de Jérusalem* (Paris, 1934-6), p. 287, speaks of "une nation franco-syrienne". For a summary of these views, see R.C. Smail, *Crusading Warfare 1097-1193* (Cambridge, 1956), pp. 40-6.

[4] J. Prawer, *The Latin Kingdom of Jerusalem: European Colonialism in the Middle Ages* (London, 1972), p. 232; also p. 230: "If the crucial test of human endeavour is the comparison of aims and results, the policy of the crusaders towards oriental Christendom was a total failure"; and pp. 503-33; idem, "The Roots of Medieval Colonialism", in *The Meeting of Two Worlds: Cultural Exchange between East and West during the Period of the Crusades*, ed. V.P. Goss (Kalamazoo, 1986), pp. 23-38. A critique of both colonial and "integrationist" models is given by R. Ellenblum, *Frankish Rural Settlement in the Latin Kingdom of Jerusalem* (Cambridge, 1998), pp. 3-41.

[5] J. Prawer, "Social Classes in the Crusader States: the Franks", in *History of the Crusades*, general ed. K. Setton, v, *The Impact of the Crusades on the Near East*, ed. N.P. Zacour and H.W. Hazard (Madison, Wis., 1985), pp. 119-21.

[6] C. Halperin, "The Ideology of Silence: Prejudice and Pragmatism on the Medieval Frontier", *Comparative Studies in Society and History*, 26 (1984), pp. 455-9.

[7] M. Mann, *The Sources of Social Power*, I, *A History of Power from the Beginning to AD 1760* (Cambridge, 1986), p. 13.

encompassing at given moments, political, economic, or religious realities, then it must be obvious that the degree of "colonialism" in the Frankish interaction with the indigenous peoples defies a simple characterization. Historians, however, look at societies as dynamic, rather than static constructions, and one of the problems in reaching a definition about crusader "colonialism" is that the answer depends on when, as well as where, one looks. Frankish attitudes toward the indigenous peoples changed, and vice versa: Usāma ibn Munqid famously observed that the longer a Frank had lived in the East, the more civilized he became.[8]

One of the distinctive features of most of the writing about the indigenous people has been the assumption that they can easily be divided into neat categories.[9] The most obvious such division is a religious one, between Muslims and Christians. The indigenous Christians are then subdivided further according to religious confession: Greek Orthodox, Syrian Orthodox, Armenian, Georgian. A closer look at these divisions, however, reveals the difficulty in defining identities among the native population. The most numerous group of indigenous Christians was Greek Orthodox in confession, but among these a further distinction must be made between the ethnic Greeks of Antioch and the much larger number of Arabic-speaking Orthodox in the Kingdom of Jerusalem itself. Culturally, these Christians were Arab, and scarcely distinguishable in dress and manners from the Muslims; but ethnically they were native to what had once been the Roman provinces of Palestine and Syria. They were Greek Orthodox, but not Greek; Arabic-speaking, but not Muslim; Christian inhabitants of a Christian state, yet subject to the rule of conquerors.

Even the vocabulary of reference to the indigenous Christians is a source of confusion. The Arabic-speaking Orthodox were known in Arabic sources as "Melkites", a nomenclature that was taken up by nineteenth-century European scholars. The Frankish sources, however, usually call them *Suriani*, Syrians, when referring to their activities or status as an ethnic group, and *Graeci*, Greeks, when speaking of religious confession. Both definitions invite confusion. Calling them "Syrians" may mislead one to group them with a different religious affiliation, and one to which only a minority of the native Christians belonged — the Syrian

---

[8] *Memoirs of an Arab-Syrian Gentleman, or an Arab Knight in the Crusades*, trans. P.K. Hitti (Beirut, 1964), p. 163.

[9] For example, Smail, *Crusading Warfare* (see n. 3), pp. 40-63; Prawer, "Social Classes in the Crusader States: The 'Minorities'", in *History of the Crusades*, ed. Setton, v (see n. 5), pp. 65-70.

Orthodox Church, known to westerners as the Jacobite Church. Calling them "Greeks" may accurately reflect their religious confession, but hardly their ethnicity or status within the ecclesiology of the Levant.

The marginal position occupied by the native Orthodox is exemplified by the relationship between bishops and their flock in the ecclesiastical establishment. The expulsion of Orthodox bishops from their sees by the crusaders after 1099, and their replacement by Latins, has been cited as an example of the colonial oppression of the indigenous religious identity.[10] Yet the bishops who went into exile returned, as far as we can judge, whence they had come — to Constantinople.[11] The pre-crusade bishops were not, so far as we know, members of the indigenous Orthodox community, but Greeks, selected for appointment to their sees by the patriarch of Constantinople from among the higher clergy of the Byzantine Empire. An ethnic and linguistic division was thus observed within the Orthodox Church between the bishops and their flock.

Given the fluidity between their ethnic and religious identities, the vocabulary of margins offers an alternative model to that of colonialism by which to understand the Latin attitude to the native Christians. In what follows, I will use three Latin sources, ranging in date from 1168/87 to 1283, to explore further some of the conceptual difficulties encountered by Franks in understanding the Christians under their rule, and to ask what such categorization of the native Christians can tell us about the nature of crusader society.

From the last quarter of the twelfth century onward, western pilgrimage accounts tend to include brief passages on the contemporary inhabitants of the Holy Land. The earliest such passage occurs in the anonymous *Tractatus de locis et statu sancte terre*, written probably 1168/1187.[12] It begins by describing the Franks, or Latins: "a warlike

---

[10] E.g. J. Pahlitzsch, "The Greek Orthodox Church in the First Kingdom of Jerusalem", in *Patterns of the Past, Prospects for the Future: The Christian Heritage of the Holy Land*, ed. T. Hummel, K. Hintlian and U. Carmesund (London, 1999), pp. 199-200.

[11] Hamilton, *Latin Church*, pp. 7, 16, for Symeon II and John the Oxite, patriarch of Antioch; and pp. 159-60 for the general situation. John VIII, who had been bishop of Tyre, fled to crusader Jerusalem in 1105 when he was ejected from his city by the Fatimids. Although elected patriarch of Jerusalem by the native Orthodox, in 1106/7 he went to live in Constantinople, probably because of the anti-Latin treatises he wrote around that time, J. Pahlitzsch, "Die Bedeutung der Azymenfrage für die Beziehung zwischen griechisch-orthodoxer und lateinischer Kirche in den Kreuzfahrerstaaten", in *Die Folgen der Kreuzzüge für die orientalischen Religionsgemeinschaften*, ed. W. Beltz, Hallesche Beiträge zur Orientwissenschaft, 22 (Halle, 1996), pp. 75-92.

[12] Kedar, "The *Tractatus*", pp. 111-33, with the edition of the *Tractatus* from British Library Royal MS 14.C. X at pp. 123-31.

people, trained in the use of arms, who go about bare-headed and alone among all people shave their beards. They are called Latins because they use the Latin language and profess obedience to the Roman Church. They are pure Catholics."[13] This lapidary description sets a kind of standard according to which the other peoples can be judged. The Armenians, for example, are quite well trained in war, but disagree with both Latins and Greeks on matters of religious custom. They use their own language. The Georgians are highly skilled in war and cultivate flowing beards. Both clerics and laymen wear hats, though of different shapes. They imitate the Greeks in religious custom, but use their own language. The Syrians (Arabic-speaking Orthodox) are described as useless in war, wearing beards but not in the Greek fashion. In matters of religion they are halfway between the Latins and Greeks, but follow Greek custom and belief. They use Arabic as a spoken language, but Greek in their liturgy. Everywhere they are found, they pay tribute to some other power.[14]

This list of ethnic and religious characterizations is found, with only slight variations, in dozens of copies over the next hundred years. So close are they textually that the most recent research by Benjamin Kedar has demonstrated that they are variants of the same original rather than different pilgrimage accounts.[15] The *Tractatus* was not the first text to describe these characteristics of ethnic groups in the Levant. William of Tyre, for example, characteristically describes the Greeks as "effeminate", "prone to giving ambiguous answers", and compares them to snakes.[16] But William uses these pejorative adjectives in the context of a narrative in which he judges them appropriate. The *Tractatus* seems to initiate a genre of systematic categorization of ethnic and religious groups according to characteristics with which those groups were already associated. About a hundred years after the *Tractatus*, the *Descriptio Terrae Sanctae* by Burchard of Mount Sion (1280-3) clearly borrows from this tradition.[17] Burchard devotes a section of his account

---

[13] *Tractatus*, p. 124.
[14] *Tractatus*, pp. 124-5.
[15] Kedar, "The *Tractatus*", pp. 111-22.
[16] William of Tyre, *Chronicon*, XVII, 17, XXII, 12 (effeminate); XVIII, 22, 31 (ambiguous answers); XXII, 13 (snakes), pp. 785, 843, 856-7, 1021, 1024.
[17] Burchard of Mount Sion, *Descriptio Terrae Sanctae*, in *Peregrinatores medii aevi quatuor*, ed. J.C.M. Laurent (Leipzig, 1864), discussed by A. Grabois, "Christian Pilgrims in the Thirteenth Century and the Latin Kingdom of Jerusalem: Burchard of Mount Sion", in *Outremer: Studies in the History of the Crusading Kingdom of Jerusalem*, ed. B.Z. Kedar, H.E. Mayer and R.C. Smail (Jerusalem, 1982), pp. 285-96. An old tradition, as reported in Aubrey Stewart's translation of Burchard for the Palestine Pilgrims Text Society, 12 (1896), IV, has it that he spent ten years in the Holy Land, but Grabois makes no mention of this.

to the constituent peoples of the Holy Land. Of the native Orthodox (*Suriani*), he remarks:

> "The whole land is full of these people. They are Christians, but keep no faith with the Latins. They dress wretchedly; they are mean and give no alms. They live among Muslims and are often their servants. They are indistinguishable in dress from the Muslims, except that they wear a woollen girdle."[18]

The most fully developed version of this genre is found in the *Historia orientalis* of Jacques de Vitry, written in stages from 1219 to 1226, during the period when he was bishop of Acre.[19] Jacques was better informed about the theological positions represented by religious customs than most other exponents of the genre. When he berates the native Orthodox for using leavened bread in the Eucharist, he is able to denounce not simply custom but the Orthodox theology from which the custom derived. However, the conceptual link in Jacques' mind between religious custom and belief is not always clear. Jacques despises the Jacobites, for example, for practising circumcision, for failure to use auricular confession, and for branding the sign of the cross on their children's heads or arms, but these customs have little to do with the theological origins of the Jacobite Church or the Monophysite beliefs that Jacques proceeds to criticise.[20]

Confusion between ethnic custom and theology also characterises the *Tractatus*. This, for example, is the description of the Greeks:

> "They are divided from the Roman Church; they are clever men, but insufficiently trained in war, for which they carry long spears; they are wrong about the articles of faith, notably in saying that the Holy Spirit proceeds not from the Father and Son but only from the Father, and they offer Mass with leavened bread, and err in many other ways. They have their own language."[21]

It is not easy to unpick the tightly-knit strands of this description in order to arrive at a conceptual understanding of the basis of western prejudices against the native peoples. It is clear, however, that one index of ethnicity was theological belief or confessional affiliation. Adherence to the Roman Church, for example, was the index commonly used by William of Tyre to define the Frankish inhabitants of the Levant, who are called *Latini* rather than *Franci*.[22] That a theological tradition should

---

[18] Burchard of Mount Sion, *Descriptio Terrae Sanctae* (see n. 17), p. 89.
[19] Jacques de Vitry, *Historia orientalis*.
[20] Jacques de Vitry, *Historia orientalis*, LXXVI, 145.
[21] *Tractatus*, p. 124.
[22] A.V. Murray, "Ethnic Identity in the Crusader States: The Frankish Race and the Settlement of Outremer", in *Concepts of National Identity in the Middle Ages*, ed. S. Forde, L. Johnson and A.V. Murray, Leeds Texts and Monographs, New Series 14

have been understood as the index of religious custom is not surprising; but the linkage in the author's mind to ethnic customs is more difficult to grasp.

Perhaps the most obvious point to make about these texts is that the characterization of the Arabic-speaking Christians is universally negative. Something can be found to say in praise of each of the other groupings: they are pious, or astute, or effective fighters. The native Orthodox, in contrast, are described only in order to be criticized: they are poor fighters, their appearance is wretched, they are servile, mean, duplicitous. So much is obvious even from a cursory reading of the texts. When we examine the categories according to which the native peoples are characterized, it becomes possible to arrange them into a kind of "taxonomy of otherness". Such a taxonomy is in no way intended to represent an authoritative reading of these texts, but is offered rather as an illustration of my use of the term "marginal" to describe western perceptions of the native Orthodox people. When the texts are tabulated in this way, the key to the Melkites' position appears to depend on contrast. The category of language can serve as an example. All three sources remark on the use of a national or ethnic language for both liturgical and everyday usage by Greeks, Armenians, Jacobites and Georgians; the Melkites, in contrast, use one language for the liturgy and another in everyday usage.[23] The point made by dual language usage is reinforced by the discussion of theological status. All the other groups can be described as heretical or schismatic, in varying degrees. The Melkites are characterized by both the *Tractatus* and Jacques de Vitry as vacillating in religious beliefs. According to Jacques, they profess obedience to their Latin prelates, but this is skin-deep only, and their theology remains entirely Greek Orthodox. Their religious customs, likewise, are mostly Greek, for example using leavened bread in the Eucharist; at the same time, however, they keep Saturday as their holy day, a custom borrowed

(Leeds, 1995), p. 61. This was true within the Orthodox world as well as the Latin: when the Byzantine delegates to the Council of Lyons returned home, having agreed to a formula for the union of the Churches, they were abused with cries of "You have become Franks!", H. Laurent, *Le Bienheureux Innocent V (Pierre de Tarentaise) et son temps* (Vatican, 1947), pp. 424-5.

[23] Jacques de Vitry, *Historia orientalis,* LXXV, 139 (Greeks and Melkites); LXXVI, 148 (Jacobites); LXXIX, 153-4 (Armenians); *Tractatus,* pp. 124-5; Burchard of Mount Sion, *Descriptio Terrae Sanctae* (see n. 17), pp. 91-2. This observation is only partially accurate, since Syriac was also used by some Melkite communities in the Holy Land. The use of separate languages for liturgical and everyday purposes was also, of course, characteristic of the Franks!

from the Jews.[24] The native Orthodox thus appear to live on the margins of other traditions.

This marginal position is put into sharper relief when we consider the political status of the different groups. The Armenians, Georgians and even Jacobites are characterized as occupying their own territory — in the case of the Armenians and Georgians, with the capacity to defend it by force of arms.[25] The Melkites stand alone as a people described as "servile", and "everywhere they live, tributaries of other people". The same was in fact true of the Jacobites, but Jacques de Vitry is able to assert that they occupy their own lands, because he knows that they are more concentrated in northeast Syria than in the crusaders' territory.[26]

One category that is only implicit in this taxonomy is that of ethnicity. The Greeks, Armenians and Georgians had separate ethnic identities, and these identities are recognised in the sources by their use of distinctive languages and appearance. Even the Jacobites are called by Jacques de Vitry, with some exaggeration, a "nation" — presumably, following his assertion that they occupy north-eastern Syria.[27] The Melkites alone constitute neither a nation nor a separate ethnic group, and the fact that they are scattered throughout the Near East as subjects of stronger peoples reflects this. The Melkites' political and ethnic status is thus framed in moral terms — they are "servile" because they have no lands of their own; concomitantly, they adopt language, customs and even beliefs from stronger, ethnically distinctive peoples. The political circumstances under which the native Orthodox live — as subject peoples without sovereign status of their own — is deliberately elided with the moral criticism of their customs, characteristics and even dual language usage.

This point becomes more acute when we recall the increasing importance in the West of the *origines gentium* tradition. Alan Murray has recently argued that twelfth-century western chronicles of the crusades can be read as part of a genre in which myths of national origins are articulated. "What writers such as Fulcher of Chartres and William of Tyre give us in their accounts of the crusade and the Frankish settlement is the history of a people in the making."[28] Experiences, and their retelling, serve as the historical basis for forging a new Frankish identity. Murray argues that Fulcher's use of the word *Francus* represents the

[24] Jacques de Vitry, *Historia orientalis*, LXXV, pp. 139, 142, 143-4.
[25] Jacques de Vitry, *Historia orientalis*, LXXX, p. 156 (Georgians); *Tractatus*, p. 124 (Armenians).
[26] Jacques de Vitry, *Historia orientalis*, LXXV, p. 137; LXXVI, p. 144.
[27] Jacques de Vitry, *Historia orientalis*, LXXVI, p. 144.
[28] Murray, "Ethnic Identity" (see n. 22), p. 70.

recoining of what had been an ethnically specific term for people deriving from a particular region of Europe, and its transfer to a new arena of experience. This argument is further supported by Marcus Bull's reading of the chronicles of the First Crusade, in which the use of "*Franc*-stems" (*Franci, Francigeni*) is all the more telling because of the genuine and strongly felt cultural differences between the crusade armies.[29] The self-perception of the Franks had originally derived from the myth, recorded if not invented by the seventh-century chronicler Fredegar, that they were descended from the Trojans.[30] The Franks in the Crusader States, however, formed "a race distinct from the diverse national elements from which they had sprung".[31] As Murray has noted, one component of medieval ethnogenesis was the motif of arrival and settlement in new lands, after hazardous travel from distant places. This was obviously true of the crusaders themselves, but even the Turkish enemy could be credited with such an ethnogenesis, as recounted by William of Tyre in the chapter of his chronicle entitled "De ortu et prima origine gentis Turcorum".[32] Moreover, Jacques de Vitry's location of the Jacobites' homeland throughout Asia "et totius tractus orientalis", and the Armenians' obvious place of origin in a land named for them, grants to these peoples a measure of the same ethnic integrity.[33] Such an identity, whether based on a real or invented history, was denied to the native

[29] M. Bull, "Overlapping and Competing Identities in the Frankish First Crusade", in *Le concile de Clermont et l'appel à la croisade*, Collection de l'école française de Rome, 236 (Rome, 1997), pp. 195-211, quoting for example Ralph of Caen, *Gesta Tancredi in expeditione Hierosolymitana*, RHC Occ., III (Paris, 1866), p. 651, criticising the Provençals for their failure to act *ut Franci*.

[30] *Chronicarum quae dicitur Fredgarii Scholastici libri IV, cum Continuationibus*, MGH, Scriptores rerum Merovingicarum, II (1888), pp. 46, 93; J.M. Wallace-Hadrill, *The Long-Haired Kings* (London, 1962), pp. 79-83. The extensive literature on the development of ethnic and national self-consciousness in the early Middle Ages includes H. Wolfram, "Einleitung oder Überlegungen zur Origo Gentis", in *Typen der Ethnogenese unter besonderer Berücksichtigung der Bayern*, ed. H. Wolfram and W. Pohl, 2 vols (Vienna, 1990), I, 19-33; idem, "Le genre de l'*origo gentis*", *Revue belge de philologie et d'histoire*, 68 (1990), pp. 789-801; H-D. Kahl, "Einige Beobachtungen zum Sprachgebrauch von *natio* im mittelalterlichen Latein mit Ausblicken auf das neuhochdeutsche Fremdwort 'Nation'", in *Aspekte der Nationenbildung im Mittelalter*, ed. H. Beumann and W. Schröder (Sigmaringen, 1978), pp. 65-8; see also S. Reynolds, "Medieval *origines gentium* and the Community of the Realm", *History*, 68 (1983), pp. 375-90.

[31] Murray, "Ethnic Identity" (see n. 22), p. 70.

[32] Murray, "Ethnic Identity" (see n. 22), pp. 66-9; William of Tyre, *Chronicon*, I, 7-10, pp. 114-24. See also the critical comments of Walter Goffart on the longevity of the "rhetoric of movement" tradition in the historiography of the Germanic peoples, "The Theme of '*The* Barbarian Invasions' in Late Antique and modern Historiography", in idem, *Rome's Fall and After* (London, 1989), pp. 114-6.

[33] Jacques de Vitry, *Historia orientalis*, LXXVI, p. 144.

Orthodox people, because no distinctive national origin could be found for them — they are, instead, "tributaries of other people", and only the etymological derivation of *Surianus* from *Sur* (Tyre) betrays any geographical roots.[34]

Ethnic identity is allowed, in this genre of description, to determine religious practice. Customs that deviated from the Roman norm were understandable if they derived from distinct liturgical and theological traditions, because such traditions were themselves indices of an ethnic identity. Thus the Armenians, who possessed their own distinctive language, dress and customs, were highly regarded, despite the collapse of their union with the Roman Church and the refusal of most Armenians to abandon Monophysite doctrines.[35] In contrast, the native Orthodox, though members of the same Church as the Latins, were despised because their religious customs did not appear to derive from the same root as their ethnicity.

It is the failure to achieve a distinct ethnic or religious identity that appears to determine the moral and intellectual failings assigned to the native Orthodox by Jacques de Vitry. Thus, immediately after his explanation of why the Melkites are called Syrians, Jacques gives us an insight into their character:

> "They are for the most part untrustworthy, duplicitous, and like the Greeks, as cunning as foxes. They lie and are inconsistent and treacherous, and easily seduced by bribes. They say one thing but think another; and they take robbery and theft for granted. For trifling sums of money they betray the secrets of the Christians to the Muslims, among whom they have been brought up, whose language they speak, and whose perverse customs they mostly imitate."[36]

Some of this prejudice can be understood in rhetorical terms. William of Tyre's characterization of Greeks as treacherous is taken direct from Virgil; elsewhere he uses an epithet from Juvenal.[37] The classical her-

---

[34] Jacques de Vitry, *Historia orientalis*, LXXV, p. 137.

[35] Jacques de Vitry, *Historia orientalis*, LXXIX, pp. 153-5, comments on the different customs of Armenians with regard to the Eucharist, baptism and the celebration of Christmas, but without the rancour reserved for the Melkites; he observes, moreover, that they were permitted to retain their own customs when they promised obedience to Rome. Burchard of Mount Sion, *Descriptio Terrae Sanctae* (see n. 17), pp. 91-3, commends the piety and austerity of the Armenian clergy. On the Armenians and the union with Rome, see B. Hamilton, "The Armenian Church and the Papacy at the Time of the Crusades", *Eastern Churches Review*, 10 (1978), pp. 61-87.

[36] Jacques de Vitry, *Historia orientalis*, LXXV, pp. 137-8.

[37] P.W. Edbury and J.G. Rowe, *William of Tyre: Historian of the Latin East* (Cambridge, 1988), pp. 32-8, cast some doubt on William's familiarity with some classical sources.

itage was rich in ethnographical observation about the morals, character and practices of "orientals". The Syrians, Cicero observed, were "natural slaves".[38] Their ethnic character is variously summed up in classical writing as "rascally", "fickle", "disloyal" and "shrewd"[39] — all of which find echoes in Jacques de Vitry's labels "faithless", "two-faced", "as cunning as wolves", "lying", and "treacherous".[40] Classical Roman observation of orientals' martial prowess was strikingly similar to the criticism made by the *Tractatus* and Jacques de Vitry. The Romans' judgement that effeteness made them unfit for war is found again in the laconic phrase "armis inutiles" of the *Tractatus*, and in Jacques' remark "in battle they are as useless as women". Jacques commented unfavourably, as had Roman sources, on the oriental preference for the bow and arrow over the more manly weapons of close encounter.[41] More striking is the conceptual connection made by both Roman and medieval writers between oriental weakness of character and their customary form of government. Jacques' observation that the native Orthodox have always been subject peoples to stronger powers seems to follow the judgement of Lucan that the Syrians' feebleness in war is the result of long subservience to the rule of kings.[42] Roman authors also commented on the mannerliness of the orientals compared to westerners, a trait that may be what Jacques had in mind when he criticised the native Orthodox for saying one thing while thinking another.[43]

Was Jacques, or even the author of the *Tractatus*, aware of this classical tradition? In the matter of warfare, at any rate, we need not suppose so, for even a cursory observation would have sufficed to inform a medieval critic of the prevalence of bow and arrow in the East. Not all the classical authors cited here would have been familiar to a conventional product of the Paris schools such as Jacques de Vitry; it may be, indeed, that Roman attitudes were simply not so very different from those of medieval Europeans.

[38] J.P.V.D. Balsdon, *Romans and Aliens* (London, 1979), p. 66, citing Cicero, *De provinciis consularibus*, X.
[39] Cassius Dio, *Roman History*, 77, 10, 2; Herodian, *De imperio post Marcum*, II, vii, 9; III, xi, 8, *Script. rerum Aug. Aurel.*, 31.1.
[40] Jacques de Vitry, *Historia orientalis*, LXXV, p. 137.
[41] Balsdon, *Romans and Aliens* (see n. 38), p. 61, citing *Pan. Lat.*, XII, v, 3 and XXIV, i ("timidi et imbelles"); *Tractatus*, p. 124; Jacques de Vitry, *Historia orientalis*, LXXV, p. 137.
[42] Jacques de Vitry, *Historia orientalis*, LXXV, p. 137; Lucan, *Pharsalia*, VII. 442.3. This is a judgement made even by modern historians; cf. Tenney Frank, *An Economic History of Rome* (London, 1927²), pp. 217-8.
[43] Balsdon, *Romans and Aliens* (see n. 38), p. 62; Jacques de Vitry, *Historia orientalis*, LXXV, p. 137.

If a debt to a classical tradition is noticeable, it may lie rather in the generic idea of describing other races than in specific points of comparison. There were other, more recent models for this kind of writing, though not necessarily closer at hand for Jacques de Vitry. Professor Kedar has observed that the genre in which the *Tractatus* should be placed is not that of pilgrimage literature but rather of ethnogaphic reports of exotic lands and their inhabitants.[44] When we look at the chapters in Jacques' *Historia orientalis* immediately following the description of the peoples of the Holy Land, we find accounts of natural marvels, the flora and fauna and miraculous properties of the land itself. Moreover the description of the native peoples themselves offers comparisons and contrasts with ethnographic writing of a generation earlier, notably by Gerald of Wales about the Welsh and Irish, and by Adam of Bremen about the Scandinavians. On the surface, these northern European ethnographic observations share little with Jacques' view of the native Orthodox. The northern natives are barbarous, but their barbarism is characterised by social violence, ferocity in war and pastoralism rather than agriculture. In contrast, Jacques describes the Melkites as "altogether unwarlike, and as helpless as women in battle", and says that they were kept as tributaries specifically to work the land.[45]

It is when we turn to religious identities that conceptual similarities become apparent. For although the Celts and Scandinavians were Christians, they were perceived as occupying the margins of Christianity. They not only lived on the edges of the world; they occupied a spiritual penumbra. According to William of Malmesbury, Urban II dismissed the idea that "people who live on distant islands in the frozen ocean... in the manner of beasts" could be Christians.[46] Similarly, St Bernard says of the Irish that they are "Christian in name, but pagan in fact", and John of Salisbury describes the Welsh as "rude and untamed, living like animals and despising the word of life; they nominally profess Christ but deny him in their life and customs".[47] Ethnic customs permeated

[44] Kedar, "The *Tractatus*", p. 120.

[45] Jacques de Vitry, *Historia orientalis*, LXXV, p. 138. Gerald of Wales remarks that the Irish do not conform to the normative pattern of human evolution — from the woods to the fields, from fields to towns — because, being truly bestial, they spurn agriculture and urban life alike, Giraldus Cambriensis, *Topographica Hibernica*, dist. III, x, ed. J. Dimock, in *Giraldi Cambriensis Opera*, ed. J.S. Brewer, J.F. Dimock and G.F. Warner, 8 vols, V, Rolls Series (London, 1867), p. 151.

[46] William of Malmesbury, *Gesta regum Anglorum*, I, ed. and trans R.A.B. Mynors, R.M. Thomson and M. Winterbottom, 2 vols (Oxford, 1998-9), p. 600.

[47] Bernard of Clairvaux, *Vita S. Malachiae Episcopi*, in *S. Bernardi Opera*, ed. J. Leclercq, H. Rochais and C.H. Talbot, 9 vols (Rome, 1957-77), III, 325; John of Salisbury, *Letters*, ed. W.J. Millor and H.E. Butler, rev. C.N.L. Brooke, 2 vols (London, 1979-86), I, p. 87.

through the membrane of their religious beliefs. For Gerald of Wales, these ethnic customs were an index of spiritual status: their customs of trial marriages, bride prices and — so he says — incest, made the Welsh inadequate Christians.[48] Part of the concept of "barbarism", therefore, seems to have been a religious deficiency engendered by adherence to ethnic customs.

Comparative ethnography can help us up to a point. But of course the marginal position occupied by the native Christians of the East was more acute and more threatening than that occupied by the Celts. Customs such as observing Saturday as a holy day, or enclosing wives within the household, were perceived not as generically barbaric but as specifically Jewish or Muslim. If the Holy Land was a margin of the civilised world, it was a contested margin, in which the native Christians had been, as Jacques says, "brought up with Muslims", in which boundaries between ethnicity, language and religion were dangerously permeable.

When we look beyond the narrow prejudice of Jacques' description of the native Orthodox Christians, we see a refracted political reality. Behind the accusation of vacillation and ambivalence in language lay a genuine fear. For native Orthodox people were mobile, with the ability to cross political boundaries from Frankish to Muslim control. According to a Coptic chronicle, for example, Saladin was able to enforce the surrender of the city of Jerusalem in 1187 because he had the allegiance of a Melkite inside the city — a merchant who had known Saladin from the conduct of his business in Egypt.[49]

Against such a background of suspicion, Jacques de Vitry's concern with the detail of the religious customs of native Christians in the East becomes more resonant. Customs such as the wearing of beards by priests, or the use of a single finger in blessing, or the day of the week on which one observed a fast, might appear less important to theologians than differences in doctrine. But it is precisely through such observable customs as these that a community maintains its identity. Customs are, or can become, enactments of an allegiance to a doctrine. They may even be more powerful than doctrinal discourse; as Martin Bloch once

---

[48] Giraldus Cambriensis, *Descriptio Kambriae*, II, vi, ed. J. Dimock, in *Giraldi Cambriensis Opera* (see n. 45) (1868), VI, pp. 213-4. On Gerald's ethnographic views, see R. Bartlett, *Gerald of Wales, 1146-1223* (Oxford, 1982), pp. 161-97, and in general, W.R. Jones, "The Image of the Barbarian in Medieval Europe", *Comparative Studies in Society and History*, 13 (1971), pp. 376- 407.

[49] E. Blochet, "Histoire d'Egypte de Makrisi", *Revue de l'Orient latin*, 9 (1902), pp. 29-30, n. 3.

observed, "You cannot argue with a song".[50] Thus, for example, the use of the single finger in blessing by Jacobites, a custom criticised by Jacques de Vitry, was a visual affirmation of monophysite belief. The single finger, as opposed to the three used in Latin (and Greek Orthodox) custom, symbolised the doctrine of the single nature of Christ.

The *Tractatus de locis et statu sancte terre* describes the native Orthodox as halfway between Latins and Greeks in religious matters. For Jacques this is a moral failing, indicative of an ambivalence between religious traditions, of being neither one thing nor another; hence the Melkites "say one thing but think another". Again, the underlying suspicion was real enough. Jacques' observations about the native Orthodox in the *Historia orientalis* had initially been made in a letter written soon after taking up his appointment as bishop of Acre. Here he complains that they are guilty of the Greek custom of using leavened bread, and refuse to venerate the Catholic Eucharist; and moreover that after a Catholic Mass has been said they insist on washing the altar before using it for their own worship.[51] In the letter, Jacques is writing not as an ethnographer, but as a pastor, and his polemic is informed by experience. When he went into Orthodox churches to preach, he instructed the Melkites in the Latin doctrine on the use of unleavened bread and on the procession of the Holy Spirit. They promised to reform their customs in line with Roman usage, but Jacques found afterwards that they continued to follow the very customs against which he had preached.[52] Thus, in the *Historia orientalis*, he ruefully remarks that they obey their Latin bishops "superficialiter", in words but not in their hearts.[53]

The ambivalence of the native Orthodox — their "saying one thing but thinking another" — was not simply a moral failing but a denial of episcopal authority. Because the Latin and Orthodox Churches were not separated, Jacques was the bishop of the Melkites as well as of the Frankish inhabitants of his diocese. He observed and condemned the customs and beliefs of the other native Christian groups, such as the Jacobites, but he did not attempt to reform them, because those groups fell outside his authority. The Monophysite Christians were members of a different Church, and thus had their own bishops; in a sense, they were beyond the margin. Life for the Melkites on the margin meant the impo-

---

[50] M. Bloch, "Symbols, Dance and Features of Articulation", *Archives Européens de Sociologie*, 15 (1974), p. 71.
[51] *Lettres de Jacques de Vitry*, II, ed. R.B.C. Huygens (Leiden, 1960), p. 84.
[52] *Ibid.*, p. 85.
[53] Jacques de Vitry, *Historia orientalis*, LXXV, p. 139.

sition of Latin customs and doctrines, and, perhaps most crucially, recognition by the native Orthodox clergy of the Roman primacy. Jacques' critique of the native Orthodox can be used as evidence to support both sides of the debate over crusader "colonialism". On the one hand, his contempt for the native Christians seems to indicate what Prawer called "colonial pragmatism"; on the other, the continuity of indigenous ethnic and religious customs among the native Orthodox that is self-evident from his account seems to suggest a tradition of tolerating native custom among his predecessors in the episcopal office. The weight of recent research on widely different sources of evidence, and using different methodologies — textual, archaeological, and geographical — suggests that the relationship between the Latins and the native Christians might best be summed up by a combination of both — "pragmatic tolerance", perhaps.

An example of such pragmatic tolerance concerns one of Jacques' grievances against the native Orthodox — their insistence on washing altars after the Catholic Eucharist. Clearly, such a situation could only have arisen where churches were being shared by native Orthodox and Latin communities. The most obvious examples are the great shrine churches of the Holy Sepulchre and the Nativity, to both of which were attached Orthodox and Latin monastic communities.[54] In these churches, Jacques' complaint about the washing of altars would not have applied, because the Orthodox and Latins had altars reserved for their own use. But in a smaller shrine church, such as that of 'Ain Karim, just outside Jerusalem, which was supposedly the house of John the Baptist's father Zacharias, Orthodox and Latin clergy used the same altars alternately.[55] Similar examples have been uncovered by Ronnie Ellenblum in his survey of Frankish rural settlement. 'Abud, a little to the west of Jerusalem, was one of a group of villages occupied by indigenous Christians but forming part of Latin ecclesiastical lordships. Besides the local Chris-

---

[54] H.E. Mayer, *Bistümer, Klöster und Stifte im Königreich Jerusalem*, Schriften der Monumenta Germaniae Historica, 26 (Stuttgart, 1977), pp. 406-9, argued that the Orthodox clergy only returned to the Holy Sepulchre in the 1160s, but this has been disproved by Pahlitzsch, "Greek Orthodox Church"(see n. 10), pp. 204-5. For arguments in favour of the presence of an Orthodox monastic community at Bethlehem, see A.T. Jotischky, "Manuel Comnenus and the Reunion of the Churches: The Evidence of the Conciliar Mosaics in the Church of the Nativity in Bethlehem", *Levant*, 26 (1994), pp. 216-17.

[55] The situation at 'Ain Karim is encapsulated in a surviving letter by a Byzantine theologian to the Orthodox clergy serving the church, R.J. Loenertz, "L'épître de Théorien le philosophe aux prêtres d'Oreiné", in *Mémorial Louis Petit* (Paris, 1948); on the church itself, see D. Pringle, *The Churches of the Crusader Kingdom of Jerusalem: A Corpus*, I (A-K) (Cambridge, 1993), pp. 30-8.

tians, 'Abud also had Frankish inhabitants, apparently both within the village and in fortified manor houses nearby. Archaeological surveys confirm the place-name evidence that 'Abud had only one church. A Syriac inscription of the mid eleventh century confirms its use by indigenous Christians, while the enlargement of the church by the Franks in the twelfth century suggests that it had to serve a larger population that now included Franks.[56]

Ellenblum's research indicates patterns in the spatial distribution of indigenous Christians relative to the Frankish settlers. A picture emerges of a rural Christianity in the Kingdom of Jerusalem in which resources of both interior space and landscape were often shared by the new settlers and the indigenous villagers.[57] Similar conclusions are suggested by the role of indigenous Christian monks and artists in the decoration of shrine churches, such as the church of the Nativity in the 1160s,[58] or in the hybrid court art of Jerusalem that has been described by Jaroslav Folda.[59] One might expect that the practice of sharing churches would have given rise to tensions between the indigenous Christians, who were after all a subject people, and the Frankish settlers. The example of 'Ain Karim stands almost alone, however, as evidence of such tensions in the twelfth century.[60] Why, then, did a genre of Latin writing emerge from the last quarter of the twelfth century onward, in which the native Orthodox were regarded with suspicion and contempt?

One answer is that the victory of Saladin in 1187 resulted in a shift in the relationship between Latins and native Orthodox. The picture of shared resources described by Ellenblum is largely rural, and it was the rural interior of the Kingdom that was lost in 1187, and only partially recovered from the 1190s onward. Some Melkites may have moved into the towns, but many more must have continued to live in their villages, merely exchanging Frankish domination for Muslim.[61] Accusations of

---

[56] Ellenblum, *Frankish Rural Settlement* (see n. 4), pp. 128-36; Pringle, *Churches*, I (see n. 55), pp. 18-20; for the inscription, J.T. Milik, "Inscription araméenne christo-palestinienne de 'Abud", *Liber Annuus Studii Biblici Franciscani*, 10 (1959), pp. 197-204. 'Abud seems to have been a centre for Syriac language use, to judge from the two surviving manuscripts in Syriac attributable to the village.

[57] Ellenblum, *Frankish Rural Settlement* (see n. 4), pp. 213-34.

[58] Jotischky, "Manuel Comnenus and the Reunion of the Churches" (see n. 54); L.-A. Hunt, "Art and Colonialism: The Mosaics of the Church of the Nativity in Bethlehem (1169) and the Problem of 'Crusader' Art", *DOP*, 45 (1991), pp. 69-85.

[59] J. Folda, *The Art of the Crusaders in the Holy Land, 1098-1187* (Cambridge, 1995), pp. 137- 62, for example, on the Psalter of Queen Melisende.

[60] In general, see Hamilton, *Latin Church*, pp. 159-87.

[61] William of Tyre, *Chronicon*, XXII, 29, p. 1057, describes the flight of native Orthodox in the region of Kerak into the Frankish fortress in 1183 to escape Muslim raiding; such immigration must have been frequent, but short-lived.

selling secrets to the Muslims, of hypocrisy and collusion, of a general ambivalence in loyalty, became more poignant in such a context.[62]

The disaster of 1187, the failure of the Third Crusade to recapture Jerusalem, and of the crusade of Emperor Henry VI to achieve anything, also brought about new attitudes in the West, and particularly in the papacy. Jacques himself was a papal appointee, and the letter in which he complained of lingering ethnic customs among the native Orthodox of Acre was written to the Pope.[63] His complaint can be seen as a criticism of a situation that he had inherited from his predecessors. As Bernard Hamilton has argued, the Latin bishops of the Crusader Kingdom in the twelfth century were not (with a few notable exceptions) known for their learning or grasp of canon law.[64] Brenda Bolton has recently characterised the appointments by Innocent III to sees in the Crusader States as indicative of a shift in attitude on the part of the papacy. Patriarch Aimery the Monk had "lost touch with reality";[65] in contrast, western appointments such as Albert of Vercelli, Peter of Lucedio and Jacques de Vitry himself were better attuned to papal views and imperatives. They were "typical of those men whom Innocent chose to have in his circle of friends: able, persuasive, spiritual leaders by word and example".[66] Innocent's pontificate was marked by a fresh attitude both to crusading and to the Latin East.[67] As early as 1199 Innocent had asked Patriarch Aimery for a report of the general state of the Holy Land and its inhabitants, presumably as part of the preparations for a new crusade.[68] It may reasonably be assumed that the fresh approach to the

[62] But see Roger of Wendover, *Flores Historiarum*, ed. H.G. Hewlett, Rolls Series (London, 1886), I, p. 219, for the story of a native Orthodox nun who escaped from Jerusalem to give intelligence on Saladin's defences to Richard I; and *Itinerarium Regis Ricardi*, v, 53-4, ed. W. Stubbs, Rolls Series (London, 1864), pp. 376-7, for evidence of friendship toward the crusaders from the Orthodox coadjutor bishop of Lydda and the abbot of Mar Sabas. For background, see A.T. Jotischky, "The Fate of the Orthodox Church in Jerusalem at the End of the Twelfth Century", in *Patterns of the Past* (see n. 10), pp. 179-94.

[63] M. Coens, "Jacques de Vitry", *Bibliographie Nationale de Belgique*, XXXI (Brussels, 1962), cols 465-74; B. Bolton, "Serpent in the Dust — Sparrow on the Housetop: Attitudes to Jerusalem and the Holy Land in the Circle of Pope Innocent III", in *The Holy Land, Holy Lands and Christian History*, ed. R.N. Swanson, Studies in Church History, 36 (Woodbridge, 2000), p. 162.

[64] Hamilton, *Latin Church*, pp. 134-5.

[65] Bolton, "Serpent in the Dust" (see n. 63), p. 160.

[66] *Ibid.*, p. 179.

[67] On Innocent and crusading, see C.J. Tyerman, *The Invention of the Crusades* (London, 1998), pp. 35-6; J. Sayers, *Innocent III, Leader of Europe 1198-1216* (London, 1994), pp. 164-71.

[68] Bolton, "Serpent in the Dust" (see n. 63), pp. 158-60, quotes from Innocent's letters in order to demonstrate the context of this request. The response sent by Aimery,

problems of the Latin East characterised by Innocent III's pontificate included a changed attitude toward the indigenous Orthodox Christians under Latin rule.

Conquests by crusaders between 1191 and 1204 also altered the relationship between the Franks and the native Christians. By the time Jacques de Vitry arrived in Acre, Cyprus and Constantinople, with their huge Orthodox populations, were under Latin rule. The effect of these conquests was to direct papal attention to Orthodox religious customs as never before. Innocent III had to send instructions, recommendations and demands to the Latin bishops in the eastern Mediterranean, to deal with administrative problems created by absorbing Orthodox communities under Latin supervision. Among these problems was the question of duties normally, under Orthodox canonical tradition, carried out by Orthodox parish clergy, but which were in the Latin Church reserved for bishops.[69] The Orthodox practice of having confirmations performed by clergy even seems to have been adopted by some Latin clergy.[70] Another problem was whether to recognize ordinations carried out by Orthodox bishops; Innocent III demanded that Orthodox clergy who were to serve in diocese under Latin bishops should be ordained by Latins.[71] Greek bishops, apparently, were also prone to confer all four canonical orders on prospective clergy at the same time, instead of at appropriately staged intervals.[72] Before the 1190s, in contrast, there had been effectively no papal supervision of the Latin Church in the Crusader States over its dealings with the indigenous Christians. Only after encountering Orthodoxy on a wider scale from the 1190s onward did the papacy recognize the anomaly represented by the marginal Christians in the Levant. In the twelfth-century Kingdom of Jerusalem, the marginal Christians were accepted as part of a new polity and a new society. Jacques de Vitry's remarks about the indigenous Christians represent a more sharply defined state, in which marginality was looked on with suspicion. The

---

known as *Narratio Ierosolimitane patriarche*, has had a complex editorial history, and was interpolated into Jacques de Vitry's *Historia orientalis* by his seventeenth-century editor, Bongars. Kedar, "The *Tractatus*", pp. 112-22, distinguished this from the text of the *Tractatus* discussed in this paper.

[69] In Laodicea, for example, an Orthodox priest called Sala had in the 1160s caused trouble for the Latin bishop, Gerard, by continuing to dedicate cemeteries, A.T. Jotischky, "Gerard of Nazareth, Mary Magdalene and Latin Relations with the Greek Orthodox in the Crusader East in the Twelfth Century", *Levant*, 29 (1997), pp. 217-26.

[70] *Registrum Innocentii III*, PL 214, col. 772.

[71] *Pontificia Commissio ad redigendum Codicem Iuris Canonici Orientalis: Fontes*, III, *Acta Innocentii papae III (1198-1216)*, ed. T. Haluscynski (Vatican, 1944), p. 208.

[72] *Registrum Innocentii III*, PL 215, col. 407.

"pragmatic tolerance" that had brought about shared churches in the countryside and decorative programmes at shrines, a system of coadjutor bishops for the Orthodox people, and a revival of Orthodox monasticism under the crusaders, was abandoned in the thirteenth century. A people with no distinct ethnic origin, no language of their own, and customs and beliefs drawn from different peoples, was no longer welcome.

ABBREVIATIONS USED IN THE FOOTNOTES

Kedar, "The *Tractatus*"
    B.Z. Kedar, "The *Tractatus de locis et statu sancte terre Ierosolimitane*", in *The Crusades and their Sources: Essays Presented to Bernard Hamilton*, ed. John France and W.G. Zajac (Aldershot, 1998), pp. 111-33.

Tractatus   *Tractatus de locis et statu sancte terre Ierosolimitane*, the edition of the *Tractatus* from British Library Royal MS 14.C.X in Kedar, "The *Tractatus*", pp. 123-31.

copy as we find it in the Cambrai manuscript ends in 1155.³ The first part of the text contains passages from the *Vita Norberti* (the so-called version B) and the *Continuatio Laudunensis*.⁴ For contemporary events the material has partly been collected from oral sources from the year 1140 onwards. Unfortunately the text is very succinct, also when dealing with contemporary events.

The *Continuatio Praemonstratensis* is of value because of its wide interest: Western European history, the history of the Crusader States and the history of Byzantium. This historical text makes clear how these worlds were interrelated, in a friendly or in a hostile way, and how news travelled easily and quickly from one country to another, even if the channels of information are not explicitly mentioned. Sometimes the author refers to oral sources. When he discusses events in the Crusader States he sometimes says "ut aiunt" or "dicunt", which suggests that the information may be more or less contemporary or was supplied by contemporaries.⁵ These oral sources were undoubtedly people who travelled from East to West and from West to East. It is therefore interesting and important to look more closely at the activities of the Praemonstratensian Order which quickly spread over Western Europe. Bishop Bartholomew of Laon, who had been very helpful to find an isolated place for Norbert and his brothers to live, is mentioned several times. During his episcopate he propagated the Christian faith in far-away areas, including Outremer. It is no wonder then that in 1131, according to the *Continuatio Praemonstratensis,* Premonstratensian brothers were sent to Syria and Palestine where they founded several abbeys.⁶ The mother house in Prémontré had plenty of opportunities to send news abroad and to receive news from abroad, as far as the East, and so did the various daughter houses. This news could include so-called *petite histoire* as well as news about political ambitions and achievements. Examples of

---

³ *Catalogue général des manuscrits des bibliothèques publiques,* XVII, *Cambrai,* ed. A. Molinier (Paris, 1891), no. 965 (863), pp. 399-401; P.N. Backmund, *Die mittelalterliche Geschichtsschreiber des Prämonstratenserordens* (Averbode, 1972), p. 253, suggests the abbey of St Martin, Laon, as the lieu of origin. Both editions are preceded by an introduction about the various *Continuationes.*

⁴ The passages are indicated by the editor. The *Vita Norberti,* version B, has been published in the *AASS* Iunii, I (1695), pp. 807-45; the *Cont. Praem.* does not offer important information about the origins of the *Vita,* see W.M. Grauwen, *Norbertus, aartsbisschop van Maagdenburg (1126-34)* (Brussels, 1978), pp. 11-2.

⁵ *Cont. Praem.,* MGH SS, VI, p. 454; PL 160, c. 376.

⁶ *Cont. Praem.,* MGH SS, VI, pp. 448, 450; PL 160, c. 363, 370; they were not explicitly sent by the Pope as has sometimes been thought, cf. B.Z. Kedar, *Crusade and Mission* (Princeton, 1984), p. 134, n. 127, who could have referred to the *Continuatio Praemonstratensis* for their arrival in the East.

both categories will be discussed here in order to try to see the *Continuatio Praemonstratensis* in a better light and obtain a better view of its historical value.

The first example dealing with what seems to be of minor importance to Western Europeans, was the death of the Byzantine Emperor John Comnenus in 1143, somewhere in the neighbourhood of Antioch. For western rulers in the East, however, his death may not just have been *petite histoire*.

"[A.D. 1141] Imperator Constantinopolitanus, Antiochia aliquandiu obsessa, pacem tandem cum principe fecit, et civitatem intravit; sed venationi insistens, dum arcum vehementius intendit, toxicata sagitta a semetipso vulneratus in sinistra manu, obiit, captis ante nonnullis Turcorum presidiis. Et post eum filius ejus Manuel imperium sumpsit."[7]

The Byzantine Emperor besieged Antioch, former Byzantine territory, which was now a Frankish princedom. Eventually the Emperor had made peace with his liegeman Raymond of Antioch. He was about to restore his authority over Antioch and possibly over Jerusalem as well.[8] When hunting he was mortally wounded fighting a boar. The *Continuatio Praemonstratensis* says that the Emperor hit himself in the left hand with a poisoned arrow. None of the contemporary or later sources, Latin or Greek or other, has this specific detail about the left hand. William of Tyre who was in Europe at the time, says that the Emperor hit himself in the hand with which he was tending the bow.[9] Two later French historians, Guillaume de Nangis who was active in Saint Denis in the second half of the thirteenth century, and the anonymous author of the *Chronicon Universale* of Laon repeat the passage as we find it in the *Continuatio Praemonstratensis*.[10] Why this interest in the death of a Byzantine

---

[7] *Cont. Praem.*, MGH SS, VI, p. 452; PL 160, c. 373.

[8] S. Runciman, *A History of the Crusades* (Harmondsworth, 1971, etc.), II, p. 224; R. Browning, "The Death of John II Comnenus", *Byzantion*, 31 (1961), pp. 229-35.

[9] For a survey of these sources see *ibid*.

[10] Guillaume de Nangis, *Chronicon*, in *Recueil des historiens des Gaules et de la France*, ed. M. Bouquet (Paris, 1840), XX, p. 732), gives the passage almost verbatim, except for the fact that he confuses John Comnenus with Manuel Comnenus; for Guillaume de Nangis, see *Lexikon des Mittelalters*. The *Universal Chronicle* of Laon was probably compiled in the Abbey of St Martin, Laon, and is only partially published. It gives the passage almost verbatim, but the name of the Byzantine emperor is here Alexius, which suggests that the *Vorlage* was unclear or simply spoke of the "imperator", MS Berlin, Deutsche Staatsbibliothek, Phillipps 1880, fol. 130v; MS Paris, Bibliothèque Nationale, Lat. 5011, fol. 138; for the Chronicle of Laon, see *Chronicon universale anonymi Laudunensis, Von 1154 bis zum Schluss (1219)*, ed. A. Cartellieri and W. Stechele (Leipzig and Paris, 1909) (partial edition).

emperor? Did the Emperor indeed send a relic of the True Cross to the church of St Martin in Laon? His death may have been fortunate for the Crusader States where, according to some historians, a war between the Greeks and Latins was about to break out.[11] The Greek Emperor was overlord of these territories.

John Comnenus was succeeded by his son Manuel, even though his elder son Isaac in Constantinople was still alive. Manuel was known for his dealings with the Latins, which could be to the advantage of the Crusader States. Doubts have been cast upon the circumstances of John's death by R. Browning, who referred to two unpublished Greek contemporary texts which suggest this. Could it be that the information about the Emperor wounding himself, with the addition of some details, was spread quickly to avoid unpleasant rumours or suspicions? *Petite histoire* or "high" politics, the answer has to remain in suspense for the moment. Other Greek sources may confirm these suspicions in future.[12] Under the year 1143 then follows, according to the *Continuatio Praemonstratensis*, the hunting accident of Fulk of Anjou who had left the West to marry Melisende, daughter of Baldwin II of Jerusalem and his Armenian wife Morphia. He too died of a hunting accident as if to parallel the death of John Comnenus.

Since they had arrived in Southern Italy the Normans had formed a permanent threat to the Byzantine Empire. In the year 1147, when the crusaders had just left Constantinople to proceed to Asia Minor, Roger II of Sicily attacked the Peloponnese where he devastated towns and villages and took much booty and many prisoners. From Thebes and Corinth he abducted silk weavers as is known from western and eastern sources.[13] According to the *Continuatio Praemonstratensis* the reason for the Sicil-

---

[11] P.N. Backmund, *Monasticon Praemonstratense* (Straubing, 1952), II, p. 509, but I have not been able to confirm this gift and it is not mentioned in the *Chronicon Universale* of Laon.

[12] For Manuel and his contacts with the Latins, see William of Tyre, *Chronicon*, XV, 22-23, pp. 704-6, for the Latins in the Greek camp who supported Manuel (*A History of Deeds Done beyond the Sea*, Engl. trans. E.A. Babcock and A.C. Krey (New York, 1943), inaccessible), and Michael Italos, *Lettres et discours*, ed. P. Gautier (Paris, 1972), p. 286, where he is said to have commanded a Latin contingent in the army; see also P. Magdalino, *The Empire of Manuel I Komnenos, 1143-1180* (Cambridge, 1993), p. 41, and Browning, "Death of John II Comnenus" (see n. 8), pp. 231-4.

[13] K. Ciggaar, "Chrétien de Troyes et la 'matière byzantine': Les demoiselles du Château de Pesme Aventure", *Cahiers de Civilisation Médiévale*, 32 (1989), pp. 325-31, esp. p. 328; D. Jacoby, "Silk in Western Byzantium before the Fourth Crusade", *Byzantinische Zeitschrift*, 84/85 (1991/1992), p. 462 ff.

ian attack was the imprisonment by the Greek Emperor of Sicilian envoys, sent to make peace.

> "[A.D. 1148] Manuel rex Grecorum nuntios regis Siciliae, quos ad eum pro exequendo pacis foedere miserat, detinuit mancipatus carcere. Unde iratus Rogerus, misso navali exercitu, Corinthum spoliavit cum quibusdam aliis civitatibus et castellis in Grecia; et infinitam sumens diversi generis paludamentorum et vestis preciosae substantiam cum auri et argenti copia, captivavit et de Grecis nonnulla milia."[14]

However, nothing is known about an official war between Byzantium and the Normans of Sicily. This made J. Chalandon doubt the authenticity of the information given by the *Continuatio Praemonstratensis*.[15] One wonders where this information comes from. Did the Normans offer a sort of peace to stop their incursions? And what did they want to achieve by doing so? What did they want in return? I should like to make the suggestion that the information, true or untrue, comes from Louis VII and his entourage when they returned to France after the Second Crusade (see also below). This could also explain the "wrong" dates in the chronicle for some of these events like the death of John Comnenus. At a certain distance of time chronological errors can easily develop. The negative description of the Byzantines and their Emperor who, according to the French and the *Continuatio Praemonstratensis*, had betrayed the French crusaders when they travelled through Asia Minor — "Franci per deserta Asiae dolo et astu Grecorum et crebro assultu Turcorum detrimenta maxima patiuntur" — precedes immediately the passage discussing the Norman action.[16] It was Roger II of Sicily who received King Louis VII returning from Palestine. The King had been captured by a Greek fleet and was liberated by the Sicilian fleet under the command of George of Antioch. His reception by the King of Sicily and by the Pope was a good occasion to exchange information from various parts of the world. It cannot be excluded that Roger II used a pretext for invading Byzantine territory. Both Louis and Roger had their own negative views on the Greek Emperor. Now they could join forces to strengthen the negative image of the Greek Emperor. Another story which most likely comes from such an interview of the two Kings is the story of George of Antioch (from an Orthodox family in Antioch and now serving Roger II), who attacked some Greek provinces, and

---

[14] *Cont. Praem.*, MGH SS, VI, p. 453; PL 160, c. 375.
[15] F. Chalandon, *Les Comnène: Jean II Comnène (1118-1143) et Manuel I Comnène* (Paris, 1912; reprint New York, 1971), p. 317, n. 1.
[16] *Cont. Praem.*, MGH SS, VI, p. 453; PL 160, c. 375.

even Constantinople. He devastated its suburbs and made a sort of mock attack on the imperial palace by shooting golden arrows.

> "[A.D. 1149] Ludovicus rex Francorum a Palestina navigans, ut in patriam rediret, Grecorum naves incurrit. Cumque ab eis imperatori Curfolium obsidenti presentandus deducitur, Georgius dux navium regis Siciliae eos aggreditur. Siquidem vastatis et spoliatis Grecorum provinciis, usque ad ipsam urbem regiam Constantinopolim accedens, sagittas aureas in palatium imperatoris jecerat, et incensis suburbanis, de fructu ortorum regis violenter tulerat. Unde rediens, naves Grecorum incurrit, captis Ludovicum regem eripuit, sed captos regis obtentu dimittit."[17]

Fairy-like as the information about the golden arrows seems, it is nevertheless a true story. Corroboration comes from an unsuspected witness, the serious Greek historian Nicetas Choniates (*ca.* 1155-1215/16). In his *Historia* this one time imperial secretary inserted fragments from earlier historical writers, which he probably found in the imperial library or archives. Nicetas tells us that the arrows had been dipped into gold and that the Emperor had laughed about it.[18] There was some boasting in the Norman camp when this story was told, because the arrows were not made of gold but were gilded. Nevertheless it was a spectacular thing to do. Why the use of golden arrows? Was there some sort of respect for the Byzantine Emperor, possibly on behalf of George of Antioch himself? This also goes for the stealing of fruit from the imperial gardens in a suburb, instead of laying waste these gardens or orchards as was a common procedure during an enemy attack in those days. The same story, almost verbatim, can be found in two French sources, the *Chronicon Universale* of Laon and in the *Speculum historiale* of Vincent de Beauvais, including the golden arrows, whereas Guillaume de Nangis does the same but changes the arrows into "sagittas igneas" (fire-arrows).[19] The attack on the imperial palace in Constantinople, including the shooting of arrows, was known in the Crusader States and in the Arab world.[20] We may safely conclude that the information about golden

[17] *Cont. Praem.*, MGH SS, VI, p. 454; PL 160, c. 375.

[18] Nicetas Choniates, *Historia*, ed. J.-L. van Dieten (Berlin, 1975), p. 99; ed. I. Bekker (Bonn, 1885), pp. 130-1; German trans. F. Grabler, *Die Krone der Komnenen* (Graz etc., 1958), p. 138: such arrows had to be prepared in advance; see also Magdalino, *Empire of Manuel I Komnenos* (see n. 12), p. 56 and n. 105.

[19] Guillaume de Nangis, *Chronicon* (see n. 10), p. 734, under the year 1149; Vincent de Beauvais, *Speculum historiale* (Douai, 1626; reprint Graz, 1965), XXVII, ch. cxxvi, p. 1141, under the year 1149; MS Berolinensis, fol. 132.

[20] E.g. J.-B. Chabot, *Chronique de Michel le Syrien, patriarche d'Antioche (1166-1199)*, 4 vols (Paris, 1910; reprint Brussels, 1960), III, p. 282; Ibn al-Athir, *Somme des Histoires*, with French trans., RHC Or., I, p. 477.

arrows could only have come from an insider. True, there was some boasting on the part of the Normans who more than once wanted to show off their newly acquired riches, but this time the story was almost real. It is again a detail in the text of the *Continuatio Praemonstratensis* which confirms its authenticity and its reliability. King Louis VII may have played a role in the transmission of this tale and of other historical events to France, which by some fortune are only mentioned in our text.[21] In Saint-Denis, at an unknown date, the golden arrows became "sagittas igneas", and were copied as such by Guillaume de Nangis.

Details of the *petite histoire* do not play a role in the third group of fragments in which Queen Melisende of Jerusalem and her activities are described. In western sources the second wife of Fulk of Anjou is not often mentioned and thus the interest of the *Continuatio Praemonstratensis* in the Queen of Jerusalem deserves our attention, even if she is not referred to by her proper name.[22] A few lines after the story of the death of John Comnenus, her husband's death — which was also caused by a hunting accident as we have seen — is mentioned. Melisende, a half-Armenian by her mother, was to share power with her infant son Baldwin III.

In 1129 Fulk had come to the East where he was to become ruler of Jerusalem when his father in law would come to die. The *Continuatio Praemonstratensis* does not give this information but we find it in the work of Guillaume de Nangis.[23] More interesting is the description of the arrival in Palestine of Alfonso of Toulouse who had certain rights to Tripoli:

> "[A.D. 1148] Hildefonsus comes de Sancti Egidii cum navali exercitu Palestinam applicuit, et cum magnum quid facturus speraretur, reginae ut aiunt dolo male potionatus, apud Cesaream Palestinae moritur. Filius ejus adolescens quoddam castrum comitis Tripolitani patruelis sui ingreditur, sed dolo ejusdem cum sorore a Turcis captivatur."[24]

---

[21] See e.g. *Cont. Praem.*, MGH SS, VI, p. 454; PL 160, c. 376, where the Emperors Conrad and Manuel are plotting against Roger II of Sicily in 1149.

[22] H.E. Mayer, "Fontevrault und Bethanien: Kirchliches Leben in Anjou und Jerusalem im 12. Jahrhundert", *Zeitschrift für Kirchengeschichte*, 102 (1991), p. 36, where several members of the royal family of Jerusalem are mentioned by name in the obituary: Fulk, Baldwin II, Baldwin III, Iveta, Hodierna and Alice (sisters of Melisende), but not Melisende herself or her son Amalric. It is not likely that she is commemorated in one of the many unpublished obituaries in France.

[23] See below.

[24] J. Richard, *Le comté de Tripoli sous la dynastie toulousaine (1102-1187)* (Paris, 1945), pp. 6-7, blames Eleonore for the poisoning of Alfonso, but this cannot be concluded from the text; the young lady seems to have ended up in the harem of Nureddin, cf. H.E. Mayer, "Studies in the History of Queen Melisende of Jerusalem", *DOP*, 26 (1972), p. 160.

The Queen of Jerusalem is accused of having poisoned a reputed crusader who could have menaced the position of her sister, the Count of Tripoli's wife. She is also blamed for her intriguing which caused the imprisonment of Alfonso's son and daughter by the Turks. Until recently the work of Guillaume de Nangis was the only source for the poisoning of Alfonso. The *Continuatio Praemonstratensis* is also used by H.E. Mayer who sees in its author a "fierce enemy of Melisende".[25]

The *Continuatio Praemonstratensis* then proceeds to the civil war in Jerusalem between Melisende and her son. The latter had come of age but was hardly allowed to rule the Kingdom. The *Continuatio Praemonstratensis* places the events in the year 1152:

> "[A.D. 1152] Regina Jerosolimorum justo familiarius ad inimicos Dei se habente, filius ejus Balduinus rex contra eam insurgit, et obsessis captisque ejus munitionibus, in urbem sanctam intrare ab ipsa secundo prohibitus, tandem violenter ingreditur; eamque in arce obsidens, facta pace Neapolim ei dimittit, reliquam regni partem sibi retinet."[26]

Here the text is almost contemporary with events and gives the year 1152 for the civil war. E.H. Mayer has come to the conclusion that these events took place in 1152, using the *Continuatio Praemonstratensis* as corroborating evidence.[27] The Queen had to give in and she retired to Nablus leaving the reign to her son Baldwin III. In this passage we can clearly see that the Cambrai manuscript is a copy of another manuscript. The expression *justo familiarius ad inimicos Dei* is a contradiction in terms and seems a copyist's misreading or misinterpretation. The Queen of Jerusalem is again accused of immoral behaviour, making common cause with the enemy. It is clear that this western text is very negative about her, whereas William of Tyre, writing in Outremer after the events had taken place, is positive about the Queen.[28] The former author, or possibly the copyist of the Cambrai manuscript, apparently did not live long enough (or was insufficiently informed) to mention an important gift of Melisende to the abbey of Prémontré. R. Hiestand has drawn attention to an entry in the obituary of Prémontré where Melisende is said to have donated, at an unknown date, liturgical vessels (a golden

---

[25] Runciman, *History of the Crusades* (see n. 8), pp. 280, 355, for the release of the son; Mayer, "History of Queen Melisende" (see n. 24), p. 160. William of Tyre, *Chronicon*, XVIII, 25, ll. 43-5, p. 849.

[26] *Cont. Praem.*, MGH SS, VI, p. 455; PL 160, c. 378.

[27] Mayer, "History of Queen Melisende" (see n. 24), p. 95.

[28] *Ibid.*, passim; William of Tyre, *Chronicon*, XV, 27, ll. 43-4, p. 711, calls her "dominam Milissendam deo amabilem reginam" when he refers to the period shortly after her husband's death, which does not necessarily mean that she had a good character.

chalice and a silver incense burner) and precious vestments, the "capella Melisendis", among them a "tunicam de samith".[29] How should one explain such an important gift given in order to be included in the abbey's prayers, especially in the context of the negative image which the Queen apparently had in Premonstratensian circles? It seems to be a gift much too precious to be given to a monastery in Western Europe with which the royal family in Jerusalem is not known to have had any connections, and find a place in its obituary. True, the Queen was generous to the Church and patronized religious art and religious institutions in Outremer, as we know from several donations and from her exquisitely illustrated Psalter, but this does not explain the connection with Prémontré. Her sister Iveta, abbess of Bethany in Palestine, had sent a gift to Fontevrault in order to be mentioned in its prayers, but a pyxis filled with relics is of a different order.[30] We know that Bernard of Clairvaux wrote a letter to Melisende to ask her to be kind to the Premonstratensian brothers who came to Palestine. However, this letter was probably written in the early days of their arrival in Outremer.[31]

We have to look at the events of 1152 which are mentioned explicitly in the *Continuatio Praemonstratensis*, and at the ensuing peace. Unfortunately we know nothing about the reconciliation and the peace settlement between Melisende and her son. From this silence B. Hamilton concluded that the civil war was ended by "some unnamed peacemakers, perhaps churchmen". William of Tyre wrote his work in the early 1170s and by then the names, which at first were deliberately "ignored", were slowly "forgotten". Queen Melisende had died in 1161 or 1162.[32] Could these anonymous churchmen have been members of the Premon-

---

[29] R. Hiestand, "Königin Melisendis von Jerusalem und Prémontré — Einige Nachträge zum Thema: Die Prämonstratenser und das Hl. Land", *Analecta Praemonstratensia*, 71 (1995), pp. 77-82, for the "Capella Melisendis reginae"; R. van Waefelghem, "Obituaire de l'abbaye de Prémontré", *Analectes de l'ordre de Prémontré*, 5-8 (1909-12); also published separately (Louvain, 1913), p. 177. One wonders what happened to the precious liturgical garments, one of which was explicitly called as made of samith, i.e. silk. The Order was not allowed to have silken garments, cf. P.F. Lefèvre and W.M. Grauwen, *Les Statuts de Prémontré au milieu du XIIe siècle* (Averbode, 1978), p. 51, "albas ornatas de pallio vel serico non habebimus".

[30] Mayer, Fontevrault und Bethanien (see n. 22), pp. 35-6; see also J. Chartrou, *L'Anjou de 1109 à 1151: Foulque de Jérusalem et Geoffroi Plantegenet* (Paris, 1928), p. 239, n. 1.

[31] *Sancti Bernardi opera*, VIII, *Epistolae*, ed. J. Leclercq and H. Richais (Rome, 1977), p. 299, no. 355; PL 182, c. 557-8; his death is mentioned in the *Cont. Praem.*, MGH SS, VI, p. 455; PL 160, c. 378.

[32] B. Hamilton, "Women in the Crusader States: The Queens of Jerusalem (1100-1190)", in *Medieval Women*, ed. D. Baker (Oxford, 1978), p. 153; see Hiestand, "Königin Melisendis" (see n. 29), p. 79, n. 12.

stratensian Order who were active in Outremer? During the reign of Baldwin II (1118-31), Melisende's father, the Premonstratensian Order had received the shrine of St Samuel on Mountjoie, near Jerusalem. This gift corroborates the sending of Premonstratensian brothers to Palestine.[33] The abbey of SS Joseph and Habacuc near Ramlah and Diospolis was in existence in 1154 when its Abbot, Amalricus of Floreffe, was elected bishop of Sidon.[34] The promotion of the Abbot suggests that the nominee was in favour with the King who had to approve the nomination. It may have been a remuneration for services rendered in recent times. It cannot be excluded that Amalricus of Floreffe was one of these peacemakers, especially since the Military Orders had been siding with the Queen. Amalricus is favourably judged by William of Tyre who calls him a simple and God loving man, a man of excellent company, "egregie conversationis", a qualification he reserves for only twelve people in his huge work.[35] The Queen could honourably retire to Nablus where in the 1180s we find confirmation of the gift of a sanctuary to the Premonstratensians. Whoever the peacemakers were, Melisende had to express her gratitude for the honourable peace treaty and make her contribution to the parties involved. It is my guess that Amalricus, a close friend of Norbert of Xanten and possibly embarrassed with the gift (see also below), suggested that it should be sent to Prémontré in France, where the mother house could well do with some *religiosa* for its new church. There was plenty of opportunity to carry such a gift to the West. The new Bishop himself travelled to Rome a year later. It was not necessarily a gift in relation to Melisende's death. In the present context it is remarkable that both mother and son are given an entry in the obituary of Prémontré where a new church was under construction.[36]

We have seen that Guillaume de Nangis' *Chronicon* offers some minor but interesting deviations from the fragments of the *Continuatio Praemonstratensis* which have been discussed here. The golden arrows were changed into incendiary arrows and the doubtful expression about

[33] H.E. Mayer, "Sankt Samuel auf dem Freudenberge und sein Besitz nach einem unbekannten Diplom König Balduins V.", *Quellen und Forschungen aus italienischen Archiven und Bibliotheken*, 44 (1964), pp. 35-71; *Cont. Praem.*, MGH SS, VI, p. 450, PL 160, c. 370.

[34] William of Tyre, *Chronicon*, XVII, 26, l. 47, p. 797.

[35] *Ibid.*, XVII, 26, ll. 42-8, p. 797; see also *Instrumenta lexicologica latina*, fasc. 32, *Willelmus Tyrensis archiepiscopus* (Turnhout, 1986), s.v. "egregie", "conversationis".

[36] *Ibid.*, XVIII, 6, l. 27, p. 818; van Waefelghem, "Obituaire" (see n. 29), pp. 43, 177; M. Plouvier, *L'abbaye de Prémontré aux XVIIe et XVIIIe siècles* (Louvain, 1985), I, pp. 19, 22-3, 28-9.

Melisende's familiarity with the enemy, "justo familiarius ad inimicos Dei", is rendered as "ad inimicos fidei familiarius", which makes more sense. The *Chronicon Laudunense* speaks of "multo familiarius", which must have been the initiative of a copyist.[37] In contrast to the *Continuatio Praemonstratensis*, Guillaume de Nangis speaks of Fulk's departure for the Holy Land and gives interesting details about him:

> "[A.D.1128] Fulco comes Andegavis relinquens comitatum andegavensem Gaufrido filio suo, et in Suriam proficiscens accepit in uxorem Milisandem primogenitam filiam Balduini regis Jerusalem..." "[A.D. 1143] In festo sancti Martini aestivalis, dum Fulco rex jerosolymitanus venatum iret, et leporem insequeretur, equo cespitante ruens mortuus est, per miraculum rupto collo; ipse enim, ut tradunt aliqui, antequam Rex esset Jerusalem, quamdiu comitatum andegavensem tenuit, ecclesiam Sancti Martini turonensis in quantum potuit infestavit. Cui ita mortuo Balduinus filius ejus cum matre Milisandi regina regnavit."[38]

The differences between the various texts suggest that there was a common *Vorlage*, possibly even two that served as their model and source of information. The earliest known text which used the model was the *Continuatio Praemonstratensis* as we know it today. At an earlier stage the *Continuatio Laudunensis* may also have used this hypothetical CONTINUATIO PRAEMONSTRATENSIS*.[39] It is my hypothesis that the *Continuatio Praemonstratensis*, the *Chronicon Universale* of Laon and the *Speculum historiale* of Vincent of Beauvais derive, directly or indirectly, from a text which we may call the CONTINUATIO PRAEMONSTRATENSIS*, a text written in Prémontré itself and in which the foundation of a new church should have been mentioned. The *Chronicon* of Guillaume de Nangis may have been modelled on a twinsister of it in the library of Saint-Denis.

The mother house of the Order of Prémontré must have written her own history and kept her own annals. Its library had an inventory of the relics and riches in its possession and one or more manuscripts of the

---

[37] The Berlin manuscript has a corrupted and illegible word, *Chronicon universale anonymi Laudunensis* (see n. 10), p. 1; Vincent de Beauvais, *Speculum historiale* (see n. 19), *ibid*, under the year 1151, gives the passage verbatim as in the *Cont. Praem.*

[38] Guillaume de Nangis, *Chronicon* (see n. 10), pp. 728, 732. Fulk's generosity for St Martin raises the question of the sponsorship of the crusader icon on which three Greek and three Latin saints — St Martin, St Leonard and St Laurence — are depicted. St Martin of Tours was revered by Fulk and St Leonard (patron of prisoners) was a saint from the nearby Limousin, which could suggest a link between the royal family in Jerusalem and this icon, now on Mount Sinai, cf. K. Weitzmann, "Icon Painting in the Crusader Kingdom", *DOP*, 20 (1966), p. 329, reprint in *idem*, *Studies in the Arts at Sinai* (Princeton, 1982), no. XII, p. 329.

[39] see Grauwen, *Norbertus* (see n. 4), pp. 11-2.

Vita of St Norbert, a cherished text. Its cartulary certainly contained interesting information as well.[40] The obituaries of Prémontré have been published and they indicate that Prémontré had rich and royal benefactors, like the kings of France, the counts of Champagne and others, among whom figured Queen Melisende of Jerusalem.[41] During the French Revolution the library and treasury of the abbey were destroyed, stolen and dispersed. Remnants of the library and the archives found their way into the Bibliothèques Municipales of Laon and Soissons. In the early nineteenth century a number of manuscripts disappeared from the library in Soissons, among them a twelfth-century manuscript containing a *Chronica* of Sigebert de Gembloux.[42] It is not unlikely that this manuscript contained the hypothetical CONTINUATIO PRAEMONSTRATENSIS*. This text may have contained more information on the royal gift from Jerusalem. Only by reading between the lines can we explain the discrepancy between the obituary of Prémontré and the silence in the *Continuatio Praemonstratensis* about the gift of the Queen of Jerusalem, a silence which can be "explained" by the premature death of its compiler or by his (persisting) grievance against Queen Melisende.[43]

Interesting details about the death of John Comnenus, the Sicilian attack on Constantinople and the malicious dealings of the Queen of Jerusalem must have reached the abbey by returning crusaders among whom Louis VII himself. These details are sometimes confirmed by Byzantine sources. In Antioch the French King had visited his wife's uncle Ray-

---

[40] *Catalogue général des manuscrits des bibliothèques publiques de France: Départements* (Paris, 1885), III, A. Molinier, pp. 75-6, no. 12, a twelfth-century *Vita Norberti*; Backmund, Monasticon Praemonstratense (see n. 11), p. 524.

[41] Van Waefelghem, "Obituaire" (see n. 29), p. 26 for Thibaud de Champagne, p. 31 for King Ladislaus of Bohemia, p. 153 for King Louis VI of France, p. 155 for Gertrud, Countess of Bohemia, p. 184 for Otto of Freising, p. 180 for the Empress Mathilda, p. 195 for Constance, second wife of King Louis VII of France.

[42] *Catalogue général des manuscrits des bibliothèques publiques de France: Départements* (see n. 40), III, p. 70, no. 22.

[43] The mixed feelings about Queen Melisende may eventually have influenced the illustration programme of William of Tyre's work in which originally he must have had a say, see e.g. J. Folda, *Crusader Manuscript illumination at Saint-Jean d'Acre, 1275-1291* (Princeton, 1976), who gives a selection of the illustrated manuscripts showing a certain diversity of pictures for Fulk riding out for hunting with or without Melisende and the coronation scenes of Fulk and Baldwin III: see ills 12, 14, 107, 109, 129, 131, 153, 155, 167, 181 (coronation of Baldwin III and Melisende, Paris, BN, Fr., 779, French version of the text, written in the third quarter of the thirteenth century in Paris), see ills 189, 194, 233, 235, 267, 268, 278, 296.

mond de Poitiers, ruler of the princedom. During his return journey he visited Roger II of Sicily. There was plenty of opportunity to get hold of "gossip".

Brothers of the Premonstratensian Order were active in Western Europe and in Outremer. They had their own network for information about the political situation in the Kingdom of Jerusalem and they possibly played their own role in the complicated political events of 1152 when a civil war in Palestine threatened the very existence of the Crusader States. Royalties and royal news travelled fast and frequently in both ways. Information in the *Continuatio Praemonstratensis* should not only be considered at its face value but also in the wider context of the Premonstratensian Order and its contacts with rulers in East and in West. The reception of the *Continuatio Praemonstratensis* (or its *Vorlage*) in the *Chronicon Universale* of Laon and in the *Speculum historiale* of Vincent of Beauvais are another indication that medieval historians judged it as a valuable historical source.

GEORGIANS AND GREEKS IN JERUSALEM (1099–1310)

Johannes Pahlitzsch

The history of Jerusalem in the period from the foundation of the Crusader Kingdom in 1099 until the beginning of the fourteenth century is marked by dramatic changes: in 1187 the Holy City was conquered by Saladin, 1228 saw its return to the Latins, in 1244 it was sacked by the Khwarizmians. Although under Mamluk rule since the 1250s, Jerusalem was nevertheless raided several times by the Mongols. In this period Georgia and the Byzantine Empire also underwent far-reaching changes. To which extent was the situation of the Georgian and Greek communities in Jerusalem and their relations to the respective rulers marked by these developments? Both belonged to the Orthodox Church. Were their mutual relations influenced by political events? Can we assume, as René Janin did, that "pendant le XIIIe et le XIVe siècle, la communauté géorgienne toute-puissante remplace peu à peu la communauté grecque persécutée par les Mamelouks"?[1]

From the fifth century onwards, close ties existed between the Georgian Church and Jerusalem, based for one on the fact that pilgrimages to Jerusalem became customary in Georgia and for the other on the permanent presence of Georgian monks in the Holy Land.[2] After the temporary decline of Georgian power due to the Arab conquests, a new phase began in Jerusalem around 1038 with the foundation of the monastery of the Holy Cross.[3] At the time of the Seldjuk rule in Jerusalem between

---

[1] René Janin, "Les Géorgiens à Jérusalem", *Échos d'Orient*, 16 (1913), p. 34.

[2] Gregory Peradze, "An Account of the Georgian Monks and Monasteries in Palestine as Revealed in the Writings of Non-Georgian Pilgrims", *Georgica*, 1 (1937), no. 4 and 5, pp. 181-246; Kalistrat Salia, "Les moines et les monastères géorgiens à l'étranger", *Bedi Kartlisa: Revue de kartvéologie*, 34-35 (1960), pp. 30-59; Amnon Linder, "Christian Communities in Jerusalem", in *The History of Jerusalem: The Early Muslim Period 638-1099*, ed. Joshua Prawer and Haggai Ben-Shammai (Jerusalem and New York, 1996), pp. 121-62; Johannes Pahlitzsch, "Die Bedeutung Jerusalems für Königtum und Kirche in Georgien zur Zeit der Kreuzzüge im Vergleich zu Armenien", in *Jerusalem in der christlichen Spiritualität des Mittelalters*, ed. Walther Brandmüller (forthcoming).

[3] Kalistrat Salia, *History of the Georgian Nation* (Paris, 1983), pp. 132-46. For the monastery of the Holy Cross cf. K. Lübeck, "Das Kloster zum hl. Kreuze bei Jerusalem", *Der Katholik*, 94 (1914), pp. 355-69; Elene Metreveli, *Masalebi Ierusalimis k'art'uli koloniis istoriisat'vis* [Materials for the History of the Georgian Colony in Jerusalem] (Tbilisi, 1962) (I am indebted to Dr A. Chotiwari and Dr A. Nadiraschwili for the transla-

The importance of the monastery of the Holy Cross for Mamluk-Georgian relations is shown by the fact that, when relations were re-established under Sultan an-Nāṣir Muḥammad, the restitution of the monastery was the first step taken. Several Arab historians give contradictory accounts of this event, dating it either 705/1305-6 or 710/1310-11.[33] These accounts are well known to scholars who have worked on the history of the monastery of the Holy Cross, such as Dito T. Gocholeishvili and Davit Ninize, and it is widely assumed that two embassies were sent to Cairo.[34] But these interdependent sources have until now been used quite uncritically. It is therefore necessary to try to establish the relationship of the various accounts. The oldest contemporary historian is Baybars al-Manṣūrī (d. 725/1325), who records that in 705/1305-6, a Georgian embassy came to Constantinople on its way to Cairo. The Byzantine Emperor Andronikos II named *Alāshkarī* (i.e Laskaris) in the Arab chronicle, sent an envoy of his own who accompanied the Georgians. They arrived in Alexandria and travelled on to the Sublime Porte to hand a letter to the Sultan.[35] In this letter the Sultan was asked to give the monastery of the Holy Cross, in which a mosque (*masjid*) with a minaret had been built some time before, back to the Georgians. The Sultan granted the request and returned the monastery to the Georgians.[36]

However, the Copt Mufaḍḍal Ibn Abī Faḍā'il, who completed his chronicle in 759/1357-58, dates the restitution to the year 710.[37] He records that an embassy from Andronikos II (also named Laskaris/

more detailed account of the complex relations between the Mamluks and the two Georgian Kingdoms cf. Müller and Pahlitzsch, "Sultan Baybars I and the Georgians" (see n. 3).

[33] The Arabic text of these sources is given in the appendix.

[34] Dito T. Gocholeishvili, *XIV-XV ss. arabi istorikosebis cnobebi sak'art'velos shesakheb* [Information of Arab Historians of the fourteenth and fifteenth centuries on Georgia] (Tbilisi, 1988), pp. 33-9, dates the restitution at 1310; Davit Ninize, "Aus der Geschichte des Kampfes um die Befreiung des Kreuzklosters zu Jerusalem", *Georgica*, 18 (1995), pp. 5-13, pleads for 1305, on the grounds of his analysis of Georgian history at the beginning of the fourteenth century. He also gives references for older Georgian literature on this topic. Cf. also Elene Metreveli, *Masalebi Ierusalimis* (see n. 3), pp. 43-5; Butrus Abu-Manneh, "The Georgians in Jerusalem in the Mamluk Period", in *Egypt and Palestine: A Millennium of Association (868-1948)*, ed. Amos Cohen and Gabriel Baer (Jerusalem, 1984), pp. 103-4.

[35] Whether the letter was written by the Georgian King or by Andronikos is not told by Baybars al-Manṣūrī.

[36] Baybars al-Manṣūrī al ad-Dawādār, *Zubdat al-fikra fī ta'rīḫ al-hijra: History of the Early Mamluk Period*, ed. Donald S. Richards, Bibliotheca Islamica, 42 (Beirut, 1988), pp. 385-6.

[37] Cf. Johannes den Heijer, "Coptic Historiography in the Fāṭimid, Ayyūbid and Early Mamlūk Periods", *Medieval Encounters*, 2 (1996), pp. 67-98.

Alāshkarī) arrives together with Georgian envoys at the Sublime Porte to ask for the restitution of the monastery of the Holy Cross. He tells us that it was Šayk Ḥaḍir who took over the monastery and states more correctly than Baybars al-Manṣūrī that he turned it into a *zāwiya* — not a mosque. Thus far the construction of Ibn Abī Faḍā'il's account corresponds to Baybars al-Manṣūrī's. Then he adds new information: firstly, the monastery had been restituted in accordance with the *fatwas* of some jurists which declared that the expropriation had not been permitted by law ("fa-u'īdat ilayhim bi-muqtaḍā fatāwā al-'ulamā' annahu lā yajūzu iġtiṣābihā").[38] Secondly, the Byzantine Emperor asked that the *ahl aḍ-ḍimma* in Egypt be treated according to custom and that their churches be reopened. The Sultan granted this request as well. And thirdly, the Sultan allowed the Christians to sit face forward in the saddle. Before that they had only been allowed to ride side-saddle.[39] In his chronicle, Ibn Abī Faḍā'il several times names Baybars al-Manṣūrī as his source. But he uses him in a flexible manner, embellishing these passages with additional information without mentioning that these constitute additions to the original.[40] In the case in question, Ibn Abī Faḍā'il does not tell us on which source he depends but it seems likely that he proceeded in just the same way.

Badr ad-Dīn al-'Aynī (762-855/1361-1451) also made considerable use of Baybars al-Manṣūrī's historical work in his chronicle *'Iqd al-jumān*.[41] For the year 705 he cites the account of Baybars al-Manṣūrī verbatim. Then he adds another paragraph which is almost identical to Ibn Abī Faḍā'il: al-'Aynī refers to Šayk Ḥaḍir in just the same words but names Ibn Kaṯīr as his source. The mention of the *fatwas* is slightly abridged. Nothing is said in al-'Aynī's chronicle about the request of the Byzantine Emperor for the Egyptian *ahl aḍ-ḍimma*, but the concluding

---

[38] As already mentioned, the rights of the Georgian monks had been recognised by the Muslim *qāḍī* court only a few years before the expulsion of the monks (see n. 27). Donald P. Little, "Communal Strife in Late Mamlūk Jerusalem", *Islamic Law and Society*, 6 (1999), pp. 69-96, demonstrates that jurists and politicians at the highest level could be mobilized to assert Mamluk interests when destabilizing conflicts arose among the different communities in Jerusalem. Thus the prohibition by the local officials and jurists for the rebuilding of a synagogue or a church could develop into a conflict between the jurisdiction of the sultanate and the judicial establishment of Jerusalem.

[39] Mufaḍḍal Ibn Abī Faḍā'il, *an-Nahj as-sadīd wa-d-durr al-farīd fī mā ba'd ta'rīḥ Ibn al-'Amīd*, PO XX, fasc. 1: Moufazzal ibn Abil-Fazaïl, *Histoire des Sultans Mamlouks* (fasc. III), ed. and trans. E. Blochet (Paris, 1928; reprint Turnhout, 1974), pp. 701-2.

[40] Donald P. Little, *An Introduction to Mamluk Historiography* (Wiesbaden, 1970), p. 35; Amitai-Preiss, "Mongol Raids into Palestine" (see n. 26), pp. 244-5; Richards in the introduction to Baybars al-Manṣūrī, *Zubdat al-fikra* (see n. 36), p. XXII.

[41] *Ibid.*, pp. XXII-XXIV.

passage on the riding of horses is again more or less the same as in Ibn Abī Faḍāʾil's work.[42] All in all the second paragraph reads as if it were a commentary to the first, naming the one who expropriated the monastery and turned it into a *zāwiya*, and telling us about the legal procedure. Al-ʿAynī apparently put two versions together without ensuring that they were congruent.

The date of 705 is confirmed by the account in al-Maqrīzī's (766-845/ 1364-1441) *Kitāb al-sulūk*. He records that envoys of the Byzantine Emperor ("malik al-Qusṭanṭiniyya") arrived together with envoys of the Georgian King in the year 705. They delivered presents and a letter containing the plea for the reopening of the monastery of the Holy Cross so that the Georgians could make the pilgrimage to it. In return, the Georgians promised to support the Sultan whenever he needed it. The Sultan ordered the monastery to be reopened, which was done, and the envoys were sent back.[43] This account seems to be independent from Baybars al-Manṣūrī and Ibn Abī Faḍāʾil.

However, for Rajab 710/November-December 1310 al-ʿAynī and al-Maqrīzī record another embassy being sent to the Sultan. But al-ʿAynī's account is almost identical with Ibn Abī Faḍāʾil's. Thus he repeats partly his own account of the restitution in 705.[44] The same holds true for al-Maqrīzī as a careful comparison between the various sources reveals. His account of how the envoys were sent to the Sultan and of their request is similar to Ibn Abī Faḍāʾil's. He has, however, assimilated the wording to his own version of the year 705. The expropriation by Ḫaḍir is mentioned as in Ibn Abī Faḍāʾil's work. But without making any reference to the jurists' *fatwas* al-Maqrīzī just states: "A mosque has been built in the 'church' and the dissolution of this 'mosque' is impossible" ("buniya fīhā [i.e. fī l-kanīsa] masjid, wa-lā yumkin naqḍ ḏālika").[45] This is contrary to the results of the embassy of 705 as reported also by al-Maqrīzī himself. Maybe he disliked the idea of the jurists making a decision in favour of the Christians fearing the establishment of a pre-

[42] Badr ad-Dīn Maḥmūd al-ʿAynī, *ʿIqd al-jumān fī tarīḫ ahl az-zamān*, ed. Muḥammad Muḥammad Amīn, IV (Cairo, 1992), pp. 378-9.

[43] Taqī ad-Dīn Aḥmad b. ʿAlī al-Maqrīzī, *Kitāb as-sulūk li-maʿrifat duwal al-mulūk*, ed. Muḥammad Muṣṭafā Ziyāda, II, part 1 (Cairo, 1941), p. 17 (Quatremère, *Histoire des Sultans Mamlouks* (see n. 32), II, part 2, p. 255).

[44] The edition of al-ʿAynī's *ʿIqd al-jumān* ends with the year 709. Gocholeishvili, *XIV-XV ss. arabi istorikosebis* (see n. 34), p. 38 n. 73, gives the text of a St Petersburg manuscript.

[45] Ibn Abī Faḍāʾil's statement: "wa-jaʿalahā zāwiya… fa-uʿīdat ilayhim bi-muqtaḍā fatāwā al-ʿulamāʾ annahu lā yajūzu iġtiṣābihā" (cf. n. 39) has been twisted by al-Maqrīzī with a few modifications to mean just the opposite.

cedent. Then he goes on to record that the church of the Melkites in Egypt ("al-kanīsa al-malikiyya bi-Miṣr") and the church of the Copts as well as the synagogue in Cairo were reopened on the orders of the Sultan. This could be a revision of Ibn Abī Faḍā'il's report of the Byzantine Emperor's plea to treat the *ahl aḏ-ḏimma* according to custom and to reopen their churches. Or al-Maqrīzī is referring to other expropriations of Šayḵ Ḥaḍir who had turned the great Jewish synagogue in Damascus into a Sufi convent (*zāwiya*) and the Greek Orthodox church in Alexandria into a *madrasa*.[46] He concludes this paragraph with the statement on permission to ride face forward.[47] Although al-Maqrīzī has revised Ibn Abī Faḍā'il's version, the dependence of the fifteenth-century historian on his Coptic predecessor is proven by the identical composition of both accounts.

All these various sources are interdependent, with the exception of al-Maqrīzī's account of the embassy of 705. However, while so many texts are as yet unpublished, their relationship can only be guessed. As Donald Richards puts it: "The general situation is complicated with, as it appears, many historians all writing at the same, or roughly the same, time and all sharing information and exhibiting textual interdependence."[48] Maybe al-ʿAynī and al-Maqrīzī borrowed, not from Ibn Abī Faḍā'il, but from a yet unknown common source. At any rate, the comparison between the various texts reveals that, with the exception of al-Maqrīzī's first account, they are all founded on the same — partly enlarged — model. It can thus be concluded that there was only one group of envoys sent to ask for the restitution of the monastery of the Holy Cross. On the basis of Baybars al-Manṣūrī's chronological priority and al-Maqrīzī's independent first account, this embassy must be dated to 705. It might be that Ibn Abī Faḍā'il or his source made a mistake in dating this Byzantine-Georgian embassy to 710.[49] Al-ʿAynī and al-Maqrīzī then came across the accounts of two groups of envoys: one dated 705 as recorded by Baybars al-Manṣūrī and al-Maqrīzī's unknown

---

[46] Cf. Ibn Šaddād, *Taʾrīḫ al-Malik aẓ-Ẓāhir* (see n. 29), pp. 59, 273-4.

[47] Al-Maqrīzī, *Kitāb as-sulūk* (see n. 32), II, part 1, p. 90.

[48] Richards in the introduction to Baybars al-Manṣūrī, *Zubdat al-fikra* (see n. 36), p. XXIII.

[49] Indeed it seems very likely that envoys were sent to an-Nāṣir Muḥammad, after he had assumed power for a third time in 709, with the objective of asking for the confirmation of the Georgian rights in Jerusalem: Although a few sheets of the beginning of the document VII.B. 1/5 of the archive of the Greek Orthodox Patriarchate (dated 710) are missing, this most likely refers to the monastery of the Holy Cross. Agamemnon Tselikas, Καταγραφὴ τοῦ ἀρχείου τοῦ πατριαρχείου Ἱεροσολύμων, Δελτίο τοῦ ἱστορικοῦ καὶ παλαιογραφικοῦ ἀρχείου ε' (Athens, 1992), p. 396. For the archive and the catalogue cf. Pahlitzsch, *Graeci und Suriani* (see n. 7), pp. 232-4.

independent source, and another one dated 710, recorded by Ibn Abī Faḍā'il or his model. Thus both fifteenth-century historians were led to think that there had been two embassies.

The re-establishment of Mamluk-Georgian relations could only happen as the Mamluk-Mongol conflict seemed to come to an end, with the sending of a conciliatory letter by the Ilkhan Öljeitü in 1305 to Sultan an-Nāṣir Muḥammad.[50] The execution in 1314 of the Georgian St Nicolas by the Mamluk governor of Syria Tankiz in Damascus is no contradiction. His *vita*, contained in the Georgian Synaxar, describes vividly how Nicolas had himself provoked this execution by repeatedly and publicly insulting Islam. Furthermore, the responsibility of the Melkite Metropolitan of Damascus for the Georgian Saint becomes apparent in the several, and initially even successful, attempts to free Nicolas from imprisonment by the Muslims, the result of his provocations.[51]

How then had the situation of the Greeks evolved after the catastrophe of 1244? Did they also suffer from Mamluk persecution? We have hardly any information on the history of the Greek Church in the second half of the thirteenth century. A few colophons in MS Sabas 144 from the library of the Greek Orthodox Patriarchate of Jerusalem, a Greek gospel dated 1019, grant us some insights into the volatile situation. This codex, which was most likely produced in the monastery of St Sabas and has remained in the Holy Land until today, contains various Greek and Arab notes. According to an Arab comment, the Archbishop of Caesarea consecrated the manuscript in 1281. In Greek, we read that a nun named Matrona purchased it from the "booty" of Acre, which clearly means that this happened after the city had been taken by the Mamluks in 1291. Matrona made a gift of the manuscript to St Mary's Cloister called "της Αλαμανα". The principal house of the Teutonic Order thus fell to the Orthodox after the crusaders had been driven from Palestine. Under Patriarch Sophronios III (after 1281 — before 1303),[52] the manuscript was donated to the cloister, now designated as *dayr alamāna* in Arabic. Another Arab note by Patriarch Gregorios II, dating from 1322, describes the further history of the manuscript: originally, the manuscript had

---

[50] Öljeitü, however, apparently only wanted to gain time while attempting to put together an alliance with western rulers against the Mamluks: Reuven Amitai-Preiss, "Mongol Imperial Ideology and the Ilkhanid War against the Mamluks", in *The Mongol Empire and its Legacy*, ed. *idem* and David O. Morgan, Islamic History and Civilization: Studies and Texts, 24 (Leiden, Boston and Cologne, 1999), p. 69.

[51] A summary of the *vita* is given in Tarchnishvili and Assfalg, *Geschichte der kirchlichen georgischen Literatur* (see n. 30), pp. 417-8.

[52] For Sophronios cf. Venance Grumel, "La chronologie des patriarches grecs de Jérusalem au XIIIe siècle", *Revue des études byzantines*, 20 (1962), pp. 197-201; and Pahlitzsch, *Graeci und Suriani* (see n. 7), p. 351.

been donated to St Mary's Cloister, called *alamāna*. "In the year of the Tartars" ("sanat at-tartar"), i.e. that of the Mongols, it was robbed from the cloister and then bought back by the believers, who donated it to the Anastasis, in whose possession it still is today.[53] The looting by the Mongols probably refers to the incursions of the Mongols against the Christian populace, described by Baybars al-Manṣūri and the Georgian chronicle, *The Life of Kartli*. These took place during the short-lived Mongol conquest of Palestine in 1300.[54]

The Orthodox patriarchs continued to reside in Jerusalem and still played a role in the Orthodox world. In particular, this is shown by one episode which took place during the disputes, held after the Council of Lyons in 1274 within the Byzantine Church, concerning the Union of the Orthodox and the Latin Churches. The Patriarch of Constantinople, Joseph, went to Jerusalem as leader of the anti-unionist party in order to persuade Patriarch Gregory of Jerusalem to plot against the Emperor. Later, Gregory had a treatise published attacking the doctrine of the unionist John Bekkos.[55] The Greek Orthodox Church of Jerusalem retained its political importance for two closely connected reasons. For one, the Holy Land and the Holy City never ceased to be the most attractive destination for Orthodox pilgrims; the Church of Jerusalem was held in special veneration by the Orthodox as being founded by Jesus Christ himself.[56] On the other hand, the importance of the city played a signifi-

[53] For the manuscript cf. *ibid.*, pp. 228 and 350-1.

[54] Ibn Abī Faḍāʾil, *an-Nahj as-sadīd*, PO XIV, fasc. 3: Moufazzal ibn Abil-Fazaïl, *Histoire des Sultans Mamlouks* (fasc. 2) (Paris, 1920; reprint Turnhout, 1984), pp. 502-3, mentions Baybars al-Manṣūrī, *Zubdat al-fikra* (see n. 36), pp. 343-4, as his source but, without telling us that this is not in the original, adds that the Mongols "killed both Muslims and Christians"; *Histoire de la Géorgie*, trans. M. Brosset (St Petersburg, 1849), p. 631. Amitai-Preiss, "Mongol Raids into Palestine" (see n. 26), pp. 244-7, carefully analyses the various sources for the raiding of Jerusalem; cf. also Richard B. Rose, "Jerusalem and Jihad — The Devotion of the Iberian Nation to Jerusalem: A Footnote on the Role of the Georgians in Late Medieval Jerusalem", *Proche-Orient Chrétien*, 41 (1991), p. 22.

[55] For the plot against the union cf. Georgios Pachymeres, *Relationes historici*, ed. Albert Failler, trans. Vitalien Laurent (Paris, 1984), book 6, c. 1, pp. 544-7; Vitalien Laurent, "Le serment antilatin du patriarche Joseph Ier (Juin 1273)", *Échos d'Orient*, 26 (1927), p. 404; Donald M. Nicol, "The Greeks and the Union of the Churches: The Preliminaries to the Second Council of Lyon, 1261-1274", in *Medieval Studies, presented to A. Gwynn*, ed. J. A. Watt a.o. (Dublin, 1961), p. 470. For the treatise that was written by Georgios Moschabar on Patriarch Gregory's instructions cf. Vitalien Laurent, "Un polémiste grec de la fin du XIIIe siècle: La vie et les oeuvres de Georges Moschabar", *Échos d'Orient*, 28 (1929), pp. 153-5.

[56] For Greek pilgrims to the Holy Land from the eightht/ninth century until the sixteenth century cf. Andreas Külzer, *Peregrinatio graeca in terram sanctam: Studien zu Pilgerführern und Reisebeschreibungen über Syrien, Palästina und den Sinai aus byzantinischer und metabyzantinischer Zeit*, Studien und Texte zur Byzantinistik, 2 (Frankfurt a.M., Berlin etc., 1994).

cant role for the Orthodox Church when it rejected the Roman pope's idea of primacy. Already before the Crusades, the Church of Jerusalem had borne the honorary title of "Mother of all Churches" in the Orthodox world — a title its patriarchs continued to use during their exile in Constantinople. When the Roman Church placed a claim on this title, the Orthodox Church promptly and unmistakably refuted this usurpation, arguing that this title could refer only to Jerusalem, where Christ himself had founded the Church. Nearly all of the sources dating back to the thirteenth century and dealing with this discussion, transmit this argument.[57]

We know a bit more about Patriarch Athanasios III, who held office in the early fourteenth century. When a certain Gabriel Broulas filed a complaint against Athanasios before the Emperor and the Patriarch of Constantinople around 1308, an imperial commission of inquiry was sent to Jerusalem which — presumably in cooperation with a local synod — removed Athanasios from office and elevated Gabriel to patriarch. Athanasios then turned to the Emperor himself, who cancelled his envoys' decision and reinstated Athanasios.[58] The Jerusalem Church, then, was clearly still part of the Byzantine Imperial Church and the Emperor and the Patriarch of Constantinople were actively involved in Jerusalem affairs.

A prerequisite for these close ties of the Patriarchate of Jerusalem to Constantinople was the fact that Byzantine relations to the Mamluks in general were good.[59] The Mamluks' main interest was to prevent any

---

[57] Patriarch John X. of Constantinople for one argues accordingly in answer to a letter by Pope Innocent III in 1199, cf. Donald M. Nicol, "The Papal Scandal", in *The Orthodox Churches and the West: Papers Read at the Fourteenth Summer Meeting and the Fifteenth Winter Meeting of the Ecclesiastical History Society*, ed. Derek Baker (Oxford, 1976), pp. 146-7; Jan L. van Dieten, "Das Lateinische Kaiserreich von Konstantinopel und die Verhandlungen über kirchliche Wiedervereinigung", in *The Latin Empire*, ed. Victoria D. van Aalst and Krijnie N. Ciggaar (Hernen, 1990), pp. 105-7.

[58] Venance Grumel, "Notes de chronologie patriarcale: Un synchronisme de patriarches (Constantinople, Alexandrie, Antioche, Jérusalem) dans un rouleau liturgique de l'Athos (XIVe s.)", in *Mélanges offerts au père René Mouterde pour son 80e anniversaire*, II, Mélanges de l'Université Saint Joseph, 38 (1962), pp. 264-7.

[59] For the Mamluk-Byzantine relations in the late thirteenth and early fourteenth century cf. Marius Canard, "Un traité entre Byzance et l'Égypte au XIIIe siècle et les relations de Michel Paléologue avec les sultans mamlūks Baibars et Qalā'ūn", in *Mélanges Gaudefroy-Demombynes* (Cairo, 1937); reprint in *idem, Byzance et les musulmans du Proche Orient* (London, 1973), pp. 197-224; Pia Schmid, *Die diplomatischen Beziehungen zwischen Konstantinopel und Kairo zu Beginn des 14 Jahrhunderts im Rahmen der Auseinandersetzungen Byzanz — Islam* (Diss. Munich, 1956); Peter M. Holt, *The Age of the Crusades: The Near East from the Eleventh Century to 1517* (London, 1986), pp. 159-63; see also n. 61.

harm being done to the import of military slaves from the northern Caucasus Mountains.[60] The Byzantine Emperor, on the other hand, was specifically interested in maintaining good relations with his powerful neighbour, the Golden Horde, that was allied to the Mamluks.[61] In view of the Georgians' political weakness and the consolidation of the Byzantine Empire under Michael Palaiologos (1258-82) and his son Andronikos II (1282-1328), Byzantium could thus regain its role as protector of the Orthodox Christians in the Holy Land. As already mentioned, the restitution of the monastery of the Holy Cross in 1305-6 was effected with the participation of the Byzantine Empire.[62] In return, Andronikos obviously hoped for the support of the Georgians against his enemies, since he sent an embassy to the King of Georgia, asking him for an army against the Catalans at about the same time as the Byzantine-Georgian envoys were in Egypt.[63] According to Chrysostomos Papadopoulos, the Georgians also gained Calvary by Byzantine mediation in 1308.[64] That the position of the Greek patriarch as ecclesiastical leader in Jerusalem was not questioned, is demonstrated by a decree issued by Sultan an-Nāṣir Muḥammad to Patriarch Athanasios III, dating from the early fourteenth century, in which we find the clause that the possessions of Georgian monks who had died would pass to the Greek patriarch.[65]

---

[60] Andrew Ehrenkreutz, "Strategic Implications of the Slave Trade between Genoa and Mamluk Egypt in the Second Half of the Thirteenth Century", in *The Islamic Middle East, 700-1900: Studies in Economic and Social History*, ed. A. L. Udovitch (Princeton, 1981), pp. 340-1.

[61] Amitai-Preiss, *Mongols and Mamluks* (see n. 23), pp. 91-4. Cf. also Bruce G. Lippard, *The Mongols and Byzantium, 1243-1341* (dissertation, Indiana University, 1983).

[62] For the restitution of the monastery cf. above n. 36.

[63] *Regesten der Kaiserurkunden des oströmischen Reiches von 565-1453*, part 4, *Regesten von 1282-1341*, ed. Franz Dölger (Munich and Berlin, 1960). Angeliki E. Laiou, *Constantinople and the Latins: The Policy of Andronicus II 1282-1328* (Cambridge, Mass., 1972), p. 175.

[64] Papadopoulos, "Ἡ ἱερὰ μονὴ τοῦ Σταυροῦ" (see n. 4), p. 655. In the short description of the Mamluk decree ("ὁρισμός", i.e. marsūm) dated 7th of Shawwāl 707/ 31st of April 1308 in Anastasios Papadopoulos-Kerameus, Ἀνάλεκτα Ἱεροσολυμιτικῆς σταχυολογίας, IV (St Petersburg, 1894; reprint Brussels, 1963), p. 441, it is just said that Golgotha became the property of the Georgians. Janin, "Géorgiens à Jérusalem" (see n. 1), p. 34; Peradze, "An Account of the Georgian Monks and Monasteries" (see n. 2), p. 188; Schmid, *Diplomatischen Beziehungen zwischen Konstantinopel und Kairo* (see n. 59), pp. 203-4; and the *Regesten der Kaiserurkunden*, no. 2311, provide no new evidence for Byzantine mediation. For the history of the dispute between Georgians and Armenians about the ownership of Calvary cf. Donald S. Richards, "Arabic Documents from the Monastery of St James in Jerusalem including a Mamluk Report on the Ownership of Calvary", *Revue des études arméniennes*, 21 (1988-89), pp. 455-69.

[65] Document no. VII.B. 7/501 (Rajab 713/November-December 1313), lines 24-7; Tselikas, Καταγραφὴ τοῦ ἀρχείου τοῦ πατριαρχείου Ἱεροσολύμων (see n. 49), p. 472.

In conclusion, it can be said that the situation of the Greek and Georgian Christians resident in Jerusalem or travelling there as pilgrims, essentially depended on the political events and developments in their home countries and on the relationship of their own rulers to the respective powers in Palestine. However, the relations of Greeks and Georgians amongst each other were not influenced in any recognizable way by political changes, at least not until the beginning of the fourteenth century.

APPENDIX

Arabic Sources on the Restitution of the Monastery of the Holy Cross

I. Baybars al-Manṣūrī, *Zubdat al-fikra* (pp. 385-6):

وفيها [سنة ٧٠٥] وصلت رسل من جهة ملك الكرج إلى القسطنطينية لقصد الأبواب الشريفة فجهّز الاشكري معهم رسولاً من عنده وأرسلهم فوصلوا في البحر إلى ثغر الإسكندرية ومنها إلى الأبواب السلطانية برسالة يسألون فيها أن تعاد إليهم كنيسة معروفة بهم بالقدس الشريفة يسمى المصلّبة كانت قد أخذت منهم مذ مدّة وبنى فيها مسجد بميدنة فأعيدت إليهم وردّت ضالّتهم عليهم.

II. Ibn Abī al-Faḍāʾil, *an-Nahj as-sadīd* (pp. 701-2):

فيها [سنة ٧١٠] وصلت رسل الاشكري وصحبتهم رسل الكرج إلى الأبواب الشريفة يسألون اعادة الكنيسة بالمصلّبة بالقدس الشريف إليهم. و كان الشيخ خضر قد انتزعها في الدولة الظاهرية و جعلها زاوية كما تقدّم فأعيدت إليهم بمقتضى فتاوى العلماء أنّه لا يجوز اغتصابه. وسأل الاشكري اجراء أهل الذمّة بالديار المصرية على عادتهم وفتح كنائسهم ففتحت. ورسم لهم بالاستواء في الركوب وكانوا قبل ذلك يركبون عرضاً من جهة واحدة.

III. Al-ʿAynī, *ʿIqd al-jumān* (vol. 4, pp. 378-9):

وفيها [سنة ٧٠٥] وصلت رسل من جهة ملك الكرج إلى القسطنطينية لقصد الأبواب الشريفة فجهّز الاشكري معهم رسولاً من عنده وأرسلهم فوصلوا في البحر إلى ثغر الإسكندرية ومنها إلى الأبواب الشريفة برسالة يسألون فيهالون فيها أن تعاد إليهم كنيسة معروفة بهم بالقدس الشريفة تسمى المصلّبة كانت قد أخذت

منهم منذ مدّة وبنى فيها مسجد بمئذنة فأعيدت إليهم وردّت ضالّتهم عليهم وقال ابن كثير: وكان الشيخ خضر انتزعها منهم في الدولة الظاهرية و جعلها زاوية فأعيدت عليهم بمقتضى فتاوى العلماء وأذن لهم في الاستواء في الركوب و كانوا قبل ذلك يركبون عرضاً من ناحية واحدة.

IV. Al-ʿAynī, ʿIqd al-jumān (Gocholeishvili, p. 38 n. 73):

فيها [سنة ٧١٠] في رجب وصل رسل الاشكري صاحب القسطنطينية إلى الأبواب الشريفة وصحبتهم رسل الكرج يسألون اعادة الكنيسة المصلحية [sic!] التي بالقدس إليهم. و كان الشيخ خضر في الدولة الظاهرية انتزعها من ايديهم فأعيدت بمقتضى فتاوى الشرعية.

V. Al-Maqrīzī, Kitāb as-sulūk (vol. 2, 1, p. 17):

وفيها [سنة ٧٠٥] قدم رسول ملك القسطنطينية ومعه رسول الكرج بهدايا و كتاب يتضمّن الشفاعة في فتح الكنيسة المصلّبة بالقدس لزيارة الكرج لها وأنّ الكرج تكون في طاعة السلطان وعوناً له متى احتاج إليهم. فكتب بفتح الكنيسة ففتحت وأعيد الرسول بالجواب.

VI. Al-Maqrīzī, Kitāb as-sulūk (vol. 2, 1, p. 90):

و[في سنة ٧١٠] قدم رسول ألاشكري ورسل ملك الكرج بهدايا سنية في رجب وسألوا فتح الكنيسة المصلّبة بالقدس. فكتب الجواب بأن هذه الكنيسة غلّقت من الأيام الظاهرية على يد الشيخ جضر وبنى فيها مسجد ولا يمكن نقض ذلك. ورسم أن تفتحت لهم كنيسة الملكية بمصر و كنيسة اليعاقبة التي بالقاهرة و كنيسة اليهود. و أذن لهم أن يركبون على الاستواء.

below the official meetings between the Syriac Orthodox high clergy and Latin kings or patriarchs.[4]

Among these the encounters between Syriac Orthodox and military orders present one starting point: in the three great Syriac Orthodox chronicles, namely the one by the Patriarch Michael (d. 1199), the one by the anonymous author of the chronicle ad a. 1234, and the chronicle by the *maphrian*, Gregorius Bar ʿEbrōyō (known in the West as Bar Hebraeus, d. 1286), some 25 passages mention the military orders.[5] Without already being able to solve all the textual and factual problems posed by these passages, the known Syriac material shall be evaluated and presented here to foster further interdisciplinary discussion between medievalists and orientalists.[6]

As will be seen, the Syriac Orthodox became aware of the military orders immediately after they were founded and accepted them as one of the Latin forces in the Levant. They were well informed about the spiritual concept of the military orders. Contrary to expectations they, apparently, had no objections to it. One could have expected otherwise: the members of the military orders — in the Levant most prominently the Knights Templar and the Hospitallers —[7] were men who combined reli-

---

[4] The since then often quoted passages were gathered by P. Kawerau, *Die Jakobitische Kirche im Zeitalter der Syrischen Renaissance: Idee und Wirklichkeit*, Berliner Byzantinische Arbeiten, 3 (Berlin, 1960), pp. 82-5. For new sources see H. Kaufhold, "Zur syrischen Kirchengeschichte des 12. Jahrhunderts: Neue Quellen über Theodoros bar Wahbûn", *Or. Chr.*, 74 (1990), pp. 115-51; A.B. Schmidt and P. Halfter, "Der Brief Papst Innozenz II. an den armenischen Katholikos Gregor III.: Ein wenig beachtetes Dokument zur Geschichte der Synode von Jerusalem (Ostern 1141)", *Annuarium Historiae Concilium*, 31 (1999), pp. 50-71.

[5] BE CE occ.; BE CP; AA 1234 CE/CP II; M (III). Apart from the introductions consult also A. Baumstark, *Geschichte der syrischen Literatur* (Bonn, 1922), pp. 298-300, 302, 312-20; J.-M. Fiey, "Esquisse d'une bibliographie de Bar Hebraeus", *Parole de l'Orient*, 13 (1988), pp. 279-312; A.B. Schmidt, "Die zweifache armenische Rezension der syrischen Chronik Michael des Großen", *Le Muséon*, 109 (1996), pp. 299-319; L.I. Conrad, "The Arabic Bar Hebraeus", *Parole de l'Orient*, 19 (1994), pp. 318-78.

[6] Indices given by the editors and translators of the Syriac chronicles in this case do not prove to be reliable: M 595-7 (III, 201-3); M 598 (III, 207-8); M 612-3 (III, 231); M 614 (III, 235-6); M 644 (III, 287); BE CP 319 (279-80), compare the Armenian revision: *Chronique de Michel le Grand*, Langlois, p. 310 (*lacuna* in the chronicle of Michael); BE CP 323 (283), compare *Chronique de Michel le Grand*, Langlois, p. 314 (*lacuna* in the chronicle of Michael); BE CP 330 (288), AA 1234 CP II 188-9 (141-2); M 720 (III, 379); BE CP 354 (308-9); M 734 (III, 404); AA 1234 CP II 198 (148); BE CP 373-4 (324-5); BE CP 390 (337); BE CP 430 (370); AA 1234 CP II 518 (171); BE CP 442 (379), BE CP 444 (381), BE CP 454 (389), BE CP 462-3 (396); BE CP 543-4 (463); BE CE occ. 669 (670), BE CP 578-9 (492-3).

[7] See J. Riley-Smith, *The Knights of St. John in Jerusalem and Cyprus c. 1050-1310: A History of the Order of the Hospital of St. John of Jerusalem*, 1 (London, 1967); M. Barber, *The New Knighthood: A History of the Order of the Temple* (Cambridge,

gious life and military service. As a form of *vita religiosa* this must have been unheard of within Oriental Christian communities, as indeed it was within Latin Christian communities.[8] Even for the members of the military orders themselves, their specific form of life could pose theological and social problems.[9] It is therefore worth noting that the Syriac chroniclers never seem to have been inclined to share the Latin's theological reservations.

Equally surprising is a report indicating that Syriac Orthodox and members of the military orders were killed side by side far up in the north-east of Syria. Both observations consequently lead to the question about the Syriac Orthodox's own attitude towards war, which has not yet been investigated systematically.[10] No exhaustive answer shall be attempted here, since the very existence of military involvement of Syriac Orthodox has not received the attention it deserves. These military activities, however, shall be interpreted as the context in which the Syriac reports about the military orders make sense.

II

The majority of the passages in the Syriac chronicles deal with military history. Involvement of Syriac Orthodox is not reported. The first well-

---

1994); for further reading consult K. Elm, "Die Spiritualität der geistlichen Ritterorden des Mittelalters: Forschungsstand und Forschungsprobleme", in *Militia Christi e Crociata nei secoli XI-XIII*, Miscellanea del Centro di studi medioevali, 13 (Milan, 1992), pp. 477-518; A. Luttrell, "The Military Orders: Some definitions", in *Militia Sancti Sepulcri — Idea e istituzioni: Atti del Colloquio Internazionale tenuto presso la Pontificia università del Laterano 10-12 aprile 1996*, ed. K. Elm and C.D. Fonseca (Vatican City, 1998), pp. 77-88.

[8] See, however, similiar institutions in a similar context, the early militant confraternities in Spain: N. Jaspert, "Frühformen der geistlichen Ritterorden und die Kreuzzugsbewegung auf der Iberischen Halbinsel", in *Europa an der Wende vom 11. zum 12. Jahrhundert: Beiträge zu Ehren von Werner Goez*, ed. K. Herbers (Stuttgart, 2001), pp. 90-116. I would like to thank N. Jaspert for reviewing the present paper.

[9] They had to face criticism as well as their own doubts. Exhortations are known to have come from the most approved authorities of the time, see Bernard of Clairvaux, *De laude novae militiae*, *S. Bernardi Opera*, ed. J. Leclercq and H.M. Rochais, III (Rome, 1963), pp. 207-38. J. Leclercq, "Un document sur les débuts des Templiers", *Revue d'Histoire Ecclésiastique,* 52 (1957), pp. 81-91; see also R. Hiestand, "Kardinalbischof Matthäus von Albano, das Konzil von Troyes und die Entstehung des Templerordens", *Zeitschrift für Kirchengeschichte*, 91 (1988), pp. 295-323, p. 296 for further references.

[10] See, however, A. Palmer, "De overwinning van het kruis en het probleem van de christelijke nederlaag: Kruistochten en djihaad in Byzantijnse en Syrisch-orthodoxe ogen", in *Heilige oorlogen: Een onderzoek naar historische en hedendaagse vormen van collectief religieus geweld*, ed. H. Bakker and M. Gosman (Kampen, 1991), pp. 84-109.

known battle to be mentioned is not, as could be expected, the siege of Damascus in 1148,[11] but the conquest of Ascalon in 1153.[12] The next incident mentioned is the battle between Reynald of Châtillon and Prince Thoros of Armenia in Alexandrette in 1156.[13] It is followed by the battle of Ḥarīm in 1164,[14] Montgisard in 1177,[15] the battle on the river Litani in 1179,[16] and Ḥaṭṭin in 1187.[17] The military orders are further mentioned in the context of consultations between Richard Lionheart and Malik al-ʿĀdil in 1191,[18] the siege of Damietta in 1219 and 1221,[19] and the conquest of Acre in 1291.[20] Here the military orders are depicted more or less like other military powers, who were involved in collecting tribute, in the assault and the defence of towns, and in political negotiations.[21] Where the chroniclers gathered their knowledge about these battles is a source-critical problem as yet unsolved.[22] The passages in question, however, sometimes clearly show Latin[23] and sometimes Muslim provenance.[24]

Another more general conclusion can be gained from this first glance. Michael and Bar ʿEbrōyō were born in areas of Muslim domination. Michael visited the territories of the Latins several times at the start of his administration, and Bar ʿEbrōyō lived there for part of his earlier life.[25] The anonymous is known for his excellent sources for the history

---

[11] M 639 (III, 276); BE CP 313 (274); AA 1234 CP II 149 (112).

[12] BE CP 319 (279-80); *Chronique de Michel le Grand*, Langlois, 310 (*lacuna* in the chronicle of Michael); AA 1234 CP II 155-6 (116-7) does not mention them.

[13] BE CP 323 (283); compare *Chronique de Michel le Grand*, Langlois, 314 (*lacuna* in the chronicle of Michael).

[14] BE CP 330 (288).

[15] AA 1234 CP II 188-9 (141-2); M 709-10 (III, 375) does not mention them, neither does BE CP 353-4 (207-8).

[16] M 720 (III, 379); BE CP 354 (308-9).

[17] M 734 (III, 404); AA 1234 CP II 198 (148); BE CP 373-4 (324-5).

[18] BE CP 390 (337).

[19] AA 1234 CP II 518 (171).

[20] BE CP 578-9 (492-3).

[21] See also BE CP 430 (730), 444 (381), 454 (389), 462-3 (396), 543-4 (463).

[22] Michael's secular sources for the twelfth century are virtually unknown, see the introduction of Chabot to M (I), xxxv-xxxvi; P. Kawerau, "Barbarossas Tod nach ʿImād ad-Dīn und Michael Syrus", *Or. Chr.*, 48 (1964), pp. 135-42; for Bar ʿEbrōyō see the recent studies of Herman Teule, esp., "The Crusaders in Barhebraeus' Syriac and Arabic Secular Chronicles: A Different Approach", in *East and West in the Crusader States*, I, pp. 39-49.

[23] At least I would like to suggest this for BE CP 323 (283), which must stem from Michael (now *lacuna*): compare *Chronique de Michel le Grand*, Langlois, p. 314.

[24] BE CP 373-4 (324-5), who preferred this version to that of M 734 (III, 404).

[25] W. Hage, *Theologische Realenzyklopädie*, XXII (1992), pp. 710-2, s.v. Michael der Syrer; H. Teule, in *Encyclopedia of Iran*, VIII (1997), pp. 13-5, s.v. Ebn al-ʿEbrī.

of Edessa, which is why he is widely assumed to be of Edessenian origin.[26] Be it as it may, he was certainly born after the loss of the County of Edessa to the Muslims but was in Jerusalem when it fell to Saladin in 1187.[27] Hence, he must have seen members of the military orders and the places where they stayed in Jerusalem and elsewhere. The chroniclers' starting position being quite equal in this respect, their interest in the military orders turns out to be less so.

The anonymous chronicler mentions the military orders only three times. He was also misinformed about their actions. After all, his intellectual world is not concerned with the West. He records, not whether scholars knew Greek but whether they knew Arabic;[28] in fact, he was mainly interested in Arabic culture and the Oriental world. No direct contacts between him and Latins of any position can be detected.

The bulk of the passages is offered by the chronicle of Bar ʿEbrōyō, which is only partly due to the *lacunae* in the chronicle of Michael.[29] Most of them concern military history. Some of the passages by Michael, discussed in the following, apparently did not find Bar ʿEbrōyō's interest.

III

Michael the Great describes the origin and early history of the military orders. The passage in question is inserted into his chronicle ad a. 1118 or 1119. It is distinguished by a headline, "tašʿitō da-frēr aḥe frangē", that is to say, "a narrative about the *frēr*, the Frankish brethren". Compared to other narratives in Michael's chronicle, no stylistic change can be perceived. From the way the development of the Knights Templar is presented, the narration must have been written in the second half of the twelfth century and before the battle of Ḥaṭṭin in 1187. This is congruent with the assumption made on other grounds that this part of the chronicle must have been written after the year 1165.[30] There is no positive

---

[26] Fiey in his introduction to AA 1234 CE/CP II, vii-viii again discussed the evidence concluding with: "Il semble que l'on puisse répondre sans hésiter que l'écrivain était Édessénien."

[27] AA 1234 CP II 200 (150).

[28] AA 1234 CE II 302 (226); AA 1234 CE II 309 (231).

[29] Two passages can be traced, see above notes 11, 12. Concerning the *lacunae* consult Chabot, Introduction in M (I), lx-lxii.

[30] D. Weltecke, "Mōr Michael der Große (1126-1199): Die Beschreibung der Zeiten" (unpublished dissertation, Berlin, 1999), pp. 127-30.

proof, however, that Michael himself was the author of this narration and in all probability he used second hand information.

Scholars do not hold this account of the origin of the *frēr* in high esteem as to the information it provides about the early history of the Knights Templar.[31] For the present survey, however, another feature comes to light: although the account does not relate any direct encounter between Syriac Orthodox and members of the military orders, it leaves the impression that such encounters must have taken place.

The narration starts off by reporting the first steps of the history of the Knights Templar:

> "In the beginning of the reign of *Bagduin* II [=Balwin II (1118-1131)] a Frankish man came from Rome to Jerusalem to pray. He had taken a vow not to go back to his own lands but rather, after helping the King in his battles for three years, he — and the 30 knights, who were with him — would become monks and would fulfil their lives there, in Jerusalem. And when the King and his magnates saw that they succeeded in the battles and virtuously helped the city during their service in these three years, they advised him, instead of becoming a monk and only saving his own soul, to serve in the army together with those, who would accompany him, and to protect those places from brigands. And when he accepted this advice, this man, whose name was Hū d-Payn and also those 30 knights agreed and came with him, the King gave them the house of Solomon for habitation and villages for their livelihood. And likewise the Patriarch gave to them some of the villages of the Church."[32]

Whereas this passage describes the assignment of the brethren as an unspecified military service on behalf of the city of Jerusalem, a second definition of their purpose is presented at the end of the narration: "Although they have been founded for the sake of the pilgrims, whom they guarded on the streets, later on they also set off with the kings for the battles against the Turks."[33]

This account reveals some apologetic elements: The virtuous Hugh de Payen and his knights were coaxed into military service with a very convincing argument. Instead of selfishly saving only their own souls by leading the contemplative life of the monks, they are asked to do more,

---

[31] Compare Barber, *New Knighthood* (see n. 7), pp. 6, 7, 10; A. Luttrell, "The Earliest Templars", in *Autour de la Première Croisade: Actes du Colloque de la Society for the Study of the Crusades and the Latin East (Clermont-Ferrand, 22-25 Juin 1995)*, ed. M. Balard (Paris, 1996), pp. 193-202.

[32] M 595-6 (III, 201). Concerning the dates of foundation see Hiestand, "Kardinalbischof Matthäus von Albano" (see n. 9). For a recent discussion of the sources of the origins see Luttrell "Earliest Templars" (see n. 31).

[33] M 596 (III, 203).

to join in good service for others. "Service" (*tešmeštō*) appears to be a keyword of the text. Military service is not only equated to religious service but fighting becomes a form of worship, as, in fact, it was in the conceptions of the military orders:[34] "And when it is ordered to go to a place to die, he has no right to say: 'I don't go!' but as he promised, until death, he labours in this service for faith" ("tešmeštō hōdē d-haymōnūtō").[35]

But to whom is this apology directed? The Orientals were not an interested party here, and their approval or disapproval of the way of life of the Knights Templar was of little concern to the Latin authorities. The passage, then, might rather preserve an argument of the early internal Latin conflicts connected with this new form of religious life and its specific discrepancy between the desire for contemplation and military duty.[36]

As to their religious way of life Michael's account reads: "And they defined their way of life by these rules, to live monastically [*dayrō'īt*]: that they have no women and do not go to the baths; and that they will never purchase anything separately, but give their entire property to the community."[37]

By *dayrō'īt* the Syriac Orthodox writer does not mean monasticism in the Latin sense. In the West, the previous four centuries had brought a great differentiation of rules, customs, statutes, and orders of monks and regular canons, whereas Syriac Orthodox forms of religious life remained individual and flexible. The term only refers to religious life in the community in contrast to the life of the anchorites. It is exactly this aspect of their life being a communal one which is repeatedly stressed, as the narrator says that all the new members, "sons of kings, and kings, magnates, and humble men are united with them in the brotherhood, which is a spiritual one" ("methayadīn ʿamhūn b-aḥūtō d-ak hōdē rūḥōnōytō").[38]

Both *aḥō*, the *terminus technicus* for the *frēr*, and *aḥūtō* are well established as terms for religious relationships in the Syriac Orthodox culture.[39] Nevertheless some informant must have explained the fact that

[34] See above notes 7 and 8.
[35] M 596 (III, 202).
[36] Compare esp. Leclerq, "Un document" (see n. 9), pp. 86-9.
[37] M 596 (III, 201).
[38] M 596 (III, 201), the sentence is unclear, perhaps incomplete.
[39] For some references see R. Payne-Smith, *Thesaurus Syriacus*, I (Oxford, 1897; reprint New York, 1981), pp. 110-1, who states "Praesertim Christiani se invicem fratres nominaverunt... postea coenobitae monachique nomen sibi assumpserunt, unde Angl. friars...", and *ibid*., pp. 111-2. Kawerau, *Jakobitische Kirche* (see n. 4), pp. 122-3, and the studies he used were unaware of this fact.

the life of the *frēr* was organized as a spiritual *confraternitas*[40] and he took pains to translate the Latin and French words. The narrator is also informed about some further peculiarities of Latin religious life: "Their habits [*amnē*] and their rules [*qōnunē*] are written down and are arranged."[41] The Syriac Orthodox tradition does not distinguish between rules and customs as written documents to regulate religious life, yet the narrator faithfully records both words. Again, someone apparently stressed these facts and translated the terms in question.[42]

Bearing in mind these translations of words and features of social life, one conceives a certain dialogue. As the narration unfolds and further details about the life of the brethren are related — revealing an amalgamation of features of the Knights Templar and the Hospitallers — two directions of dialogue become evident. The Syriac Orthodox would ask about aspects familiar to him from his own culture and religious experience: How does one become a *frēr*?[43] Do they really have no property of their own?[44] What clothes do they have apart from their white cloak? What do they eat?[45] How do they earn their livelihood and who does the work for them? The author records all information with equanimity, even the following one:

> "And for everybody who dies they celebrate 40 masses, and feed the poor for him for 40 days, every day 40 souls. And his memory will be kept in

[40] See Hiestand "Kardinalbischof Matthäus von Albano" (see n. 9).

[41] M 596 (III, 202).

[42] See *La Règle du Temple*, ed. H. Curzon (Paris, 1886); *Die ursprüngliche Templerregel*, ed. G. Schnürer, Studien und Darstellungen aus dem Gebiete der Geschichte, 3/1-2 (Freiburg, Br., 1903); *Cartulaire général de l'ordre du Temple 1119?-1150: Recueil des chartes et des bulles relatives à l'ordre du Temple*, ed. Marquis d'Albon (Paris, 1913); *Cartulaire général de l'ordre des Hospitaliers de St. Jean de Jérusalem (1100-1300)*, ed. J. Delaville le Roulx (Paris, 1894-1906). S. Cerrini, "A New Edition of the Latin and French Rule of the Temple", in *The Military Orders*, II, *Welfare and Warfare*, ed. H. Nicholson (Aldershot, 1998), pp. 207-15.

[43] Michael 596 (III, 202): "Everybody who comes to be a brother with them is rejected for one year. During that time [not: "On lui lit les règles par sept fois…"] the rules are read to him, and during the whole time he is told 'See to it that you do not deceive yourself, in case you are not able to live up to the fulfilment of these rules. Do penance and return to your home!' At the end of that year they say the prayers above the one, who accepts it and promises to carry the burden, as they clothe him in their habit."

[44] Michael 596 (III, 202): "They observe however the following custom that nobody is allowed to possess anything for himself, neither a house, nor money, nor other properties…. And if someone is found to have concealed something from the community, or, when he dies, it is discovered that he had something which he did not give to the community, they do not even spread the clothes, which consist of one simple white habit, over [him] for the funeral."

[45] Michael 597 (III, 202): "Their food is as follows: on Sundays, on Tuesdays and on Thursdays they eat meat, and the rest of the week milk, eggs, and cheese, but only the priests and the deacons who are serving in the churches drink whine with their bread every day of the week."

the masses of their churches in all eternity. And those who die in the battles, they count among the martyrs."

But in addition to these aspects, the Syriac Orthodox learns some features of the Latin way of organising religious life which he would never ask about because there is no equivalent in his own culture. Apart from the documents regulating their lives, these features include most prominently the centralised hierarchy of the knights and their strict rules of obedience and communal life.[46]

A specific feature of the narration requires explanation: if someone neglects the vows he took upon him, "... without mercy and without any intercession he dies by the sword".[47] This is obviously a dramatisation of the actual facts as is the description of the recruits of the new order, who are supposed to be "sons of kings, and kings, magnates and humble men".[48] Dramatisation is one of the prominent features of the narration.[49] This feature seems to allow some further considerations: if the initial informant had been a Knight Templar he would deliberately have been telling lies. However, the informant was probably not a Knight Templar. Rather, there seems to be a considerable distance between the chronicler and the initial cross-cultural dialogue.

At the same time, the dramatisation underlines even more strongly the rules and the asceticism of the knights, as well as the widespread recognition of their virtuousness and their fame. This feature, then, has apologetic effects as well.

IV

This narration about the early history of the *frēr* is followed by another one, concentrating on charity.[50] Here many of the features of the first

---

[46] Michael 596 (III, 202): "... and nobody is allowed to go out without the permission of the prior [*rīsō*], or to sleep anywhere else but in their house or to eat bread but at the communal table." Michael 597 (III, 202): "And in every city and in every village where they have a house there is a prior or a commander, and according to his command they all serve, each in his own occupation. The one prior common to them all is in Jerusalem. He is the one who rules over all of them, while on no account shall anybody be in charge over anything particular himself." See A. Forey, "Rank and Authority in the Military Orders during the Twelfth and Thirteenth Century", *Studia Monastica*, 40 (1998), pp. 291-327.

[47] M 596 (III, 202).

[48] M 596 (III, 201).

[49] Perhaps dramatisation is also responsible for the rise of numbers of the first members, which time and again puzzled scholars working with this passage, see above note 33.

[50] M 598 (III, 207-8).

account reappear; therefore the interpretation just given can now be tested for its validity. As indicated, Michael does not distinguish between the different military orders and only has one set of designations at his disposal, which makes it impossible to identify the *frēr* mentioned in his chronicle.[51]

In the year 1120, the narrator tells us, there was a severe famine in Jerusalem, and the *frēr*, whose custom it was to distribute food to the poor, were prepared to face death together with them and to share the small remains of their wheat with them. Then a miracle took place and they were able to feed everybody. "And this miracle was proclaimed everywhere for the glory of God."[52]

Again apology makes itself felt, this time described as a proclamation, which also reached the Syriac Orthodox. They were now, in fact, an interested party as they, too, were part of the religious and social landscape of Jerusalem affected by the rule of the Latins. Even if this account cannot at present be corroborated, the historical situation where Latins saw the need to legitimate their position towards their oriental Christian subjects is certainly genuine: Michael claims to be an eyewitness to the proclamation of the successful battle of Montgisard in the Principality of Antioch. Thus he learned a certain Latin version of the events, stressing divine support and hence, legitimate Latin warfare and rule.[53]

Again the use of specific terms reveals the ultimate origin of this piece of information: "... these *frēr*, that is to say 'brethren', those who call themselves *DAWYH* [ܕܐܘܝܗ] which is *alōhōyē*."[54] Jean-Baptiste Chabot, the French translator of Michael's chronicle, translated *alōhōyē* with *divin*, which seems to be a surprising self-designation for the humble *commilitones*. In fact, Michael obviously uses the same term by which the Templars are known from Arabic texts, *ad-dāwiyya*. Apparently this term cannot be derived from the Arabic and therefore different suggestions for loan words from outside have been put forward. Hitti explained the Arabic term as a Syriac loan word, as an arabisation of the

---

[51] Unlike the anonymous, Bar 'Ebrōyō again occasionally uses the term *aḥē* as Michael does.

[52] M 598 (III, 207).

[53] One wonders in which language this proclamation was made: M 718-9 (III, 375); compare BE CP 353-4 (207-8), who copied the account but preferred not to conclude with Michael's testimony but with quotations from a Muslim source, and a Muslim proclamation of the outcome of the battle issued in Egypt, which further stresses the importance of this medium.

[54] M 598 (III, 207).

Syriac *dōwē*, *dōwyō*.⁵⁵ But this derivation has been dismissed. Another hypothesis supposes Arabic *dāwiyya* to be the arabised Latin word *devotus* or rather, French *dévot*.⁵⁶

The Syriac sources corroborate this thesis. The anonymous and Bar ʿEbrōyō clearly use an Arabic loan word. Michael's spelling is a little different. He presents *DAWYH* as a term the brethren use themselves and translates it. His translation of the term *alōhōyō* should indeed be interpreted as "belonging to the god, sacred" instead of Chabot's *divin*. *Dévot*, therefore, is the original term. But *DAWYH* is a phonetic transcription of the *arabised* term. The Syrian again heard an intermediary, who in this case spoke Arabic.

V

The next two passages to be mentioned report actual contact between Syriac Orthodox and members of the military orders. Inserted ad a. 1130 in the chronicle of Michael the Great is the story of the rather restless Bishop of Segestan, who deserted his diocese in this year and was excommunicated because of that.⁵⁷ Time and again he is provided with a new see and livelihood, conspicuously with the help of a Latin, Jocelyn II, Count of Edessa, who strongly interfered in Syriac Orthodox affairs.⁵⁸ But the Bishop continued to fail and was expelled by the faithful. After 1138:

> "... he continued to wander about from one place to another and went to Jerusalem, and as he could not bear it in our monastery, which is there, he joined the Franks who are called *frēr*, and finally he fell into an oven and burnt."⁵⁹

No identification of these brethren with either of the military orders can be attempted here. But one would like to know why, of all the possibilities he could have chosen, it would be attractive for the Bishop from

---

⁵⁵ Ph.K. Hitti, *History of the Arabs: From the Earliest Times to the Present* (London etc., 1970¹⁰), p. 644, n. 3: "Ar. Dâwîyah, corruption of a Syriac word for 'poor', the original name of the order in Latin being *Pauperes commilitones Christi* (Poor Knights of Christ)." William Budge was not aware of the meaning of this term; he consequently translated it "wretched Brethren"; compare BE CP in his translation, 324 etc.

⁵⁶ St.R. Humphreys, *EI²*, Supplement fasc. 3-4 (1981), pp. 204-6, s.v. Dāwiyya and Isbitāriyya; H. Hein, "Der Deutsche Orden bei den arabischen Historikern der Kreuzzugszeit", *Der Islam*, 76 (1999), pp. 148-54.

⁵⁷ M 612-3 (III, 231-2).
⁵⁸ M 612 (III, 231), 628 (III, 259).
⁵⁹ M 613 (III, 232).

afar to join the brethren in Jerusalem. Neither Armenians nor Copts would accept him, and maybe the Latin monastic orders settled in and about Jerusalem decided not to accept him either.[60] At first sight, this passage is proof only for an isolated spontaneous encounter between Syriac Orthodox and brethren.

There are, however, more clues for connecting pieces in the triangle formed by the military orders, Jocelyn II, and Syriac Orthodox of the County of Edessa, and they are all the more welcome since little is known of the activity of the military orders in this area.[61] One of them is provided by the following lemma ad a. 1133. It alludes to some activity of the *frēr* far up in the north or even outside the Crusader States.[62] "During the time when this eclipse took place, that is to say the darkness of the sun, 40 knights *frēr* were slain and with them 400 other Christians and the deacon Bar QRYA."

---

[60] The miaphysitic sister-churches usually accepted each other's verdicts during the twelfth century as can be seen in a Coptic and in a Syriac Orthodox conflict; see G. Graf, *Ein Reformversuch innerhalb der koptischen Kirche im zwölften Jahrhundert* (Paderborn, 1923). Theodor bar Wahbūn had to leave the monastery of the Armenians in Jerusalem where he sought refuge and was accepted in Cilicia only after the conflict between the Catholicos and Patriarch Michael aggravated, see Kaufhold, "Zur syrischen Kirchengeschichte" (see n. 4). Prof. H.E. Mayer doubts that this encounter is historical and comments: Why should the Latin institution have accepted him, as he probably had nothing to offer? The motive of a bishop falling into an oven is also rather suspicious. This being true, the evidence leaves no room for doubt that the term *frēr* before the arrival of the mendicants can only refer to members of the military orders. Whether or not the narration is considered to be historical requires explanation.

[61] The first settlement of the Hospital dates back to the reign of Baldwin II, perhaps even to the time when he was Count of Edessa. Jocelyn II's first known donation dates from 1134, see *Regesta Regni Hierosolymitani (MXCVIII-MCCXCI)*, ed. R. Röhricht [= *RRH*] (Oenipointi, 1904), n. 206, 137b, 151. Concerning *RRH*, n. 390 see H.E. Mayer, *Varia Antiochena*, MGH Studien und Texte, 6 (Hanover, 1993), pp. 65-74, who dates the original chart to 1143, and *ibid.*, pp. 114-7, n. 3. I would like to thank Prof. H.E. Mayer for correcting this note and for the following reference: R. Hiestand, "Ein unbekanntes Privileg Fürst Bohemunds II. von Antiochia für das Hospital von März 1127 und die Frühgeschichte der antiochenischen Fürstenkanzlei", *Archiv für Diplomatik*, 43 (1998), pp. 27-46. See also C. Cahen, *La Syrie du Nord à l'Époque des Croisades et la Principauté franque d'Antioche* (Paris, 1940), pp. 510-26.

[62] M 614 (III, 235-6). See *Bartholomaei de Cotton monachi Norwicensis Historia Anglicana (A.D. 449-1298)* etc., ed. H.R. Luard (London, 1859), ad a. 1133, 62: "Eodem anno interfecti sunt omnes milites Templi. Eodem anno tenebrae factae sunt in Anglia et terraemotus; sol similis factus est lunae tertiae." *Matthaei Parisiensis monachi Sancti Albani chronica majora*, ed. H.R. Luard, II (London, 1874), p. 159: "Anno Domini MCXXXIII. Tenebrae factae sunt in Anglia, et terra mota est; sol similis factus lunae tertiae ... . Interfecti sunt omnes milites Templi Domini." Usually these passages are identified with the defeat of Damascus in 1129 mentioned among others by William of Tyre, *Chronicon*, pp. 13, 26. See M.L. Bulst-hiele, *Sacrae Domus Militiae Templi Hierosolymitani Magistri: Untersuchungen zur Geschichte des Templerordens 1118/19-1314* (Göttingen, 1974), p. 28, n. 39 and others.

No indication is given as to how this killing came about or where it took place. But some pages earlier the deacon is identified.[63] He belonged to the Benē QRYA, who were entangled in a fierce conflict with the Benē KMRA, concerning land property in the vicinity of the Euphrates. The Benē KMRA was the family of the Syriac Orthodox Patriarch Athanasius VII. The Emir of Amid became involved and the conflict aggravated into a veritable feud. The anonymous relates that the Patriarch was kept in Amid against his will and that he could take leave only after the diplomatic efforts of a certain Syriac Orthodox named Michael bar Šūmōnō, official of the Edessenian administration, second to Jocelyn II himself, who seems to have threatened the Emir with raids.[64] Hence, the anonymous alludes to military activity of Latins. The context is a little different, since the Count took the side of the Patriarch whereas the *frēr* perhaps fought with the Benē QRYA, but nevertheless the report of the anonymous corroborates the passage in Michael's chronicle.[65]

After the fall of Edessa conditions changed. In 1148 an event took place which brought the future Patriarch Michael, then 22 years of age, involuntarily into direct contact with the *frēr*:[66] the assault by Count Jocelyn II and his Armenian-Latin troops on the rich monastery Mōr Barṣawmō.[67] According to Michael, the attack has to be seen in the context of skirmishes provoked by the concurrence of Danishmendids and Latins in the border region, taking their toll on several Syriac Orthodox monasteries.[68] Following Michael's account, the priests accompanying Jocelyn apparently went straight into the church to loot, and afterwards Jocelyn "... ordered his soldiers to inspect the cells and to collect everything to be found in gold, and silver, and brass, and iron, and garments, and carpets".[69]

---

[63] M 602 (III, 213).

[64] AA 1234 CE II, 302 (226).

[65] Ten years earlier a Latin-Armenian contingent, also from Edessa, was active in the northern region for different reasons, see G. Dédéyan, "Un projet de colonisation arménienne dans le royaume latin de Jérusalem sous Amaury Ier (1162-1174)", in *Le partage du monde: Échanges et colonisation dans la méditerranée médiévale*, ed. M. Balard et A. Ducellier, Byzantina Sorbonensia, 17 (Paris, 1998), pp. 101-40, p. 105.

[66] See Kawerau, *Jakobitische Kirche* (see n. 4), p. 84 etc.

[67] E. Honigmann, *Le couvent de Barsauma et le patriarcat jacobite d'Antioche et de Syrie*, CSCO, 146, Subs.7 (Louvain, 1954); H. Kaufhold, "Notes on the Late History of the Barsauma Monastery", Hugoye (http://syrcom.cua.edu/Hugoye), 3,2.

[68] M 644 (III, 287).

[69] M 644 (III, 287).

These "Frankish scholars" were the well-trained and multilingual *fratres ordinis praedicatorum*, the Dominicans, who had recently arrived in the Levant and apparently maintained close relations with the Copts. They offered Ignatius their service suggesting that they settle the matter peacefully but the Patriarch went ahead in spite of them and ordained the *Abūna*.

> "And the *Per-per sūrōyē* heard about this and burned with anger and went to the brethren Knights Templar and Hospitallers [*dōwayē w-asbtaryē*] and agitated them and gathered their entire chapter. And they came to the Patriarch in great anger and sat down without saluting him. And the head of the brother scholars started and said to the Patriarch: 'I tell you: who are you? Neither was the city once bought by your wealth nor did you rule it with your sword, but as a stranger you came to us, and for the sake of Christ we received you in love and honoured you. And when you consulted us because of this unlawful act we forbade you. But you held us in contempt and trampled on our word. So why then and how did you do this, tell us boldly!' On the Patriarch fell fear because of them and he was struck dumb and his face became pale and his lips white. And he did not know what to answer them."[80]

Then the helpless Patriarch and Bishop Dionysius standing next to him discussed the situation in Syriac. Dionysius, who had acted as the Patriarch's messenger, took the risk of pretending that the venerable brother scholar had given his consent or that at least he, Dionysius, had understood thus. "Then the noble Franks [i.e. the hierarchy of the knights] said to the head of the brethren: 'Truly you don't know Arabic as you should do, and neither does this Bishop.'"[81] Mutual excuses were exchanged, and the matter was settled. The Patriarch thanked his Bishop for relieving him "from the accusation of these tyrants".[82]

This story is narrated rather vividly. It is difficult to evade the strong image of those armoured and fierce looking men, roaring at the intimidated Patriarch. With its moments of irony and ruse it seems fit for the amusement among like-minded people. And Bishop Dionysius was a good story-teller, whose testimony Bar 'Ebrōyō records several times.[83] Still, there is no reason to challenge the factual solidity of the account.

---

[80] BE CE occ. 659-61 (660-2).

[81] BE CE occ. 663 (664).

[82] *Ibid.* Kawerau, *Jakobitische Kirche* (see n. 4), p. 85, considered this passage to be significant, although it rather contradicts his concept of good relations.

[83] BE CE occ. 637 (638). It is the same Dionysius *sōbō* BE mentioned several times (Abbeloos and Lamy erred in assuming two personalities), whom he apparently knew personally and who died in the year 1273, see CE occ. 697 (698), 745 (746), 771 (772).

Ignatius III David, who is often presented as the Syriac Orthodox patriarch in union with Rome,[84] — information not corroborated by Bar ʿEbrōyō — is shown here in his utter administrative weakness. The Latin brother scholars, on the other hand, apparently feel entitled to forced action against the Patriarch and to direct church regimen. And they use the knights and their armed authority to support their cause.[85]

VII

Michael the Great reports that knights were killed together with Syriac Orthodox during an eclipse of the sun. One of the dead had been a deacon. Michael's sources for these accounts are unknown. Therefore some further circumstantial evidence shall be examined in this context. Military involvement of Christians in Muslim wars had caused new legal problems, concerning the role of the clergy in particular: from Bishop Jacob of Edessa's (d. 708) answers to some such questions,[86] two specific historical situations can be discerned. Firstly, the lower clergy resorted to military service as a means to survive in times of severe hardship. Secondly, all inhabitants of the cities were obliged to take part in the defence of the walls in case of war. The Muslim authorities forced the clergy to join the defenders.

Jacob's ruling was mild and compassionate. The deacons should be readmitted to service after some time. Jacob left it to the clergymen to decide for themselves whether they wanted to go back to service after having been forced to kill on the ramparts, and in his view it was ultimately for God to decide whether it was a sin to kill under these circumstances.

---

[84] See Cahen, *Syrie du Nord* (see n. 61), pp. 681-8; Hamilton, *Latin Church*, p. 350. Because of BE's silence on this matter and because no consequence of the assumed union was ever traced Teule, "It is not Right to Call Ourselves Orthodox" (see n. 76), voices again doubts.

[85] They obviously occupied the position of the traditional secular and clerical powers in Jerusalem, who demonstrated little interest for the city during the interregnum, see Hamilton, *Latin Church*, pp. 258-61; see also J. Pahlitzsch, *Graeci und Suriani im Palästina der Kreuzfahrerzeit: Beiträge und Quellen zur Geschichte des griechisch-orthodoxen Patriarchats von Jerusalem*, Berliner Historische Studien, 33 (Berlin, 2001), pp. 259-89. I would like to thank Dr J. Pahlitzsch for critical advice concerning the following paragraph.

[86] Additional questions of Addai, translated by R. Hoyland, *Seeing Islam as Others Saw It: A Survey and Evaluation of Christian, Jewish and Zoroastrian Writings of Early Islam*, Studies in Late Antiquity and Early Islam, 13 (Princeton, 1997), pp. 605-6.

Although Christian and Jewish minorities were generally excluded from military service by Muslim law, Syriac Orthodox also carried weapons in the twelfth and thirteenth centuries.[87] This fact is mentioned in the context of the fierce war between Turkomans and Kurds, which took place in the 1280s. According to Bar ʿEbrōyō and Michael the Great, the Turkomans invaded regions in Greater Armenia after they had defeated all the Kurds in Syria. Bar ʿEbrōyō's report reads:

> "... and from Tel-Besmy in the County of Mardin 170 of our Syriac men were killed, and of the village Amrun in the country of Qlaudia under authority of Melitene 200 of our young men [ṭlōyē] who carry weapons were killed."[88]

This passage is explicit about the Syriac Orthodox carrying weapons. But Bar ʿEbrōyō does not only quote Michael the Great in this passage. He also interprets Michael's account to some extent, for Michael himself reports the incident as follows:

> "And after that, when the governors saw that their countries were desolated because of the Kurds passing through, every one of them in his own country began to attack the Turkomans as there was war and killing all over Cappadocia and in the country of Melitene. At that time, when the Turkomans invaded the region of Qlaudia, the governor rose against them for war, and from the village and from the rest of the country about 200 young men were killed in the war."[89]

To Bar ʿEbrōyō it was clear that Syriac Orthodox were actively involved in the fighting, even if Michael the Great hesitates to be explicit about their actions. Michael's account explains his uneasiness:[90] the military command was in Turkish and Armenian hands.

Michael reports another case of Syriac Orthodox taking part in military action:

> "In the year 1449 [1138] when Edessa was almost under siege by the Turks, who were frequently raiding and did not permit its inhabitants to go in and out freely, there assembled in Samosata a multitude of people because of that to provide it with supplies, and with them Frankish horsemen and 300 Romans; altogether there were almost 4000 men, amongst whom was Abū Saʿd, a deacon, physician, and philosopher. As they trav-

---

[87] Concerning legal treatment of this fact by Muslim lawyers see A. Fattal, *Le statut légal des non-musulmans en pays d'Islam*, Recherches publiées sous la direction de l'Institut de lettres orientales de Beyrouth, 10 (Beyrouth, 1958), pp. 232-3, and his historical evidence pp. 233-6. See also A.S. Tritton, *The Caliphs and their Non-Muslim Subjects: A Critical Study of the Covenant of ʿUmar*, Islam and the Muslim World, 14 (London, 1930; reprint London 1970), pp. 185-6.
[88] BE CP 370 (321-2).
[89] M 733 (III, 402).
[90] BE CP 370 (321-2).

elled forth, an ambush of the Turks assaulted them in the night. This had been Ḥusam ad-Dīn, the head of Mardin. Then a multitude of them were killed and all the rest were led away as slaves, he, Abū Saʿd, and Michael bar Šūmōnō,[91] and his son. And Abū Saʿd had not been able to forecast the events of that day by the craft of the futile astronomy."[92]

Again Michael bar Šūmōnō, who was also involved in the affair between the Emir of Amid and Jocelyn II, is mentioned here. Michael bar Šūmōnō, the administrator, was none other than the brother of Basilius bar Šūmōnō (d. 1169), at that time Metropolitan of Edessa.[93] Basilius was accused of having taken the bishopric out of Jocelyn's hands, an accusation he rejected in a written answer.[94]

The assembly seems to have pursued the interests of all parties affected by the Turkish actions against Edessa, the Latins being one of them. But the presence of the Latin horsemen is unambiguous evidence that the supreme command was theirs. Hence, Syriac Orthodox were fighting under Latin command just like they probably had done in the year 1133. Joint military action, must then, in all probability, also have been the situation in the north of the county in the year 1133.

It should also be noticed that in the year 1138 a deacon was again involved. The reports of the spectacular sieges of the time reveal that the clergy, and especially the bishops, gained specific functions. They were engaged in the exhortation, and even in the command of the defenders of the cities, and they were targets for diplomatic efforts from the attackers.[95]

Jocelyn II is said to have forced Basilius bar Šūmōnō to join him in his attempt to recapture the citadel of Edessa in 1146.[96] Basilius also took part in the first defence of the city in 1144, as did the bishops of the Latins and the Armenians. According to the Syriac sources, the three of them in fact shared the command.[97] As to the people fighting on the

---

[91] Sic! Compare Chabot's commentary to M (III, 246), who prefers the reading of the chronicle of Bar ʿEbrōyō, see next note.

[92] M 622 (III, 264); BE CP 302 (265) continues: "Present with them was Abū Saʿd, a deacon, physician and philosopher, and Michael bar Šmūnō [sic! see previous note] and his son. And he, Ṭemurtaš, also took the castle of KSWS from the Franks."

[93] AA 1234 CE II, 305 (229).

[94] M 628 (III, 259).

[95] M 586 (III, 185-6), 648 (III, 295-6). See also BE CE or. 405 (406), where a *maphrian* is related fighting on horseback in the year 1231.

[96] AA 1234 CP II, 140 (105).

[97] AA 1234 CP II, 120 (90); M 631 (III, 262). See A. Rücker, "Aus der Geschichte der Jakobitischen Kirche von Edessa in der Zeit der Kreuzfahrer", *Or. Chr.*, 3. Ser. 10 = 32 (1935), pp. 124-39; Basilius, because of his subsequent collaboration with the new Turkish overlords, was accused of treason by Edessenians, as Michael reports, and was imprisoned for three years in Hromqla by Jocelyn II, M 638 (III, 277); see also Baumstark, *Geschichte* (see n. 5), p. 293.

walls, all three of the chroniclers assure that everyone without exception took his or her specific position in this situation.[98] Michael (and, by using his account, Bar ʿEbrōyō) also reports military engagement of monks: "And the people of the city — old and young, men and women, and the monks from the mountains — were standing on the walls and were fighting."[99]

Michael mentions an additional incident in this context:

> "During the first capture of Edessa, Bishop Basilius, who was ʿAbbas, was killed together with many; he had been Bishop of Mardin and had left his diocese and returned to live on the mountain of Edessa and there he was crowned."[100]

The passage is ambiguous. It is said that Basilius died a violent death, which is interpreted as martyrdom, and that he was not alone at this moment. One might only assume that Basilius faced death while defending the city; however, no action of the virtuous monk is explicitly stated.

Be it as it may, there are more clues to the fact that monks were not altogether alien to the use of force. In the monastery of Mōr Barṣawmō the memory of an assault lingered on, when about 300 Armenian brigands roamed the area of Melitene in the summer of 1066, looting villages and monasteries. In contrast to the year 1148, the intentions of the brigands were disclosed in time. A provisional guard, consisting of refugees from the region of Qlaudia camping on the hillside, "mighty men from Tel-Tūrō",[101] fought them off. But still a number of monks and *mšaʿbdē* were caught in an ambush, when they made their way home from Melitene from temporary exile two months later. There was an exchange of arrows, and three monks and two *mšaʿbdē* were killed. After citing their names, Michael the Great concludes: "The reader may pray for them, because they killed the murderers, and they were killed on behalf of the holy monastery."[102]

---

[98] AA 1234 CP II, 121 (91); BE CP 305 (268); M 630 (III, 261).
[99] M 630 (III, 261).
[100] M 630 (III, 263).
[101] Michael 574 (III, 163). It should be noted that several of the incidents recorded here point to the regions of Qlaudia and Gargar in the northeast of Melitene and at the eastern shores of the Euphrates.
[102] M 575 (III, 164), compare AA 1234 CP II, 46 (33), who relates an assault dated to 1045, when a few hundred Kurds were supposed to have been involved. No action of defence is mentioned.

Obviously monks joined armed action in serious cases of assault, and this could develop into outright war.[103] The monastery of Mōr Barṣawmō was fortified in the forty years to come, as is well known,[104] and it became a desirable fortress for Turkish and Latin forces alike. As a fortress it must have organised means of defence by manpower, for which there is some evidence: the monastery provided foot soldiers for the Emir of Melitene in the year 1242. Whether it did so voluntarily or not remains an open question.

> "The head of Melitene collected his troops, 500 horsemen, and for his assistance he took as well some of the *mša'bdē* of the monastery Mōr Barsawmō, proved men, 50 foot soldiers, archers, and they went to meet the Turkomans, and those from Bet Rūmōyē were defeated, and none of the *mša'bdē* escaped except for some few."[105]

In Bar 'Ebrōyō's narration there is some stress on the fact that these men had practise in bow shooting. Their social status is more clearly defined than that of the *ṭlōyē* mentioned above. In the present case they were *mša'bdē* of the monastery. William Budge and Jean-Baptiste Chabot used "subjects" or "serfs" as a translation. They agree with Robert Payne-Smith who suggested "mancipia monasterii" for *mša'bdē d-'umrō*.[106] But in this context the term needs further investigation.

Apparently they were employed as armed guardians as were the *nōṭūrē* (guardians) Barṣawmō and Eliah, whose names Michael records for the sake of memorial prayer.[107] At least in Mōr Barṣawmō *mša'bdē* seem to have been employed as guardians on a regular basis. In the insecure position Syriac Orthodox held between Turks, Kurds, Armenians and Latins, they surely chose those entrusted with guardianship very carefully. In fact, the *mša'bdē* of Mōr Barṣawmō in the twelfth century originated from the same villages and could argue with the monks on an equal level: in 1149 refugees from Gargar camped at Mōr Barṣawmō in

---

[103] BE CP 516-7 (440-1) records the dramatic attack on the monastery Mōr Mattai by Kurds in 1261, an incident to which Tritton, *The Caliphs and their Non-Muslim Subjects* (see n. 87), p. 186 already pointed.

[104] M 575 (III, 164). See Honigman, *Couvent de Barsauma* (see n. 67); H. Hellenkemper, *Burgen der Kreuzritterzeit in der Grafschaft Edessa und im Königreich Kleinarmenien: Studien zur Historischen Siedlungsgeographie Südost-Kleinasiens*, Geographica Historica, 1 (Bonn, 1976); idem, "Kirchen und Klöster in der nördlichen Euphratensia: Studien zur Religion und Kultur Kleinasiens", in *Festschrift für Friedrich Karl Dörner*, ed. S. Sahin, E. Schwertheim and J. Wagner (Leiden, 1978), pp. 389-414.

[105] BE CP 474 (405), see also BE CE occ. 773 (774).

[106] Although *ṭlōyē* could also be servants a decision is at present not possible. For *mša'bdē* compare Payne-Smith, *Thesaurus Syriacus*, II (see n. 39), pp. 2771-2.

[107] Michael 575 (III, 164).

search for shelter against Turkish raids. Some of the monks, concerned for piety and afraid of becoming the next victims, wanted to expel them from the confines of the monastery.

> "However, because there were monks and *mša'bdē* in the monastery who were countrymen of those refugees, they could not expel them. Then two parties were formed in the monastery: those who said 'it would be better to hand over these people', and those who cried 'we will not hand them over!', and they were close to fighting and swords."[108]

Conditions under which armed guardians, fellow countrymen and possibly even relatives of monks under constant military pressure, could have been held in the state of *mancipia* are hard to imagine.

CONCLUSION

In Michael's account of the early history of the *frēr* one notices some dispassionate interest. It reveals the existence of intercultural dialogue on the forms and terms of religious life. As to his attitude, Michael presents the knights as people who were good to the poor, and even if they were not good to the Syriac Orthodox, they at least refrained from doing them any harm.

Intercultural dialogue produced cultural knowledge on the side of the Syriac Orthodox: scholars of religious orders will find unambiguous transcultural proof that the knights were not monks but brethren in the Syriac sources.[109] Still, in the year 1138, the former Bishop of Segestan is said to have taken the house of the *frēr* as an appropriate abode for a monk, as he was one himself. Clearly, the Syriac Orthodox accepted that the *frēr* led a religious life. At the same time the specific spirituality of the military orders, which equated military and religious service, was known and apparently not objected to by the Syriac Orthodox.

Traces of direct Latin apology for the military orders were discovered. Latin apologetic proclamations to their subjects emerge as another context of intercultural contact. Was it a mere coincidence that these reached the Syriac Orthodox? It seems that, unlike Armenians and Greek Orthodox, they never did matter much to the Latins, neither as friend nor foe. At least this seems to be the message of the silence and the attitude of superiority expressed by the Latin sources.

---

[108] M 647 (III, 290-1).
[109] Hiestand "Kardinalbischof Matthäus von Albano" (see n. 9), p. 298.

In Bar ʿEbrōyō's report, it is the knights and the newly arrived brother scholars, the Dominicans in Jerusalem, who look down on the Syriac Orthodox Patriarch as a stranger. He describes intercultural contact too, but on unequal levels. The impact of these different forms of cultural contact on the Latin side cannot be assessed at present.

The case of the anonymous chronicler, his mentality so entirely different from that of Michael and also the differences between him and Bar ʿEbrōyō, indicate a factor which should always be taken into account when the relationship between the Latins and the Syriac Orthodox is discussed: strong regional and individual differences may be expected.

All in all, there are not sufficient data to reconstruct a development in the mutual relations. Neither of the chroniclers decided to focus on cases of formal alliance between Syriac Orthodox and military orders. The relevant reports seem to have slipped into their works by chance. The note about the ousted Bishop is a telling exception, supporting the overall impression. But the small passages scattered throughout the chronicles, which are more dense in the fourth decade of the twelfth century and again in the third and fourth decade of the thirteenth century, form a rough picture, which raises further questions.

It comes as a small surprise that the passages about contact with the brethren point to the County of Edessa, the Principality of Antioch, Cilicia, and to the city of Jerusalem. But activity of the military orders in the County of Edessa in connection with Syriac Orthodox matters of concern and together with Syriac Orthodox (auxiliary) troops in the year 1133, does come rather unexpectedly. In order to evaluate this dark passage in the chronicle of the Patriarch Michael, digressions were needed to analyse this particular coalition more closely.

Since this incident was recorded within a context of cooperation between members of the family Bar Šūmōnō both in the secular and the ecclesiastical administration of Edessa and the Count, and since further evidence was found to prove that Syriac Orthodox fought under Latin command in this area, it cannot easily be dismissed. In this context new questions about Latin administration and warfare should be asked. Neither Muslim nor Latin overlords could do without the military support of auxiliary troops. This also resulted in military cooperation with Syriac Orthodox, sometimes voluntary, sometimes undoubtedly less so. Neither Muslims nor Latins provided sufficient security for the Syriac Orthodox subjects against third parties. They were rather apt to turn violently against them. Syriac Orthodox could not afford to be the passive subjects, the non-fighting civilians they are usually taken for today. They had to look for means of defending themselves.

Some preliminary suggestions can be offered here as to how this was done in cities and monasteries. In this context military activity by members of the Syriac Orthodox secular clergy and by monks (as well as women) was mentioned. Their involvement in war seems consistent with their vital social functions in the infrastructure of the communities; as to the historical, theological and legal consequences, further study is needed. A hypothesis for the lack of objections to the spirituality of the military orders on the part of the Syriac Orthodox chroniclers was put forward. Their societies were not conceptionalised along the lines of the three *ordines* of *oratores*, *bellatores*, and *laboratores*. Hence, the spirituality of the military orders, which was undermining the western concept, could not cause the same irritation in the Syriac world.[110]

That so little should be known about these contacts is only partly due to the state of research. Apparently this is an area of a very volatile nature, ambiguous for both lords and subjects. The analysis of the chroniclers' reports revealed some uneasiness on their part to be outspoken about this subject.

It is true that the relations between Syriac Orthodox and Latins are generally described as cordial. Apart from the fact that this assumed cordiality always contradicted the overall disinterest of the Latin sources, what exactly does "cordiality" mean in this context? It is certainly not fit to serve as a historical category. Neither is it fit to qualify relations like these, maintained by people on unequal levels of power, bound by temporary common interests. The memory of the particular relations discussed in the present paper at least was cherished by neither of the two parties.

ABBREVIATIONS USED IN THE FOOTNOTES

BE CE occ.   *Gregorii Barhebrei Chronicon Ecclesiasticum*, I-II, ed. and trans. J.B. Abbeloos and Th.J. Lamy (Louvain, 1872, 1874), Syriac text and Latin trans.

BE CP   *Gregorii Barhebraeis Chronicon Syriacum*, ed. P. Bedjan (Paris, 1890); *The Chronography of Gregory Abu'l Faraj, the Son of Aaron, the Hebrew Physician, Commonly Known as Bar*

---

[110] See G. Duby, *Les trois ordres ou l'imaginaire du féodalisme* (Paris, 1978) for the theological foundation of this concept in the eleventh century. O.G. Oexle, "Die funktionale Dreiteilung als Deutungsschema der sozialen Wirklichkeit in der ständischen Gesellschaft des Mittelalters", in *Ständische Gesellschaft und soziale Mobilität*, ed. W. Schulze, Schriften des historischen Kollegs: Kolloquien, 12 (Munich, 1987), pp. 65-117.

                Hebraeus: Being the First Part of His Political History of the World, trans. E.W. Budge (Oxford and London, 1932), Syriac text and English trans.

AA 1234 CE/CP II
                Anonymi auctoris chronicon ad annum Christi 1234 pertinens, ed. J.B. Chabot, CSCO, 82, SS 37 (Louvain, 1953); *Anonymi auctoris chronicon ad a. C. 1234 pertinens*, II, trans. A. Abouna, introd., notes and index J.M. Fiey, CSCO, 354, SS 154 (Louvain, 1974), Syriac text and French trans.

Chronique de Michel le Grand, Langlois
                Chronique de Michel le Grand, Patriarche des Syriens Jacobites: Trad. pour la première fois sur la version arménienne du prêtre Ischôk (Venice, 1868).

History of the Holy Church
                History of the Patriarchs of the Egyptian Church, Known as the History of the Holy Church, acc. To MS Arabe 302 Bibliothèque Nationale, Paris foll. 287v-355r, IV, 2, Cyril III Ibn Laklak (1216-1243), trans. and ann. A. Khater and O.H.E. KHS- Burmester (Cairo, 1974), Arabic text and English trans.

M (III)   *Chronique de Michel le Syrien, Patriarche Jacobite d'Antioche (1166-1199)*, ed. J.B. Chabot, 4 vols (Paris, 1899-1924; reprint Brussels, 1963), Syriac text (III French trans.).

"THE LETTER OF LOVE AND CONCORD" BETWEEN ROME AND ARMENIA

A Case of Forgery from the Crusader Period

Mane Erna Shirinian*

During the crusader period many literary forgeries were created, both in the West and in the East. One of them is the forged document, known in Armenian literature as *Dashants T'ught* (The Letter of Concord or Alliance). It appeared in Cilicia in the form of a letter, preserved in many MSS[1] under the following title: "The Letter of Love and Concord between the Emperor Constantine the Great and St Silvester, the Supreme Pope, and the King of Armenia Trdat and St Gregory the Illuminator, Composed in the Year of the Lord 316".

This Letter, which is not very well-known in western scholarly circles, is similar to the famous forgery called the *Donatio* of Constantine. Both these documents are based on the same idea — the supremacy of Rome — and both are forged documents of the Emperor Constantine the Great, by which large privileges and rich possessions were conferred on the Pope and the Roman Church; in the case of the Letter, on the Armenian Catholicos and Church as well. The Letter had various redactions and found its way into some later redactions of Agathangelos.

Though this document is obviously a forgery, it deserves to be closely examined. This is also true for other forged writings because substitution of false documents was quite the fashion in the Middle Ages and it is impossible to ignore them. Besides, even in a forged form they provide important information in different fields concerning both Armenia and the West. The problem of forgeries is complicated because they are often laced with genuine information or based upon loose traditions. Sometimes the source can be recognized but very often it has been lost. It should also be noted that forgeries have a rather protracted history.

Substitution of false writings became an accepted practice from the first century onwards starting, for example, with the numerous

---

* For the abbreviations used in the footnotes see the end of this article.
[1] For example Mashtots' Matenadaran, Yerevan, MSS Armenian 516 (seventeenth century), 1520 (fifteenth century), 1920 (sixteenth century), 2272 (seventeenth/eighteenth century), 3078 (sixteenth-seventeenth century) etc.

Pseudo-Aristotelian or Pseudo-Pythagorean writings. Nevertheless, at the time their existence was well-rationalized and there were even standard methods for treating forgeries, which are, for example, attested in the interesting manuscript containing a "Commentary on Aristotle's Categories".[2] The lack of historical sense and the widespread presence of falsifications became more prevalent in the Middle Ages. The medieval practices of creating and treating sources has always been a great obstacle to the progress of historical study. As a consequence, in the light of the problems of early historiography, very little information concerning the legal history of the Eastern and Western Churches or the papacy is available. During the Middle Ages, it was quite difficult to evaluate all the sources of information, to distinguish genuine writings from apocryphal ones or to check those at hand, due to the popular legendary mind-set of the Middle Ages towards ecclesiastical antiquity. Even a casual glance at the fields of philosophy or theology of the Middle Ages makes it manifest that, during the Middle Ages, scholars were more successful in systematizing theology and writing commentaries than they were in the field of historiography.

Due to this medieval approach, there are many spurious or forged documents. But forgeries differ. One should not confuse the forgery composed in order to fill a gap in history (e.g. *The Decrees* of Pseudo-Isidore published between 847 and 852) with those that fabricated the signatures of the Roman popes or other officials. In the first case, medieval Christian scholarly practices played a role, since citations were not as necessary as in (antique) classical times, compilation was not considered plagiarism and, in any event, it was not easy to distinguish compilation from plagiarism.

[2] Mashtots' Matenadaran, Yerevan, MS 1930. The "Commentary on Aristotle's Categories" is ascribed to David the Invincible or Elias. It is a translation from Greek, preserved only in Armenian. It was found by H. Manandian, who made the *editio princeps*, *Eliasi imastasiri Meknoutiwn Storogouteanc' Aristoteli* (St Petersburg, 1911); cf. also H. Manandian, *Hunaban dproc'e ew nra zargac'man shrdzannere* (Vienna, 1928). In 1980 S. Arevshatian re-edited it, *Davit Anhaxt, Sahmank' imastasirutean* (Yerevan, 1980). Because of its Hellenizing style it must be a translation from the Greek. The MS is defective and starts with a ten-pages long text, which is of great interest because it has apparently been taken from another unknown translation from Greek which treats seven modes of *airesis* — *herdzuats*. Manandian published these pages as an appendix to his book; Arevshatian omitted them. For the substitution of false writings see Lazar Parbeci, *Patmut'iwn Hayoc' ew Tught' ar Vahan Mamikonean* (Yerevan, 1982), p. 13: "Stupid authors often use to write their weak-minded writings under a famous name." For the translation of a significant part of the text (Elias, p. 148; cf. also MS 1930, 9r-9v) see the attachment to this article.

Forgeries especially flourished in the ninth century and at the time of the crusades. A forgery such as the one composed by the Patriarch of Constantinople could be mentioned as an example of great learning and skill in the ninth-century. The forged "Genealogy" of Photius convinced the Emperor Basil — an Armenian by origin — that the latter belonged to the Armenian royal family of Arshakuni and that they were relatives; thanks to this forgery, Photius returned to his patriarchal see.[3] Such methods were widespread in the diplomatic service as well.[4]

The "Letter of Concord or Alliance" is based upon the historical tradition of the visit of the Armenians to Rome in the beginning of the fourth century. It has not received the proper attention of experts and a critical edition has not been published. The pro-Roman character of this writing also played a significant role in this: non-Catholics used to reject it as "an apocryphal, spurious document"[5] while the Catholics — including Armenian Catholics — gratefully accepted the tradition of *unitas et concordia* between Rome and Armenia.[6] However, the main reason for drawing attention to that tradition was always political.[7]

---

[3] M.E. Shirinian, "Genealogy by Patriarch Photius and *History of Armenians* by Movses Khorenac'i", in *Ashtanak*, 1 (Yerevan, 1995), pp. 85-96, esp. pp. 71-80 [in Armenian]. Interesting is that according to the "claim of Nicholas I, the document ought to have been supported by texts from the fifth and sixth centuries". Cf. "The Letter of Love and Concord". Hence, it might be possible that Photius was affected by this claim and the main source which he brings forward in his "Genealogy" seems to belong to the fifth-sixth centuries.

[4] For example, it applied in the "Acta rescripta" — documents compiled from extracts or remnants of the originals, which themselves or their ancient copies, had been damaged or lost. Cf. A. Giry, *Manuel de diplomatique* (Paris, 1894), pp. 12, 867, etc.

[5] M. Ormanian, *The Church of Armenia*, trans. from the French edition by G. Margar Gregory (London and Oxford, 1915), p. 15.

[6] It is not always a case of confession, e.g., L.S. Kogyan, himself a Catholic, considered this letter a forgery: *L'Eglise Arménienne* (Beirut, 1961), pp. 86-8.

[7] The Letter was especially needed in the second half of seventeenth century, when the Roman Church, with France, was fighting the Reformation and its influences in the East. For the Armenians, its "resurrection" could be a salvation for their ominous political situation. Several editions of the document were published in Italy. For the *editio princeps* (Venice, 1683) of the Armenian text (with Italian trans. by Hovhannes Holov) see H. Anasian (*XXVII-rd dari azatagrakan sharzhumnern Arevmtyan Hayastanum* [The Emancipatory Movements in Western Armenia in the Seventeenth Century] (Yerevan, 1961), p. 51), who found it back in Mashtots Matenadaran, MS no. 2272, as pp. 215r-36r (this MS also contains other printed texts). The Italian translation bears the title: "Lettera dell'Amicitia e dell'Unione di Constantino gran Cesare, e di S. Silvestro Sommo Pontefice [sic!], e di Tridade Re dell' Armenia, e di S. Gregorio Illuminatore...". The *editio princeps* is, however, not mentioned in bibliographies (G. Zarphanalean, *Haykakan matenagituit'iwn* (Venice, 1883), pp. 148-9; R.W. Thomson, *A Bibliography of Classical Armenian Literature to 1500 AD* (Turnhout, 1995), p. 149). Other editions appeared in 1690, 1695 and 1700, all in Venice. The first one also contains the Italian translation, possibly a reprint of the *editio princeps*. Inaccessible is the 1695 edition, *Lettera dell'Amici-*

Rome's interest in Armenia, the aforementioned historical tradition and the Letter are well attested in the activities of *De Propaganda Fide*. One of its representatives was the famous Armenologist C. Galanus, who translated the Letter into Latin.[8]

In 1824, in Constantinople, Dzhanik Amira printed the Letter as an appendix to the *History of Armenia* by Agathangelos. Among Armenologists lively disputes and confrontations arose, concerning its authenticity. As a result, two more publications of this document appeared: the "Confirmation of the Authenticity of the 'Letter of Concord'"[9] and its "Refutation"'.[10]

Though the Letter claims to have been written in 316, scholars agree that it is a forged document[11] because it makes references to the period of the crusades; it is believed to have been written between the eleventh and thirteenth centuries in Cilicia. In a sense, it is a kind of declaration of political orientation, on the basis of the old Armenian tradition about the alliance between Armenia and Rome.

CONTENTS OF THE LETTER

The Letter starts with introductory remarks,[12] saying that this is the testament of the Emperor Constantine the Great. Then the text itself is presented on behalf of Constantine, who declares that he ordered Pope Silvester to sign this document. The Letter continues with the journey of Trdat and Gregory to Rome. This part is a repetition of Agathangelos'

---

tia e dell'Unione, Appresso Bortoli, con Licenza dei Superiori. Zarphanalean, p. 149, writes that it contains only the Armenian text, but Thomson, p. 149, points out that it also contains the Italian translation. The third edition is mentioned by Hovhannisian, 1957, p. 80.

[8] C. Galanus, *Conciliatio ecclesiae Armenae cum Romana*, I (Rome, 1690), pp. 31-5. In the same year this work was published in Armenian translation. *Autographum Amoris et Concordiae* by C. Galanus, in *Sacrorum conciliorum nova et amplissima collectio*, ed. J.D. Mansi (reprint Graz, 1960), II, p. 461.

[9] *Dashanc' t'ght'i stuguteann hastatut'iwn, erkasirut'eamb Matt'eos, srbazan Kat'oghikos amenayn Hayoc'*, *Jrak'agh*, I (Moscow, 1860), pp. 237-44; 253-60.

[10] Shahnazareanc', 1862.

[11] It was already noted in the seventeenth century: *Histoire critique de la créance et des coutumes des nations du Levant*, ed. Sr. de Moni (Frankfurt, 1631), p. 134. See also K.V. Chahnazarian, *Réfutation de la prétendue alliance entre s. Grégoire et s. Sylvestre* (Paris, 1862), p. 11 ff.; Hovhannisian, 1957, pp. 58-80; Anasian, *XXVII-rd dari azatagrakan sharzhumnern* (see n. 7), pp. 49-52; Kogyan, *L'Eglise Arménienne* (see n. 6), pp. 86-7; R.W. Thomson, "Constantine and Trdat in Armenian Tradition", *Acta Orientalia*, L, fasc. 1-3 (1997), pp. 277-89.

[12] Shahnazareanc', 1862, p. 11; MS 2272, 215r-224r.

passage about the same journey, with some additions. In this forgery, the Pope of Rome is especially praised; he is honoured with distinctions such as "the successor of the 'chief' Apostles Peter and Paul, who has *the heavenly and earthly keys* of power, from the West to the East over all the nations of Christendom..."[13] This wording seems to have been drawn from the *Donatio Constantini* which states: "et tibi dabo *claves regni caelorum*; quodcumque ligaveris *super terram*, erit ligatum et in caelis, et quodcumque solveris *super terram*, erit solutum et in caelis."[14]

The Pope should have primacy over the other holy patriarchs and not only over all believers but also over the Emperor. Here Constantine pronounces the names of patriarchs and saints: "We truly believe that there are seven pillars of the world in our time: St Silvester in the West and St Gregory in the East. St Antonius in the South and St Nicolas in the North. And St Macarius in Jerusalem. And St Jacob in Nisibis. And St Ephrem in Edessa."[15]

The Armenian Catholicos and the King are similarly glorified and receive privileges and incredible gifts;[16] they are called "beloved brothers and true friends of our Eminent Power".[17] According to the Letter, the Emperor crowned King Trdat, calling him "p'arawor frers mer Trdates"[18] and granted him many privileges,[19] e.g. the right to possess the place where Christ was born in Bethlehem[20] and a piece of the True Cross.[21] Moreover, Constantine declares that he himself is the ruler of the West and that Trdat will reign over the East.[22] Trdat on his part, at the request of Constantine the Great ("I asked King Trdat to give me..."), gave him 300 fine warriors called "armens"; these should be guards in his palace day and night and should form the vanguard in time of war.[23]

---

[13] Shahnazareanc', 1862, p. 12; MS 2272, 222v.

[14] Ch.B. Coleman, *The Treatise of Lorenzo Valla on the Donation of Constantine* (Renaissance Society of America, 1993), p. 232.

[15] MS 2272, 226v; Shahnazareanc', 1862, p. 23 — in this version the names of St Macarius in Jerusalem and St Ephrem in Edessa are omitted, while MS 3078 has all these names (211r).

[16] Shahnazareanc', 1862, pp. 16-8, 27; MS 2272, 219v-220v; cf. MS 3078, 214r.

[17] Shahnazareanc', 1862, p. 12; MS 2272, 218v.

[18] "Our illustrious brother Trdat", Shahnazareanc', 1862, p. 20; MS 2272, 224v. In other places just Armenian *eghbayr* — "brother" attached to the name of Trdat, which always occurs with praising epithets.

[19] Shahnazareanc', 1862, pp. 16-8; MS 2272, 219v-220v, 223v, 226v.

[20] Shahnazareanc', 1862, p. 18; MS 2272, 223v.

[21] Shahnazareanc', 1862, p. 29; MS 2272, 226v.

[22] Shahnazareanc', 1862, p. 16; MS 2272, 219v.

[23] Shahnazareanc', 1862, p. 18; MS 2272, 223v-224r.

It is also stated that in Rome, Silvester endowed Gregory (who is called "a living martyr")[24] with patriarchal status and declared him to be equal in honour to the Sees of Jerusalem, Antioch and Alexandria;[25] furthermore, the patriarchs of these Sees should be ordained in accordance with his will and decision and confess to him as to the chief representative of the Pope in Asia Minor.[26] The Armenian Catholicos should ordain the Georgian and the Albanian catholicoses.[27]

The Letter also says that major privileges were granted to the Church and the clergy, including exemption from all kinds of taxes, and it questions the applicability of taxes, duties and rights to the Latin and Armenian population ("azatk' ew anharkk' linic'in yamenic' dimosakanac' harkac'n ark'uni"[28] or "italac'ik' ew hayk' amenek'ean anglxaharkk' linc'in"[29]). The passages concerning taxes not only reflect the situation of the Armenians, saying that they were not prescribed to the land,[30] but there are references to other nations as well. Indeed, in the Cilician Armenian Kingdom, the Church enjoyed some of the privileges referred to in the Letter; the Kingdom was, for example, tax-exempt.[31] But the privileged position of the Armenian Church in relation to other Eastern Churches, as presented in this document, is a fiction.

The alliance of love and concord between, on the one side, the Aryan[32] (*sic!*) Dalmatians (as the Latins are called in the Letter[33]) or

---

[24] Shahnazareanc', 1862, p. 12; MS 2272, 218v; 222v. Note that the same epithet is given by Nerses the Gracious: see Th. van Lint, "Seeking Meaning in Catastrophe, Nersēs Šnorhali's Lament on Edessa", *East and West in the Crusader States*, II, p. 54.

[25] Shahnazareanc', 1862, p. 24; MS 2272, 227v-228v; it said that Silvester endowed Gregory with the status of *Pap ew Patriark' ew Hayrapet* — "the Pope, the Patriarch and the Patriarch". The last word *Hayrapet* is a lexical calque from the Greek *patriarchs*, so it has the same meaning as the previous word.

[26] Shahnazareanc', 1862, p. 25; MS. 2272, 228v.

[27] Shahnazareanc', 1862, p. 25; MS 2272, 228v; MS 3078, 212v.

[28] Shahnazareanc', 1862, p. 23; MS 2272, 226v-227v.

[29] Shahnazareanc', 1862, p. 23; MS 2272, 227v. For example, the Letter states that "only Dalmatians and Armenians are free from capitations [poll-taxes]; all other nations and languages, who are conquered by us and Armenians should pay the capitations" ("glxahark").

[30] And it is a truth, as we know from V. Langlois, *Essai historique et critique sur la constitution sociale et politique de l'Arménie sous les rois de la Dynastie Roupénienne* (St Petersburg, 1860), p. 46. See also V. Langlois, *Le Trésor des Chartes d'Arménie* (Venice, 1863), p. 33, that Armenian peasants in Cilicia were more like western settlers and were not prescribed to the land as, for example, Muslims or Christians (Greeks, Syrians and others who were parishioners).

[31] On taxes cf. also the Greek *Vita Silvestri*, Combefis, p. 279 (for the Armenian translation of the Greek *Vita Silvestri* see Ter-Movsesian, p. 733).

[32] Shahnazareanc', 1862, p. 14; MS 2272, 217v.

[33] Shahnazareanc', 1862, pp. 14, 18, 23 etc.; MS 2272, 217v. For "Dalmatians" see Agathangelos, History, p. 409 and p. 500, n. 2.

Latins and, on the other side, the Invincible Torgomians (i.e. Armenians) was bound to continue until the end of the world.[34] It is also said that three lamps were placed "in Jerusalem in memory of the Latins, the Armenians and the Greeks."[35] At the end, the document informs us that this pact was written in Latin by the order of the Emperor Constantine and Pope Silvester and that there are two copies of this document. One of them was placed by Constantine, Silvester, Trdat and St Gregory in the Royal *shambrn*[36] (= *chambre*); another copy, equivalent to the first, was translated by Agathangelos and taken to Armenia.[37]

STYLISTIC ELEMENTS

One of the peculiarities of the Letter is that it has many loan words (mainly for technical terms) from different languages, including Latin (*pretorin*[38] — *praetorium*; *signaiwk'*[39] — *signis*; *burkaniay* — *vulcanus*[40]), Greek (*xruske*[41] — χρυσός (nom., m.); *falok'* — φάλος (nom., m.)[42]; *protopaps*[43] — πρωτοπαπάς (nom., m.); *zproton Armenian*[44] — πρῶτος) and French (*frer*[45] — *frère*). There are also loan words from Persian and Tartarian.[46] The technical terms from Greek and Latin make one think that the author used documents written in these languages. The loan words give some information about the author: his knowledge of the Armenian language was apparently imperfect but he knew several languages to some extent. Therefore the author could certainly have been a person living in Cilicia.

[34] Shahnazareanc', 1862, p. 14; MS 2272, 217v.
[35] Shahnazareanc', 1862, p. 28; MS 2272, 230v.
[36] In MS 3078 (216r) this French word is replaced by the incomprehensible *dzmambarn*.
[37] Shahnazareanc', 1862, p. 30; MS 2272, 217v; MS 3078, 216r; MS 516, 19v.
[38] Shahnazareanc', 1862, p. 24; MS 2272, 227v.
[39] Shahnazareanc', 1862, p. 17; MS 2272, 219v.
[40] Shahnazareanc', 1862, p. 24; MS 2272, 227v.
[41] Shahnazareanc', 1862, p. 17; MS 2272, 219v.
[42] Shahnazareanc', 1862, p. 17; MS 2272, 219v. Surprisingly, the rare word φάλος — "the peak of the Helmet" usually describing Homeric heroes, appears here. Note that all these loan words have Armenian endings, e. g. here *-ok'* (as well as *-iwk'*, here the ending of the Armenian instrumentalis, plural).
[43] Shahnazareanc', 1862, p. 24; MS 2272, 227v.
[44] Shahnazareanc', 1862, p. 18; MS 2272, 223v.
[45] Shahnazareanc', 1862, p. 14; MS 2272, 224v, cf. also 217v: *girs zays grec'ak' mimeanc' frerk's*.
[46] Shahnazareanc', 1862, pp. 92-7.

The Letter and Constantine's Vision

The Letter contains many elements of a legendary character. One of them is the prophetic utterance by Constantine the Great, conveyed to him by God, about the future of the Armenian nation. According to this prophecy, the "house" of the family of the Arshakunies (from which King Trdat descended) would be removed from Armenia by the Armenian nobles and the Armenians would be captured and go through terrible times until God would save them at the hands of Constantine's progeny; but that would be in a very distant future.[47] In his book, A. Hovhannisian examines the plot of this prophecy and its connections with similar predictions, such as the prophecies of SS Nerses, Agathon and Methodius which were known outside Armenia.[48] Traces of these predictions are found in sources from the seventh-eighth centuries.[49] It is noteworthy that these prophecies are not only discussed in Armenian sources.[50] Among them, Hovhannisian mentions St Sahak's Vision,[51] which seems to have many common elements with Constantine's Vision. Surprisingly, the Vision of St Sahak penetrated into the works of Byzantine authors, for example into Theophanes Continuatus.[52] Moreover, the part of the vision which deals with the family of the Arshakunies is closely connected with the information in the "Genealogy" composed by Patriarch Photius, and critics consider that it appeared in Byzantine literature, thanks to Photius and his forged "Genealogy".[53]

---

[47] Shahnazareanc', 1862, pp. 18-9; MS 2272, 223v-224v.

[48] Hovhannisian, 1957, pp. 63, 76 ff. Very recently another article by Thomson appeared in which this topic is also discussed: R.W. Thomson, "The Crusaders through Armenian Eyes", *DOP* (2001), pp. 77-82.

[49] For example, the Vision of Constantine is found in Georgian translation in a MS of the seventh-eighth centuries: Hovhannisian, 1957, p. 76; N. Marr, *Iz poezdki na Afon* (1899), p. 33.

[50] Otto Freising, *Die Weltchronik*, Teubner, VII, p. 33; Saint Martin, Mémoires historiques et géographiques sur l'Arménie (Paris, 1819), II, p. 432. There is a strong connection with the prophecy of Agathon (more often rendered as "Agadron" and as a rule he is called "invincible philosopher"), which is attested in many Armenian MSS. According to all these obscure but interesting prophecies, the salvation of the Armenians will come from the West.

[51] Hovhannisian, 1957, p. 37.

[52] H. Bartikian, *Teop'anesi Sharunakogh* (Yerevan, 1990), p. 143; cf. also *idem*, *Kostandin Tsiranatsin* (Yerevan, 1970), p. 51; M.E. Shirinian, *"Genealogy" by Patriarch Photius and "History of Armenians" by Movses Khorenac'i*, Ashtanak, I (Yerevan, 1995), p. 95.

[53] Bartikian, *Kostandin Tsiranatsin* (see n. 52), pp. 51, 265-266, n. 66; cf. also *idem*, *Teop'anesi Sharunako* (see n. 52), pp. 143, 344, n. 60.

Vita Silvestri and the Donatio Constantini

When speaking about the patriarchal sees the author of the Letter mentions neither the See of Constantinople, nor even the See of Ephesus, which was equivalent to the already mentioned Sees of Jerusalem, Antioch and Alexandria, before it bequeathed its rights to the See of Constantinople. This could mean that the document was composed after the crusaders' conquest of Constantinople in 1204, as some critics suppose.[54] However, this omission seems to be deliberate; it follows another spurious writing — the Greek *Vita Silvestri*, in which Constantinople was also omitted.[55] It is comprehensible in both cases: both texts being spurious and pro-Roman, a period was chosen when Constantinople was not even founded — the right time for praising the supremacy of Rome and simultaneously diminishing the role of Constantinople as much as possible.

There are more traces connected with the Greek *Vita Silvestri*. For example, the privileges granted to the Pope and the recognition of the primacy of the Episcopal See of Rome over other Churches, is taken from the legends of Silvester. The Letter repeats the story about Silvester's slaying of the dragon, adding that King Trdat defeated another dragon.[56] The remarks of Constantine about his ablution from the terrible leprosy called *zeghap'andean*[57] is also taken from the Greek *Vita Silvestri* — ἐλεφαντικῇ.[58] It is notable that the obscure and bizarre words about the doctors who were unable to cure Constantine of leprosy with the pejorative meaning "arioghkeann kaxardk' ew Marsikeann bzhishk"[59] (cf. Gr. "οἱ μάγοι οἱ λεγόμενοι ἀρίολοι καὶ οἱ ἐπαοιδοὶ καὶ οἱ Μαρσικοὶ ἰατροί"),[60] are here replaced by the no less pejorative, but more clear for that time, "yartark'n jemaranin ew sop'isteayk'n sokrateank'" ("skilled from the Academy and Socratic sophists"), i.e. Greek philosophers.

Does this mean that one of the sources of the Letter is the Greek *Vita Silvestri*? It is possible to think that the author of the Letter used only its

[54] E.g., Hovhannisian, 1957, p. 70.
[55] The Armenian translation of the Greek *Vita Silvestri* does not name it either, while the revision of this translation does not omit it (Ter-Movsesian, p. 693).
[56] Shahnazareanc', 1862, pp. 19-20; MS 2272, 224v.
[57] Shahnazareanc', 1862, p. 22; MS 2272, 226v.
[58] Combefis, p. 273. In the Armenian translation: *eghap'antakan*, Ter-Movsesian, p. 722; in the revision *eghap'andakan* (ibid.).
[59] Ter-Movsesian, p. 722; cf. in the revision: *ariokean kaxardk' ew aristokeann bzhishk* (ibid).
[60] Combefis, p. 273.

Armenian translation or revision. But if so, why did he not render the borrowed words in the same way as in the Armenian text? And how are the similarities with the *Donatio Constantini* to be explained? The following example clearly demonstrates that the author of the forged Letter used the Greek text (or, at least, if we agree that the Letter was translated, that he used the original). In the Letter, in the story about the slaying of the dragon, we read: "Dardzeal er vishap mi mets vnasakar i Kapetolin"[61] (Near the Capitolium the big and harmful dragon again appeared). In the *Vita Silvestri* it says: "Ἦν δράκων παμμεγέθης ἐν τῷ Ταρπείῳ ὄρει, ἔνθα τὸ Καπετώλιον ἵδρυται"[62] ("There was a very big dragon on Mount Tarpeios, where the Capitolium was situated"). In the Armenian translation of the *Vita* we read: "Vishap er mets yoyzh i Tarson lerinn, yorum ew tajar goyr nma"[63] ("There was a very big dragon on Mount Tarson, on which the temple stood"). Moreover, the word *Capitolium*, which is present in the Letter as well as in the Greek *Vita Silvestri*, is also missing in the revision: "Vishap er mets yoyzh i Tarson lerinn"[64] ("There was a very big dragon on Mount Tarson").

The scholars who studied the sources of this forgery do not mention the *Vita Silvestri* and the *Donatio Constantini*. Some sources and studies on the "Letter of Love and Concord" are examined in Shahnazareanc's book[65] and in the articles by Matt'eos Catholikos[66] and Thomson.[67]

However, several other writings are noteworthy:

1. A text under the same title: "The Pact between Trdat and Constantine", translated into Armenian from Greek (as it states) by the order of Chortuanel Tornikian in 1080.[68] Here Gregory the Illuminator tells us about the journey to Rome. It also says that "the alliance and concord was concluded between the Armenians and the Franks". The word "Franks" in this sentence shows that the document could not

---

[61] Shahnazareanc', 1862, p. 19; MS 2272, 224v.

[62] Combefis, p. 269.

[63] Ter-Movsesian, pp. 704-5.

[64] Ter-Movsesian, pp. 704-5. Cf. also the famous phrase "τουτω νικα", which is present here as well (Shahnazareanc', 1862, p. 22; MS 2272, 210v), and has similarities with the Armenian *Vita Silvestri* (Ter-Movsesian, p. 715; in the Greek text this passage is omitted). For more information about the sign of the cross that appeared in the sky and its reflection in the Armenian sources, see M. van Esbroeck, *Legends about Constantine in Armenian. Classical Armenian Culture*, ed. Th.J. Samuelian, Armenian Texts and Studies, 4 (University of Pennsylvania, 1982), pp. 79-101.

[65] Shahnazareanc', 1862, pp. 64-111.

[66] *Dashanc' t'ght'i stugut'eann hastatut'iwn* (see n. 9), pp. 240-4.

[67] Thomson, "Constantine and Trdat" (see n. 11); see also *idem*, "Crusaders through Armenian Eyes" (see n. 48), pp. 71-82.

[68] Hovhannisian, 1957, p. 76.

have been written before the crusades[69] because, in the Armenian milieu, this word, meaning all Catholics, became current only in the crusader period.

2. In his letter to Pope Urban VIII (*sedit* 1185-87), the officiating Armenian Catholicos Movses recognized the papal supremacy and expressed a desire for a renewal of the love and unity that had existed between St Gregory the Illuminator and Pope Silvester.[70]
3. In the "History of the first invasion by Lank-T'amur" by Step'anos and Nerses Metsop'ec'i, the large privileges and gifts granted to Trdat and Gregory by Constantine and Silvester are mentioned.[71]
4. In a spurious writing, preserved only in Armenian, the alliance between Armenia and Rome and the journeys to Rome and Jerusalem are largely discussed.[72]

THE JOURNEYS TO ROME AND JERUSALEM

As has been noted above, all Armenian sources of the Letter, as well as the Letter itself, are based upon the historical tradition about Gregory and Trdat's journey to Rome. From the very beginning of Armenian literature, many authors make reference to this journey. The most extensive passage is found in the History of Agathangelos, who describes this journey in ten paragraphs (873-883), without mentioning Silvester by name:

"When the Emperor Constantine, established by God and honourable holder of the throne, and the great Patriarch, archbishop[73] of the imperial

---

[69] Hovhannisian, 1957, pp. 76-7.
[70] *Armeno-Turcica: Selected Studies*, ed. E. Schütz (Indiana University, 1998), p. 288.
[71] Levon Xachikian, *Ashxatut'yunner*, I (Yerevan, 1995), pp. 283, 285.
[72] G. Frasson, *Pseudo Epiphanii Sermo de Antichristo*, Bibliotheca Armeniaca, 2 (Venice, 1976), pp. 20, 22, 24-6, 38-42, 54, etc.
[73] Cf. Agathangelos, History, p. 500, n. 2. The titles "patriarch" and "archbishop" are confusing. In the fourth-fifth centuries the word "patriarch" was merely used as an honorary epithet for any venerable bishop. This title gradually developed before it became a technical term and was used officially as a Christian title of honour for Pope Leo I in a letter of Theodosius II (408-50; Mansi, VI, 68). There are many examples of its application to bishops of a special dignity, e.g. in "On the Numerous Progeny of the Ancients", ascribed to Eusebius; Gregory of Nazianzus, in Orat. XLII, 23, says: "the elder bishops, or more rightly, the patriarchs"; Evagrius, *Ecclesiastical History*, III, 9; Sokrates, *Ecclesiastical History*, VII, 31, p. 379, 14 (but not in V, 8, p. 280, 21 because the Armenian translation has *hayrapetutiwn* (p. 419), which means that instead of *patriarchas, patriarchia* should be read. This reading was somehow missed in the new edition of *Sokrates, Kirchengeschichte*, ed. G.Ch. Hansen and M. Shirinian (Berlin, 1995), but Hansen accepted it, because he has grammatical, prosorythmical and other proofs that here the

court, who was called Eusebius, heard this, with great love they honoured them and went out to meet them."[74]

"... they were honoured with great solicitude and splendid pomp by the court and the ecclesiastical officials and the honourable princes of the city"[75]

"Then they took their leave from the purpled Augusti and the holy Catholicos, being greeted by the Church and the notable princes..."[76]

The name of Eusebius here is confusing because, according to both the tradition and Agathangelos, Armenians decided to visit Constantine after his conversion and at that time Eusebius was not yet pope. Silvester is not always specifically named in Agathangelos' passages,[77] but it is understood — and this goes for other sources as well — that Pope Silvester is meant whenever reference is made to the head of the Church of Rome at that time. In many other Armenian sources dealing with this journey, Silvester is specifically named. That is why, in the "Letter of Concord", the author tries to improve the place where Eusebius is referred to: "And by the order of Eusebius, the Great Pope of Romans, the successor of the supreme, called Silvester, signed."[78]

The sources and studies on this historical tradition are too numerous to be treated here thoroughly; many have been examined by Thomson.[79] In later narratives, the historical tradition antedating the forged Letter has been so mixed up with the details of the Letter that it is not easy to determine what is authentic and what is not. Moreover, in certain instances, even when the source of a text is the Letter but the text itself contains significant details that are absent in the Letter, certain additional details also appear to be authentic. One such example is the case of the thirteenth-century historian, Kirakos Gandzakec'i, who, in his "History", sets forth a large passage with details that are attested neither by the Letter nor by the earlier sources on the same topic:[80] he enumer-

---

context seems to corroborate *patriarchia*). The second title, archbishop, is more obscure for that time.

[74] Agathangelos, *History*, par. 875, p. 409.

[75] Agathangelos, *History*, par. 879, p. 413.

[76] Agathangelos, *History*., par. 880, p. 413.

[77] The name of Silvester is found in the Greek *Life of Gregory* by Agathangelos: G. Garitte, *Documents pour l'étude du livre d'Agathange*, Studi e Testi, 127 (Vatican City, 1946).

[78] Shahnazareanc', 1862, p. 12; MS 2272, 222v.

[79] Thomson, "Constantine and Trdat" (see n. 11); R.W. Thomson, "Crusaders through Armenian Eyes" (see n. 48), pp. 71-82.

[80] *Kirakos Gandzakec'i Patmut'iwn hayots*, ed. K. Melik-Ohandzanian (Yerevan, 1961), pp. 5, 11.

ates the possessions in Jerusalem[81] — Golgotha, the place of Christ's Crucifixion, St James, and a place for the liturgy at the tomb of the Holy Anastasis — which were granted to the Armenians by Constantine and Silvester.[82]

To the same tradition belongs the account of the journey of St Silvester and Gregory the Illuminator to Jerusalem when they divided the Holy places between the Latins, Armenians and Greeks. Some of these places belong to the Armenians up to the present day.

While critics in general agree on the non-authentic character of the Letter, they are divided into two camps concerning the crucial question: is the historical tradition completely legendary or is there some authentic information in it? This question eludes any easy answers because of the thorough blending of mythic and historic elements. In my opinion, however, it probably contains some authentic information. Some experts who reject the authenticity of this tradition, suggest that it is an adaptation of the visit of Trdat I to the court of Nero in Rome in the first century A.D.;[83] others who are not satisfied with all the Armenian sources say that there is no proof in other works. Kogyan[84] stresses that if such a tradition really existed, it would have been noted by Eusebius of Caesarea. He quotes from the *Vita Constantini*, book I, chapter 43, which Gatrjean[85] considered proof of Eusebius' knowledge about that journey, but it is not clear what he means, as there is no mention of the journey in this book. There is, however, another passage in the same work, book IV, chapter 7, under the title "Ambassadors from various barbarous nations receive presents from the Emperor",[86] which could be used as a proof that visits to the Emperor's palace were very common at that time. Eusebius describes how ambassadors from all nations continually arrived and brought their most valuable gifts. Then he continues that he himself sometimes stood beside the entrance of the imperial palace and observed a wild cortege of barbarians with various vestments and deco-

---

[81] On the visit of Constantine and Trdat to Jerusalem see also Vardan Vardapet Bardzrberdc'i: *Sopherk Haykakank'* (Venice, 1853-1861), vol. v, *Grigor Lusaworich*, pp. 78-9.

[82] See Thomson, "Constantine and Trdat" (see n. 11), pp. 285-6.

[83] See, for example, Hovhannisian, 1957; cf. Thomson, "Constantine and Trdat" (see n. 11), pp. 277-89.

[84] It is a pity that this useful book with its large bibliography is written in a tendentiously pro-Catholic manner solely as a response to or a refutation of Ormanian's, *Church of Armenia* (see n. 5).

[85] H. Gatrjean, *The Holy Massbooks of the Armenians* (Vienna, 1897), p. 65.

[86] *Eusebii Pamphili De Vita Constantini libri IV et Panegyricus atque Constantini ad sanctorum coetum oratio.* (Leipzig, 1830), p. 253.

rations.[87] He describes their hair and beards, the colour of their skin and their costumes in detail and among them he even distinguishes representatives of the Blemmyan tribes, Indians and Ethiopians. Then he describes the gifts they brought with them and tells us that they offered their services and allegiance to the Emperor. He also notes that the Emperor received these presents separately and carefully and also honoured the noblest among them.[88] This description resembles Agathangelos', when he depicts the visit of Trdat and Gregory to Rome. There is no mention of the Armenians but neither is there an exact mention of any other nation. Eusebius only mentioned exotic representatives. And so one can conjecture that the Armenian leaders were among the visitors to Rome.

THE ALLIANCE BETWEEN ARMENIA AND ROME

Another very well known and widely quoted passage, this time from his *Ecclesiastical History*, may serve as a proof of Eusebius' knowledge about the alliance between Armenia and Rome:

> "In addition to this the tyrant was compelled to go to war with the Armenians, who had been friends and allies of the Romans from ancient times.[89] As they were also Christians and zealous in their piety toward the Deity, the enemy of God had attempted to compel them to sacrifice to idols and demons and had thus made friends foes, and allies enemies."[90]

There are other examples as well, showing that in the beginning of the fourth century the Armenian Church was developing in the same context as the Church of Rome. It is accepted as genuine that in the time of Silvester the first martyrologies were composed and the first martyries were built. This information is given in the Greek *Vita Silvestri* for the first time but similar information about the martyrs and martyries in the Armenian tradition is to be found in Agathangelos' work.[91] This is a reason to conclude that in the beginning of the fourth century the first martyrology of Armenian martyrs was composed.[92] Moreover, the informa-

---

[87] *Ibid.*, pp. 253-4.
[88] *Ibid.*
[89] Cf. Greek, W. Bright, *Eusebius' Ecclesiastical History* (Oxford, 1945), p. 317; and Armenian, A. Jarean, *Evsebiosi Kesarac'woy Patmut'iwn Ekeghec'woy* (Venice, 1877), p. 688.
[90] Bright, *Eusebius' Ecclesiastical History* (see n. 90), pp. IX, 8.
[91] Agathangelos, *History*, p. 415.
[92] *Ibid.*, cf. "…in the province of Ayrarat at the city of Vagharshapat and the martyr's resting-places."

tion about martyrs in Armenia at that time is even richer, e.g. the martyrdom of Rhipsime, Gaiane and their companions who fled from the persecution of Diocletian and obtained asylum in Armenia where they were tortured and made saints and where their *vitae* were written. Why did they chose Armenia? This is yet one more obvious example of the close relationship between Armenia and Rome at the beginning of the fourth century.

The early alliance between Armenia and Rome is also attested in non-Armenian sources, which seem to be influenced either by this Letter or by historical tradition. After his visit to Armenia in the fifteenth century, Hans Schildberger, a German traveller, gave more details about this tradition from the narratives which he had heard on his travels and which are absent in the Letter. In the eighteenth century, Charles Cocquelines, an able scholar who had been engaged by the publisher to re-edit the six volumes of Cherubini's *bullarium* from Leo I to Clement X, presents the following passage:

> "Sane Armeniorum gens numero amplissima, as prope infinita; antiquitate et nomine celeberrima, Christianae Religionis studio et constantia supra universos Orientis Populos laudatissima, cum initio nascentis Ecclesiae gloriosis Apostolis Bartholomaeo et Thaddaeo docentibus, evangelicam degustasset Fidem, ac deinde Beati Silvestri Pontificis et Constantini Magni Imperatoris tempore, publico omnium consensu una cum Rege suo Tiridate (ita videtur dicendum) ut apud eos traditum est, recepisset, ac tanta praeterea veneratione, Pontificem Romanum omni tempore est prosecuta."[93]

It seems fair to say that the Armenian sources are based on a strong historical tradition, sometimes commingled with documents of a more legendary, spurious character or even forgeries, such as the "Letter of Love and Concord". But the main conclusion is that in the first half of the fourth century Armenia had close relations with Rome. Indeed, it was a peaceful and flourishing time for Armenia, as Coleman noted:

> "In Armenia, the reign of Trdat (Tiridates), a contemporary of Constantine, was a time of glorious national revival. The Roman government then and for some time after, supported the Armenian kingdom against the Persians, and the country had a breathing spell before its final political dismemberment."[94]

---

[93] Charles Cocquelines, IV, 78-80. Cf. also: "... nulla Natio, nullus Populus promptius, alacriusve eis (sc. Cruciatis) suppetias tulit, quam Armenii, qui viris, equis, armis, commeatu, consilio, ac denique omni ope Christianos sacro illo in bello fortissime ac fidelissime iuverant."

[94] Coleman, *Treatise of Lorenzo Valla* (see n. 14), p. 157.

One could even say that, being in "love and concord" with Rome, as evidenced in the "History" of Agathangelos, and having the primacy of the official adoption of Christianity, as Sozomenos reported, Armenia was at that time still a powerful state, the memory of which the Armenians carried forward through their history, from time to time trying to revive it. The peculiarities of that period should also be taken into account; when the Christian Church was establishing its official position, Christianity did not yet have a strong political influence (i.e. political issues were in the field of accepting or rejecting the Christian religion, rather than between the countries which accepted Christianity). The question was not: "where do you come from?", but: "are you a Christian or not?" A very good example is Gregory the Illuminator. He was of origin Parthian but lived in Caesarea and had Greek learning and a Byzantine education. He was in close relationship with Rome and became the person who enlightened Armenia, and the first "living" Armenian martyr. Another impressive example is the aforementioned escape of 40 virgins from the persecution of Diocletian and their asylum in Armenia. There were Armenian martyrs in Asia Minor in the third century who used to have Greek names and spoke Greek, using Armenian as a secret language when needed.[95]

Armenia, as a country that officially accepted Christianity in the beginning of the fourth century, must have had quite close relations with Rome until confessional — in fact, political — questions arose between them. Indeed, the Romans helped both Gregory the Illuminator and King Trdat to ascend their thrones.[96] Moreover, after the successful battle in 297, when the Roman and the Armenian armies together defeated the Persians, they signed a peace treaty for 40 years in Nisibis in 298.[97]

Apart from the historical tradition concerning the journey of St Silvester and Gregory the Illuminator to Rome, the Letter, as we have seen above, has a strong connection with the *Vita Silvestri,* which was widespread in Armenia. In some sense, it is even the repetition of the story of how the Greek *Vita Silvestri* — as well as other works, for example, the *Donatio Constantini* — were composed. Hence, this letter is an illustration of the motives behind the appearance of the Greek *Vita Silvestri* in the Armenian milieu.

[95] See H. Bartikian, "Christianity in Armenia Minor", *Historical Philological Journal* (Yerevan, 2001), pp. 3-43.
[96] There was another candidate — Albianos — who pretended to become Catholicos of Armenia.
[97] N.G. Adontz, *Armenia in the Period of Justinian,* transl. with partial revisions N.G. Garsoian (Louvain, 1970), p. 349.

The texts commonly referred to as *Vita Silvestri* have not been properly studied[98] and have no satisfactory editions. As a rule, experts mention them in the context of other topics, such as legends about Constantine,[99] the Symmachian forgeries, the Decretals of Pseudo-Isidore, the *Donatio Constantini*, etc. This is comprehensible, as they are closely connected with each other and were later even incorporated into each other.[100] Another reason for the neglect of the *Silvestri* texts is the fact that they are considered non-historical, have different versions and exist in numerous manuscripts.[101]

The most interesting aspect is that the Roman legend about Constantine's baptism by Silvester has been so mixed up with elements of its oriental versions that it is virtually impossible to uncover its original core without studying all these versions. Moreover, both the Latin original and the Greek translation have been preserved in different versions. The Syriac and Armenian translations were made from the Greek. Later, the short recension of the translation appeared in the Armenian milieu, at the same time figuring as part — namely the beginning — of a completely different writing: the "Short Recension of the Armenian Translation of Socrates' Ecclesiastical History".[102]

It is clear that the creation of the legend of Silvester served several purposes: for the East it was the Orthodox rehabilitation of the Emperor; for the West the aggrandizement of the papacy was of primary concern. Why did such a pro-Roman work appear in Armenia and how did the legend of Silvester spread in the Armenian milieu? It is true that it appeared in Armenia in the form of the "Story about the life of St Silvester", but it is also true that there are numerous references to Silvester in Armenian historiography before and after the appearance of the Armenian translation of the *Vita Silvestri*.

[98] The exception is W. Pohlkamp who deals with the Latin text and has written a few articles on this topic; see G. Fowden, *The Last Days of Constantine: Oppositional Versions and their Influence* (Princeton, 1994), p. 154, n. 43; idem, "Textfassungen, literarische Formen und geschichtliche Funktionen der romischen Silvester-Akten", *Francia*, 19 (1992), pp. 15-96.

[99] For example, Fowden, *Last Days of Constantine* (see n. 99); S.N.C. Lieu, *Constantine: History, Historiography and Legend* (London and New York, 1998).

[100] G. Cenni, *Monumenta Dominationis Pontificiae Romae*, I (Rome, 1760), pp. 304-6.

[101] W. Levison, "Konstantinische Schenkung und Silvester-Legende", in *Miscellanea Francesco Ehrle*, Studi e Testi, Bibliotheca Apostolica Vaticana (Rome, 1924), p. 166.

[102] For more details see M.E. Shirinian, "The Concise Version of the Old-Armenian Translation of Socrates Scholasticus' Ecclesiastical History", *Vizantijskij Vremennik*, 43 (1982), pp. 231-41 [in Russian]; idem, "Ricerche sulla storia ecclesiastica di Socrate Scolastico e sulle sue versione Armene", *Annali di Ca'Foscari*, XXXIII, 3 (1994), Serie orientale, 25, pp. 151-67.

Armenian sources designate January 2nd as the feast of Silvester, as is also the case in some versions of the Greek *Vita Silvestri*. In Armenian literature, the story about the baptism of Constantine by Silvester is found in the Greek Life of Gregory,[103] in the History of the Armenians by Movses Khorenac'i and in some other writings. In the Armenian tradition, Silvester is also closely associated with the Council of Nicaea — perhaps the most authoritative Council for the Armenian Church doctrine — which Silvester helped to organize with the Emperor Constantine.[104]

In the Armenian sources, Silvester is mentioned, not only in connection with the semi-legendary and semi-genuine historical events from the times when the Christian Church was establishing its official position, but also from a dogmatic point of view. The Armenian authors frequently quote Silvester and his testimonies in support of their own views on dogma. For example, Vardan Aygekc'i brought forward citations from the Armenian translation of the Greek *Vita Silvestri* under the title: "The Testimonies by Silvester, Patriarch of Rome".[105]

Not only Pope Silvester but also Pope Julius is mentioned in this book.[106] Moreover, these two popes are not the only popes mentioned in Armenian sources. A quite well-attested canonical list existed, a list of the ecclesiastical dignitaries and authors that should be accepted as "The Pillars of Faith", set forth by Samuel Kamrjadzorec'i (940?-1010?) in his "Apologetic Epistle" and addressed to Theodorus Metropolitan.[107] It presents, besides Silvester, other popes of Rome: St Clement I (*sedit* 88-97), St Julius I (*sedit* 337-52), St Damasus I (*sedit* 366-83) and St Celestine I (*sedit* 422-32). From this list one can see that all the persons included by the Armenians in their Canon[108] lived before the Council of Chalcedon and that their confessional points of view coincide with the Nicene Creed, to which the Armenians tried to be faithful throughout their subsequent history. That also means that, during the papacy of the above-mentioned popes, Armenia did not have a confessional problem with Rome.

---

[103] G. Garitte, *La Narratio de rebus Armeniae*, Subsidia, IV (Louvain, 1952).

[104] In general, scholars agree on this. Actually, the documents of the Sixth General Synod (680) affirm that the Council of Nicaea was convened by the Emperor and Pope Silvester (Mansi, Coll. Conc., XI, 661).

[105] *Vardan Aygekc'i, Girk' hastatut'ean ev armat havatoy* (Yerevan, 1998), pp. 780-2.

[106] *Ibid.*; cf. also pp. 12, 65, 85-8, 325-7, esp. 86, 327.

[107] *The Book of Letters* (Jerusalem, 1994) [in Armenian], pp. 555-6.

[108] In this case the etymology of the word *kanon* — loan word from Greek —, "straight rod, bar", becomes more symbolic for the Armenians, who tried to keep their balance in complicated political situations and confessional questions which would become serious problems for the Armenians.

Moreover, "The Letter of Love and Concord", being a blend of historical and mythical elements, provides a partial explanation for the appearance of the Greek *Vita Silvestri*: it is the same story adapted to the Armenian milieu. All the sources, then, can be seen as part of the same interconnected web of texts. They all originate in another, non-Armenian, pro-Roman tradition based on the real *Vita beati Silvestri*, which, at the beginning of the sixth century, served as a basis for various improvisations and forgeries, the first and foremost of which was the Greek *Vita Silvestri*.

We see a solid tradition of historical facts, well attested in the Armenian sources, which "underwent curious developments",[109] such as "The Letter of Love and Concord", which has been criticized on good grounds. M. Ormanian has explained well enough why this forgery was instigated:

> "As to the supposed license granted by Silvester, it rests on no more than an apocryphal document, which was fabricated by the Armenians at the time of the Crusaders. The object of that document was to protect the independence of the See of Armenia without offending the *amour propre* of the papacy, and at the same time to invoke the aid of the Crusaders in the interests of their kingdom in Cilicia. Moreover, all historical, chronological, critical, and philological information at our disposal unite in declaring the spuriousness of this document, which no longer finds a defender."[110]

But the main reason why such a document appeared was the concept of *unitas et concordia*, which, indeed, was desirable for both Byzantium and the West, for acceptance of their supremacy. This concept was not new; over the centuries, Byzantium and Rome, competing with each other, tried to get all other Churches on their own side. In particular, it became powerful during the eleventh-twelfth centuries, turning into the main political orientation for Byzantium and one of the constituent parts of the crusaders' programme. From 1166-1176 onwards, Manuel Comnenus, "sought to unite the whole of Christendom under his protection and conducted discussions about Church unity, not merely with the Pope, but also with the leaders of the non-Chalcedonian Churches of the East".[111] The negotiations of the Byzantine Emperor with the Armenians[112] were very successful. The conditions were discussed at the Synod

---

[109] Thomson, "Constantine and Trdat" (see n. 11), p. 278.

[110] Ormanian, *Church of Armenia* (see n. 5), p. 15.

[111] B. Hamilton, "Aimery of Limoges, Latin Patriarch of Antioch (c. 1142-c. 1196) and the Unity of the Churches", in *East and West in the Crusader States*, II, p. 4.

[112] When I speak about the "Armenians" I mean the Armenians in Cilicia because Greater Armenia was under Muslim rule.

of Hromqla in 1179 (for example, it was agreed that the Byzantine Emperor would ordain the Armenian Catholicos). But the death of Manuel I put an end to the possibility, however slight, of a union between the Byzantine and Armenian Churches.

Meanwhile, the contacts of Armenia with Rome were becoming more active. Disappointed by the aggressive policy of Byzantium, Armenians believed that the salvation for the whole of Christendom would come from the West, especially from Rome. The Catholicos of Armenia, Gregory III, and then Gregory IV, negotiated with the Papacy: "In c. 1184 the Catholicos Gregory IV, who had hitherto been a supporter of union with the Byzantines, sent an embassy headed by Bishop Gregory to Pope Lucius III... The Armenian Church had last made friendly overtures to the Papacy forty years before."[113]

This situation of permanent negotiations with the Papacy and the coming and departing delegations suggests that it was the right time for the creation of a forgery such as the Letter. In the crusader period, the Armenian Kingdom of Cilicia hoped to find support in this forgery because it demonstrated the ancient connection between the Catholic and Armenian Churches and the close ties between them and their secular leaders at the onset of the formation of their Churches.

ATTACHMENT

"Commentary on Aristotle's Categories" (*Eliasi imastasiri Meknoutiwn Storogouteanc' Aristoteli*, ed. H. Manandian (St Petersburg, 1911), p. 148):

"There are four categories of substitutions of texts: either because of the ambition of a king, as it happened with the king of the Libyans when he desired to have some of Aristotle's texts. He gave many treasures and that is why some people, out of fear or greed, sat down and wrote false texts and buried them in a stack to make them old, and brought them to him as a gift. The same happened when another king, Philadelphus, desired the texts of Ptolemy. He gave much money so that they would bring him such texts. This is one way in which texts are altered.

The second category was applied because of the positive disposition of pupils towards their teacher. For example, Pythagoreans ascribed their writings to their teacher, Pythagoras, and wrote down the name of Pythagoras.

---

[113] Hamilton, "Aimery of Limoges" (see n. 111), p. 9.

And the third category of conversion of texts were practices as follows: authors composed their own doctrines and in order to attract readers they ascribed them to Aristotle or Plato, i.e. to famous persons.

In the fourth category the conversion of texts occurs because of homonymity. Because not only Aristotle wrote 'categories', but also Theophrastes and Alexander; and the homonymity caused errors. Thus texts are altered in four different ways. This being so, it must be known that the false texts should be separated from the authentic ones by three different principles: either according to thoughts and words, or according to persons or according to teachings. As to ideas and words, we will say how to compare: for the writings of Aristotle are rich in ideas and poor in words..."

ABBREVIATIONS USED IN THE FOOTNOTES

Agathangelos, History
    Agathangelos, *History of the Armenians*, transl. R.W. Thomson (Albany, 1976).
Combefis   F. Combefis, *Illustrium Christi Martyrum lecti triumphi, Vetustis Graecorum Monumentis consignati* (Paris, 1660).
Hovhannisian, 1957
    A. Hovhannisian, *Drvagner azatagrakan mt'k'i patmut'yan, Girk' I- in (*Yerevan, 1957).
Shahnazareanc', 1862
    K.V. Shahnazareanc', *Dashanc' t'ghtoc' k'nnut'iwnn u herk'ume (*Paris, 1862). [= K.V. Chahnazarian, *Réfutation de la prétendue alliance entre s. Grégoire et s. Sylvestre* (Paris, 1862)].
Ter-Movsesian
    M. Ter-Movsesian, *Sokratay Sk'olastikosi ekeghec'akan Patmut'iwn ew Patmut'iwn varuc' srboyn Sighbestrosi episkoposi Hrovmay* (Vagharshapat, 1897).

SAINT LOUIS AND THE EAST SYRIANS, THE DREAM OF A TERRESTRIAL EMPIRE

EAST SYRIAN ATTITUDES TO THE WEST

HERMAN TEULE*

INTRODUCTION

One of the most popular writings among the Chaldean Christians of the last two centuries is the so-called *Book of the Magnet*. The original language of this work was probably Arabic, but it was mostly read in a Syriac translation, which survives in a great number of manuscripts.[1] The author is Patriarch Joseph II (1696-1712), who wrote it in the city of Amid (today Diarbakır in Eastern Turkey) in the year 1703. His aim was to provide the faithful under his pastoral care with some guidelines as to how to behave as good Christians. It is surprising to read in the Syriac version, that one of those good Christians much venerated by the Patriarch and held as an example to his flock was "Lowisios qaddišā", also spelled "Lōbis", "King of France",[2] who, according to Joseph, considered the place of his baptism as the most honourable place in his kingdom, since the baptismal font had added "Christian" to his name. This public recognition of his Christian beliefs and convictions was much appreciated by Patriarch Joseph. This is to be interpreted against the background of Christians living in a minority situation, who sometimes had great difficulties in expressing their Christian identity. Apparently, Joseph alludes to Saint Louis IX (1215-70), known for his public recognition of Christian values and for his holiness as well as for his participation in the Seventh and Eighth Crusades.

When Joseph was Patriarch, life was not easy for the Christians in the region of Diarbakır. There were only limited possibilities for educa-

---

* For the abbreviations used in the footnotes see the end of this article.
[1] On the *Book of the Magnet* and Joseph II, see *GCAL*, IV, pp. 100-4; R. Macuch, *Geschichte der spät- und neusyrischen Literatur* (Berlin and New York, 1976), pp. 42-4; and H. Teule, "Joseph II, Patriarch of the Chaldeans and the Book of the Magnet", in *Festschrift*, ed. R. Ebied and H. Teule, Eastern Christian Studies (Louvain, forthcoming). The *Book of the Magnet* is still unedited. I use MS Mingana Syriac 491.
[2] MS Mingana Syriac 491, fol. 6r, line 20; cf. fol. 15r.

tion — Joseph himself complains that he had to take lessons in a Muslim school in order to have access to learning — and the Christians were heavily taxed by the local Ottoman authorities. One can easily understand that the image of a powerful Christian king greatly appealed to Christians living in such conditions. Such a mythical monarch, however, was usually given the name Constantine, also by the East Syrians, who associated Constantine, or more generally, the Greeks, with any power that could free them from the yoke of the Muslims. Thus we read in the poem, "On Revealed Truth", written by the Chaldean priest Joseph of Telkepe in the year 1663: "that [God] save us from the Ishmaelites..., may our Lord re-establish the Greeks, that He establish the Greeks in our days."[3]

Is the idea of naming this mythical figure "Saint Louis" instead of "Constantine" a personal devotion of Patriarch Joseph or should it be traced back to the crusader period and the former contacts between the East Syrian community, the crusaders and the powerful monarchs of the West?

In order to answer this question we should look at the intensity and, more importantly, at the nature of these encounters: to what extent had the East Syrians or Nestorians of the twelfth and thirteenth centuries been exposed to influences from the West, so that in a later period the name of St Louis could become a symbol of the better times of the past? Unfortunately, most studies about the relations of the crusaders and Eastern Christians are focused on the contacts with the Greek Orthodox, the West Syrians or "Jacobites",[4] the Maronites and the Copts. This is understandable since the latter minorities were, of course, more numerous in the Crusader States than the East Syrians. The heartland of these "Nestorians" was Eastern Mesopotamia, situated outside crusader territory, and their presence in the Frankish states was rather marginal. This, however, does not mean that they were totally absent from crusader lands, took no interest in the crusaders nor received any attention from the Franks, as also appears from the works of B. Hamilton and Marshall W. Baldwin.[5] The aim of the present article is to investigate some of the

---

[3] Cf. A. Mengozzi, *Israel of Alqosh and Joseph of Telkepe — A Story in Truthful Language: Religious Poems in Vernacular Syriac (North Iraq, 17th Century)*, CSCO, 230-1 (Louvain, 2002), pp. 80-1 (pp. 184-5). For the theme of Hülagu and his wife Doquz Khatun as the new Constantine and Helen, see Fiey, *Mongols*, p. 23.

[4] See Hamilton, *Latin Church*, p. 209.

[5] M.W. Baldwin, "Missions to the East in the Thirteenth and Fourteenth Centuries" in, *A History of the Crusades*, v, *The Impact of the Crusades on the Near East*, ed. K. Setton (Madison, Wisc., 1985), pp. 452-518.

East Syrian documents related to the presence of Western Christians in the Middle East, paying attention more particularly to their theological content. Next, we shall return to the issue of St Louis and his image in the later East Syrian tradition. By way of introduction, we briefly discuss the marginal East Syrian presence in the Crusader States themselves.

THE SOURCES

For our investigation we have the following sources at our disposal.
1. A number of East Syrian works of a historical and theological nature.
1.1. The *kitāb al-Majdal* (the Book of the Tower). According to Georg Graf, the *Book of the Tower*, a theological and spiritual encyclopedia in seven parts, was composed in the middle of the twelfth century, which would make it an important source for our knowledge of the East Syrians in the early crusader times. Two recent studies[6] have convincingly argued that it should be dated to the early eleventh century, that is to the period before the crusaders. The *Book of the Tower*, however, contains a historical section (in part V.2) on the Nestorian patriarchs up to ʿAbdišoʿ III, who died in 1147. Most probably this is an update by a subsequent reader, or even readers, wishing to continue the chronicle up to their own time. We can use this Patriarchal Chronicle, since it gives some information about Nestorian episcopal sees in crusader territories.[7]
1.2 There exists a comparable work, which was erroneously also designated by Graf, on the authority of J.S. Assemani's *Bibliotheca orientalis*, as "Book of the Tower". This work, divided into five parts, is known in Arabic under different titles: *asfār al-asrār* (the Books of the Mysteries), *kitāb al-taʾrīḫ* (the Book of History), *kitāb al-tawārīḫ* (the Book of Dates) and *risālat al-Burhān wa l-Iršād* (a Treatise of Demonstration and Guidance), though the last title is more appropriately applied only to the first part.[8] It was composed by the priest Ṣalībā b. Yuḥannā al-Mawṣilī in 1332, possibly on the Isle of Cyprus.[9] It is a theological and

---

[6] B. Holmberg, "A Reconsideration of the kitāb al-Maǧdal", in *Actes du 4e congrès international d'études arabes chrétiennes (Cambridge, Septembre 1992)*, ed. Khalil Samir Khalil, *Parole de l'Orient*, 18 (1993), pp. 256-62; and especially Landron, pp. 99-108.

[7] This chronicle was edited by Gismondi (I).

[8] A presentation of this work is given in Landron, p. 140 and especially in Wright-Cook, *Catalogue*, with a description of MS Add. 2889, pp. 754-92. Book I can be consulted in Gianazza, "Traité".

[9] From the colophon of MS Paris Ar. 204 we know that Ṣalībā was in Famagusta in the year 1336, cf. G. Troupeau, *Catalogue des manuscrits arabes: Manuscrits chrétiens*, I (Paris, 1972), p. 173.

historical compendium, the first part of which is explicitly intended for the Christians of the West, and, like the *kitāb al-Majdal*, contains a historical section on the Nestorian patriarchs.[10]

Apart from the relevant — be it scarce — information found in this section, this compendium is especially important, since it is no less than an exhortation to love between the East Syrians and their western brothers. Besides the ecumenical theories developed by Ṣalībā himself, it also contains a number of extracts taken from the writings of some East Syrian theologians, including those who sent some doctrinal letters to the Pope, such as the Metropolitan of Nisibis, Išoʿyahb b. Malkon. These Arabic extracts may help us to better understand the doctrinal letters composed by these authors and preserved in Latin translations (see *infra*, nr 3.).

2. *Tašʿitā d-Mār Yahbalāhā qatolikā d-madnḥā wa-d-rabbān Ṣawmā saʿorā gawānāyā* (The History of Mar Yahbalāhā, Catholicos of the East, and of Rabban Ṣawmā, visitor general). This work, written in Syriac between 1317 and 1319, not only gives a description of the life of Yahbalāhā III (d. 1317), the Mongol Patriarch-Catholicos of the Church of the East at the end of the crusader period, but in particular a description of the journey of the monk Ṣawmā, sent as an envoy of both the Mongol King Argun and of Yahbalāhā to the Pope and to the western Christian leaders in order to ask their assistance for the liberation of Jerusalem.[11] This source should be complemented by the reports of other eastern embassies visiting the West.

3. Letters, declarations and creeds, written by different East Syrian dignitaries and theologians, and intended for the Pope or other western leaders, such as St Louis. These documents were originally composed in Arabic or maybe Syriac, the languages of the authors, but Latin translations had to be made for the intended recipients and this was done by members of the Latin clergy in the Crusader States themselves.[12] On account of the sometimes euphoric attitude of some western missionaries who interpreted any proof of openness and friendliness of the Oriental Christians as a step towards Rome,[13] these Latin translations should be read with circumspection.

---

[10] This section was edited by Gismondi (II).

[11] This work was edited by Bedjan, *Hist. Yahbalāhā*; there exists a recent Italian translation by Borbone, *Storia*, with an elaborate introduction and commentary.

[12] They can easily be consulted in *CICO*, III, III and IV. Cf. Giamil, pp. 1-12.

[13] For the West Syrians, see H. Teule, "It is Not Right to Call Ourselves Orthodox and the Others Heretics: Ecumenical Attitudes in the Jacobite Church in the Time of the Crusaders", in *East and West in the Crusader States*, II, pp. 13-29, on p. 23.

4. The Oriental sources should be complemented by some western documents: a number of letters sent by the Pope to the Mongol leaders or, more importantly, the local ecclesiastical authorities and, secondly, the travel reports of European pilgrims and missionaries, such as Burchard of Mount Sion, James of Vitry, Oliver of Paderborn and others.

THE EAST SYRIAN PRESENCE IN THE CRUSADER STATES

We have only incidental information about the Nestorians in crusader territory. As appears from various documents, Jerusalem was the see of a bishop or even a metropolitan.[14] In a letter to Pope Innocent IV, written by a certain "Rabban Ata", a representative of the East Syrian Catholicos Sabrišoʿ V (1226-56), and preserved in Latin, the author asks the Pope to protect the Nestorian Archbishop (*Archiepiscopus*) of Jerusalem. Unfortunately, he does not give his full name, but only the initial "I".[15] The Patriarchal Chronicle of the *Books of the Mysteries* mentions "Abraham, Metropolitan of Jerusalem" as one of the bishops attending the consecration of Patriarch Yahbalāhā III in 1281.[16] In the *History of Mār Yahbalāhā*, however, this Abraham is called "Metropolitan of Tripoli and Jerusalem".[17] It is probable that in the crusader period Jerusalem had no higher status than a suffragan diocese, since the *Book of Canon Law*, composed by ʿAbdišoʿ of Nisibis in 1316, speaks of "a Metropolitan of Damascus, Jerusalem and the coastal cities".[18]

This Nestorian presence in Jerusalem is confirmed by the observations of some western travelers. The priest John of Würzburg visited Jerusalem in the sixties or seventies of the twelfth century. In his

[14] For the East Syrian Episcopal sees, see especially Fiey, "Oriens Christianus", pp. 43-145.
[15] *CICO*, III, IV, pp. 95-8 and Giamil, p. 6. On this letter, see *infra*.
[16] Gismondi, II, p. 124 (72).
[17] *Hist. Yahbalāhā*, p. 37.
[18] Cf. the canonical work of ʿAbdišoʿ of Nisibis (*Ṭukkās d-dinē w-nāmosē ʿedtānāyē*). The relevant canon can be found in J.B. Chabot, *Synodicon orientale* (Paris, 1912), p. 619. This was also the situation before the crusaders arrived in the Mashreq, cf. *The Summary of Ecclesiastical Events* (*Muḫtaṣar al-aḫbār al- bīʿiyah*, ed. B. Haddad (Baghdad, 2000), a recently discovered East Syrian Church history up to the year 1007, which mentions Jerusalem as one of the suffragan sees of Damascus. Cf. O. Meinardus, "A Note on the Nestorians in Jerusalem", *Or. Chr.*, 51 (1967), pp. 123-9. Meinardus mentions a certain Peter of Beth Garmai as having been Metropolitan of Jerusalem in the latter part of the thirteenth century with no less than four suffragan bishops. This information is however based on the unreliable *Statistique inédite de l'ancienne Eglise Chaldéo-Nestorienne*, ed. P. Aziz (Beyrouth, 1909).

Descriptio Terrae Sanctae,[19] he mentions the Nestorians as one of the many nations present in the Holy City, unfortunately without any further explanation. The Saxon Dominican, Burchard of Mount Sion, who visited Jerusalem towards the end of the thirteenth century, refers in the same general way to "Nestorians and Jacobites and the like, so named after certain heretics, who were once their chiefs".[20] James of Vitry, in his *Historia orientalis*, mentions the Nestorians of the Holy Land, whose "detestable heresy" he describes according to the classical theological standards, accusing them of accepting two different persons in Christ, without, however, giving information about their local situation.[21] In his *Letters,* he writes that he had met with Nestorians in Acre, who had no bishop and were heretical.[22] In both works, he is much interested in the fact that most Nestorians lived in the mighty kingdom of the legendary Prester John whom he considered to be a possible ally of the crusaders. Nestorians in Acre are also mentioned in Rabban Ata's letter to Pope Innocent IV, as well as in an *assise* issued after the recapture of the city in 1191 by Richard the Lionhearted.[23]

There must also have been some Nestorians in Tripoli. Apart from Abraham, Metropolitan of Tripoli and Jerusalem, mentioned above, we know that the West Syrian scholars and future *maphrians*, Gregory Bar ʿEbrōyō (d. 1286) and Ṣalībā bar Yaʿqūb Wagih (d. 1258), studied rhetoric and medicine with the Nestorian *rhêtor* Jacob.[24] Rabban Ata, too, knows of Nestorians in Tripoli, as does Burchard of Mount Sion.[25]

---

[19] Ed. in PL 155, col. 1055-90, esp. 1088 and *Peregrinationes tres,* ed. R.B.C. Huygens (Turnhout, 1994), p. 137 f.

[20] Burchard of Mount Sion, *Description of the Holy Land*, trans. A. Stewart, Palestine Pilgrims Text Society, 12 (London, 1896), IV, p. 104 (quoted in Meinardus, "Note on the Nestorians" (see n. 18), p. 125). It should, however, be noted that Burchard had a remarkably open attitude to the lesser Oriental Churches and did not consider the Nestorians heretical, cf. Hamilton, *Latin Church*, p. 359.

[21] Jacques de Vitry, *Historia orientalis*, pp. 1-258; ch. 77 (pp. 148-50) is devoted to the Nestorians. For further information about the situation of Eastern and Oriental Christians in the Latin Kingdom of Jerusalem, see J. Pahlitzsch and D. Weltecke, "Konflikte zwischen den nicht-lateinischen Kirchen im Königreich Jerusalem", in *Jerusalem im Hoch- und Spätmittelalter — Konflikte und Konfliktbewältigung: Vorstellungen und Vergegenwärtigungen*, ed. D. Bauer, Kl. Herbers and N. Jaspers (Frankfurt and New York, 2001), pp. 119-45.

[22] Jacques de Vitry, *Lettres de la Cinquième Croisade*, ed. R.B.C. Huygens, trans. G. Duchet-Suchaux (Turnhout, 1998), pp. 50 and 70.

[23] See J. Prawer, *The History of the Jews in the Latin Kingdom of Jerusalem* (Oxford, 1988), p. 261. In this edict, the Nestorians are mentioned among the Eastern Christian communities, which are no longer allowed to trade in the old quarter of the city.

[24] *Chron. ecclesiasticum*, II, col. 667.

[25] Cf. Hamilton, *Latin Church*, p. 209, n. 6.

A reference to Nestorians in Antioch is found in the letter of Rabban Ata, as well as in a western source, sc. the *Historia Damiatina* of Oliver of Paderborn, who mentions a Nestorian church there.[26] In a letter to the Latin Patriarch of Antioch, Pope Gregory mentions the fact that some Nestorians and Jacobites revert to obedience to the Roman Church.[27]

According to the Patriarchal Chronicle of the *Books of the Mysteries*, Edessa would have had a Nestorian metropolitan at the beginning of the fourteenth century.[28] It is not certain whether this also reflects the situation in crusader times. Edessa is not mentioned in the Patriarchal Chronicle of the *Book of the Tower*.

Tarsus appears to have been a Metropolitan See in the fifteenth century. Timothy, who accepted the Catholic faith under Pope Eugenius IV on the Isle of Cyprus, called himself Metropolitan of Tarsus.[29] Since the Nestorian Bishop of Damascus, Elias, mentions Tarsus as a suffragan see of Damascus at the beginning of the tenth century, it is also possible that there were some Nestorians living in Tarsus in crusader times.

Finally, due to the bad situation in which the Nestorian Christians found themselves in the fourteenth century, after the Mongols had embraced Islam, some of them had fled to Cyprus. This was the case of the priest Ṣalībā b.Yuḥannā al-Mawṣilī, the author of the *Books of the Mysteries*, mentioned above, who was in Famagusta in the year 1336. The Nestorians even possessed a church in this city, built in 1359 after the model of the churches of southern France. In 1326, Pope John XXII had already invited both the (titular) Latin Patriarch of Jerusalem, Raymond Bequin and Hugo, King of Cyprus, to combat the errors and heresies of the Nestorians in Cyprus.[30] And finally, in 1455, Timothy, Metropolitan of Tarsus, adopted Catholicism in Cyprus.[31]

---

[26] Quoted in Hamilton, *Latin Church*, p. 356.
[27] *CICO*, III, III, p. 312 (letter dated to 9.3.1238)
[28] Gismondi, II, p. 126.
[29] Giamil, p. 10.
[30] *CICO*, III, VII.2 (*Acta Iohannis XXII (1317-1334)*) (Rome, 1952), p. 176 (letters dated to 1.10.1326). Cf. V. De Wilde, "Bequin", in *Dictionnaire d'histoire et géographie ecclésiastiques*, VI (Paris, 1934), col. 307-8. According to the Pope, the heresy of the Nestorians consisted of their acceptance of two persons (*personas*) in Christ, who was only the adoptive Son of God.
[31] Cf. Fiey, "Oriens Christianus", p. 71.

teenth century bearing the name Ensoaib/Išoʿyahb.[40] Išoʿyahb b. Malkon is a relatively unknown author. He wrote mostly in Arabic, less in Syriac.[41] Among his writings, we find several theological treatises which are useful for the interpretation of his *libellus de fide,* sent by Simeon to the Pope.

This creed is essentially a short christological treatise. Three points are important. The letter begins by stating that Christ is perfect God and perfect man, united in one person ("una persona"). At the end of the letter, the author uses a more technical vocabulary, mentioning that the one Christ and Son exists in two natures but is one "individuum" and one person ("unus Christus, unus filius, res duarum naturarum divinitatis et humanitatis, unum individuum, una persona"). Unfortunately, the term *individuum* is not explained. It has, however, remained unnoticed that the original text of this creed is preserved in the theological encyclopaedia, the *asfār al-asrār* of Ṣalībā b. Yuḥannā already mentioned.[42] It appears that the Latin text is a literal translation from the Arabic, which reads: "masīḥ wāḥid, ibn wāḥid ḏū ṭabīʿatayn lāhūtiyyah wa-nāsūtiyyah šaḫṣ wāḥid farsūf wāḥid". Thus, *individuum* translates the Arabic term šaḫṣ, which in Christological texts is normally used to indicate the one person of Christ and is synonymous with the originally Greco-Syriac term, *farsūf* (< Syr.: *parṣopā*), also used to indicate the one person in Christ. This emphasis on the oneness of Christ in two natures is remarkable, since the author refrains from mentioning the classical Nestorian expression of the duality of *qnomē*, frequently rendered by "substances" or "hypostasis", which had earned them the reproach of dividing Christ into two persons. The fact that Išoʿyahb, neither here nor in the original Arabic text, makes any reference to the delicate term *qnoma*, can possibly be interpreted as an attempt to give a presentation of the Nestorian christology, which would be acceptable to the Latins and avoid any misunderstandings. This is probably also the reason why he does not call his Church "Nestorian", but speaks in a neutral way of "al-Naṣārā al-Suryāniyyūn al-mašāriqah" ("East Syrian Christians"). It would have been interesting to compare this creed with the refutation by Išoʿyahb of the reproach formulated by the Jacobite Patriarch that the Nestorians profess two substances (*jawharān* and *qnumān*) in the person of Christ.

[40] J.-M. Fiey, Nisibe, *Métropole syriaque orientale et ses suffragants des origines à nos jours,* CSCO, 388 (Louvain, 1977), pp. 105-7.
[41] A. Baumstark, *Geschichte der syrischen Literatur* (Bonn, 1922), p. 309, GCAL, II, pp. 208-10. Landron, p. 135.
[42] It was edited by J.S. Assemanus, *Bibl. or.,* III, 1, pp. 295-6 (on the basis of Vat. ar. 110, olim MS Scand. 41).

The text of this refutation is preserved in MS Vat. Ar. 180 (olim 49, thirteenth century), but, unfortunately, precisely the passage concerning his explanation of the appropriate christological terminology seems to be missing.[43] However, it seems highly improbable that Išoʿyahb would have entirely given up the classical Nestorian formula of the christological dogma, since other more or less contemporary theological documents defend it, such as e.g. the *ktābā d-margānitā* (the Book of the Pearl) by one of Išoʿyahb's successors to the throne of Nisibis, ʿAbdišoʿ b. Brikā (d. 1318), who carefully explains the traditional "Nestorian" wording of the christological dogma, distinguishing it from the formula used by the Chalcedonians, including the Franks, whom he mentions explicitly.[44]

The second issue in Išoʿyahb's letter is that of adoptionism, one of the classical reproaches by the Latins to the Nestorians.[45] Išoʿyahb carefully explains that his Church does not adhere to this heresy, stating that the union between Christ's humanity and divinity took place at the moment of the Angel's Annunciation to Mary. He was not first merely a pure man, whose humanity was later united to his divinity ("non fuit prius homo purus et post unitus deitati"). The Arabic text even stresses that this is the "traditional, apostolic belief" of the Church of the East.

The third issue, related to the former one, is the likewise classical point of controversy of "Mary, Mother of God". Išoʿyahb does not use objections of principle in defending the traditional Nestorian reluctance to use this expression. To him, it seems more a question of a clear and unequivocal terminology. The Nestorian term "Mother of Christ" is preferable, since the Chalcedonian (and Jacobite)[46] "Mother of God" might make some foolish persons think that Mary is the Mother of the Holy Trinity, "God" being the term currently used to indicate Trinity. On account of the rejection of adoptionism, Christ being perfect God and perfect Man from the very moment of the conception, the term "Mother of Christ" has no significance other than what the Chalcedonians intend to express with "Mother of God". However, in another document, the *risālat al-bayān* (the Book of Proof), fragments of which are also preserved in the *asfār al-asrār*, and which was directed against the Coptic theologian Severus b. al-Muqaffaʿ, he shows himself less inclined

---

[43] *Bibl. or.*, pp. 297-303, esp. p. 301. Cf. *GCAL*, II, p. 245.

[44] See below, Concluding remarks, "Faithfulness to the Tradition".

[45] See e.g. the remarks on the Nestorian christology in *Liber peregrinationis*, p. 136-8. Cf. the remarks of Pope John XXII, *CICO*, III, VII.2 (see n. 30).

[46] The same argumentation is found in the profession of faith intended for the Jacobites, see *Bibl. or.*, p. 301.

to compromise and defends the view that only the expression "Mother of Christ" is acceptable, since the term "Mother of God" is not found in the Gospel, the basis of the Christian faith.[47]

By way of a conclusion, we may state that Išo'yahb's letter is an attempt to explain the Nestorian christology. In order not to shock the ears of his theological opponents, he avoids using the expression of two *qnomē* in Christ. This element distinguishes his letter from some other East Syrian theological treatises, such as the *Book of the Pearl*, which also try to explain the Nestorian wording of the christological dogma in terms understandable by the Chalcedonians, but without giving up the traditional emphasis on the duality of *qnomē*.[48]

3. *Rabban Ṣawmā*

In the History of Mar Yahbalāhā,[49] we find that during his first visit to Rome (1287), Yahbalāhā's envoy, Rabban Ṣawmā, is invited by the cardinals to explain his faith and to present a creed of his Church. In matters of christology, Ṣawmā simply repeats the classical Nestorian wording of the dogma, that the Son is perfect God and perfect Man, two natures (*kyānin*), two *qnomīn* and one Person (*parṣopā*). This did not provoke any remark from the cardinals, who seemed more interested in the question of the *filioque*. Here, Rabban Ṣawmā again professes the traditional teaching of his Church, that the Father is the source of both the Son and the Spirit, explaining to the cardinals that it is irrational to assume, as they seemed to do, that the Father is the source of the Son and the latter the source of the Spirit. The matter is not pursued, however, since Rabban Ṣawmā declares that he has not come to Rome for discussions, but in order to receive the blessing of the Pope. During his second visit to Rome, after the election of Nicolas IV, who was one of the cardinals who had assisted at the theological encounter of the first visit, there were no more theological discussions and, at his request, the new Pope allowed Rabban Ṣawmā to celebrate mass according to the East Syrian rite and, on another occasion, he even admitted him to Communion.

The Syriac description of the encounter with the cardinals was only composed at some later date[50] after the return of Rabban Ṣawmā to the

---

[47] Text of this refutation in MS Paris Ar. 6744, fol. 190v-192v; cf. Wright-Cook, *Catalogue*, p. 788; and *GCAL*, II, p. 209.

[48] For other treatises avoiding to mention the duality of *qnomē*, see note 71. About the *Book of the Pearl*, see below Concluding Remarks.

[49] *Hist. Yahbalāhā*, p. 59.

[50] On the date of the composition, see the introduction by Borbone, *Storia*, p. 17.

East. It was based on the personal notes made by Rabban Ṣawmā himself in Persian. Even if we assume that the anonymous author of the History did not give a fully accurate report of the discussion in Rome,[51] the fact that he thought it important to emphasise the way in which a prominent member of his Church defended the classical christological terminology and trinitarian theology in his encounter with Latin theologians without making concessions to the cardinals reveals the theological position of some Nestorians by the end of the thirteenth or the beginning of the fourteenth century and their attitude towards the Latin theologians.

4. Mar Yahbalāhā III (1281-1317)

As we can read in his biography,[52] Catholicos Yahbalāhā was elected head of the East Syrian Church on account of his Ongüt origins and his familiarity with the language and customs of the Mongol leaders. Yahbalāhā himself was reluctant to accept this dignity on account of his poor theological training and weak knowledge of the Syriac language, which are also reported by the West Syrian Bar ʿEbrōyō.[53] Ten years later, according to Riccoldo da Monte Croce, his fellow bishops were shocked at the ease with which the Catholicos gave in to the arguments of the Dominican friar and accused him of being a Frank and even an adversary of Nestorius.[54]

This friendly disposition towards the Latin Christians is certainly one of the characteristics of Yahbalāhā. In order to determine if this also meant that he was actually prepared to make concessions to Latin theology, we have to investigate the declarations sent by him to Rome.

Two such documents are preserved.[55] The first was intended for Pope Boniface VIII and can be dated to the year 1302, the second was sent to his successor, Benedict IX in 1304.

---

[51] Cf. *Hist. Yahbalāhā*, p. 85 f., where the author mentions that he sometimes had to condense Ṣawmā's report.
[52] Cf. *Hist. Yahbalāhā*, p. 33.
[53] *Chron. ecclesiasticum*, III, col. 453.
[54] *Liber peregrinationis*, pp. 152-4.
[55] Yahbalāhā had already sent some earlier letters to the Pope, as appears from *Hist. Yahbalāhā*, p. 77. They do not seem to have been preserved. They undoubtedly dealt with the situation in Jerusalem, the recapture of which was one of the reasons why the monk Ṣawmā had been sent to Europe (cf. p. 58). The Pope (Nicholas IV) sent Ṣawmā back with a patent giving Yahbalāhā patriarchal authority over all Oriental Christians. This is at least what we can read in *Hist. Yahbalāhā*, p. 84. The letter, preserved in Nicholas IV's registers (dated 7.4.1288) and intended as an answer to the letters of Yahbalāhā, does not mention this. Yahbalāhā is addressed merely as "episcopus in partibus Orientis". The letter contains a Roman Catholic profession of faith, which Yahbalāhā is invited to accept.

Apart from the short introduction and the final greetings which are in Syriac, the first letter is only preserved in Arabic. There seems to be no Latin translation. It is basically a letter of courtesy to the Pope, who is respectfully addressed as "keeper of the Keys of the Kingdom [of Heaven], sun of the Christian nation, fifth evangelist", etc. The author does not discuss theological subjects or submit a profession of faith. He presents himself as Catholicos, Patriarch of the East.[56] Tisserand considers this letter as a proof of how sincerely Yahbalāhā was in favour of a union with Rome.[57]

The second letter, on the contrary, is an important theological document. Again, the original language is Arabic with, according to the East Syrian customs of the time, a short introductory and concluding formula in Syriac.[58] It was translated into Latin by the Dominican Friar Jacques d'Arles-sur-Tech, who had brought to the Catholicos news of the election of the new Pope Benedict.[59] In the profession of faith, which is the core of the letter, Yahbalāhā explains the mystery of Trinity by his Church's classical imagery[60] of the Sun, the Ray and the Warmth. The Latin translation reads as follows:

> "(Credimus in) Unam Deitatem. Patrem generantem, Filium genitum, Spiritum Sanctum procedentem. Unum Dominum: unum adoratum creatorem rerum visibilium et invisibilium, infigurabilem, incorporeum et inimaginabilem super omnem intellectum: immensum et incomprehensibilem

---

This profession does not deal explicitly with the differences between the Nestorian and the Roman Catholic Church, but is more of a standard creed, which had already been sent by Clement IV to Emperor Michael VIII Paleologus in 1267. It recognizes the Patriarchal privileges only in very general terms and most probably only the four classical eastern patriarchal sees are meant. One year later, the Pope sent Yahbalāhā the same creed a second time (text of both letters in *CICO*, III, v.2, pp. 128-31 and 148-9). Several other eastern and Oriental dignitaries also received it. Cf. J. Richard, "La mission en Europe de Rabban Cauma et l'union des Eglises", *XII Convegno Volta* (Rome, 1957), reprint in J. Richard, *Orient et Occident au Moyen-Age: Contacts et relations (XIIe-XVe s.)*, Variorum Reprints (London, 1976), XXII, esp. p. 163.

[56] Ed. and Italian trans. in L. Bottini, "Due lettere inedite del patriarca mar Yahbalaha III (1281- 1317)", *Rivista degli studi orientali* (1992), pp. 239-56. Yahbalāhā calls himself Yahbalāhā "al-ġarīb" (the stranger). Bottini considers this to be an allusion to the Ongüt origins of the Patriarch. It is, however, a translation of the Syriac *aksnāyā*, which is a current term to indicate a monk, someone who is, spiritually, a foreigner to anything in this world. Cf. Borbone, *Storia*, p. 236.

[57] E. Tisserand, "L'église nestorienne", in *Dictionnaire de théologie catholique* XI,1, col. 223.

[58] Also ed. and transl. by Bottini, "Due lettere" (see n. 56).

[59] The Latin text can be found in J.B. Chabot, *Histoire du Patriarche Mar Jabalaha III et du moine Rabban Cauma*, trans. from Syriac (Paris, 1895), pp. 249-55; and in Giamil, p. 5 ff.

[60] R. Haddad, *La trinité chez les théologiens arabes (750-1050)* (Paris, 1985), p. 119.

propter humani intellectus debilitatem. Quapropter ad aliquam fidelium manuductionem dicimus et confitemur ipsum Patrem generantem sive loquentem, filium autem genitum sive Verbum, Spiritum autem Sanctum tam Verbi quam loquentis esse spiritum, sive vitam. Et propter hoc scriptum est in principio Genesis: Dixit Deus faciamus hominem ad imaginem et similitudinem nostram. Sicut etiam videmus in sole ipsum corpus solare, et radium sive lucem ab ipso exeuntem, et calorem ab utroque manantem ... "

"(We believe) in One Godhead. The Father engendering, the Son begotten, the Holy Spirit proceeding. One Lord, one adored creator of things visible and invisible, beyond representation, incorporeal and unimaginable, above all intellect, immense and incomprehensible on account of the weakness of our human mind. Therefore, for the guidance of the faithful, we say and profess that the Father is engendering or speaking, the Son is begotten or the Word, *the Holy Spirit, however, the Spirit or life from both the Word and the One who speaks.* Therefore, it is written in the beginning of Genesis: God said, let us make man in our image and after our likeness [Gen. 1:26]. As, in the [light of] the sun, we see the body of the sun itself, and the ray or the light which comes out from it, and the *warmth emanating from both* ..."

According to this Latin translation, Yahbalāhā even twice expresses his belief in the proceeding of the Spirit from both the Father and the Son, which would be in contradiction with the views defended by his envoy Rabban Ṣawmā in Rome.

Comparing this passage to the Arabic original, however, one finds that here the mystery of Trinity is only evoked in much less explicit terms:

"We believe in One Lord, eternal, wise, living, good, mighty,[61] one substance [*jawhar*], three persons [*aqānīm*], Father, Son and Holy Spirit, One God, the Father engendering, the Son begotten and the Holy Spirit proceeding [*munbaʿiṯ*],[62] one Lord, one adored One, Creator of what is visible and invisible, who is [incorporeal],[63] incomparable, to whom there is no likeness or equality, whom thoughts cannot define nor intellects comprise. Rather, on account of the weakness of the human knowledge, which falls short of understanding its truth, it is said that the Father is analogous to the soul, the Sun to the Word and the Spirit to Life.[64] For this reason God has said at the beginning of the Tora: 'Come, let us create man after our image

---

[61] For the attributes *hakīm* (wise), *hayy* (living), *jawād* (good) and *qādir* (mighty), see *ibid.*, p. 205 ff. Yahbalāhā follows the traditional Christian Arabic Trinitarian vocabulary.

[62] This is the normal term especially used by the Nestorians to indicate the procession of the Spirit from the Father, see *ibid.*, p. 240.

[63] Conjecture on the basis of the Latin translation, the Arabic text being illegible.

[64] The same trilogy is expressed by the Nestorian Elias of Nisibis, who, however, employs *nuṭq* to express the Word instead of *al-kalima* used by Yahbalāhā, cf Haddad, *La trinité* (see n. 60), p. 126.

affection and love among the Sons of the Baptism; that he may make us abide by the tenderness and love in our hearts for the other communities of the Christian nation... May God by his guidance bring everyone to the Truth and inspire them to work according to his intentions."[70]

The presupposition is evidently that this should be possible on the basis of mutual esteem and respect for both the eastern and western traditions, which have equal validity. This is confirmed when we look at the subsequent — unfortunately, still unedited — parts of the *Book of the Mysteries*. Though some authors quoted by Ṣalībā seem, like Išoʿyahb b. Malkon, to avoid speaking about two *qnomē* in Christ,[71] we also find passages which emphasize the traditional Nestorian terminology of the union in Christ. Thus, Ṣalībā himself discusses the differences of the Christian communities (*firaq*) regarding the union of Christ's divinity and humanity.[72] He states unambiguously that the best opinion is the belief of the East Syrian Christians, who hold that:

> "the eternal Son, that is God the Word, one of the three holy eternal persons [*al-aqānīm*], was united with the man taken from the pure Virgin, the Lady Mary the Virgin, not in substance nor in qunūm, but in the propriety of the sonship, of power [*qudra*] and sovereignty [*sulṭān*]. This means that the substance of the eternal Son and the substance of the man taken from the Lady Mary remain preserved. Likewise their two *qnome*. And their union happens in the propriety of the sonship and of power... Therefore we say about Christ that he is two substances [*jawharān*] and two *qnome* [*qnumān*], one Son, one Person [*šaḫs*], one Christ."

This and comparable passages put Ṣalībā's openness to the Western Christians into the right perspective. It did not imply abandoning the traditional formulas of the East Syrian Creed, although this was clearly what was expected by the contemporary Roman eclesiastical authorities, as can be seen in the letters of Pope John XXII (1317-34) to King Hugo of Cyprus already mentioned.[73]

CONCLUDING REMARKS

Faithfulness to the Tradition

Like Ṣalībā, the East Syrian Church leaders were generally well-disposed towards the Western Christians. One of the reasons was cer-

[70] Gianazza, "Traité", p. 627.
[71] Cf. the so-called *Creed of the Eastern Christians* (= Nestorians), translated from Syriac into Arabic, found in the *Book of the Mysteries*, MS Par. Ar. 6744, fol. 26v-27v, which only speaks about two substances (*jawharān*) united in one person (*šaḫs*).
[72] MS Par. Ar. 6744, 168v-169v; Wright-Cook, *Catalogue*, p. 783 ff.
[73] See the references mentioned in footnote 30.

tainly political; the East Syrians needed help from the West, as appears from the letter of Rabban Ata quoted above, or the requests by Rabban Ṣawmā, Yahbalāhā's envoy to the King of France.[74] It did not mean however that their theologians would therefore be prepared to give up speaking of two *qnome* in Christ or accept calling Mary Mother of God. Most theological treatises of this time were traditional in this respect and defended the classical positions. Some theologians of the Church of the East had, however, come to realize that the traditional differences in the wording of the christological dogma were no longer lines of division between the Churches. Thus, ʿAbdišoʿ of Nisibis seemed prepared to accept the validity of the western Chalcedonian christology, which speaks of only one *qnomā,* since he holds that in Greek, the language used at the Council of Chalcedon, the terms *qnomā* and *parṣopā* (hypostasis and prosopon) have exactly the same meaning, which is not the case in Syriac.[75] Apparently, for ʿAbdišoʿ, both formulas (the Greek "one *hypostasis-qnoma*" and the Syriac "two *qnomē*") are both acceptable and there is no reason to submit to the Chalcedonian formula, as he also makes clear with respect to the use of the term *theotokos* and *christotokos*, the latter of which is preferable. This might also be the reason why Ṣalībā speaks about the westerners and the members of the Church of the East as *equals*, between whom there is "no difference or separation, except in distance and difference of languages".[76]

Saint Louis

We have to return to the problem of St Louis, mentioned in the *Book of the Magnet* by Patriarch Joseph II. At first sight, it seems quite possible that the name of St Louis was transmitted by generations of East Syrians from the time of the crusaders up to the period of Joseph. We know that on several occasions the East Syrians had been in direct contact with the holy monarch. The embassy sent to St Louis by the highest-ranking Mongol representative in Iran, Aljijidai, when the former was staying in

---

[74] Cf. *Hist. Yahbalāhā*, p. 68. When asked by the French King for the reasons of his journey, Rabban Ṣawmā replies: "I have been sent for the question of Jerusalem."

[75] See his *ktābā d-marganitā* (Book of the Pearl; with tendentious Latin translation), in *Scriptorum veterum nova collectio*, ed. by A. Mai (Rome, 1838), X, pp. 317-66, esp. 328b-9. Unfortunately, Mai did not edit ch. III.5 and 6, dealing with the same issues. ʿAbdišoʿ is well informed about the crusaders' theological positions: he mentions the issue of the *filioque* and the use of unleavened bread in the Eucharist.

[76] Gianazza, "Traité", pp. 582-3. This notwithstanding his preference for the Nestorian terminology, as seen above.

Cyprus in 1248, was probably lead by two Nestorian monks.[77] St Louis' envoy to the Mongol court, Friar André de Longjumeau, was much interested in the Nestorian Church, representatives of which he had already met on a previous mission for Innocent IV. In 1270, Abaqa, son of Hülagu and, like his father, generally praised by the Oriental Christians, sent a letter to St Louis about the liberation of Jerusalem.[78] This was the year of the King's death, but about fifteen years later during his visit to Paris the envoy of Yahbalāhā III, Rabban Ṣawmā was shown the only recently finished church of Saint-Denis with the tombs of the French kings.[79] He also visited the Sainte Chapelle, built to the order of St Louis to house the Crown of Thorns and other relics that the monarch had brought from Constantinople.

Since the more recent literature of the East Syrians has not yet been studied properly, it is difficult to prove that, when with the acceptance of Islam by the Mongols, history took a course different from the one that had been hoped by the East Syrians, these contacts with the West lingered on in their minds and literature, so that the name of St Louis, like that of Constantine, could become the symbol of a powerful Christian nation.

In the case, however, of the *Book of the Magnet* and Patriarch Joseph II — and here, scholarly research also takes a different course than had been anticipated — it seems that the Chaldeans of this period became familiar with the name of St Louis, not from the stories circulating in their own community and dating back to the crusader times, but rather by the direct contacts with Latin missionaries. In the early eighteenth century, Diarbakır, the city where Joseph wrote his *Book of the Magnet*, these were mainly French Capuchine Fathers, who may have provided him with the kind of devotional literature, which was popular in seventeenth-century France and in which the name of St Louis frequently recurs. One may think e.g. of *l'introduction à la vie dévote* de François de Sales or comparable writings, which in this period were massively translated into Arabic and which allowed the Oriental clergy — after centuries of isolation — to renew contact with the West and the Latin Church.[80]

---

[77] Fiey, *Mongols,* p. 12. Fiey does not exclude the possibility that both monks were Jacobites.

[78] Fiey, *Mongols*, p. 35.

[79] *Hist. Yahbalāhā,* p. 70. Cf. Chabot, *Histoire du Patriarche Mar Jabalaha* (see n. 59), p. 79, note 2.

[80] Cf. Teule, *Joseph II* (see n. 1).

ABBREVIATIONS USED IN THE FOOTNOTES

Bibl. or.   J.S. Assemanus, *Bibliotheca orientalis,* III, 1 (Rome, 1725).
Borbone, *Storia*
         P.G. Borbone, *Storia di Mar Yahballaha e di Rabban Sauma: Un orientale in Ocidente ai tempi di Marco Polo* (Torino, 2000).
Chron. ecclesiasticum
         Gregorii Barhebraei Chronicon ecclesiasticum, ed. J.-B. Abbeloos and Th. Lamy, 3 vols (Paris and Louvain, 1874).
CICO, III, III and IV
         Pontificia Commissio ad redigendum codicem iuris canonici orientalis, Fontes, series III, III, *Acta Honorii III et Gregorii IX* (Rome, 1950); IV, *Acta Innocentii PP IV* (Rome, 1962).
Fiey, *Mongols*
         J.-M. Fiey, *Chrétiens syriaques sous les Mongols (Il-Khanat de Perse, XIIIe-XIVe s.),* CSCO, 362 (Louvain, 1975).
Fiey, "Oriens Christianus"
         J.M. Fiey, "Pour un Oriens Christianus Novus: Répertoire des diocèses syriaques orientaux et occidentaux", in *Beiruter Texte und Studien,* 49 (Beirut, 1993).
GCALG.   Graf, *Geschichte der christlichen arabischen Literatur,* 5 vols, Studi e Testi, 118, 133, 146, 147, 152 (Città del Vaticano, 1944-53).
Giamil   S. Giamil, *Genuinae relationes inter sedem apostolicam et Assyriorum Orientalium seu Chaldeorum Ecclesiam* (Rome, 1912).
Gianazza, "Traité"
         Gianmaria Gianazza, "Traité de la démonstration et de la direction: Kitāb al-burhān wa-l-irshād de Ṣalībā ibn Yuḥannā al-Mawṣilī", critical edition and trans., *Parole de l'Orient,* 22 (1997), pp. 567-629.
Gismondi, I H. Gismondi, *Maris Amri et Slibae De patriarchis Nestorianorum Commentaria,* I, *Maris textus Arabicus; Maris versio Latina* (Rome, 1899).
Gismondi, II H. Gismondi, *Maris Amri et Slibae De patriarchis Nestorianorum Commentaria,* II, *Amri et Slibae textus* (Rome, 1896) ; *Amri et Slibae versio* (Rome, 1899).
Hist. Yahbalāhā
         P. Bedjan, *Histoire de Mar Jab-alaha, patriarche, et de Raban Sauma* (Paris and Leipzig, 1895[2]).
Landron B. Landron, *Chrétiens et musulmans en Irak: Attitudes Nestoriennes vis-à-vis de l'Islam* (Paris, 1994).
Liber peregrinationis
         "Riccold de Monte Croce — Pérégrination en Terre Sainte et au Proche Orient: Texte latin et traduction; Lettres sur la chute de Saint-Jean d'Acre: Traduction", ed. R. Kappler, in *Textes et traductions des classiques français du Moyen Âge,* 4 (Paris, 1997).

Wright-Cook, *Catalogue*
> W. Wright and S. Cook, *A Catalogue of the Syriac Manuscripts Preserved in the Library of the University of Cambridge*, II (Cambridge, 1901).

THE ALEXANDRIAN CRUSADE (1365) AND THE MAMLŪK SOURCES

REASSESSMENT OF THE *KITĀB AL-ILMĀM* OF AN-NUWAYRĪ AL-ISKANDARĀNĪ
(D. A.D. 1372)

Jo Van Steenbergen[*]

The crusade that Peter I of Lusignan, King of Cyprus and Jerusalem from 1358 until 1369,[1] embarked upon in October 1365 has already aroused a considerable number of scholarly controversies. In recent times, the works of Azīz S. Atiya[2] and Peter W. Edbury[3] in particular were very notable in this respect. Nevertheless, several issues still remain open for research and consideration — or reconsideration —, particularly concerning the Muslim historiography on the event. One of these issues, I believe, is that of the appreciation of the most elaborate Muslim reproduction in the encyclopaedia of the eyewitness an-Nuwayrī al-Iskandarānī of the conquest and sack of Alexandria in 1365. This description of the last convulsions of the Crusades in Egypt was regarded by such an authority as A.S. Atiya as "the most valuable source material on the Crusade of Alexandria from the Egyptian point of view".[4] It is the intention of this paper to show that this is a dangerous assumption and that, though an-Nuwayrī's contribution is indeed very valuable, it still requires a very critical approach.

King Peter I prepared his crusade against the Mamlūks of Egypt very thoroughly, travelling around in Europe from 1362 until 1365 and seeking financial and practical support at the illustrious European courts of his time.[5] He finally gathered with his allies at the island of Rhodes in August 1365[6] and the entire fleet set sail on the 4th of October. Only

---
[*] For the abbreviations used in the footnotes see the end of this article.
[1] See H.D. Purcell, *Cyprus* (New York and Washington, 1969), p. 133.
[2] A.S. Atiya, "The Crusade in the Fourteenth Century", in *A History of the Crusades*, ed. K.M. Setton, III, *The Fourteenth and Fifteenth Centuries*, ed. H.W. Hazard (Madison, Wisc., 1975), pp. 3-26.
[3] Edbury, *Kingdom of Cyprus*; idem, "Crusading Policy", pp. 90-105.
[4] Atiya, *A Fourteenth Century Encyclopedist*, pp. 18, 38.
[5] Edbury, *Kingdom of Cyprus*, p. 161; idem, "Crusading Policy", pp. 92-3; Atiya, "Crusade" (see n. 2), pp. 14-5.
[6] Edbury, *Kingdom of Cyprus*, p. 166.

then, did Peter make known to his companions that their goal was an attack on Alexandria.[7]

As was persuasively suggested by Peter Edbury, this expedition had little or nothing to do with Christian motives of recovery of the Holy Land. On the contrary, its motives seem to have been purely commercial. The changing trade routes and the economic effects of the Black Death threatened Cyprus' commercial position, while the economic element at the same time favoured the Mamlūk Empire in Egypt and in particular its most important Mediterranean port, Alexandria.[8] According to Edbury, Peter I

> "hoped to achieve one of two things: to capture and hold the city so that in future he and his kingdom would derive profit from its commerce, or if... permanent occupation was not feasible, to destroy Alexandria in the naive expectation that its commercial wealth would revert to Famagusta."[9]

What do Mamlūk sources tell us about the ensuing attack on and sack of their Mediterranean port al-Iskandarīyya, and what is the value of their accounts? After careful study, I ended up with five major historiographical sources that provide ample details. However, a comparison of their accounts made clear that only three versions of this event actually survived in Muslim historiography. These versions and their sources will be presented and analysed here and in the light of this analysis, the version that was traditionally considered the most authoritative Muslim account of the Cypriote conquest and sack of Alexandria in 1365 — i.e. that in the encyclopaedia of the eyewitness an-Nuwayrī al-Iskandarānī — will be reconsidered.[10]

As Atiya informs us in his study *A Fourteenth Century Encyclopedist*, Muḥammad b. Qāsim b. Muḥammad an-Nuwayrī al-Iskandarānī lived in fourteenth-century Alexandria as a copyist of manuscripts for the rich Muslim merchants of that city, a profession which made him very familiar with the classical Arabic literature.[11] He died in Alexandria in A.D.

---

[7] *Ibid.*, p. 167.

[8] *Ibid.*, pp. 152-3; Edbury, "Crusading Policy", pp. 95-7; R. Irwin, *The Middle East in the Middle Ages: The Early Mamlūk Sultanate, 1250-1382* (London, 1986), p. 145.

[9] Edbury, "Crusading Policy", p. 97.

[10] Atiya, *A Fourteenth Century Encyclopedist*, pp. 18, 38. See also M. Müller-Wiener, *Eine Stadtgeschichte Alexandrias von 564/1169 bis in die Mitte des 9./15. Jahrhunderts: Verwaltung und innerstädtischen Organisationsformen*, Islamkundliche Untersuchungen, 159 (Berlin, 1992), p. 46, where an-Nuwayrī al-Iskandarānī is used as the sole authority to describe the attack and sack of Alexandria in 1365.

[11] Atiya, *A Fourteenth Century Encyclopedist*, pp. 11-2.

1372, so he definitely was an eyewitness and contemporary of Peter's sack of his city. It was after this event that he decided to write down what he had seen and heard, under the title *Kitāb al-Ilmām bi l-I'lām fī mā ǧarat bihi l-aḥkām wa l-umūr al-muqḍīyya fī waq'at al-Iskandarīyya* (The Book of Gleanings to become informed of what was entailed by the predicaments and the accomplished facts regarding the event of Alexandria). His rich background, however, made him diverge a lot from his central theme and digress on any subject known in his time, so that in the end his report of the sack of Alexandria turned out to be imbedded in a richly documented encyclopaedia of six volumes and about 2,641 pages in the Hyderabad-edition.[12] This made Atiya state that "an-Nuwayrī's work must be regarded as a storehouse, perhaps a disorganized storehouse, of valuable treasure heaped around a central event which happened to be the sack of Alexandria in 1365".[13] In the course of his report, an-Nuwayrī informs us that his main reason for writing it was his love for the city of Alexandria and the disgust he had felt when he saw what the "Franks" had done to her.[14] He provides us with a mass of data gathered from his own experience or compiled from reports of other eyewitnesses.[15] Concerning the general character of his encyclopaedia, Atiya already noticed that "His approach appears to be that of a story teller with an emphasis on the dramatic and the legendary rather than a realistic record";[16] an-Nuwayrī was also an almost fanatic religious Muslim, who indicated the will of God as the main cause of the sack of Alexandria.[17] His fanaticism and personal involvement might clearly bias and influence his writings. Nevertheless Atiya still describes an-Nuwayrī as a foremost historical authority on the account of this crusade, not only owing to the paramount importance of his story in quantity, but also in quality.[18]

In an-Nuwayrī's version, 70 Venetian tradeships ("tuǧǧār al-Banādiqa") appeared before Alexandria on Wednesday 20 Muḥarram 767. Fourteen were manned by Venetians and two by Genoese, ten came from Rhodes, five from France and Cypriots manned the remainder. When they did not enter the harbour, the inhabitants of Alexandria felt something was wrong and panic began to spread.[19] On the next day,

---

[12] an-Nuwayrī, *Kitāb al-Ilmām*.
[13] Atiya, *A Fourteenth Century Encyclopedist*, p. 13.
[14] an-Nuwayrī, *Kitāb al-Ilmām*, II, pp. 219-20.
[15] Atiya, *A Fourteenth Century Encyclopedist*, p. 28.
[16] Atiya, *A Fourteenth Century Encyclopedist*, p. 17.
[17] an-Nuwayrī, *Kitāb al-Ilmām*, II, p. 92.
[18] Atiya, *A Fourteenth Century Encyclopedist*, p. 18.
[19] an-Nuwayrī, *Kitāb al-Ilmām*, II, pp. 136-7; 230.

Thursday 21 Muḥarram, Peter I and his fleet entered the western harbour of Alexandria, Baḥr as-Silsila, but when they tried to disembark, they were driven away by the Muslim defenders and their arrows.[20]

On the morning of Friday 22 Muḥarram, many Muslims came out, trusting the defence of their city, and they spread on al-Ǧazīra, the long peninsula in front of the city. Even merchants selling food went around among them. In their recklessness, some even insulted the "Franks", apparently without getting any reaction.[21] When some people protested to the governor's substitute, the amir Ǧanġarā, against this dangerous situation, their warnings were brushed aside.[22] Meanwhile spies had informed Peter of the opportunity this situation offered him, and a first ship was sent ahead. A skirmish in the water ensued between this first ship and some Muslims, which was won by the former. This enabled the men to go ashore, followed by the rest of their crusader troops.[23]

Then an-Nuwayrī informs us of the horror that ensued, the mostly unarmed Muslims panicking and trying to return to the safe city-walls, while some perished heroically defending themselves and their partners-in-distress with whatever they could lay their hands on. This complete chaos enabled the "Franks" to take the beach easily.[24] The amir Ǧanġarā also had to flee back to the city, where he gathered the city treasure and sent all "Frankish" merchants who were in Alexandria to Damanhūr.

The crusaders meanwhile attacked the walls, but were driven back by the Muslim defenders and their arrows.[25] The crusaders then went to the eastern harbour, where they found the walls undefended and no moat to hinder the approach. Consequently they were able to force the gate at that side of the wall — the Customs Gate, Bāb ad-Dīwān. Through this gate, they were then able to climb the walls and attack the defenders.[26] An-Nuwayrī tells us that the reason for this easy capture of Alexandria was the fact that the Customs Gate had also been locked for the Alexandrians themselves, to protect the merchandise that was kept there. Consequently, the defenders had been unable to man this gate and its adjacent walls. Later on — so an-Nuwayrī remarks — the officer in charge of this gate would be convicted for treason and for handing the city to Peter.[27]

---

[20] an-Nuwayrī, *Kitāb al-Ilmām*, I, p. 112; II, pp. 137-9.
[21] an-Nuwayrī, *Kitāb al-Ilmām*, II, pp. 139-41.
[22] an-Nuwayrī, *Kitāb al-Ilmām*, II, pp. 143-5.
[23] an-Nuwayrī, *Kitāb al-Ilmām*, II, pp. 141-2, 146.
[24] an-Nuwayrī, *Kitāb al-Ilmām*, II, pp. 147-51.
[25] an-Nuwayrī, *Kitāb al-Ilmām*, II, pp. 155-6.
[26] an-Nuwayrī, *Kitāb al-Ilmām*, II, p. 157.
[27] an-Nuwayrī, *Kitāb al-Ilmām*, II, p. 158.

Then many inhabitants of Alexandria were murdered or captured, while others fled to the countryside through one of the gates of the city or by using their turbans to climb down the walls.[28] According to an-Nuwayrī, the crusaders kept killing, violating, robbing and sacking from Friday-evening until Saturday, when they moved their abundant spoils as well as five thousand prisoners to their ships. An-Nuwayrī states that when the crusaders spent the night on their ships, the city was also plundered by the Bedouins who entered it. The fleet finally sailed away on Thursday 28 Muḥarram 767, eight days after it had arrived, when they saw Yalbuġa l-Ḥāṣṣakī, the commander of the Egyptian army, arriving in Alexandria with his relief force.[29]

Badr ad-Dīn Abū Muḥammad Maḥmūd b. Aḥmad b. Mūsā al-ʿAynī was born on 21 July 1361 in ʿAynṭāb, a city close to Aleppo. In 1399, he moved to Cairo where his knowledge of Turkish gave him access to the ruling circles. He occupied several high positions in the religious administration of Cairo, where he died on 28 December 1451. His major historical work was his multi-volume *ʿIqd al-Ǧumān fī Tārīḫ Ahl az-Zamān* (A Pearl Necklace of the History of the People of the Time), a universal history of the world — mostly on Egypt and Syria — from Creation until al-ʿAynī's own time.[30]

In the course of his chronicle, al-ʿAynī mentions the conquest of Alexandria by "the lord of Cyprus" ("ṣāḥib Qubrus") and 70 warships, carrying more than 30,000 "Franks".[31] Unfortunately, however, most of the attention in al-ʿAynī's account — which is a second version of this event — goes to the Cairene scene and the reaction of the sultan and the commander of his army, Yalbuġa l-Ḥāṣṣakī.[32]

Nevertheless, al-ʿAynī informs us that these "Franks" arrived near Alexandria on Friday 23 Muḥarram 767 AH/10 October A.D. 1365. They proceeded until right outside the city, where they started fighting the people of Alexandria, who had come out to stop them. However the "Franks" also attacked the Muslims from an ambush, which caused the

---

[28] an-Nuwayrī, *Kitāb al-Ilmām*, II, pp. 162-4.
[29] an-Nuwayrī, *Kitāb al-Ilmām*, II, pp. 166, 171-3, 178, 179, 269-70.
[30] W. Marçais, "al-ʿAynī", in *EI²*, I, p. 814; Brockelmann, *Geschichte*, ii, pp. 52-3; S II, pp. 50-1; F. Wüstenfeld, *Die Geschichtsschreiber der Araber*, Burt Franklin Research and Source Work Ser., 50 (New York, 1964), p. 489; Little, "Historiography", pp. 437-8.
[31] al-ʿAynī, *ʿIqd al-Ǧumān fī Tārīḫ Ahl az-Zamān*, XXIV/1, MS Cairo, National Library, 1584 *Tārīḫ*, p. 138.
[32] al-ʿAynī, *ʿIqd*, XXIV/1, pp. 138-9.

bour, where the walls seem to have been abandoned by their defenders ("wa ḫalat al-aswār mina l-ḥumā"). With ladders, they climbed these walls, took the city and burned down the armoury.[42] Meanwhile, the inhabitants tried to flee and got jammed at one of the gates, Bāb ar-Rašīd, which was burned. Al-Maqrīzī informs us that this jam killed an innumerable number of people ("mā lā yaqaʻu ʻalayhi ḥaṣrun").[43] The amir Ġanġarā — at that moment in charge of the city — took the contents of the city's treasure together with 50 imprisoned European merchants with him when he fled to Damanhūr in the Delta. And so the city was left entirely to the crusaders.[44]

The King of Cyprus then entered the city and he had it sacked, destroyed and burned. The crusaders were said to have treated the remaining population very harshly ("istalama bi s-sayf"), killing many, also Christians, and capturing a great many of them. They continued doing this until the morning of Sunday, 25 Muḥarram/12 October, when they returned to their ships with their booty and 5,000 prisoners. When the commander of the Egyptian army, Yalbuġa l-Ḥāṣṣakī, and his relief force arrived in Alexandria on Thursday ("yawm al-ḫamīs"), the crusaders sailed away with their booty and prisoners.[45]

A clear echo of this account by al-Maqrīzī can be found in the chronicle of the Mamlūk historiographer Zayn ad-Dīn Abu l-Barakāt Muḥammad b. Aḥmad Ibn Iyās al-Ḥanafī, who was born on 9 June 1448 and who died in 1524, a couple of years after the conquest of Egypt by the Ottomans. His writings were also mainly historical, and although his most important chronicle *Badāʼiʻ az-Zuhūr fī Waqāʼiʻ ad-Duhūr* (Marvellous Blossoms among Events of the Times) concentrates especially on the decline and fall of the Mamlūk Empire, it yet also contains a short account of the sack of Alexandria.[46]

His summary of events is so brief, that he forgets to mention the events of Thursday and Friday and simply antedates the complete story of the conquest of Alexandria to Wednesday 21/8, but then wrongly naming Ṣafar/November as the month concerned. He only informs us that on that day the "Franks" came to Alexandria in 70 ships under the

---

[42] al-Maqrīzī, *Sulūk*, III/1, p. 106.
[43] al-Maqrīzī, *Sulūk*, III/1, p. 106.
[44] al-Maqrīzī, *Sulūk*, III/1, p. 106.
[45] al-Maqrīzī, *Sulūk*, III/1, pp. 106-7.
[46] W.M. Brinner, "Ibn Iyās", in *EI²*, III, pp. 835-7; Brockelmann, *Geschichte*, II, p. 295; S II, pp. 405-6; Wüstenfeld, *Geschichtsschreiber der Araber* (see n. 30), p. 513; Little, "Historiography", pp. 440-1.

command of the lord of Cyprus and that they took the city. The continuation of his story looks like a copied summary — almost word for word — of al-Maqrīzī.[47]

After this presentation of the Mamlūk sources on the sack of Alexandria by Peter I of Lusignan and his allies in October 1365, we must undoubtedly agree with Atiya that an-Nuwayrī's version is the most elaborate one. For instance, it mentions numerous details of Muslim heroes and their fights and skirmishes with "Franks" and it lists all the major demolitions and plunderings inside Alexandria. In all 44 pages of an-Nuwayrī's encyclopaedia were dedicated entirely to the event,[48] while al-ʿAynī and al-Maqrīzī only gave two and four pages of information respectively.[49]

But what is the actual value and the historiographical quality of this elaborate contemporary version? And what is the value and quality of the two other later versions? A résumé of the most important differences and similarities might help to clarify this. For an accurate assessment of the results of this comparison the issues that are here considered for comparison are also looked at from an angle independent of Mamlūk historiography: the stories of the attack and sack of Alexandria as they can be read in the chronicle *La Prise d'Alexandrie ou Chronique du Roi Pierre Ier de Lusignan* by the French musician and historiographer Guillaume de Machaut (1300-77),[50] and in the history of the Lusignan dynasty of Cyprus by Leontios Makhairas (*ca.* 1380-*ca.* 1450), i.e. the *Recital concerning the Sweet Land of Cyprus entitled "Chronicle"*.[51]

Both al-Maqrīzī and an-Nuwayrī mention the appearance of 70 or 80 Venetian ships on Wednesday.[52] Both mention the fact that inhabitants of

---

[47] Ibn Iyās, *Badāʾiʿ az-Zuhūr fī Waqāʾiʿ ad-Duhūr*, I/2, ed. M. Muṣṭafā, Bibliotheca Islamica, 5a2 (Wiesbaden, 1974), pp. 21-3.

[48] an-Nuwayrī, *Kitāb al-Ilmām*, II, pp. 136-79.

[49] al-ʿAynī, *ʿIqd*, XXIV/1, pp. 137-9; al-Maqrīzī, *Sulūk*, III/1, pp. 104-7.

[50] Guillaume de Machaut, *Prise d'Alexandrie*, pp. 56-110; *Lexikon des Mittelalters*, IV (München and Zürich, 1989), pp. 1781-2. De Machaut is even said to have been a participant in and therefore eyewitness of these events (Atiya, *A Fourteenth Century Encyclopedist*, p. 7).

[51] Leontios Makhairas, *Chronicle*; on the work and the author, see the Introduction, II, pp. 1-24; *Lexikon des Mittelalters*, VI (München and Zürich, 1993), p. 58. We want to make the observation here that the stories both these chronicles tell are, of course, not to be regarded as a standard of historical truth for our Mamlūk sources in the light of the following comparison; rather they are used here just like the Mamlūk sources to help us reassessing the true value of the one source that is often treated as such a standard of historical value for the Alexandrian Crusade, an-Nuwayrī's *Kitāb al-Ilmām*.

[52] al-Maqrīzī, *Sulūk*, III/1, p. 105; an-Nuwayrī, *Kitāb al-Ilmām*, II, p. 230; al-ʿAynī, *ʿIqd*, XXIV/1, p. 138.

Alexandria spread on the peninsula on Friday.[53] Another common element was the ensuing skirmish between one crusader ship and some Muslims in the surf, which actually started the conquest of Alexandria.[54] We find an echo of both these elements in al-ʿAynī's report, when he mentions the clash between the crusaders and the inhabitants of Alexandria who had come out to stop these crusaders.[55] All three versions then equally mention how many Alexandrians were killed, either during the fight or when fleeing back to the city.[56] There is also general agreement between these versions on how the Franks violated, captured and killed many, Muslims and non-Muslims alike, and how they plundered and destroyed Alexandria.[57] Finally, the sources agree on the fact that after the sack of the city, the crusaders remained on their ships in the harbour for a couple of days until a relief force from Cairo approached or entered the city.[58]

Clearly, all versions agree on the general line of events concerning the sack of Alexandria. Compared with the "western" version of Guillaume de Machaut and Leontios Makhairas, this general line indeed proves to be very reliable.[59] However, despite this general conformity, some major differences are also very significant. First of all, the dating of the event in these Muslim records poses a problem. Though both an-Nuwayrī and al-Maqrīzī agree that the crusader ships appeared before the Alexandrian coast on a Wednesday and that the real conquest of the city followed two days later, on Friday, they differ on the dates they give. While an-Nuwayrī clearly indicates this Wednesday as Wednesday 20 Muḥarram 767, al-Maqrīzī informs us that this day was Wednesday 21 Muḥarram 767, a dating which can also be derived from al-ʿAynī's statement that the date of the following crucial Friday was 23 Muḥarram 767. If we convert these dates to the Christian era 20 Muḥarram corresponds according to the Wüstenfeld-Mahler-tables[60] with Tuesday 7 October,

---

[53] al-Maqrīzī, *Sulūk*, III/1, p. 105; an-Nuwayrī, *Kitāb al-Ilmām*, II, pp. 139-40.

[54] al-Maqrīzī, *Sulūk*, III/1, p. 105; an-Nuwayrī, *Kitāb al-Ilmām*, II, p. 146.

[55] al-ʿAynī, *ʿIqd*, XXIV/1, p. 138.

[56] al-Maqrīzī, *Sulūk*, III/1, pp. 105-6; an-Nuwayrī, *Kitāb al-Ilmām*, II, pp. 146-7; al-ʿAynī, *ʿIqd*, XXIV/1, p. 138.

[57] al-Maqrīzī, *Sulūk*, III/1, p. 105; an-Nuwayrī, *Kitāb al-Ilmām*, II, p. 146; al-ʿAynī, *ʿIqd*, XXIV/1, p. 138.

[58] al-Maqrīzī, *Sulūk*, III/1, pp. 106-7; an-Nuwayrī, *Kitāb al-Ilmām*, II, pp. 162-4, 166, 171-3, 178, 256; al-ʿAynī, *ʿIqd*, XXIV/1, p. 138.

[59] Guillaume de Machaut, *Prise d'Alexandrie*, pp. 56-110; Leontios Makhairas, *Chronicle*, pp. 150-5.

[60] B. Spuler, *Wüstenfeld-Mahler'sche Vergleichungs-Tabellen zur muslimischen und iranischen Zeitrechnung mit Tafeln zur Umrechnung Orient-Christlichen Ären: Dritte, verbesserte und erweiterte Auflage der "Vergleichungs-Tabellen der mohammedanischen und christlichen Zeitrechnung"* (Wiesbaden, 1961), p. 17.

while 21 Muḥarram indeed corresponds with Wednesday 8 October. Then again comparing these data with the "western" versions of the event in the chronicles of Guillaume de Machaut and Leontios Makhairas, we can firmly state that, strangely enough, our eyewitness an-Nuwayrī was one day wrong. For Guillaume de Machaut informs us that de crusaders tried to disembark in the harbour of Alexandria "En un juedi, ce m'est avis, Jour de la feste St. Denis" — dated by his editor De Mas Latrie as Thursday 9 October —[61] and Makhairas also gives Thursday 9 October as the day of arrival of the Franks.[62] Consequently, the preceding Wednesday had to be 8 October or 21 Muḥarram, as attested by al-Maqrīzī and indicated by al-ʿAynī. Clearly, our eyewitness an-Nuwayrī was wrong here.

Though this minor mistake should not question the value of the content of an-Nuwayrī's report, I believe that this false dating reveals that al-Maqrīzī and al-ʿAynī must have used other sources than the report of an-Nuwayrī regarding the sack of Alexandria. This fact makes al-Maqrīzī's version of the events in particular at least as important as an-Nuwayrī's. Nevertheless, al-Maqrīzī also seems partially to have used an-Nuwayrī or a common source, for although he follows his own correct dating during his entire record of the sack, he surprisingly makes the same mistake as an-Nuwayrī in the end when he informs his reader of the date on which the crusaders sailed away from Alexandria. Al-Maqrīzī — as an-Nuwayrī — gives Thursday 28 Muḥarram as this date, though 28 Muḥarram in fact corresponds with Wednesday 15 October.

Other issues that attest to the equally valuable character of al-Maqrīzī's account, are the following:

Both authors differ considerably regarding the events of the second day, Thursday, after the arrival of the Franks in Alexandria. Al-Maqrīzī makes short work of this day, informing us that the Alexandrians came outside the walls to confront the crusaders, but these refused to react all day long and they even seemed to have remained quiet during the following night.[63] An-Nuwayrī al-Iskandarānī on the contrary states that Peter and his crusader-fleet entered the western harbour of Alexandria, Baḥr as-Silsila, on that day and that they even disembarked. But the Alexandrian defence from the walls and its clouds of arrows prevented them from approaching and eventually they were driven back to their

[61] Guillaume de Machaut, *Prise d'Alexandrie*, p. 67.
[62] Leontios Makhairas, *Chronicle*, p. 150 (Greek), p. 151 (English).
[63] al-Maqrīzī, *Sulūk*, III/1, p. 105.

ships.⁶⁴ Guillaume de Machaut, however, gives us a story that is very similar to that of al-Maqrīzī.⁶⁵ Leontios Makhairas' story, finally, remains somewhat blurred with regard to the days on which the different events took place, because of the relative briefness of its account (actually only three paragraphs). Nevertheless he also mentions that "then the Saracens came down to the shore, nigh ten thousand of them, horsemen and foot soldiers, to defend the harbour".⁶⁶

Consequently, it is again al-Maqrīzī's account that looks the soundest and most acceptable in this respect. Why did an-Nuwayrī write down a story that looks quite the opposite from reality. We suggest that his afore-mentioned general preference for the legendary and the dramatic⁶⁷ and perhaps also his pride as a devoted Muslim and Alexandrian played tricks on him.

Another matter which similarly questions an-Nuwayrī's reliability, concerns the tactics the crusaders used to surprise and overpower the Alexandrians when they started their fatal attack on the city on Friday. Al-Maqrīzī records clearly that a group of "Franks" had already secretly disembarked with their horses during the preceding night and that they were hiding in one of the graveyards, secretly awaiting the attack of their allies to surprise the defenders from this ambush ("kamanū fi t-turab"). On Friday then, the "Franks" started very tactically by sending one ship ahead, enticing the Alexandrians to come outside. During the following skirmish, when many Alexandrians actually did come outside to help their colleagues or to proceed without care to the lighthouse, the ambush opened up and the "Franks" launched their real attack. The hiding knights raised their trumpets and attacked the Alexandrians in the back, while arrows were shot from the approaching fleet. Panic spread among the defenceless Alexandrians, who tried to flee back to the walls. This chaos enabled the Franks to take the beach and attack the city-gates.⁶⁸ This ambush-story is summarized in al-ʿAynī's version⁶⁹ and an-Nu-

---

⁶⁴ an-Nuwayrī, *Kitāb al-Ilmām*, I, p. 112; II, pp. 137-9.

⁶⁵ "Or le gart cils qui fist la nue! Qu'einsois qu'eussent but ne mengié, furent li anemy logié, devant le viés port, à tel route, qu'il couvroient la terre toute ... . Tant en y ot grant quantité qui empeschierent le descendre de ses vaissiaus et terre prendre" (Guillaume de Machaut, *Prise d'Alexandrie*, p. 67).

⁶⁶ Leontios Makhairas, *Chronicle*, p. 151; surprisingly, however, he goes on by saying "and they failed". This seems, however, to point at their general defeat rather than to a specific event on this day, as no mention is made of that and the Franks are still supposed to be on their ships.

⁶⁷ Atiya, *A Fourteenth Century Encyclopedist*, p. 17.

⁶⁸ al-Maqrīzī, *Sulūk*, III/1, pp. 105-6.

⁶⁹ al-ʿAynī, *ʿIqd*, XXIV/1, p. 138.

wayrī's report makes no mention of this ambush at all. According to the latter, it were spies that had informed Peter of the defenceless position of many Alexandrians outside the city, enabling him to overpower them easily. An-Nuwayrī consequently puts the loss of the city down to the incapability of the substitute-governor and his advisors, and also to the brutality of the infidel King Peter, who attacked and butchered harmless citizens.[70] When again comparing these two versions with the account of Guillaume de Machaut, we see that the latter's coincides most with al-Maqrīzī's report: Guillaume informs us that while Peter and his crusaders fought the Muslims heroically in the western harbour, the Hospitallers had secretly disembarked in the eastern harbour. From there they attacked the Alexandrians in the back, which created great panic and caused their flight back to the city.[71] Makhairas refers to these tactics only in passing by saying that the Alexandrians, who had been very confident of their superiority at first, "were seized with great terror, and many Saracens fled" when they suddenly saw that horses had been landed too.[72]

Again we see how an-Nuwayrī seems to have given his own version of reality, more befitting his own personal motives.

More examples of such dissimilarities between an-Nuwayrī and the other chronicles exist. They all point in the same direction as the before-mentioned issues. Though an-Nuwayrī's encyclopaedia provides us with an unparalleled amount of data and details, these should not be taken for granted simply because an-Nuwayrī was an eyewitness himself and because he used the testimonies of other eyewitnesses. His version of the sack of Alexandria should be treated with a lot of historical criticism, keeping in mind that he did not so much — as Atiya stated — "stands out as a foremost historical authority ... [on] the Cypriot attack on and brief occupation of Alexandria in 1365",[73] but on the contrary that his blind faith and "his approach ... of a story teller with an emphasis on the dramatic and the legendary"[74] certainly and clearly also extended to his

---

[70] an-Nuwayrī, *Kitāb al-Ilmām*, II, pp. 139-47.
[71] "Il avoit un port à senestre, devant la cité d'Alixandre, où Dieux fist venir et descendre de Rodes le bon amiral, et les freres de l'Opital, ..., ils abillierent leurs chevaus, et issirent de leurs vaissiaus, sans avoir nul empechement; Puis se meïrent en bataille; ... Et quant li Sarazin veïrent les nostres qui les ecloïrent, en l'eure tournerent en fuie..." (Guillaume de Machaut, *La Prise d'Alexandre*, pp. 68-77).
[72] Leontios Makhairas, *Chronicle*, pp. 151, 153.
[73] Atiya, *A Fourteenth Century Encyclopedist*, p. 18.
[74] Atiya, *A Fourteenth Century Encyclopedist*, p. 17.

EIN ZIMMER MIT BLICK AUF DAS MEER
Einige wenig beachtete Aspekte der Pilgerreisen ins Hl. Land im 12. und 13. Jahrhundert *

RUDOLF HIESTAND

Am 16. September 1184 kam eine kleine Karawane von Damaskus her über den Golan an der Kreuzfahrerburg Toron vorbei, wo der Übergang ins christliche Gebiet lag und die aus dem Maghreb stammenden Mekkapilger, nicht aber die Händler, einen Dinar und einen *qirat* bezahlen mussten. Zwei Tage später, am 18. September, befanden sie sich vor den Toren von Akkon. Man führte sie zur *duana*, dem Zoll, der sich in einem Khan für Händler und Reisende befand, vor dessen Eingang auf teppichbelegten Bänken mit elfenbeinernem, goldverziertem Schreibgerät christliche Beamte sassen. Die Erleichterung war gross, als diese sich wie auch ihr Vorgesetzter, der Pächter des Zolls, des Arabischen in Wort und Schrift mächtig erwiesen. So waren die Formalitäten rasch erledigt — »alles spielte sich höflich und zuvorkommend ab, ohne Grobheiten oder Handgreiflichkeiten.«[1] Während die Händler ihre Waren im Obergeschoss des Khans zu deponieren hatten, waren die Pilger wie unser Berichterstatter, der aus Valencia oder Jativa stammende Sekretär (*kātib*) des Herrschers von Granada, Ibn Jubayr (1145-1217), und seine Gefährten frei, sich zu bewegen, wie sie wollten, und konnten nun ein Schiff für die Rückreise suchen[2].

Doch es stellte sich das erste Problem eines jeden Reisenden bis heute nach der Ankunft am Zielort, es reichte nicht aus, diesen erreicht zu haben, sondern es galt nun, eine Unterkunft für die Zeit des Aufenthaltes von noch unbestimmter Dauer zu finden: es war — ich zitiere wieder wörtlich — »ein Zimmer bei einer Christin mit Blick auf das

---

* Für Abkürzungen sehe pp. 163-4.

[1] Ibn Jubayr, p. 354: »Tout cela se fit avec politesse et courtoisie, sans brutalité ni bousculade.« Zu Ibn Jubayr vgl. *ibid.*, pp. 129; Ch. Pellat, *Encyclopédie de l'Islam*, III (Leiden-Paris, 1975²), pp. 777-9; A. Gateau, »Quelques observations sur l'intérêt du voyage d'Ibn Jubayr pour l'histoire de la navigation en Méditerranée au XIIe siècle«, *Hespéris*, 36 (1949), pp. 289-312. Die französische Übersetzung ist der englischen von R. J. C. Broadhurst (London, 1952) vorzuziehen.

[2] Ibn Jubayr, p. 354.

[3] Ibn Jubayr, p. 354: »Nous allons loger dans une chambre que nous louons d'une

Meer.«[3] Diese kurze Angabe weist auf einen wenig beachtetes Aspekt der mittelalterlichen Pilgerreisen in das Hl. Land, mit dem sich eine ganze Reihe von Erscheinungen verbindet, die man gerne als »interkulturell« bezeichnet.

Über die Motive der Pilgerfahrten, über manche technische Fragen, über die Wahrnehmung der anderen Welt, in die die Pilger kamen, ist in den letzten Jahrzehnten viel gearbeitet worden.[4] Doch über diese erste Frage, die während der folgenden Tage, Wochen, Monate auf jeder Etappe immer wieder neu zu lösen war, eben die Unterkunft, findet sich nur wenig, und die mit ihr, wo und wie immer sie gelöst wurde, unausweichlich verbundenen Auswirkungen scheinen kaum beachtet worden zu sein.[5] Dies liegt gewiss auch an den Quellen. Die im 12. und 13. Jahrhundert zu Dutzenden entstehenden Pilgerführer und Beschreibungen des Hl. Landes,[6] manche nur in einem einzigen Exemplar, andere als eigentliche Bestseller dutzend- ja hundertfach überliefert wie das Werk des Rorgo Fretellus,[7] sind weitgehend stereotypisch, da es nicht darauf ankam, eigene Eindrücke wiederzugeben, sondern möglichst »objektiv« Namen der Orte, ihre Identifikation mit biblischen Erzählungen, die Himmelsrichtungen und Distanzen festzuhalten.

Diese Texte sind daher oft schwer datierbar, und Hinweise auf den »Alltag« fehlen in ihnen fast völlig. Dabei bricht nicht selten ein durchaus persönlicher Tenor genau dann ab, wenn nach eingehenden Schilderungen von Stürmen, Piraten usw. während der Überfahrt die syrische Küste erreicht ist. In diesem Augenblick macht das Individuum dem

---

chrétienne face à la mer.«

[4] Aus der fast uferlos gewordenen Literatur seien nur angeführt: N. Ohler, *Reisen im Mittelalter* (Düsseldorf und Zürich, 1999); L. Kriss-Rettenbeck, *Wallfahrt kennt keine Grenzen* (München und Zürich, 1982), U. Ganz-Blättler, *Andacht und Abenteuer: Berichte europäischer Jerusalem- und Santiago-Pilger (1320-1520)* (Tübingen, 1990); Jean Richard, *Les récits de voyage et de pèlerinage*, Typologie des Sources médiévales, 38 (Turnhout, 1981), je mit umfangreichen Literaturangaben.

[5] Zum Unterkunftproblem für Pilger, aber für das Hl. Land auf das Johanniter-Hospital beschränkt, das sehr früh gerade nicht mehr als »Gasthaus« diente (vgl. unten), vgl. N. Ohler, *Pilgerleben im Mittelalter zwischen Andacht und Abenteuer* (Freiburg, 1994), pp. 123-54.

[6] Vgl. S. de Sandoli, *Itinera Hierosolymitana crucesignatorum (saec. XII-XIII)*, Studium Biblicum Franciscanum, Collectio maior, 24, 4 Bde. (Jerusalem, 1978-84), z.T. fehlerhaft nach überholten Editionen. Für die handschriftliche Überlieferung und Verbreitung immer noch unentbehrlich: R. Röhricht, *Bibliotheca geographica Palaestinae* (Berlin, 1890; Nachdruck mit Ergänzungen, Jerusalem, 1963).

[7] P. C. Boeren, *Rorgo Fretellus de Nazareth et sa description de la Terre Sainte*, Koninklijke Nederlandse Akademie van Wetenschapen, Afdeling Letterkunde, Verhandelingen, n.s., 105 (Amsterdam, 1980), und Einleitung; Röhricht, *Bibliotheca* (wie Anm. 6), pp. 33-5.

Heilsgeschehen Platz, was so weit gehen kann, dass ein Amen eingefügt wird, bevor der Bericht weiter geht. In der Folge heisst es dann höchstens noch »darauf gingen wir...«, »dann kamen wir...«, häufig tritt sogar an die Stelle des Erzählers in der ersten Person der gleichsam distanzierte Berichterstatter in der dritten Person.[8] Dies gilt schon für den ersten dieser Pilgerberichte aus der Zeit nach 1099, denjenigen des Engländers Saewulf aus dem Jahre 1103. Das Kriterium wenigstens stellenweise persönlich gehaltener Darstellung erfüllen aus dem 12. Jahrhundert neben dem Russen Daniel aus den Jahren 1106/07 wenigstens in Ansätzen nur die beiden Deutschen Johannes von Würzburg und Theodericus aus den Jahren 1166 bzw. 1175 und aus dem 13. Jahrhundert wieder zwei Deutsche Wilbrand von Oldenburg und der *magister* Thietmar.[9] Weshalb dies so ist, ob für sie das Hl. Land eine besonders fremde Welt war, so dass sie manches festhielten, was für französische und italienische Pilger bereits in den üblichen Erfahrungshorizont gehörte, ob sie besondere Sensibilität besassen, lässt sich nicht mehr entscheiden. Erst im Spätmittelalter nahmen unter den nach dem Verlust Akkons veränderten Bedingungen solche praktischen Begleitumstände einen grösseren Raum ein, wurde die Reise als solche wichtig, nicht nur was man gesehen hatte.[10] Doch dies soll uns hier nicht weiter beschäftigen. Man müsste diese veränderte Haltung wohl auch dadurch erklären, dass erst der massenhafte Kontakt in der Zeit der Kreuzzüge in tieferem Sinne das Bewusstsein für das Anderssein und für ein kulturelles Innen und Aussen geschärft hatte.[11]

Wer heute eine Reise in ferne Länder tun will, hat zwei Möglichkeiten: er kann einfach mit mehr oder weniger gefüllter Börse bzw. Scheckkarte sich von Tag zu Tag selber um Vorankommen, Verpflegung und Unterkunft bemühen, oder er kann ein Pauschalangebot erwerben, das ihn — mit vielen Zwischenstufen — eines Teil oder aller Sorge und Mühe, gegebenenfalls selbst für Freizeitgestaltung und Unterhaltung

[8] Saewulf, in *Peregrinationes tres*, pp. 58-77, z.B. p. 63, l. 48; p. 72, l. 461.
[9] Daniel; Johannes von Würzburg, vgl. A. Grabois, »Le pèlerin occidental à l'époque des croisades et ses réalités: La relation de pèlerinage de Jean de Wurtzbourg«, in *Mélanges E. R. Labande* (Poitiers, 1974), pp. 367-76; Theodericus; Wilbrand von Oldenburg, *Peregrinatio*, in *Peregrinatores Terrae Sanctae quattuor* (Leipzig, 1873²), pp. 159-91; Thietmar, in *Peregrinatores*, ed. Laurent (diese Ausgabe ist der bei Sandoli wiederabgedruckten, lückenhaften von 1867 unbedingt vorzuziehen (wie Anm. 6)).
[10] Vgl. A. Esch, »Gemeinsames Erleben — Individueller Bericht: Vier Parallelberichte aus einer Reisegruppe von Jerusalempilgern 1480«, *Zeitschrift für historische Forschung*, 11 (1984), pp. 385-416.
[11] Zur Alterität vgl. F. Wolfzettel, »Die Entdeckung des 'Anderen' aus dem Geist der Kreuzzüge«, in *Die Begegnung des Westens mit dem Osten*, ed. O. Engels und P. Schreiner (Sigmaringen, 1993), pp. 273-98.

enthebt. Von solchen Verheissungen des modernen Tourismus war der mittelalterliche Pilger weit entfernt, ob sein Ziel nun Santiago, Rom, Jerusalem oder Mekka oder nur Aachen oder Trier war. Nur wer, wie es bald nach 1100 zunehmend der Fall wurde, den Weg ins Hl. Land wählte, musste sich um eine Schiffspassage kümmern, die ihn ohne eigenes Zutun an die Küste Syriens brachte.[12] Was sich jedoch in keinem Fall im Voraus sicherstellen liess, war die Unterkunft. Ein Pilger sah sich daher entsprechend dem Ziel seiner Wallfahrt, den Stätten, »wo die Füsse des Herrn gewandelt hatten«, vom ersten Tage an in der Situation des vertrauten Wortes aus den Evangelien: »Der Sohn des Menschen hat nicht, wo er sein Haupt hinlegen soll« (Matth. 8, 20), und damit bereits ein Stück weit in der Nachfolge des Herrn.

Die Frage der Unterkunft hatte mit den Kreuzzügen in zweifacher Hinsicht eine neue Dimension erhalten. Im Frühmittelalter gab es in der abendländischen Welt keine auf die entgeltliche Unterbringung von Reisenden eingerichteten Beherbergungsbetriebe oder Gasthäuser, die, wie Hans Conrad Peyer in einem schönen Buch gezeigt hat, für den Westen eine »Erfindung« bzw. ein Fortschritt des 12./13. Jahrhunderts sind.[13] Als Unterkunft dienten den Reisenden welcher Art auch immer, soweit sie nicht Gäste von Bekannten waren, vor allem die Klöster, die nach der Regel Benedikts Fremden offenstehen mussten.[14] Am Ende des 11. Jahrhunderts begannen an den am stärksten begangenen Wegen aus den Klöstern, die zunehmend funktionell und finanziell überfordert waren, Hospize ausgegliedert oder neu gegründet zu werden, ähnlich den im byzantinischen Bereich seit je bestehenden Xenodochien und den gegen Entgelt bereitstehenden sog. *mitata*.[15] Das berühmteste Beispiel solcher

---

[12] Dazu J. H. Pryor, *Geography, Technology and War: Studies in the Maritime History of the Mediterranean, 649-1571* (Cambridge, 1988); und *idem*, »Introduction« zur Edition von Saewulf, *Peregrinationes tres*, pp. 34-57.

[13] H. C. Peyer, *Von der Gastfreundschaft zum Gasthaus: Studien zur Gastlichkeit im Mittelalter*, Schriften der MGH, 31 (Hannover, 1987); *Gastfreundschaft, Taverne und Gasthaus*, ed. H.C. Peyer, Schriften des Historischen Kollegs, 3 (München, 1983), mit L. Schmugge, »Zu den Anfängen des organisierten Pilgerverkehrs und zur Unterbringung und Verpflegung von Pilgern im Mittelalter« (pp. 37-60); *idem*, »Die Anfänge des organisierten Pilgerverkehrs im Mittelalter«, *Quellen und Forschungen aus italienischen Archiven und Bibliotheken*, 64 (1984), pp. 1-83; H. C. Peyer, »Gastfreundschaft und kommerzielle Gastlichkeit im Mittelalter«, *Historische Zeitschrift*, 235 (1982), pp. 265-88.

[14] *Regula s. Benedicti*, c. 54, ed. A. de Vogüé, Sources chrétiennes, 182 (Paris, 1972), p. 610.

[15] Zu den *hospitia* vgl. S. Reicke, *Das deutsche Spital im Mittelalter und sein Recht* (Stuttgart, 1932); D. Jetter, *Geschichte des Hospitals*, bisher 6 Bde. (Wien, 1966-1987) und *idem*, *Das europäische Hospital* (Köln, 1986); zu vielen einzelnen Institutionen *Dizionario degli Istituti di Perfezione*, bisher 9 Bde. (Roma, 1974ff.); zu den Xenodochien vor allem D. Constantelos, *Byzantine Philanthropy and Social Welfare* (New

neuen Einrichtungen war das in Jerusalem von Amalfitanern um 1070 gegründete Hospiz, das die Keimzelle des Johanniterordens wurde,[16] mit einem zweiten Hospiz für Frauen gleich daneben. Es folgten das Hospital der Deutschen, solche für Ungarn, Spanier, Bretonen, Engländer, während des dritten Kreuzzuges das Feldspital der Deutschen vor Akkon, das zum Deutschen Orden wurde. Neben solchen nationalen Einrichtungen entstanden andere an heilsgeschichtlich oder verkehrstechnisch wichtigen Orten, in Sebaste, auf dem Pilgerberg bei Tripolis, in Antiochia, in Tell Basher/Turbessel an der Strasse nach Edessa, nachdem schon, wenig beachtet, auf Vorhaltungen der Kreuzfahrer der Basileus Alexios I. im Frühjahr 1097 die Errichtung eines lateinischen Klosters und Hospitiums in Nikäa für die künftigen Pilger auf dem nun wieder freigelegten Weg nach Jerusalem versprochen hatte.[17] Ob das Kloster-Hospiz in Adrianopel/Edirne auf der Strasse durch den Balkan schon 1096/1097 entstand oder erst während des zweiten Kreuzzuges, muss offenbleiben, ebenso seit wann es in Konstantinopel selbst das Hospiz S. Maria Alemannorum gab.[18]

Das auf Klöstern und *hospitia* an den Wegen zu den Wallfahrtsorten und an diesen selbst beruhende frühmittelalterliche Unterbringungssystem wurde für die Jerusalem-Wallfahrt nach 1100 wie gesagt aus zwei Gründen gesprengt, einem quantitativen und einem strukturellen. Einerseits brachte die Massenbewegung im Laufe des 12. Jahrhunderts sechs-, insgesamt wohl siebenstellige Zahlen von Menschen jeglichen Alters und beiderlei Geschlechts auf dem *iter Terrae Sanctae* bzw. *iter Hierosolymitanum* in den Osten. Damit sind nicht die Kreuzfahrer gemeint, die seit 1095 auf päpstliche Aufrufe hin aufbrachen, um das Erbe Christi militärisch zu befreien, dann zu verteidigen, schliesslich wiederzugewinnen, sondern die eigentlichen *peregrini*. Nach einer oft angeführten Stelle sah der deutsche Pilger Theodericus in der Osterzeit 1175 von der

---

Brunswick, N.J., 1968) und T.S. Miller, *The Birth of the Hospital in the Byzantine Empire* (Baltimore und London, 1985); *Oxford Dictionary of Byzantium* (New York u.a., 1991), III, col. 2208 f.

[16] Vgl. Jonathan Riley-Smith, *The Order of St. John in Jerusalem and Cyprus, c. 1050-1310* (London, 1967); R. Hiestand, »Die Anfänge der Johanniter«, in *Die geistlichen Ritterorden Europas im Mittelalter*, Vorträge und Forschungen, 26 (Sigmaringen, 1980), pp. 31-80.

[17] *Le »Liber« de Raymond d'Aguilers*, ed. J.H. und L.L. Hill, Documents relatifs à l'histoire des croisades, 9 (Paris, 1969), p. 44: »promiserat, quod... monasterium et hospitium pauperibus Francorum ibi faceret.« Dass weitere Zeugnisse fehlen, dürfte auch an der bereits erwähnten Verlagerung der Pilgerrouten vom Land- auf den Seeweg liegen.

[18] Vgl. zu ihm J. Delaville le Roulx, *Cartulaire général de l'ordre des Hospitaliers de St-Jean de Jérusalem* (Paris, 1894-1906), I, p. 229, No. 321; p. 231, No. 326.

in den Bergen Judäas gelegenen Quarantena, dem Ort des vierzigtägigen Fastens Jesu und der Versuchung, nach eigener Schätzung in der Jordanebene 60 000 Menschen,[19] doch eine noch grössere Zahl eben erst angekommener, d.h. wohl mit dem Frühjahrspassagium, habe in Jerusalem geweilt.[20] Zusammen waren dies also weit über 100 000 Personen, eine Zahl, die durchaus an moderne Verkehrsströmen in der Hauptreisezeit gemahnt. Allein in Akkon sollen damals am Mittwoch der Osterwoche ausser der *Buza*, auf der Theodericus hin- und zurückreiste, einem Schiffstyp, der schon gegen 2000 Passagiere aufnehmen konnte, 30 kleinere Schiffe gewartet haben, um Pilger wieder nach Hause zu bringen.[21]

Selbst wenn das Hospitale S. Iohannis zweitausend Betten aufgewiesen haben soll[22] und man unterstellt, dass andere Klöster und Kirchen in ihren Innenhöfen Unterkunft gewährten, so reichte dies nur für einen kleinen Teil aus. Dabei ist nicht zu vergessen, dass, wie zwei neugefundene Texte wohl endgültig festlegen,[23] das Johanniter-Hospital in der Mitte des 12. Jahrhunderts bereits nicht mehr der Unterbringung von Pilgern, sondern von *pauperes* bzw. *infirmi*, d.h. im mittelalterlichen Sinne Kranken, dauernd Pflegebedürftigen, Wöchnerinnen, ausgesetzten Säuglingen und nicht zuletzt Verwundeten aus den dauernden Kämpfen diente. Johannes von Würzburg und Theodericus wissen ebensowenig wie die Statutentexte des Hospitals von einer Unterbringung von Pilgern, wie in den Urkunden eine Verschiebung von *peregrini et pauperes* zu *infirmi* stattfand.[24]

Die Mehrzahl der Pilger übernachtete wie Teilnehmer an Feldzügen unter freiem Himmel bzw. in Zelten, was jedoch in ihrem Fall als Überlebensfrage die Wehrlosigkeit des Menschen im Schlaf aufwarf. Wie jeder Wanderer auf einsamen Wegen brauchte der Pilger während des

---

[19] Theodericus, c. 30, p. 177.

[20] *Ibid.*

[21] Theodericus, c. 40, p. 186. Zu dieser Stelle, wo früher »80« gelesen wurde, vgl. die Bemerkungen von Huygens, *Peregrinationes tres*, p. 12.

[22] Johannes von Würzburg, l. 1283 ff., p. 131: »maxima multitudo infirmorum tam mulierum quam virorum colligitur, fovetur et maxima expensa cotidie reficitur, quorum summam... ad duo milia languentium fuisse cognovi«; Theodericus, c. 13, p. 157: »numerum simul accumbentium nullo modo quivimus discernere, lectorum vero numerum millenarium vidimus excedere.«

[23] K. Klement, *»Von Krankenspeisen und Ärzten...«: Eine unbekannte Verfügung des Johannitermeisters Roger des Moulins (1177-1187) im Codex Vaticanus Latinus 4852* (Salzburg und Rom, 1996) [Diss. jur.]; und B.Z. Kedar, »A Twelfth Century Description of the Jerusalem Hospital«, in *The Military Orders: Welfare and Warfare*, ed. H. Nicholson (Aldershot, 1998), pp. 3-26.

[24] Vgl. Hiestand, »Die Anfänge« (wie Anm. 16), p. 56; und idem, *Papsturkunden für Templer und Johanniter, Neue Folge* (Göttingen, 1984), pp. 104-62.

Schlafes entweder andere, die für ihn und über ihn wachten, oder feste Mauern, die Schutz gewährten bzw. eine ausreichende Reaktionszeit sicherten, am besten beides. Schon der Russe Daniel erwähnt gleich zu Beginn seines Berichtes sozusagen als erstern Eindruck, dass es bei Lydda viele Quellen gebe — ein weiterer unentbehrlicher Faktor —, doch ruhe man dort nur mit grosser Angst, weil die Sarazenen von Askalon kämen und die Pilger umbrächten.[25] Die Frage der Sicherheit klingt auch in dem Bericht des Theodericus über die ihn der Jordanebene lagernden Pilgern an, denn er fügt hinzu, auch die jenseits des Jordans lebenden Heiden könnten die Pilger sehen, natürlich nicht nur mit guten Absichten. An dieser Stelle äussert er sich zum einzigen Mal zur Frage der Unterkunft und erwähnt, dass die Pilger in der Ebene zu übernachten pflegten,[26] um von dort zum Jordan und zur Quarantena zu gehen, aber auf drei Seiten von den Mauern eines Gartens, auf der vierten durch Wachposten der Templer und der Johanniter geschützt würden, wie er schon im vorangehenden Kapitel berichtete, dass in der Umgebung dieses sog. Abrahamsgartens viele Türme und grosse Häuser der beiden Orden zum Schutz der Pilger errichtet worden seien.[27] Auch in den Pilgerberichten wird so vor dem Spätmittelalter die Sicherheitsproblematik nur punktuell angesprochen, für den Weg von der Küste nach Jerusalem und, zweifellos unter dem Einfluss des biblischen Berichtes vom barmherzigen Samariter (Luk. 10, 33), für den Weg an den Jordan, vereinzelt auch für die Reise auf den Sinai.[28] Nicht zufällig war bekanntlich aus diesem Schutzbedürfnis der erste geistliche Ritterorden, die Templer, entstanden mit der Turris Stratonis bzw. Le Destroit an der Küste zwischen Cayphas und Haifa an der Stelle, wo die Strasse vom Meer in die von Räubern bewohnten Berge abbog und später die mächtige Anlage von Castrum peregrinorum bzw. Athlit erbaut wurde.[29]

Zu den »explodierenden« Zahlen und ihren Folgen kam für das Hl. Land ein zweiter Faktor hinzu. Im Gegensatz zu den anderen grossen

---

[25] Daniel, c. 7, p. 10.

[26] Theodericus, c. 29, p. 176.

[27] Theodericus, c. 28, p. 175: »ne in eundo vel redeundo sive ibi pernoctando a Saracenis laedantur.«

[28] Vgl. unten. Zu den Sinai-Reisen vgl. M. Labib, *Pèlerins et voyageurs au Mont Sinai* (Kairo, 1961); R. Hiestand, »Der Sinai: Tor zu anderen Welten«, in *Reisen in reale und mythische Ferne*, ed. P. Wunderli, Studia Humaniora, 22 (Düsseldorf, 1993), pp. 76-102.

[29] Districtum/Destroit scheint eines der ersten Templerforts gewesen zu sein vgl. C. N. Johns, *Pilgrims' Castle (ᶜAtlit), David's Tower (Jerusalem) and Qalᶜat ar-Rabad (ᶜAjlun)* (Aldershot, 1997), passim; R. Hiestand, »Castrum peregrinorum e la fine del dominio crociato in Siria«, in *Acri 1291: La fine della presenza degli ordini militari in Terra Santa e i nuovi orientamenti nel XIV secolo*, ed. F. Tommasi (Perugia, 1996), pp. 23-41.

Wallfahrtszentren des 11. bis 13. Jahrhunderts, wie Rom, S. Michele auf dem Gargano, Mont St-Michel und Santiago de Compostela, ging es in Jerusalem meist nicht um eine einzige Nacht, vielleicht zwei oder drei, um eine Krankheit zu überwinden. Nicht wenige der Ankömmlinge wollten längere Zeit, manche auch für immer bleiben. Dies unterschied Jerusalem grundsätzlich von den anderen Zielen: Niemand liess sich in Compostela oder auf dem Gargano nieder, sondern die Pilger besuchten das Grab des Heiligen, verrichteten ihre Gebete, hofften gegebenenfalls auf den Ablass bzw. die Erfüllung eines mit einem Gelübde verbundenen Wunsches und kehrten zurück. Man zog in der Regel auch nicht an den Tiber, um auf Dauer zu bleiben oder gar dort zu sterben. Dies alles war nur in Jerusalem der Fall, wo nach verbreiteter Annahme im Tale Josaphat am jüngsten Tage die Auferstehung und das Jüngste Gericht sein sollte,[30] und nur in Jerusalem und im Heiligen Lande konnte man das biblische *sequere me* (Matth. 8,22; 9,9) auf den Spuren des Heilsgeschehens selbst umsetzen, was schon erhebliche Zeit in Anspruch nahm, wenn man allein die in den Evangelien erwähnten Orte aufsuchen wollte, ohne diejenigen des Alten Testaments mit Sinai, Ararat — wegen der Arche Noah —, Harran usw., von dem nur ausnahmsweise aufgesuchten Ur in Chaldäa und Babylon ganz zu schweigen.

Daraus entstand eine neue Konzeption der Wallfahrt, nicht rasch alles einmal gesehen zu haben, sondern, wie Daniel schreibt, der als erster in der Kreuzfahrerzeit auch jenes Wort vom »Land, wo seine Füsse wandelten« anführt: »Noch andere, die die Wallfahrt in die heilige Stadt Jerusalem gemacht haben, kommen zurück, ohne viel gesehen zu haben, weil sie nach Hause drängen, während man doch in der Eile diese Reise nicht erfüllen noch alle heiligen Orte in der Stadt und ausserhalb aufsuchen kann.«[31] Sozusagen als Kontrapunkt, als neues Programm, hebt er hervor: »Ich, Daniel, habe nach der Ankunft in Jerusalem 16 Monate dort verbracht, und so habe ich diese heiligen Stätten besichtigen und gründlich erkundigen können.«[32]

Ein längerer Aufenthalt, wie ihn Daniel freiwillig auf sich nahm, war nicht gänzlich neu. Die Bussbücher des frühen Mittelalters kannten den mehrjährigen Aufenthalt im Hl. Land bzw. in Jerusalem als festen Tarif für schwere Verbrechen.[33] So verbrachte der bretonische Adlige Frot-

---

[30] Johannes von Würzburg, l. 746 f., p. 110.
[31] Daniel, p. 5.
[32] Daniel, c. 1, p. 5.
[33] Bussstrafenkatalog, vgl. C. Vogel, »Le pèlerinage pénitentiel«, in *Pellegrinaggi e culto dei santi* (Todi, 1963), pp. 37-94; R. Kottje, *Die Bussbücher Halitgars von Cambrai und des Hrabanus Maurus: Ihre Überlieferung und ihre Quellen* (Berlin, 1980).

mund in der Mitte des 9. Jahrhunderts nach einem Mord an Onkel und Bruder vier Jahre im Osten, doch als er auf der Rückreise in Rom um Absolution bat, schickte ihn der Papst zurück, worauf er nach weiteren vier Jahren auf eine neue Begegnung mit dem Papst verzichtete, wohl aus Furcht, noch ein drittes Mal in den Osten ziehen zu müssen. Seinen Mitbrüdern im Kloster Redon hatte er schon so genügend über seine Erlebnisse zu berichten, die sie in der Chronik des Klosters festhielten.[34] Wo er sich während dieser Jahre in Jerusalem aufhielt, wo er wie all die anderen langjährigen Busswallfahrer ein Dach über dem Kopf fand, erfahren wir freilich nicht.

In der Kreuzfahrerzeit ergab sich ein längerer Aufenthalt oft allein schon deshalb, weil sich die Rückreisen mit Rücksicht auf Witterungs- und Windverhältnisse auf zwei grosse Überfahrtszeiten im Frühjahr und im Herbst, die sogenannten *passagia*, konzentrierten.[35] Aufgebaut vom Westen her, mit Venedig an erster Stelle, gestatteten sie zwar, wenn man mit dem gleichen Schiff zurückkehren wollte, einen kurzen Besuch der heiligen Stätten, vor allem Jerusalems, vergleichbar einer heutigen Kreuzfahrt mit Landausflug, doch für einen umfassenderen Besuch, wie ihn Daniel forderte, reichte die Zeit zwischen Ankunft in Jaffa, Akkon, Tyrus und der technischen Überholung und Neuverprovantierung der Schiffe bis zur Rückfahrt nicht. Wer Weihnachten im Hl. Land erleben wollte, je nach Kirchenkalender auch Ostern und Pfingsten, musste von vornherein einen längeren Aufenthalt einrechnen und damit auch für die ganze Zeit des Aufenthaltes das Unterkunftsproblem lösen, erst recht, wer wie gesagt als Bussleistung oder aus eigenem Antrieb über Jahre blieb, aber ohne in ein Kloster einzutreten. Viele dieser Langzeitpilger gaben den Gedanken an eine Rückkehr nicht auf, sie blieben *peregrini* und liessen sich gerne von Leuten aus ihrer Heimat über die dortigen Verhältnisse unterrichten, um dann gegebenenfalls nach bestimmten Nachrichten den Aufenthalt im Osten abzubrechen.[36] Doch wo hielten sie sich auf?

Auf der höheren Ebene fanden abendländische Herrscher, die mit den Kreuzzugsheeren in den Osten kamen, in der Regel standes-

---

[34] *Gesta sanctorum Rotonensium*, in *The Monks of Redon*, ed. Caroline Brett (Woodbridge, 1989), pp. 209-13.

[35] Vgl. Pryor, *Geography* (wie Anm. 12); *idem*, »Introduction« zu *Peregrinationes tres*, pp. 48-50; die Einrichtung ist auch Ibn Jubayr bekannt, der p. 341 von einem »passage de croisade«, wohl eher des Kreuzfestes spricht, vgl. auch p. 364.

[36] Ein typisches Beispiel ist Rainerius von Pisa, R. Grégoire, *San Ranieri di Pisa (1117-1160) in un ritratto agiografico inedito del secolo XIII*, Biblioteca del »Bullettino storico Pisano«, Collana Storica, 36 (Pisa, 1990), c. 56, p. 153.

gemässe Unterkunft in den Palästen der Herren der Kreuzfahrerstaaten oder bei den Ritterorden. Ludwig VII. von Frankreich wurde mit seiner Gattin Eleonore im Jahre 1148 in Antiochia wohl im Palast des Fürsten aufgenommen,[37] was bekanntlich zu folgenreichen Problemen führte, in Jerusalem wohnte der deutsche Herrscher bei den Templern,[38] der französische Herrscher, der bis in das Frühjahr 1149 im Osten blieb, vielleicht bei den Johannitern oder als Gast des Königs in der Turris David,[39] während im Jahre 1190 Friedrich von Schwaben nach der Ankunft in Antiochia gleich die ganze Stadt und insbesondere die Burg übernahm.[40] Im Königspalast Jerusalems oder beim armenischen Erzbischof dürfte der Fürst Thoros aus Kilikien untergebracht worden sein, als er in den 1160er Jahren König Amalrich (1163-74) aufsuchte.[41] während die höchsten Vertreter der orientalischen Nationalkirchen wie der Patriarch Michael Syrus und der Katholikos Gregor der Armenier bei ihren Besuch in Jerusalem vermutlich bei den eigenen Glaubensgemeinschaften bzw. deren Vorstehern ein Dach fanden.[42] Im 13. Jahrhundert dienten in Akkon vor allem die Templerburg und das Haus des Hospitals, wohl die Herberge im Montmusard, als »Gästehaus«, weil sie zugleich Schutz gewährten.[43] Zweifellos unter diesem Gesichtspunkt wurde die Gattin Ludwigs IX. nach dem uneinnehmbaren Athlit/Castrum peregrinorum gebracht, wo sie Peter von Alençon gebar.[44] Der Bericht Wilbrands von Oldenburg, der als Gesandter Kaiser Ottos IV. in den Osten kam, erweckt den Eindruck, er sei meist bei Bischöfen oder weltlichen Herren untergebracht worden, bei Jean d'Ibelin in Beirut, dem Bischof von Tripolis usw., da er zum Teil ihre Paläste schildert und bewertet, für Antiochia den Unterschied zwischen deren schmutzigen Aussenmauern und dem Prunk im

---

[37] Wilhelm von Tyrus, *Chronicon*, XIV, 27, p. 754.

[38] Otto von Freising, *Gesta Friderici*, I 63, ed. F. J. Schmale, Freiherr vom Stein-Gedächtnisausgabe (Darmstadt, 1965), p. 264.

[39] Wilhelm von Tyrus, *Chronicon*, XVI, 28, p. 755; XVI, 29, p. 757.

[40] *Itinerarium peregrinorum*, ed. H. E. Mayer, Schriften der MGH, 18 (Hannover, 1962), pp. 302-3; weitere Zeugnisse in R. Hiestand, »'Precipua tocius christianismi columpna': Barbarossa und der Kreuzzug«, in *Friedrich Barbarossa*, ed. A. Haverkamp, Vorträge und Forschungen, 40 (Sigmaringen, 1992), p. 98, Anm. 319.

[41] *La chronique d'Ernoul et de Bernard le Trésorier*, ed. L. de Mas Latrie (Paris, 1872), pp. 25-30.

[42] Michel le Syrien, *Chronique*, Ed. und Übersetzung J. B. Chabot (Paris, 1899-1924), III, p. 332.

[43] In der Templerburg wurde der Ayyubide Ibrahim 1242 aufgenommen, bei den Johanniter fand Richard von Cornwall auf seinem Kreuzzug 1240 Aufnahme.

[44] Jean de Joinville, *La vie de Saint-Louis*, ed. J. Monfrin (Paris, 1995), § 514, p. 319.

Inneren hervorhebt, für Nikosia auf die Ähnlichkeit mit Antiochia verweist,[45] nie aber eine Stadt als ganzes schildert.

Solche Unterbringung blieb dem einfachen Pilger natürlich versagt. Blieb er aus diesem oder jenem Grund länger, stellte sich die Frage der Unterkunft neu. Wie einige Asketen in Hütten längs der Stadtmauer oder auf ihr Sommer und Winter hindurch Sonne und Kälte, Regen und Schnee zu trotzen, wenn auch mit dem Nimbus, so einen mystischen Schutz der Stadt zu bilden (Jes. 62,5 und Apok. 21), war nicht jedermanns Sache.[46] Ein festes Dach über dem Kopf war besser, was zuerst einmal die geistlichen Institutionen bieten konnten. Daniel hielt sich noch in traditioneller Form im Metochion des Hl. Sabas auf. Auch dies war freilich nicht ohne Kosten, denn die unentgeltliche Aufenthaltsdauer war begrenzt. Obwohl Daniel betont, nur über bescheidene Mittel verfügt zu haben, sagt er andererseits, nichts gespart zu haben, um möglichst alles zu erfahren, was man nicht ohne einen guten Führer und einen Dolmetscher tun könne.[47] Wie diesem liess er sicher dem Metochion selbst einen Teil seiner doch nicht spärlichen Mittel zukommen lassen, so dass er ein nicht unwillkommener Gast gewesen sein dürfte, anders als so mancher Pilger, der sich hinsichtlich der notwendigen Mittel völlig verschätzt hatte.

Mit Ausnahme Daniels geben weder Pilgerberichte noch Chroniken noch Urkunden unmittelbar Auskunft auf unsere Frage, sondern nur die bei den Historikern oft keinen besonders guten Rufen geniessenden Heiligenleben. Im Jahre 1115 oder 1117 geboren, ging ein gewisser Rainerius aus Pisa, nach einer Jugend als Musikant im Hause einer Verwandten durch einen ehemaligen Krieger Albertus Leccapecore in S. Vito in Pisa im Jahre 1136 zu einem ernsthafteren Leben bekehrt, zwar noch Kaufmann, aber heimlich bereits ein *religiosus,* Ende der 1130er Jahren ins Hl. Land, äusserlich noch um Handel zu treiben.[48] Er blieb dann über

---

[45] Wilbrand von Oldenburg, c. 5, pp. 166-7 für Beirut mit detailreicher Schilderung der Ausschmückung; für Tripolis c. 8, pp. 168-9; c. 14, p. 172 für Antiochia: »nota quod domus et palacia Antiochie foris luteam monstrant apparenciam et intra aurea et delectabili vigent existencia«; für Nikosia c. 28, p. 181: »hospicia ornatu et picturis hospiciis Antiochie sunt similima.« Auffälligerweise findet sich nichts über Akkon.

[46] Schreiben Konrads von Montferrat von 1188, September 20, in *Cartulaire,* ed. Delaville (wie Anm. 18), I, p. 531, No. 858; und *Vita Rainerii Pisani,* in *San Ranieri,* (wie Anm. 36), §26, p. 131 und öfters.

[47] Daniel, »un bon guide et un interprète«. Ein solcher sehr alter heiliger und in der Heiligen Schrift sehr bewanderter Mann habe sich in der Laura selbst befunden, der ihm die heiligen Stätten in Jerusalem und seiner Umgebung, bis zum Meer von Tiberias und auf den Thabor, nach Nazareth, Hebron und zum Jordan zeigte.

[48] Eine biographische Skizze gibt Grégoire, in *San Ranieri di Pisa* (wie Anm. 36), pp. 56-7 in der Einleitung zur Edition der *Vita Rainerii Pisani.*

zehn Jahre, z.T. durch die lateinischen Gebiete wandernd, grösstenteils hielt er sich jedoch in Jerusalem auf, zeitweise unter den erwähnten Eremiten, die er freilich wegen ihres Weintrinkens kritisiert.[49] Während der übrigen Zeit wohnte er, wie die Vita berichtet, bei einer *religiosa matrona*.[50] Das ist kein Einzelfall, sondern stellt bei genauerem Hinsehen einen verbreiteten Typ der Beherbergung dar. Wie das Wort *matrona* es andeutet, handelte es sich offensichtlich um das Haus einer Witwe, mindestens einer alleinstehenden Frau fortgeschrittenen Alters.

Solche Reisen ins Hl. Land und ein längerer Aufenthalt dort scheinen für den neuen Heiligentyp des 12. Jahrhunderts zu einer wenn auch nicht unabdingbaren, doch sehr häufigen Etappe der *formation professionnelle*, dem Weg zum *Holy Man*, zu zählen. Dies setzt einen längeren Aufenthalt voraus, für den der nun mit wacheren Augen nachfragende Leser selbstverständlich auch wissen wollte, wo der Heilige tagein tagaus seine Zeit verbracht habe. Auch bereits festetablierte kirchliche Würdenträger begegnen wir, die statt einer wie vorgesehen kurzen Wallfahrt während Jahren im Osten »hängen« blieben, so dass man sie bei ihrer Rückkehr schon nicht mehr unter den Lebenden gewähnt hatte, wie den Bischof Bonfilius von Foligno (verstorben 1115), der mit dem ersten Kreuzzug ins Hl. Land gegangen sein soll, aber erst 1104 wieder zurückkam.[51] Wo eine solche Reise nach Outremer nicht erfolgte, wie z.B. beim Eremiten Silvester von Fabriano (verstorben 1267), berichtet die Vita von einem brennenden Wunsch nach einer solchen, die sich nicht erfüllen liess, weil Gott ihn in seiner Heimat sehen wollte, doch schenkte ihm der päpstliche *pigmentarius* namens Angelus gewissermassen als Ersatz Reliquien aus dem Hl. Lande, darunter Milch der Mutter Gottes.[52]

Die Unterkunft bei einer *matrona* konnte freilich auch Gefahren mit sich bringen. Die Vita des berühmten Joachim von Fiore durch Erzbischof Lukas von Cosenza berichtet, dass auch er während der sozusagen

---

[49] *Vita Rainerii Pisani*, c. 34, p. 132.

[50] *Ibid.*, c. 35, p. 132.

[51] S. Silvester, *Historia de vita sancti Bonfilij episcopi et confessoris,* in *Agiografia Silvestrina medievale*, ed. R. Grégoire, Bibliotheca Montisfani, 8 (Fabriano, 1983), p. 273 ff. Geboren um 1040 in Osimo, durfte er nach der Rückkehr in ein eigenes Kloster in Storace, dann nach Fara (Diöz. Cingoli) gehen, wo er am 27. September 1115 starb. Freilich halten die Angaben der Vita einer Überprüfung nur teilweise stand. So soll der Aufbruch ins Hl. Land etwa zehn Jahre nach der Übernahme des Bistums erfolgt sein (c. 11, p. 300), was jedoch schon um 1082 wäre.

[52] Andreas Jacobi de Fabriano, *Vita sanctissimi Silvestri confessoris et mirifici heremitae (†1267)*, c. 4, in *Agiografia Silvestrina medievale* (wie Anm. 51), p. 54; und *ibid.*, c. 47, pp. 137-44.

obligaten Wallfahrt nach Jerusalem in einem Haus aufgenommen wurde, das einer Witwe gehörte. Sie erhält allerdings nicht den Zusatz *religiosa*. Während Joachims Gedanken ganz von dem Ort, an dem er weilte, erfüllt waren, gingen die Gedanken der Hausherrin, die vielleicht selber noch nicht vorgerückteren Alters war, angesichts des jungen Gastes in eine ganz andere Richtung. Obwohl er ein *religiosus* war, suchte sie engeren Kontakt, warf ihm eines Abends eindeutige Blicke zu und gab zu verstehen, was ihr Wunsch war. Joachim sah sich in einer schwierigen Situation, denn zu der späten Stunde konnte er das Haus nicht mehr verlassen, ein Herumtreiben auf den Gassen während der Nacht wäre ebenso unziemlich gewesen. Statt des vorbereiteten weichen Lagers wurde ein Reisighaufen die Stätte schlafloser Stunden des Gebets, bis er am frühen Morgen, sobald die Türe des Hauses geöffnet worden war, ohne sich zu verabschieden, von dannen ging.[53] Ob er die Miete im Voraus bezahlt hatte oder schuldig blieb, wird nicht berichtet, ebensowenig, wie er diese Unterkunft gefunden hatte.

Gewiss handelt es sich um eine topische Szene, die die Standhaftigkeit des (künftigen) Heiligen vor der fleischlichen Versuchung belegen soll, doch wesentlich sind wie so oft die Begleitumstände, die zweifellos zeittypisch und »echt« sind. Für die Kreuzfahrerstaaten und für die italienischen Städte stand die Unterbringung eines Pilgers im Hause einer Witwe mit der Lebenserfahrung im Einklang und wirkte damit für Leser und Hörer als glaubwürdig, ebenso wie die anderen Fakten: ein Haus wird am Abend verschlossen, man darf des Nachts nicht auf die Strassen gehen, weil dies in eine wenig empfehlenswerte Gesellschaft führt, usw.[54].

Die bisher besprochenen Beispiele betrafen abendländische Pilger, die in den Kreuzfahrerstaaten für längere Zeit Aufnahme suchten und fanden und zwar bei ebenfalls aus dem Westen stammenden Einwohnerinnen, also »Franke findet Unterkunft bei Fränkin«. Für einen Pilger, der ein vollständiges Besuchsprogramm absolvieren wollte, gab es freilich selbst in der Zeit der grössten Ausdehnung der lateinischen Herrschaft, erst recht nach dem Jahre 1187 Ziele, die ausserhalb der Kreuzfahrerstaaten lagen, wie Damaskus, das nicht nur wegen des Apostels Paulus, sondern auch wegen des Marienheiligtums in Saydnaya aufgesucht

---

[53] Lucas archiepiscopus Cosentinus, *Vita Ioachim*, AASS Mai VII, 29. Mai, p. 93: »habitu iam religioso assumpto solus fuisset apud quandam viduam hospitatus.«

[54] Vgl. die Geschichte des vorgeblich durch die Strassen von Konstantinopel streunenden Kaisers Leo VI., Liudprand von Cremona, *Antapodosis*, I 11, ed. J. Becker, MGH Script. rer. Germ. (Hannover und Leipzig, 1915), pp. 9-12.

wurde.⁵⁵ Nach 1144/46 galt dies für Edessa, nach 1187 für Jerusalem und die meisten anderen grossen Wallfahrtsorte, vor allem aber für den anderen Höhepunkt einer Wallfahrt ins Hl. Land, den Sinai. Bei solchen Reisen, wo man sich nicht nur in politisch meist feindlichen Gebieten befand, sondern auch nicht mehr ohne weiteres Aufnahme bei anderen Christen finden konnte, in jedem Fall nicht bei lateinischen Klerikern oder Mönchen, stellte sich die Frage der Unterkunft in ganz anderer Weise.

Nach einer ersten Reise in Begleitung von *Suriani* und *Sarraceni* über Sephoris nach Nazareth und Kana, dann nach Damaskus und Saydnaya,⁵⁶ die Anlass zu einem kaum auf eigener Erfahrung beruhenden Bericht über Bagdad gibt,⁵⁷ ging der *magister* Thietmar im Jahre 1217 auf die eigentlich angestrebte Sinaireise. Dazu verkleidete er sich mit etwas schlechtem Gewissen als georgischer Mönch mit einem langen Bart,⁵⁸ verbrachte zwar vier Tage in Jerusalem, doch ohne darüber viel zu sagen, weil alles bekannt sei.⁵⁹ Jenseits des Jordans nahm ihn zuerst unweit von Kerak/Petra eine *muliercula graeca* gastlich auf, worauf auf ihre Bitte in der Nacht der griechische Bischof herbeieilte und *suo ydyomate*, d.h. wohl griechisch, dem Pilger den Segen erteilte.⁶⁰ Als Thietmar nach Montréal-Shobak mit seiner von Christen und Sarazenen bewohnten Siedlung kam, die nun dem Sultan von Ägypten gehörte, heisst es: »exceptus fui hospicio de quadam vidua gallica.«⁶¹

Dreissig Jahre nach der Schlacht bei Ḥaṭṭin lebte so in Shobak eine fränkische Witwe, die, wenn wir einige Hypothesen wagen, an Ort und Stelle geblieben war und das Leben an ihrem gewohnten Ort einer Übersiedlung nach Akkon oder in eine andere Küstenstadt vorgezogen hatte. Sie warnte ihren Gast vor den Gefahren der geplanten Reise auf den Sinai und nahm die Organisation an die Hand. Als Bewohnerin von Kerak und damit in einer weit besseren Position als der Fremdling schloss sie für ihn einen Vertrag mit Beduinen, der die Klausel enthielt, Thietmar sei lebendig oder tot zurückzubringen.⁶² Man hat nicht den

---

⁵⁵ Zu Saydnaya vgl. B. Z. Kedar, in den im Druck befindlichen Akten einer Tagung über die Ritterorden in Budapest im Februar 1999.

⁵⁶ Thietmar, c. 1-7, pp. 2-20.

⁵⁷ Thietmar, c. 7, p. 19.

⁵⁸ Thietmar, c. 8, p. 20: »habitu tamquam Georgianus monachus et longa barba simulavi quod non eram.«

⁵⁹ Thietmar, c. 9, p. 26.

⁶⁰ Thietmar, c. 14, p. 36.

⁶¹ Thietmar, c. 15, p. 37.

⁶² *Ibid.*: »Ubi exceptus fui hospicio a quadam vidua Gallica, que me informavit de itinere et modo itineris per desertum usque ad montem Sinay et fecit me habere viaticum

Eindruck, dass dieser »Maklerdienst« etwas Erstmaliges gewesen wäre, eher dass diese Witwe sozusagen eine Marktlücke entdeckt hatte, die sie mit einer »Sinai Travel Agency« des beginnenden 13. Jahrhunderts zu nutzen verstand. Doch ebensowenig ist zu übersehen, dass Thietmar keineswegs überrascht schien, in Shobak noch eine Landsmännin anzutreffen, so dass offen bleiben muss, ob er im Voraus von dieser Anlaufstelle für eine Sinaireise gehört hatte. Es fällt in jedem Fall auf, dass er den Weg über Kerak wählte und nicht, wie später üblich, über Gaza oder von Alexandrien aus.[63] Es zeigte sich in der Folge rasch, wie richtig das Vorgehen gewesen war, denn welche Garantie hätte sonst in der Wüste angesichts der Probleme von Weg, Verpflegung und vor allem Wasser und angesichts räuberischer Beduinen nicht nur für Hab und Gut, sondern auch für Leib und Leben bestanden?[64] Dass diese Fränkin sich ihrerseits auf solche Weise gerne von Zeit zu Zeit in ihrer Muttersprache unterhalten konnte, dürfen wir sicher annehmen.

Rechtlich stellte der Aufenthalt in einem islamischen Gebiet für Christen, von Zentralarabien abgesehen, kein Problem dar, soweit nicht politische Gründe ins Spiel kamen. Doch es ist natürlich kein Zufall, dass Thietmar zuerst bei einer *muliercula graeca*, dann bei einer *vidua gallica* Unterkunft fand, denn das gleiche bei einer Muslimin wäre schwer vorstellbar.

Gehen wir auf die andere Seite. Wie verhält es sich mit dem Aufenthalt von Muslims in den Kreuzfahrerstaaten, und zwar nicht von Hintersassen, sondern Reisenden, Kaufleuten, gegebenenfalls Pilgern? Damit sind wir zurück bei unserem Ausgangspunkt, dem Aufenthalt des spanischen Muslim Ibn Jubayr in Akkon im September 1184. Er fand, wie wir gehört haben, Unterkunft bei einer Christin, die ihm ein Zimmer mit Blick auf das Meer vermietete. Es gab anscheinend in Akkon sozusagen als Gewerbe »Privatunterkünfte«, die man mieten konnte, je nach Ansprüchen und Börse, und nicht nur für Christen, sondern auch für Muslims.[65] Ibn Jubayr hätte auch im Khan Unterkunft nehmen können, wie er dies selber berichtet, doch wir sehen ihn als wohlhabenden Mann

---

panem bis coctum, caseos, unam passam, ficus et uinum. Conduxit mihi etiam Boidewinos cum camelis usque ad montem Sinay, quia aliis non est via nota per desertum. Quos quidem iuratos et fide et sua lege astrictos convenit hoc modo, ut me reducerent vivum vel mortuum.«

[63] *Ibid.*: »quia aliis non est via nota per desertum.«
[64] Vgl. Thietmar, c. 17, p. 40 für das Wasserproblem; c. 18, p. 41 für Räuber.
[65] Ibn Jubayr, p. 354: »Nous allons loger dans une chambre que nous louons d'une chrétienne face à la mer.«

am Hof in Damaskus und in Kairo tätig war, eine Fülle von Zeugnissen für einen fast ganz selbstverständlichen Aufenthalt von Muslims im Königreich Jerusalem.[73] Er schreibt immer wieder, »als ich in Akkon war«, »als ich in Nablus vorbeikam« usw., ging am Hofe König Fulkos (1131-43) ein- und aus,[74] brachte Anliegen vor, wohnte Gerichtssitzungen bei[75] oder war mit dem König auf der Jagd. Im Nebenbei und keineswegs als ungewöhnlich vernimmt man, der Herr von Damaskus Muʿin ad-Dīn habe sich eines Tages bei einem Besuch bei König Fulko in Akkon einen eben aus dem Westen importierten Jagdfalken schenken lassen, der freilich nachher nicht hielt, was er versprochen hatte.[76] Doch es konnte ein muslimischer Herrscher Staatsgast eines Kreuzfahrerkönigs sein — gewiss nicht das Bild, das die lateinischen Chroniken entwerfen.

Ibn Jubayr und Usāma sind, wie nochmals zu betonen ist, keine Einzelfälle: Jener gibt seinen Lesern den expliziten Rat, bei einer Wallfahrt nach Mekka und Medina in jedem Fall den Rückweg über Akkon anderen Routen vorzuziehen,[77] und wie üblich dies war, zeigt, dass auf dem Schiff, mit dem er schliesslich nach Westen fuhr, die muslimischen Passagiere von den christlichen getrennt untergebracht wurden,[78] während kein christlicher Pilger je erwähnt, auf dem Schiff, das ihn ins Hl. Land brachte, seien auch Muslims mitgereist.

Über die Unterkunft während des mehrfachen Aufenthalts im Königreich Jerusalem hören wir freilich von Usāma nur den Namen des Muslims, der in Nablus jeweils sein Gastgeber war, ein gewisser Muʿizz, der dort eine Herberge für Muslims führte,[79] auch dies wieder ein wichtiger Hinweis, so dass man wohl von der Existenz solcher Herbergen in allen grösseren Zentren des Königreichs ausgehen muss. Doch man erfährt nicht, wo er in Jerusalem und in Akkon, noch wo Muʿin ad-Dīn bei seinen Besuchen bei König Fulko in beiden Städten untergebracht worden war,[80] wohl im Königspalast oder einem anderen dem König gehörenden

---

[73] Usāma ibn Munqiḏ, *passim*.
[74] Usāma ibn Munqiḏ, pp. 110, 164 usw.
[75] Usāma ibn Munqiḏ, p. 168, bei einem Gottesurteil durch Wasser in Nablus. Ähnlich p. 93 mit Usāma als Kläger im Namen seines Herrn Muʿin ad-Dīn gegen den Herrn von Banyas mit Beschreibung des Verfahrens, das ihm durch einen Spruch von sieben Rittern recht gibt, wobei unklar bleibt, ob die am Schluss des Aufenthaltes Usāma übergebenen 400 Dinar ein persönliches Geschenk oder eine Entschädigung darstellen.
[76] Usāma ibn Munqiḏ, p. 226.
[77] Usāma ibn Munqiḏ, p. 81.
[78] Usāma ibn Munqiḏ, p. 364.
[79] Usāma ibn Munqiḏ, p. 164.
[80] Zu Muʿin ad-Dīn in Jerusalem vgl. Usāma ibn Munqiḏ, pp. 164, 168 und 226.

Gebäude, während im 13. Jahrhundert einer der letzten Ayyubiden, al-Manṣūr Ibrahim von Ḥomṣ, einige Monate in der Templerburg in Akkon als Gast im wörtlichen Sinne »überwinterte«, bis sich die politische Lage auf der anderen Seite wieder soweit geklärt hatte, dass er nach Hause zurückkehren konnte.[81] Auch ein langer Aufenthalt eines hochgestellten Muslims war daher möglich, wenn auch der Ort seiner Beherbergung nahelegt, dass man gewisse Sicherheitsvorkehrungen für geboten erachtete. Man muss eigentlich annehmen, dass auch der fränkische König nach Damaskus ging. Darüber liegen keine Nachrichten vor, doch in der Zeit Saladins waren fränkische Barone willkommene Gäste auf der anderen Seite, mit denen man über Literatur und Religion diskutierte, und selbst während des 3. Kreuzzuges entstanden enge Kontakte von Richard Löwenherz und Konrad von Montferrat mit dem Bruder Saladins al-ʿAdil.[82]

Gewiss wäre es verfehlt, die Schwierigkeiten zu übersehen, die aus diesem Nebeneinander zu leichteren, aber auch zu verheerenden Zwischenfällen führten, vor allem wenn abendländische Kreuzfahrer und Pilger eingriffen. Solche führten bekanntlich in ihrem Unverständnis für das fragile Gleichgewicht zum Ende der lateinischen Herrschaft auf dem syrischen Festland, als im Sommer 1290 lombardische Neuankömmlinge über die in Akkon weilenden muslimischen Händler herfielen.[83] Harmloser, doch nicht weniger bezeichnend ist der oft angeführte Bericht Usāmas über einen jungen Templer, der ihn beim Gebet im Templum Salomonis aus Empörung über die nach Mekka statt nach Osten ausgerichtete, »falsche« Gebetshaltung dreimal nacheinander in die nach seiner Überzeugung allein richtige Stellung zu bringen versuchte, jedesmal von Aufsicht führenden Wächtern weggeführt, die sich schliesslich entschuldigten, dass der junge Franke eben erst im Osten angekommen sei.[84]

---

[81] Vgl. den Tadel Friedrichs II.: *Historia diplomatica Friderici II*, ed. J.L.A. Huillard-Bréholles (Paris, 1852-61), VI A, p. 256: »infra claustra domorum Templi predictos soldanos et suos cum alacritate pomposa receptos, superstitiones suas cum invocatione Machometi et luxus saeculares facere Templarii paterentur.«

[82] R. Hiestand, »Lasset uns singen und tanzen — morgen ist wieder Zeit für den Kampf«, in *Anknüpfungen — Kulturgeschichte, Landesgeschichte, Zeitgeschichte: Gedenkschrift für Peter Hüttenberger* (Essen, 1995), pp. 58-72; idem, »Zur Geschichte Siziliens im 12. Jahrhundert, II«, in *Quellen und Forschungen aus italienischen Archiven und Bibliotheken*, 73 (1993), pp. 58-70.

[83] R. Röhricht, *Geschichte des Königreichs Jerusalem* (Innsbruck, 1899), pp. 1006-8; R. Grousset, *Histoire des Croisades et du royaume franc de Jérusalem*, 3 Bde. (Paris, 1934-36), III, pp. 747-50.

[84] Usāma ibn Munqiḏ, pp. 163-4.

Usāmas Erlebnis führt einen Schritt weiter. Ohne dass die christlichen Quellen es erwähnen, behielten die Muslims in den lateinisch gewordenen Städten, selbst in Jerusalem, Moscheen oder wenigstens kleine Gebetsräume in zu Kirchen um- bzw. rückgewandelten Moscheen, um dort ihre Gebet verrichten zu können, und Usāma berichtet einmal auch von einem Besuch Muʿin ad-Dīns im Felsendom. Diese Berichte von der anderen Seite bestätigend, schreibt Johannes von Würzburg über den Platz des einstigen Altars unweit des Tempels, wo einst die Juden Opfer dargebracht hätten um 1165: »manche Sarazenen kommen immer noch dorthin«, »um in der Nähe zu beten, weil der Altar gegen Süden ausgerichtet ist, so wie sie zu beten pflegen.«[85] Er fügt an, dass sie auch im Templum Domini, also im Felsendom, ihre Gebete verrichteten, obwohl sie an die Passion Christi nicht glauben, doch dort ihren Schöpfer verehren, was freilich Götzendienst (*idolatria*) sei, da sie nicht dem christlichen Glauben angehörten.[86] Seine Stimme bleibt vereinzelt; kaum ein anderer Pilgerbericht ringt sich durch, auf das »Ärgernis« einzugehen, dass selbst in Jerusalem den Muslims an bestimmten Stellen eine Ausübung ihres Glaubens zugestanden war.

Detailliert berichtet dagegen wieder von der anderen Seite Ibn Jubayr über die Situation in Akkon und Tyrus. In der nun zu einer Kirche umgewandelten Hauptmoschee von Akkon gebe es einen kleinen Raum für das rituelle Gebet,[87] und in einer anderen Moschee hätten die Christen »einen anderen Mihrab«, gemeint eine Apsis, im Ostteil errichtet, so dass nun beide sich dort gleichermassen versammelten und, wie er hervorhebt, im gleichen Raum die einen in dieser, die anderen in jener Richtung beteten.[88] Und für Tyrus berichtet er von einer Moschee, die den Muslims geblieben sei, die auch noch andere Gebetsräume in der Stadt besässen.[89]

Geht man einen Schritt weiter, so hatten Aufenthalte von Christen im islamischen Gebiet und von Muslims im christlichen Gebiet unausweichlich Nebenwirkungen. Auch wenn man gegebenenfalls auf die

---

[85] Usāma ibn Munqid, p. 164; Johannes von Würzburg, l. 320 f., p. 92: »plures Sarraceni etiam hodie causa orandi ad ipsum versus meridiem dispositum, ad quem ipsi orare solent, veniunt.« Vgl. jetzt auch Hannes Möhring, »Die Kreuzfahrer und ihre muslimischen Untertanen und die heiligen Stätten«, in *Toleranz im Mittelalter*, ed. A. Patschovsky und H. Zimmermann, Vorträge und Forschungen, 45 (Sigmaringen, 1998), pp. 129-57.

[86] Johannes von Würzburg, l. 381, p. 94: »licet fidem passionis Christi non habeant, tamen hoc Templum venerantur, cum in eo creatorem suum adorent, quo tamen pro idolatria habendum est«; das letztere mit einer inneren Distanzierung von einer so rigoristischen Auffassung.

andere Seite nur ging, um eine heilige Stätte zu sehen oder ein Schiff zu besteigen, blieben andere Eindrücke nicht aus. So schildert Thietmar tief beeindruckt die Wasserbecken in den Innenhöfen der Gebäude in Damaskus, die Wasserleitungen, den Prunk der Ausstattung, wenn er auch für Ḥammāms und Wasserbecken (»natatoria vel lavatoria quadrata vel rotunda«) sogleich die Begriffe *luxus* und *stultitia* anfügt, um wieder inneren Abstand zu gewinnen.[90] Und ganz ähnlich sieht sich Ibn Jubayr während seines Aufenthaltes in Tyrus so sehr der Faszination einer prunkvollen christlichen Hochzeit erliegen, dass er sogleich Appelle an sich selbst richtet, er dürfe die Situation, es mit Andersgläubigen zu tun zu haben, nicht vergessen.[91]

Nicht zufällig folgt unmittelbar anschliessend eine grundsätzliche Betrachtung, die im vollen Wortlaut wiedergegeben sei:

> »Es gibt für einen Muslim keine Ausrede vor Gott wegen seines Aufenthaltes in einer Stadt des Unglaubens, wenn nicht im Vorübergehen. Im Lande des Islams befindet er sich geschützt vor den Mühen und den Übeln, denen er im Lande der Christen ausgesetzt ist, der Erniedrigung und der nach Erbarmen schreienden Klage der Steuerzahler, oder etwa über den, dessen Namen Gott heilig gemacht und dessen Ruhm er erhöht hat [gemeint ist Muḥammad], Worte zu hören, die das Herz zerreissen, vor allem aus dem Munde des gemeinen Volkes und der Unwissenderen unter ihnen, der fehlenden Möglichkeit zur Reinigung, dem Leben in der Mitte der Schweine und so vielen unerlaubten Dingen und all dessen, was man gar nicht nennen oder aufzählen kann. Hütet euch, hütet euch, ihr Land zu betreten.«[92]

Wie sehr es sich um Clichés handelt, ist evident. Hatte er nicht kurz zuvor erwähnt, der Empfang beim Zoll sei ohne jede verbale oder physische Belästigung höflich und zuvorkommend abgelaufen? Hatte er nicht betont, dass er sich frei bewegen konnte? Und hatte er nicht eben berichtet, dass es in Akkon und Tyrus Moscheen gebe und die Muslims dort ungehindert beten könnten? Und hatte er nicht selber empfohlen,

---

[87] Ibn Jubayr, p. 355: »Dieu a conservé pure, dans sa mosquée principale, une place qui est restée aux musulmans, comme un petit oratoire où les étrangers d'entre eux se réunissent pour célébrer la prière rituelle.«

[88] Ibn Jubayr, p. 365: »ainsi, musulmans et chrétiens, s'y assemblent et prennent les uns une direction de prière, les autres une autre.« Möhring, »Kreuzfahrer« (wie Anm. 85), unterschätzt die für die Kreuzfahrerstaaten überlebensnotwendige Weiterexistenz von islamischen Kultstätten.

[89] Ibn Jubayr, pp. 358-9.

[90] Thietmar, c. 3, p. 10.

[91] Ibn Jubayr p. 357. Die Episode wird, soweit ich sehe, nur bei Grousset, *Histoire* (wie Anm. 83), II, p. 756, nacherzählt; für H. Prutz, *Kulturgeschichte der Kreuzzüge* (Berlin, 1883), war sie noch nicht verfügbar. Vgl. Anhang.

[92] Ibn Jubayr, pp. 359-60.

den Rückweg von Mekka über Akkon und nicht über das Rote Meer zu nehmen? Auch der Begriff »in der Mitte der Schweine« gehört zum Ritual, wie Balduin IV. als »das Schwein« und die Königinmutter Agnes als »die Muttersau« bezeichnet werden,[93] obwohl er doch gerne von ihren Beamten freundlich aufgenommen worden war.

Dass er auf seiner Reise von Damaskus nach Akkon nicht über Jerusalem ging, ist ebenso aufschlussreich. Es hat nichts mit der fränkischen Herrschaft über die Stadt zu tun, sondern al-Quds ist in seinem Bericht nur die heilige Stadt der Christen und ein geographischer Begriff, drei Tage von Akkon, acht Tage von Damaskus, einen Tag von Kerak entfernt, nirgends als eine heilige Stadt der Muslims bezeichnet, wohl aber der Christen, denn, so liest man, die Marienkirche in Damaskus komme bei ihnen an zweiter Stelle nach der Grabeskirche.[94] Von der Himmelsreise des Propheten scheint er nichts zu wissen, oder sie ist, wie für weite Teile der islamischen Welt, eine fromme Legende, keine Glaubenswahrheit.

Es sind diese inneren Diskrepanzen, die die Berichte so aufschlussreich machen. Sie mussten aufbrechen, weil der tägliche Kontakt unvermeidlich Einblicke in die Welt der Anderen öffnete, an deren Wahrnehmung man nicht vorbeikam. Unterbringung in einem Privatquartier in Akkon, in Jerusalem, in Kerak und in Shobak, ob für längere Zeit oder nur für wenige Tage, trug dazu bei. Dass man sich dennoch stets bewusst blieb, nicht nur in einer anderen Kultur, sondern in einer feindlichen Welt zu befinden, dafür sorgten die »kleinen« täglichen Erlebnisse auf den Strassen und in den Städten. Wenn den christlichen Pilgern auf dem Weg nach Sichem Sarazenen entgegenkamen, die zur Bebauung der Felder gingen, sei es für den König oder für Templer und Johanniter,[95] stimmte das Weltbild, doch wie den reisenden Muslims in den christlichen Gebieten, so begegneten den reisenden Franken in den Städten Syriens Glaubensgenossen als Gefangene.[96] Ihr Anblick allein, ob man sie dann freizukaufen versuchte, wie es Usāma von sich berichtet[97] und nach Ibn Jubayr der Zweck spezieller Legate von Muslims zugunsten maghrebinischer Glaubensgenossen gewesen sei,[98] und ebenso von einem reichen christlichen Kaufmann aus Tyrus zugunsten bei Ḥaṭṭin

---

[93] Ibn Jubayr, pp. 352, 354.
[94] Ibn Jubayr, p. 329: »la cité sainte de Jérusalem.«
[95] Theodericus, c. 41, p. 187.
[96] Thietmar, c. 3, p. 13.
[97] Usāma ibn Munqiḏ, p. 111.
[98] Ibn Jubayr, pp. 360-1.

gefangener Christen berichtet wird,[99] oder ob man ihnen nur begegnet wie Ibn Jubayr in den Strassen von Akkon und Tyrus,[100] oder Kontakt aufzunehmen versuchte wie Thietmar in Damaskus, dessen spontaner Einfall, sie in der Burg aufzusuchen, von seinem Führer freilich nicht für eine glückliche Idee gehalten wurde, so dass er sich auf einen Austausch von Briefen durch Zwischenträger beschränkt,[101] oder ob man einen Bogen um ein »Lager« solcher christlicher Gefangener am Roten Meer machte,[102] änderte nichts. Man wurde sich immer von neuem bewusst, nicht nur in einer anderen, sondern in einer feindlichen Welt zu sein. Besonders schmerzlich wurde es, bekannte Gesichter zu erkennen, wie Thietmar einen gefangenen Ritter aus Wernigerode und einen Ritter Johannes aus Quedlinburg, mit denen er aus Todesangst nicht zu sprechen wagte.[103] Bei allen Ansätzen der Bewunderung und eines ersten Wohlbefindens in der neuen Umgebung wurde man in die Wirklichkeit zurückgestossen, wobei die Basis solcher Erlebnisse durch die andauernden Kämpfe immer wieder aufgefüllt wurde. So begegneten Ibn Jubayr auf dem Weg von Damaskus nach Akkon von einem Angriff auf Nablus zurückkehrende Truppen Saladins mit Tausenden von befreiten Muslims und christlichen Gefangenen.[104]

Von Berührungsängsten, von Abschottung war dennoch selbst während der eigentlichen Kreuzzüge nichts zu spüren. An anderer Stelle wurde auf die »Fraternisierung« von Leuten der beiden Heere während des dritten Kreuzzuges hingewiesen, mit Tavernen, in denen Kreuzfahrer sich mit muslimischen Sängerinnen herumtrieben statt mit Richard Löwenherz in den Kampf zu ziehen. Der Chronist schildert eingehend den aufreizenden Schnitt der Kleider, wie auch das Treiben besonders gravierend geworden sei, wenn das Personal durch neues aus den muslimischen Gebieten ersetzt wurde.[105]

[99] Vgl. auch P. G. Schmidt, »Peregrinatio periculosa«, in *Kontinuität und Wandel: Festschrift F. Munari*, ed. U. J. Stache (Hildesheim, 1986), pp. 461-85, v. 93-6.

[100] Ibn Jubayr, p. 360: »L'une des horreurs qui frappent les yeux de quiconque habite le pays des chrétiens est la vue des prisonniers musulmans, qui trébuchent dans les fers et qui sont employés à de durs travaux et traités comme des esclaves; et aussi celle des captives musulmanes qui ont aux jambes des anneaux de fer. Les coeurs se brisent à leur vue, mais la pitié ne leur sert de rien.«

[101] Thietmar, c. 3, p. 13: »sed ductori meo visum est non esse consultum.«

[102] Thietmar, c. 17, p. 40: »quoddam castrum vidi situm, cuius castellani partim erant christiani, partim Sarraceni, christiani quidem captivi Gallici, Anglici, Latini, sed omnes, et isti et illi, piscatores Soldani de Babilonia, non agriculturam, non bellum, non aliam miliciam preterquam piscaturam exercentes, nec aliunde viventes.«

[103] Thietmar, c. 3, p. 13.

[104] Ibn Jubayr, p. 349.

[105] *Itinerarium regis Ricardi*, ed. W. Stubbs, Rolls Series, 38/1 (London, 1884), p. 285 f. und 331.

Fast unüberbrückbar blieb der religiöse Graben. Mit grösstem Abscheu erwähnt Ibn Jubayr, dass ein Reisegefährte, ein Maghrebi aus Bone, dem alten Hippo des Augustinus, der von einem reichen Damaszener Kaufmann freigekauft worden war, nach längerem Schwanken in Akkon zum Christentum übertrat.[106] Dies findet in den christlichen Berichten keinen Gegenpart. Kein Pilger berichtet von einem freiwilligen Übertritt eines anderen Pilgers aus seiner Begleitung zum Islam, obwohl es keine Einbahnstrasse war, da kanonistische Quellen offen die eherechtlichen Auswirkungen auf die zurückgelassene Frau zu regeln versuchten, wenn ihr Ehepartner während der Gefangenschaft zum Islam übertrat.[107]

Fassen wir zusammen: gewiss punktuelle Beobachtungen aus westlichen und arabischen Quellen des 12. und 13. Jahrhunderts lassen anhand der für jeden *peregrinus* existentiellen Frage der Unterkunft und ihren Auswirkungen grundlegende Strukturen und Probleme des Pilgerwesens ins Hl. Land und der Begegnung zwischen christlicher und muslimischer Welt in den Kreuzfahrerstaaten erkennen. Über die mehr technischen Aspekte: Muslim wohnt bei einer Fränkin zur Miete, lateinischer Pilger findet im islamischen Gebiet Unterkunft bei einer fränkischen Witwe und einer *muliercula graeca*, eröffnet sich eine Fülle weniger unmittelbar zu Tage tretender Einblicke in das Verhältnis von Muslims und Christen. Der persönliche Kontakt schuf jeweils gewiss individuell differierende Erkenntnisse des »Anderen«, Faszination und Abwehr zugleich, über den politischen Graben hinweg, ohne ihn je wirklich zuzuschütten oder auch nur zu überdecken. Doch um in den überlieferten Texten zu diesen inneren Aussagen vorzustossen, ergibt sich die Notwendigkeit, neben den unmittelbaren Aussagen freizulegen, was auf beiden Seiten mutatis mutandis system-, besser ideologiebedingt gesagt werden musste, was dagegen aus den gleichen Gründen nicht gesagt werden durfte, und was doch bei allen solchen tabuähnlichen Schranken dem damaligen Leser und uns unterschwellig vermittelt wird.

---

[106] Ibn Jubayr, pp. 361-2.
[107] R. Hiestand, *Papsturkunden für Kirchen im heiligen Lande: Vorarbeiten zum Oriens Pontificius III*, Abh. d. Akad. d. Wiss. Göttingen, Phil.-hist. Kl. 3., Folge Nr. 136 (1985), p. 279, n. 112; J.A. Brundage, »The Crusader's Wife: A Canonistic Quandery«, *Studia Gratiana*, 12 (1967), pp. 425-40; und *idem*, »The Crusader's Wife revisited«, *Studia Gratiana*, 14 (1967), pp. 241-51.

Anhang

Ibn Jubayr, p. 357 f.: »Es fügt sich gut, an dieser Stelle von einem Spektakel zu berichten, wo sich der Luxus dieser niedrigen Welt entfaltete und dessen wir eines Tages in Tyrus Zeuge wurden im Hafen, nämlich den Brautzug. Alle Christen, Männer und Frauen, hatten sich aus diesem Anlass versammelt und hielten sich in zwei Reihen an der Türe des Hauses der Braut auf, die man einholen ging, während Trompeten, Flöten und andere Instrumente spielten. Endlich trat sie heraus mit zögerndem Schritt sich aufrechthaltend zwischen zwei Männern, die sie links und rechts stützten und die ihre nahen Verwandten mütterlicherseits zu sein schienen. Sie hatte die stolzeste Haartracht und das grossartigste Kleid, liess Schösse von goldgewirkter Seide auf dem Boden nach sich ziehen, wie dies die Mode ihrer Kleidung ist. Auf dem Kopf trug sie ein Diadem aus Gold, das eingewickelt war in ein Haarnetz aus Goldstoff, während ein ähnliches, mit Perlen geschmückt, sich oberhalb ihrer Brust entfaltete. Stolz in ihren Kleidern und ihrem Schmuck ging sie mit sehnendem Blick voran, mit dem Schritt einer Taube oder dem Dahingleiten einer Wolke. Wir suchen Zuflucht zu Gott angesichts der eigenen Verwirrung durch einen solchen Anblick. Vor ihr gingen angesehene Männer der Christen, in ihren grossartigsten Gewändern, nach sich schleppend die Schösse ihrer Kleider, hinter ihnen die Christinnen, ihr ähnlich und gleich schritten sie wie in einer Prozession in ihren schönen Kleidern voraus und sie stolzierten daher im Luxus ihres Schmuckes. Die Instrumentenspieler gingen an der Spitze. Die Muslims und die anderen Christen bildeten auf ihrem Wege zwei Reihen von Zuschauern, die sie betrachteten, ohne Zeichen des Missfallens von sich zu geben. Man führte sie in das Haus ihres Gatten, wo man sie eintreten liess und wo man diesen Tag mit Feiern verbrachte. Es war der Zufall, der uns den Blick auf dieses prunkvolle Spektakel gewährte: bitten wir Gott, dass er uns vor der Gefahr, dadurch berührt worden zu sein, bewahre.«

Abkürzungen

Daniel   Daniel, in *Itinéraires russes en Orient*, ed. B. de Khitrowo (Genève, 1889), pp. 3-83.

Ibn Jubayr   *Les voyages d'Ibn Jobair*, Übers. M. Gaudefroy-Demombynes, Documents relatifs à l'histoire des croisades publiés par l'Académie des Inscriptions et Belles-Lettres, 4-7 (Paris, 1949-65).

Johannes von Würzburg
    Johannes von Würzburg, in *Peregrinationes tres*, pp. 78-141.

Peregrinationes tres
    Peregrinationes tres, ed. R.B.C. Huygens (Turnhout, 1994).
Theodericus Theodericus, *De locis sanctis,* in *Peregrinationes tres,* pp. 142-97.
Thietmar Magister Thietmar, *Peregrinatio,* in *Peregrinatores Terrae Sanctae quattuor,* ed. J.M.C. Laurent (Leipzig, 1873²), Anhang.
Usāma ibn Munqid
    Memoirs of an Arab-Syrian gentleman or an Arab knight in the Crusades: Memoirs of Usamah Ibn Munqidh, engl. Übers. Ph. K. Hitti (New York, 1929).

A BYZANTINE TRAVELLER TO ONE OF THE CRUSADER STATES

W.J. AERTS[*]

INTRODUCTION

In 1904, the *Byzantinische Zeitschrift* published a long and interesting poem of Konstantinos Manasses edited by Konstantin Horna.[1] It is the description of a journey made by Manasses as a member of a Byzantine delegation led by Johannes Kontostephanos, a cousin of the Emperor Manuel I (1143-1180), who, after the death of his first wife Irene (= Bertha of Sulzbach, d. 1160), hoped to find a second wife from within one of the crusader communities which had been established in the Near East. It is well-known that Manuel Komnenos was one of the few Byzantine rulers who pursued a pro-western policy. His first marriage to Bertha of Sulzbach, sister-in-law of Conrad III, was part of a policy of maintaining good relations with Germany in order to defy the threats of the Normans of Sicily.[2] However, the Second Crusade, which again passed through Byzantine territory, frustrated the effects of this policy. By recruiting a new bride from one of the crusader states, Manuel hoped to strengthen his influence in the Kingdom of Jerusalem. The Kingdom would then be able to take advantage of the protection of a military power closer in distance to them than were the western countries in order to defend themselves against the Muslims. In general the West was already experiencing great difficulty in sending supplies and warriors to the Near East. It seems that the advisers of the Byzantine court had two names in mind of young women who were being considered for the role of new empress, namely Melisende,[3] sister of Raymond III, Count of

---

[*] For the abbreviations used in the footnotes see the end of this article.

[1] Horna, pp. 313-55.

[2] See *inter alia* G. Ostrogorsky and J. Hussey, *History of the Byzantine State* (Oxford, 1968), pp. 381 ff.; A.A. Vasiliev, *History of the Byzantine Empire* (Madison and Milwaukee, 1964), II, pp. 417 ff.

[3] Johannes Kinnamos, *Epitome (Historiae)*, ed. A. Meineke, CSHB (Bonn, 1836), p. 208, 17ff., speaks highly of the beauty of this girl, but suggests that an unexpected illness eliminated her for marriage to Manuel. Neither Manasses nor William of Tyre know anything about this. Kinnamos seems to have invented this argument for smoothing away the wavering diplomacy of the Byzantine delegation(s). Cf. also Horna, p. 317. Niketas Choniates, *Historia*, ed. J.-L. van Dieten (Berlin and New York, 1975), 117, 53 ff., does not mention the delegation to Tripoli and only refers to the marriage to Maria of Antioch.

legs. The "servants of Asclepius" are powerless. Nevertheless Manasses recovers after a therapy of hot baths, but he becomes very emaciated. The third poem again ends with an evocation of the City of Constantine.

The fourth poem begins with a cry of joy because the author sees Constantinople. But could this be a fata-morgana? Is he really there, and not on Cyprus, in Paphos, Kition, or Trimythous (now Limassol)? For the first time we now hear about place-names on Cyprus, which may imply that he indeed visited these places on the south coast during his stay in the island. On the other hand, it is quite possible that Manasses mentions the names of the well-known Cyprian cities here only to parade his knowledge. In any case, the dream motif is repeated here, but this time with a fortunate result: what he now sees is indeed Constantinople! This reassuring observation gives him the strength to continue his story with the description of the journey back. A number of obscurities emerge: it is suggested that they travel through Isauria, between Cilicia and the Taurus mountains where they pass the river Drakon (Serpent). The mentioning of this river is somewhat remarkable, the more so because other historians such as Procopius and Anna Comnene locate this river in Bithynia, with the same reference to its tortuous flow. Then they cross from the town Syce in Cilicia (Manasses does not wish to say a good word about this town) to Cyprus, where much commotion has arisen as a consequence of a military attack by the Count of Tripoli,[8] furious about the fact that the Byzantine Emperor has chosen Maria of Antioch to be his wife instead of his sister Melisende. This situation is dismissed by Manasses with the well-known Byzantine haughtiness: "how will a wingless, plucked sparrow approach the eyrie of an eaglet?", or "how will a small hind frighten a furiously roaring big lion?" It seems, however, that this situation had caused a problem for the leader of the delegation, who had much trouble in escaping from the hands of the Tripolitans. He manages to arrive on Cyprus with the effect that Manasses' illness disappears as if by magic. At last they can set out on the journey back. In the relief of this moment Manasses remembers an incident which happened to him during his stay on Cyprus: On Whitsunday he goes to church. While standing there a Cypriot peasant comes in with the putrefying stench of alcohol and garlic on his breath. First, Manasses asks the man politely to move on but the peasant does not react. Manasses asks for a second time, this time more loudly. The man remains unmoved. This makes Manasses so angry that he balls his fist and strikes the man's cheek with all his force. "This moment finally the

---

[8] This attack and the attacks that followed were so serious that, in 1169, the Cypriots were unable to fulfil their obligations to King Amalric to send sufficient supplies in the context of his anti-Arabic actions: see Costas P. Kyrris, *History of Cyprus* (Nicosia, 1985), p. 210.

dung-eater pissed off", to use Manasses' own words. This remarkable incident could in all probability be explained by the peasant being deaf or not understanding the refined Constantinopolitan language of Manasses and not having a high opinion of this man from the capital! Manasses, however, continues his complaints about Cyprus: the person trapped there has little chance of escaping, it is a fortress and comparable with Hades! Besides, the one who leaves the island runs the risk of being captured by pirates, who, in their behaviour, are even worse than the devils in hell!

But be that as it may: Manasses safely returned to his beloved Constantinople with the help of Christ, who may also have helped him to escape from all the other dangers of life.

So much for the narrative contents of the poem. In the first place I would say that it is clearly an egocentric document. The greatest part deals with the author's sufferings on Cyprus. In contrast to another work, the famous Chronicle of Leontios Makhairas, who recorded the acts of the first Lusignan rulers on Cyprus and speaks of the sweet land of Cyprus, the ordeal of Manasses is very unfavourable to the island. More interesting is his description of the route to and from the Holy Land making clear that the greatest part of the journey was made on land, apparently because the sea route was too dangerous due to pirates. The poem also offers a glimpse of Byzantine diplomacy. The expedition, which took place in 1160-1161, was sent to Palestine with a special goal, but it was obviously only the leader of the delegation who was aware of that goal; the other members of the delegation heard about the mandate only on their arrival in Palestine and, even then, only after they had complained to the leader, demanding to be informed about the mission's details. Manasses' description of a number of places he visited[9] and of the climate of these places is also very interesting. His apparent home-sickness was clearly at the root of his generally unfavourable impression of the Holy Land. His compassion and admiration for Christ, who chose this land to bring about the redemption of mankind, is rather comical. It is a pity that we hear nothing about the negotiations, where they were held, or who were the negotiators, nor whether there was any result and on what terms. Other sources provide us with the information that the negotiations first took place in Tripoli and later with King Baldwin in Jerusalem, who himself was in favour of a marriage to Melisende as he feared the dominant position in the region of the Byzantines in the event of Manuel's marriage to a countess from Antioch. Manasses' poem says nothing about another

---

[9] The description of Manasses has nothing to do with descriptions such as those that have been gathered in J. Brefeld, *A Guidebook for the Jerusalem Pilgrimage in the Late Middle Ages: A Case for Computer-Aided Textual Criticism* (Hilversum, 1994).

parallel delegation to Antioch. From other sources we know that that delegation stood under the leadership of Basileios Kamateros.[10] It seems probable that the delegations were sent out independently with the Emperor's intention of making a definite choice after checking the possibilities. The remark about the furious attack of the Count of Tripoli on Cyprus makes clear that the arrangements of the Kontostephanos delegation with Baldwin and the Count of Tripoli about the wedding with Melisende were already far advanced before being cancelled.

Unfortunately, Manasses' fourth poem 36-43 is very obscure. One may suppose that these verses are the residue of a passage which was originally more detailed. Horna assumes that Manasses, having been cured by means of the warm baths, joined the returning delegation, which for some reason returned from Isauria to Cyprus. He is puzzled by the fact that no indication of departure from and returning to Cyprus is given. Manasses' information about Kontostephanos' coming to Cyprus (IV, 72) makes it clear that Cyprus was the final point of departure to Constantinople. If the Isauria episode makes any sense, one of the following chains of events becomes imaginable: Manasses was not the only member of the Kontostephanos delegation who stayed on Cyprus. On hearing that another delegation at Antioch had secured favourable results, they attempted to join this second delegation in Isauria; or, Kontostephanos, feeling that his negotiations might fail, sent (a number of members of) his delegation already back through Antioch and Isauria, whereas Manasses (and others) on Cyprus were briefed to join these members. The situation turned out to be too dangerous for the carrying out of this journey, and they crossed over (back again) from Syce to Cyprus. The very mentioning of this place-name, Syce, could be used as proof that the poem originally described such an intermediate episode. This Syce is mentioned by Theophanes, 445, 17 (De Boor), as κάστρον Συκῆς, a fortress situated on the coast of Isauria or Cilicia. *Ibid.*, 446, 24-25, Syce and Cyprus are mentioned in the same breath. A similar constellation is to be found in Anna Comnene XI, 10, 8: the fleet of Boutoumites sails out from Cyprus and is destroyed by a storm off Syce.[11] That is to say that Syce was a fairly frequently used harbour for the crossing to or from Cyprus.

Having returned to Cyprus they had to wait for Kontostephanos whose position in Tripoli (or Jerusalem) had become impossible after the tidings (or rumours) about the arrangements reached at Antioch.

---

[10] See Kinnamos, *Epitome* (see n. 3), p. 210; Horna, p. 316.

[11] In his edition of Anna Comnene, *Alexiade*, 4 vols, Les Belles Lettres (Paris, 1937-76), B. Leib mistakenly takes Syce (l.c.) for Sycae near Constantinople; E.R.A. Sewter in his English trans. of the *Alexiade*, Penguin Classics (Baltimore and Harmondsworth, 1969), places Syce correctly in Cilicia.

After an adventurous flight from the Crusaders' territory he eventually arrives on Cyprus.

It is also clear that the description of Melisende as given by Manasses was composed at the moment that she was still in the race. Perhaps this was the special role Manasses had to play: every day he went to a small chapel, where one might expect the girl to come one day to say her prayers. It is Manasses who informs Kontostephanos about the physical appearance of the girl. It is possible also therefore that the passage with the portrait of the girl survived.

As has been remarked above, this is the only poem of Manasses written in iambic trimeters,[12] and given the character of the poem I am convinced that the metre was chosen because it is the common metre in classical tragedy, and certainly in the "obliged" tragic messenger's accounts.

Some years ago I published a long article on written portraits in Byzantine literature,[13] stating that two tropes of models are dominant in Byzantium: a romantic model, taken from the romance of Achilles Tatius, and a "passport"-model as used by the first Byzantine chronographer, John Malalas (sixth century). These models are in fact genre-bound: the romantic type is found in romances and some historical works, e.g. in Psellos and Anna Comnene. The passport-model appears mostly in compilations of the Homeric epics, but by Malalas also for descriptions of political persons. In later Byzantine literature these models are combined. The striking thing in this poem of Manasses is that both models are applied one after the other, first the romantic model with its ideals of tall stature, white complexion, round brows, fair hair etc., then again the passport-model with its characteristically asyndetically connected adjectives, mostly beginning with εὐ- (well-).

In my translation I have tried to imitate, as far as I was able, the twelve-syllable iambic trimeters of the original. That is to say the end of the verse is always "masculine", with the accent on the twelfth syllable and/or on the tenth. The other syllables allow within the pattern of 2-4-6-8 (-10-12) accentuation some variation by means of choliambic shifts and the like. I ignored caesuras and in a number of cases I had recourse to anapaestic or dactylic feet.[14]

---

[12] The metric rules are conform to Byzantine standards. In a number of cases o-mikron is taken long; α, ι and υ are *ancipites*. For an analysis of the metre of this poem, see Horna, pp. 319-22.

[13] Aerts, "Das literarische Porträt", pp. 151-95.

[14] I thank my colleagues Dr Peter Hatlie and Prof. Michael Metcalf for their help and suggestions for making my English text and my translation acceptable.

Τοῦ Μανασσῆ κυροῦ Κωνσταντίνου εἰς τὴν κατὰ τὰ
Ἱεροσόλυμα ἀποδημίαν αὐτοῦ.

<Λόγος πρῶτος.>

Ἄρτι θροούσης ἐκφυγὼν ζάλης ῥόφους
καὶ τὴν ἐπαφρίζουσαν ἅλμην πραγμάτων,
ὧν μοι προεξένησεν ἁπλότης τρόπου
ἀνθρωπίνης τε κακίας ἀπειρία,
μόλις προσέσχον εὐγαλήνῳ λιμένι   5
πλουτοῦντι τερπνὴν αὖραν ἀταραξίας
καὶ δὴ βίβλων χάριτας εὑρὼν ἀφθόνους
τοὺς τῶν μελισσῶν ἀπεμιμούμην πόνους.
νυκτὸς δέ μοι κάμνοντι καὶ πονουμένῳ
κἂν ταῖν χεροῖν φέροντι τὸν Ναυκρατίτην   10
ὕπνος πελάσας καὶ βλέφαρα συγκλίνας
ἐνυπνίοις με παρέπεμψεν ἀγρίοις.

Καὶ δὴ βλέπειν ἔδοξα κατὰ τοὺς ὕπνους
τὸν πανσέβαστον ἀγχίνουν Ἰωάννην,
Κοντοστεφάνων ἐκ γένους κατηγμένον,   15
εἰς ναῦν τριήρη βάντα συντόνῳ ῥύμῃ
καὶ συνεφελκύοντα κἀμὲ πρὸς βίαν,
εἶτα ξυναθροίζοντα καὶ στραταρχίαν,
ψιλούς, ἐνόπλους, σφενδονήτας, ἱππότας
καὶ πλῆθος ἄλλο ναυτικὸν καὶ ναυμάχον,   20
ὡς πνευμάτων τυχόντες ἁπαλοπνόων
ἰθυτενῶς πλεύσαιεν εἰς Σικελίαν·
ᾤμην γὰρ αὐτὸν κατὰ τοὺς ὕπνους βλέπειν,
ὡς καὶ στρατάρχης καὶ στολάρχης ἐκρίθη.
ὢ πῶς τὰ λοιπὰ κλαύσομαί τε καὶ φράσω;   25
πολλαῖς νικηθεὶς καὶ πολυτρόποις βίαις
ἐμβὰς σὺν αὐτῷ τὴν λινόπτερον σκάφην
τὴν ἁλμυρὰν θάλασσαν ἐπλωϊζόμην.
καὶ πρῶτα μέντοι δεξιῶς ἀνηγόμην,
τοῦ πνεύματος πνέοντος ἁπαλωτέρου   30

[15] For John Kontostephanos see my Introduction.
[16] ἁπαλόπνοος is a word formed by Byzantine authors. Trapp, *LBG*, quotes Prodromos, *Rhodanthe*, 4, 368; Manasses, *Σύνοψις ἱστορική*, 208; Manasses, *Aristandros and Kallithea*, frg. III, 52, 6; and this place.

Konstantinos Manasses,
About his Journey to Jerusalem (*Hodoiporikon*)

<first poem>

Just from the vexing noise of a big storm escaped
and from the foaming ocean of my many affairs,
to which I had been treated by my simple life
which had no knowledge of mankind's vicissitudes,
I nearly reached the harbour of tranquillity,   5
where richly blew a breeze of sweet untroubledness
and I had found the abundant pleasures of my books
and I was imitating so the industry of bees,
when, working hard and toiling far beyond midnight
with in my hands writs of the man from Naukratis,   10
I was attacked by Hypnos, who did close my eyes
and carried off me for a ride on frightening dreams.

   I got the impression in my dreams that I there saw
His clever Highness august John,[15] descendant of
that famous family of Kontostephanoi: 15
he went on board a trireme ship in full career
and took together also me against my will,
assembled then commanders too and light-armed troops
and heavy soldiers, slingers and equestrians
and quantities of sailors and of brave marines   20
in order that, with friendly blowing[16] favourite winds,
they would go sailing straightaway to Sicily.
I thought, I saw the man himself in these my dreams
as a commander both of army and of fleet!
Oh, how shall I bewail and tell you all the rest?   25
Well, being vanquished by all sorts of violence
I found myself on board with him, on sail-winged[17] ship,
and so was sailing now the briny waters of the sea.

   At first I liked to be transported quietly[18]
- a friendly wind blew softly in a friendly way,   30

---

[17] The word λινόπτερος is taken from Aeschylus, *Prometheus*, 468, "λινόπτερ' ηὗρε ναυτίλων ὀχήματα".

[18] The passage 29-32 recalls a similar situation in the *Batrachomyomachia*, when the mouse rides on the back of the frog, happy as long as the bank is nearby but scared to death when the frog takes a leap: *Batrachomyomachia*, 67-77.

καὶ τοῦ πελάγους προσγελῶντος τῷ σκάφει.
ἔπειτα πικρὸς λαβράσας ἀπαρκτίας
ἔσεισε τὴν ναῦν ὡς ἐλαφρὰν φυλλάδα,
ἤγειρε φλοίσβους κυμάτων πολυρρόθων,
τὴν ὑγρὰν ἠγρίαινε δυσπνόοις πνοαῖς· 35
βρύχων ἀνεῖλκε καὶ καθεῖλκε τὴν σκάφην,
ὡς δυστάλαντος ἄνισος ζυγοστάτης,
ἄνω κάτω θέουσαν ἀστατουμένην·
ἐρρήγνυ πέτραις ὑφάλοις δυσεκβάτοις
καὶ προῦπτος ἦν κίνδυνος ἐκ τοῦ ταράχου. 40
οὐκ ἦν λιμὴν εὔορμος, οὐκ ἦν εὐδία,
οὐχ ὁλκαδοσώτειρα ναύλοχος στάσις·
τὰ πάντα θροῦς ἦν, στρόμβος, ἀντίπνους ζάλη.
ἐντεῦθεν ἡμῖν δειλία καὶ ναυτία
στήθους τε παλμὸς καὶ ταραγμὸς καρδίας, 45
ἕως πεσούσης τῆς πνοῆς τῆς δυσπνόου
μόλις προσωκείλαμεν ὅρμοις εὐδίοις.
 Τοιαῦτα τινὰ συμπλάσας καὶ σκευάσας
ὁ δυστυχῶς με συλλαβὼν ὕπνος τότε,
γοργῶς ἀπέπτη καὶ παρῆλθεν ὀξέως· 50
ἐγὼ δὲ νήψας καὶ τὸ πρᾶγμα γυμνάσας
πολλοὺς στεναγμοὺς ἀνέπεμψα βυθίους,
μή μοι τὸ πικρόν φάσμα τῶν ὀνειράτων
κακὰ προμαντεύοιτο καὶ προμηνύοι.
πάλιν δὲ πρὸς τὴν κρίσιν ἀπεμαχόμην, 55
τὴν ὄψιν ἀργὴν καὶ πλάνην μόνην κρίνων,
ψευδῶς θορυβοῦσάν με ματαίοις φόβοις.
ἡ δ᾽ ἦν ἀληθὴς καὶ προμηνύουσά μοι
τῶν συμφορῶν μου τὰς θαλάσσας καὶ ζάλας.
τί δεῖ κατατείνειν με μακροὺς λόγους; 60
 Ἠὼς μὲν ὑπέλαμπεν ἄρτι φαιδρόχρους,
ὁ δ᾽ ἀστεράρχης καὶ φεραυγὴς φωσφόρος
ἐκ γῆς ἀναβὰς τοῖς ἄνω προσωμίλει,
τὸ δ᾽ εὐθὺς εὐθὺς καὶ παρὰ πόδας φθάνει

---

[19] λαβράσας < λαβράζω. The form λαβρόομαι as used in Lycophron, 260 and 705, < λάβρος in Homerus, *Ilias*, B, 148, "furious" of wind or water, seems more logical. For verba derivativa on -οῦν and -άζειν, see A. Debrunner, *Griechische Wortbildungslehre* (Heidelberg, 1917), pp. 99-103; 118-27. "Schallwörter" in -άζειν are frequent (*ibid.*, §241).

the sea produced a lovely smile towards the ship,
but then broke out[19] a northern storm with utmost rage,
which shook the ship as if it were a weightless leaf
and roused the splashing noise of furious waves,
made wild the water[20] through the stormy gales.   35
Roaring it dragged the vessel now here up, there down,
just like the scales deprived of equilibrium:
the ship ran high and low, didn't find stability.
On submarine and hardly escapable sharp cliffs
it would break down; the dangerous turmoil was nearby!   40
There was no harbour safe to moor, fine weather gone,
no docking-place, which is salvation for a ship,[21]
no, only din and whirligig and adverse winds.
So, we were panic-struck and seized by seasickness,
there was the groaning of our breast, our throbbing heart,   45
until the frenzied hurricane died down
and we could run ashore on roads by lucid sky.

    These kinds of pictures formed and showed this sleep to me,
which at that time dragged me along annoyingly,
but hastily then flew away and disappeared!   50
Being awake and fixing whole this thing in mind
I heaved a multitude of deeply uttered sighs:
I feared, the bitter apparition of the dreams
predicted and portended me disastrous things.
But then again I would reject this argument,   55
by thinking that this vision was just fast and vague
and that it falsely frightened me with needless fears.[22]
Alas, 't was true, and it foretold me without fail
the oceans and the heavy squalls of miseries!
Why should I, though, prolong my words at greater length?   60
    No sooner Dawn appeared with all its colouring
and had the Lord of stars, bright-shining Morning Star,
ris'n from the earth and had addressed the heaven-borns,
than at the same time fell before my very feet

---

[20] "τὴν ὑγρὰν ἠγρίαινε", a play on words, made possible by the itacism.
[21] "ὁλκαδοσώτειρα ... στάσις". A new adjective on the pattern of ὁλκαδοχρίστης, a "ship-caulker", in Manetho astrologus, ed. H. Koechly (Leipzig, 1885), 4, 342.
[22] Manasses more often mentions dreams, e.g. in *Aristandros and Kallithea*, frg. VIII, 152, 1 "'Ὄνειροι γὰρ ὡς τὰ πολλὰ φαντασιοκοποῦσιν, /..."

δυσάγγελον μήνυμα μεστὸν πικρίας, 65
«σὺν τῷ σεβαστῷ συμπορευθήσῃ» λέγον
«εἰς Ἱεροσόλυμα καὶ Παλαιστίνην.»
ἐγὼ δὲ πληγεὶς ὡς μύωπι τῷ λόγῳ
οὐ συνεχύθην, οὐ προήχθην δακρῦσαι,
οὐκ ἐκβαλεῖν στάλαγμα τῶν βλεφαρίδων. 70
ταῖς ἀκοαῖς γὰρ ἐμπεσὼν πικρὸς λόγος
ψυχήν τε νεκροῖ καὶ ψύχει τὴν καρδίαν·
καὶ δακρύων μὲν ἀποκόπτεται ῥύμη,
οἱ δὲ βρυχηθμοὶ δραπέται καὶ φυγάδες·
φροῦδος στεναγμός, ἄλαλον δὲ τὸ στόμα. 75
καὶ γοῦν τὰ πολλὰ τί μάτην περιπλέκω;
    Τῆς γλυκυτάτης ἀπάρας βασιλίδος
εἶδον Νίκαιαν κάλλος αὐχοῦσαν τόπου,
εἶδον πελάγη λιπαρῶν πεδιάδων,
πόλιν μυριάνθρωπον Ἰκονιέων. 80
Κιλικίας ἔβλεψα τὴν κατοικίαν
καὶ τὰς ὑπ' αὐτὴν εὐφορωτάτας πόλεις,
καλὰς μὲν ἰδεῖν, καλλίους δὲ τὰς θέσεις.
εἰς ὄψιν ἦλθεν Ἀντιοχέων πόλις,
ἡ φαιδρότης, ἡ τέρψις, ἡ κοσμιότης 85
χωρῶν ἁπασῶν τῶν κατὰ τὴν Ἀσίαν.
ἐνωπτρισάμην καὶ τὸ κάλλος τῆς Δάφνης,
κατετρύφησα ναμάτων Κασταλίας,
νεκταρέων μὲν καὶ γλυκυτάτων πίνειν,
ψυχρῶν δὲ θίγειν καὶ διειδῶν τὴν θέαν. 90
τί δεῖ διαγράφειν με τὰς πάσας πόλεις,
Σιδῶνα, Τύρον, λιμένας Βηρυτίων,
Πτολεμαΐδα τὴν φονεύτριαν πόλιν;

[23] δυσάγγελος, see Nonnos, *Dionysiaca*, 20, 184, Theodoretus, ep. 21 (4, 1082).

[24] 71-75. This kind of physiological or philosophical explanation is fairly popular in Manasses (*Aristandros and Kallithea*, e.g. frg. VI, 121, 9 ff., "Ἐν δυσκομίστοις δὲ κακοῖς καὶ πόνοις δυσαγκάλοις / φεύγουσι καὶ τὰ δάκρυα ..."; cf. also *ibid.*, 121a) and in Prodromos, *Katomyomachia*, e.g. 51 ff., 123.

[25] Strabo, ed. A. Meineke (Leipzig, 1877), 12, 7 (= 565), describes the surroundings of Nicaea as big and prosperous, "πεδίον μέγα καὶ σφόδρα εὔδαιμον".

[26] μυριάνθρωπος, not in LSJ, but twice in Lampe.

[27] Here ἐνωπτρισάμην — literally, "I saw as in a mirror" — probably means "I saw", unless Manasses did not really visit Daphne, but saw it only from a distance.

[28] Cf. Stephanus Byzantius, *Ethnicorum quae supersunt*, ed. A. Meineke (Berlin, 1849), s.v. "Δάφνη": "Δάφνη, προάστιον ἐπισημότατον τῆς ἕω Ἀντιοχείας μητροπόλεως"; Procopius Caesariensis, *De Aedificiis*, 5, 9, 29, *Bella*, 2, 11, 4 ff.: "τότε

the fatal message[23] full of awful bitterness, 65
that said: "You shall accompany His Highness towards
Jerusalem and to the land of Palestine."
I felt myself just struck by blindness by this word
but I controlled myself and did not start to cry
nor from my eyelids did I drop one single tear! 70
For, when a bitter word invades the mind by ear,[24]
it kills the soul and wraps the heart up in a chill.
Therefore, the stream of tears is totally cut off
and all the lamentations go away in banishment,
gone is the moaning and the mouth left without speech. 75
However, why should I embrace these useless words?
    Off from my dearest city, the imperial,
I saw Nicaea, boasting of its pretty site,[25]
I saw the seas of fertile and fruitbearing plains,
I saw the town of countless men,[26] Iconium, 80
I got to see the dwellings of Cilicia
and all the prosperous cities there in that district,
lovely to see, more lovely yet for residence.
Entered my view the city of the Antiochenes,
its splendidness, civilization and the grace 85
among the multitude of towns in Asia's lands.
I had a look[27] at Daphne's very beauteous sight,[28]
pampered myself with water of Castalia's spring
not only taking drinks from its sweet, tasty well,
but also touching its refreshing, transparent stream. 90
    Why should I give descriptions of each of the towns
like Sidon, Tyrus and the harbour(s) of Beirut
and Ptolemaïs,[29] city of a murderous fame,

μὲν οὖν ἐς Δάφνην ἀνέβη (Chosroes sc.), τὸ Ἀντιοχείας προάστειον. ἔνθα δὴ τό τε ἄλσος ἐν θαύματι μεγάλῳ ἐποιήσατο καὶ τὰς τῶν ὑδάτων πηγάς· ἄμφω γὰρ ἀξιοθέατα ἐπιεικῶς ἐστι", etc. See also Strabo (see n. 25), 16, 6 (= 750), who indicates that Daphne is a small village, about 40 stades north of Antioch, with a well watered forest and an asylum dedicated to Apollo and Artemis. Johannes Phokas, who undertook a pilgrimage to the Holy Land in 1176, also gives a detailed description of Antioch and its surroundings and mentions the spring Kastalia; cf. Horna, p. 348, n. ad I 84 ff. On Phokas, see H. Hunger, *Die hochsprachliche profane Literatur der Byzantiner* (Munich, 1978) I, pp. 517, 518.

[29] Cf. Stephanus Byzantius (see n. 28), s.v. "Πτολεμαΐς": "Πτολεμαΐς, πόλις Φοινίκης. Ἐκαλεῖτο δὲ πρότερον Ἀκή, ἀπὸ τῆς ἰάσεως τοῦ γενομένου δήγματος Ἡρακλεῖ ὑπὸ ὄφεως" (medieval Acco). Strabo (see n. 25), 134 (2, 39), mentions the length of daylight in these regions: "Ἐν δὲ τοῖς Πτολεμαΐδα τὴν ἐν τῇ Φοινίκῃ καὶ

Πτολεμαΐδα τὴν φθορᾶς ἐπαξίαν,
ἐξ ἧς, Ἰησοῦ, φῶς ἀειβρύτου φάους, 95
τὴν ἡλιακὴν ἀπομαράναις φλόγα
καὶ συσκιάσαις τὴν πανόπτριαν κόρην,
ὡς μὴ ποσῶς βλέποιτο μισητῇ πόλις.
εἰς Σαμάρειαν ἦλθον, εἶδον χωρίον
πολλαῖς χαρίτων καλλοναῖς ἠνθισμένον, 100
χαρίεν ἰδεῖν, εὐφυὲς τὰ πρὸς θέσιν·
ἀὴρ καθαρός, πλημμυρίδες ὑδάτων
λεπτῶν, διειδῶν, ὑγιῶν, ἀειρρύτων·
δενδρῖτις ἡ γῆ, πάμφορος, καρποτρόφος,
[πυροτρόφος, πάγκαρπος, ἀμπελοφόρος,] 105
ἐλαιόφυτος, λαχανηφόρος, πίων·
πεδιὰς ἱππήλατος, εὐμαρεῖς δρόμοι,
λειμῶνες ἐμπρέποντες εὐόσμοις ῥόδοις·
θέσις γλυκεῖα, προσφυὴς τῷ χωρίῳ·
εἴποις ἂν ἰδών, ὡς γυνή τις φιλόπαις 110
γαλακτοφάγον ἀγκαλίζεται βρέφος.
ἐκεῖθεν ἦρται δυσανάβατος λόφος,
δυσέμβολος, δύσμαχος, οὐκ ἔχων βάσιν,
ὀξύς, τραχεινός, εἰς μακρὸν τεταμένος.
ἐντεῦθεν ἄλλος μέχρις αἰθέρος φθάνων 115
πέτρας προΐσχων ἠλιβάτους,
ὄρθιος, ἀπόκρημνος, ἀνάντης λόφος.
τὸ χωρίον δὲ τοῖν δυοῖν κεῖται μέσον,
ὡς ὑπὸ μητρὸς σπαργανούμενον βρέφος,
ὡσεὶ κορίσκη παγκάλη τηρουμένη 120
γυναικὶ φιλόπαιδι θαλαμευτρίᾳ.
  Οὕτω μὲν εἶχεν εὐφυῶς τὰ τοῦ τόπου·
τέλος δὲ λοιπὸν εἶχεν ἡμῖν ὁ δρόμος
καὶ φανεροῦσθαι τὸ κρυφίον ἤρχετο.

Σιδῶνα καὶ Τύρον ἡ μεγίστη ἡμέρα ἐστὶν ὡρῶν ἰσημερινῶν δεκατεττάρων καὶ τετάρτου". Strabo, 758 (16, 25 and 26), makes mention of a tidal wave which caused the death of a group of soldiers. Manasses emphasizes the high mortality in Ptolemaïs once more in Poem IV, 20.

[30] ἀείβρυτος, see Trapp, *LBG*, s.v.

[31] πανόπτριαν κόρην. The fem. πανόπτρια with masc. πανόπτης is mentioned in Photios, *Lexikon*, ed. S.A. Naber (Leiden, 1864/65).

[32] On Samaria, see Strabo (see n. 25), 760 (16, 34). Herodes gave it the name Sebaste. According to Stephanus Byzantius (see n. 28) it was renamed Neapolis (= Nablus). Procopius Caesariensis (see n. 28), 5, 7, 1 ff., uses the same name and has a detailed story

that Ptolemaïs, which deserves its doom and gloom,
from which, my Jesus, Light of the ever-spouting[30] Light, 95
Thou may'st make withering the fire of the sun
and shade the ever-looking, all-observing eye,[31]
lest this abominable town ever be seen!
To Samaria[32] then I went and saw the spot
which flourished through so many beautiful delights, 100
delightful city to be seen, well-fit to stay:
clean and fresh air, the water in redundant floods,
fine, transparent and healthy, with eternal flow.

The landscape full of trees which bear all kinds of fruit
[producing wheat, all sorts of crops, and many vines],[32a] 105
growing a host of olive-trees and copious greens.
A plain well-shaped for riding horse, convenient ways
and meadows, full of fragrant roses, richly adorned,
a sweet location, in agreement with the town.
You might have said, if you it saw: in such a way 110
holds in her arms a woman her milk-sucking babe.
There rises up an inaccessible high hill,
no entrance and unconquerable, without path,
with sharp and rocky peaks, a lengthy range.
Another hill, which has its crest up to the sky 115
and makes its rough steep rocks[33] extend on every side,
precipitous, with deep ravines, lies there, high-crowned.
The town itself is situated in between,
just like a babe whose mother wrapped him tightly in,
or like a lovely little girl who's taken care 120
of by a children-loving tender chambermaid.[34]

These were the fine amenities of this good place.
And here then came our journey lastly to an end
and nearer drew the secret goal to be revealed.

---

about Mount Garizim near Samaria. The Samaritans used the mountain for worshipping their gods, until Jesus had his talk with the Samaritan woman. In Christian times a church was built on the top of the mountain which was destroyed by the Samaritans and rebuilt by Justinian. The second mountain is Mount Ebal, see e.g. *Lexikon für Theologie und Kirche*, s.v. "Samaria" and "Palästina".

[32a] Deleted by Horna: absent in M, but present in V.

[33] "πέτρας ... ἠλιβάτους": Homeric, e.g. *Ilias*, O, 273; *Odyssey*, ι, 243 (of the stone put at the entrance of his cave by the Cyclop).

[34] LSJ quotes for θαλαμεύτρια only Pollux, ed. E. Bethe (Leipzig, 1900), 3, 41, "bridesmaid", here more generally "chambermaid".

φωτὸς πυριμάρμαρον ἐκφέρει σέλας
καὶ καταλάμπει καὶ διώκει τὸν ζόφον·
ἔφωσε, κατέπληξε, κατήστραψέ με.
εἶπον καθ᾽ αὑτόν· «μὴ κεραυνὸς εἰσέδυ,
μὴ τῆς σελήνης κύκλος εἰς γῆν ἐρρύη;»   165
ἀπαράμιλλος ἦν τὸ κάλλος ἡ κόρη,
ὑπὲρ τὸ γάλα καὶ καλὴ καὶ λευκόχρους,
ἐπίχαρις, σύμμετρος, εὔχρους, ξανθόθριξ,
ἀναδρομὴ σώματος ὡραϊσμένη,
φοίνικος ἔρνος — εἶπεν ἄν τις προσφόρως —   170
καλόν, νεοβλάστητον, ὀρθὸν τὴν στάσιν·
πολλὴ βαθεῖα καὶ κατάχρυσος κόμη·
εὔκυκλος ὀφρύς, εὐφυεῖς βλεφαρίδες·
ὄμμα προσηνές, ἱλαρόν, στίλβον χάριν·
καλὸν τὸ χεῖλος, εὐπερίγραπτον στόμα,   175
καλὸν τὸ χεῖλος, ὑπέρυθρον, κοκκόχρουν.
εἴ που δὲ μικρὸν μειδιᾶσαι συνέβη
διαχεθεῖσαν σωφρονικῶς τὴν κόρην,
ἰαταταὶ τὸ κάλλος οὐκ ἔχω φράσαι·
εὔτορνος ἡ ῥίς, τὴν πνοὴν ἐλευθέρα·   180
εὔρυθμος ἡ κίνησις, εὔμετρος βάσις·
ἦθος γαληνότητι συγκεκραμένον
καὶ τηλικαύτῃ προσφορώτατον κόρῃ·
παίδευσις ἀσύγκριτος, εὐγενὲς γένος·
ἐξ αἵματος γὰρ Καισάρων Ἰουλίων   185
σκηπτροκρατούντων τῶν μερῶν τῆς ἑσπέρας.
ἁπλῶς ἁπάντων τῶν καλῶν αἱ συρμάδες,
εἰς ἓν χεθεῖσαι καὶ κραθεῖσαι παγκάλως,
ἓν μίγμα τερπνὸν εἰργάσαντο τὴν κόρην
καὶ φύσεως ἄγαλμα καὶ κόσμον γένους.   190

---

[38] ἔφωσε aor. from φώσκω = φαύσκω, cf. φῶς/φάος.

[39] See Homerus, *Odyssey*, 6, 163, "φοίνικος νέον ἔρνος ἀνερχόμενον ἐνόησα".

[40] The verses 175 and 176 both start with the words "καλὸν τὸ χεῖλος", which points to a corruption. Literary portraits usually mention (the colour of) the cheeks between the eyes and mouth. Perhaps one should read in 175: "καλὸν τὸ χρῶμα", implying the common white and rosy colouring of the παρειαί or simply καλαὶ παρειαί; cf. Aerts, "Das literarische Porträt", esp. pp. 151-65 and 184.

[41] The word κοκκόχρους is a neologism.

[42] διαχεθεῖσα, a late Hellenistic form = διαχυθεῖσα < διαχέομαι = be relaxed; cf. LSJ, s.v. "διαχέω 4" and "διάχυσις".

[43] The exclamation ἰαταταί = Att. ἰατταταῖ is taken from Aristophanes, *Equites*, 1.

she spread out such a shine like brightly sparkling fire
that all the darkness she outshone and drove away.
She brightened me,[38] astounded me, and dazzled me.
I said then to myself: "did strike a thunderbolt?
Was it the lunar disc which came down to the earth?" 165
The beauty of the girl was incomparable,
and her complexion very fair, whiter than milk,
both charming and harmonious, well-skinned and blond,
her stature tall and blooming, just proportionate,
a fresh young palm-tree[39] -as one rightly would have said -, 170
a beauty, newly sprouted, bolt upright indeed
with very thick and widely floating golden hair,
well-rounded brows and with well-shapèd eyelashes,
with gentle eyes, cheerful as well, and gleaming grace.
Her cheeks[40] were beautiful, her mouth so well designed, 175
her lips were charming, crimson, red as red could be,[41]
and when it happened that she showed a little smile,
the girl who was relaxed and sensible as well,[42]
ah me! — I can't describe, how beautiful she was![43]
Well-arched her nose, her breathing free and regular,[44] 180
the way she moved was delicate, steady her gait,
her temper proved a keynote of serenity,
more than should be expected of a girl so young!
And incomparably well-bred, from noble stock:
for she sprung from the Iulius Caesar families 185
who bear the sceptres in the countries of the West.[45]
So, simply said, the threads[46] of all the beauties were
twisted together in one skein of lovely blend,
which let the maiden grow into a joyful mix
and made her Nature's statue praise her family. 190

The other form ἰατταταιάξ from the same quotation is applied by Theodoros, *Katomyomachia*, v. 193.

[44] The ability to breathe freely seems to have been a sign of health. In her description of Bohemund of Tarent, Anna Comnena (*Alexiade*, 13, 10, 4) makes a similar remark: "Καὶ ἡ ῥὶς αὐτῷ καὶ ὁ μυκτὴρ ἐλεύθερον ἔπνει τὸν ἀέρα" ("His nose and nostrils freely inhaled the air").

[45] The reference to Julius Caesar implies a dynastic relationship because to the Byzantines Julius Caesar is the first Roman emperor. At the same time, the reference resuscitates the Byzantine claims to the whole (ancient) Roman Empire.

[46] The word ἡ συρμάς is mentioned in LSJ with the meaning "snowdrift". The meaning here is clearly "threads"; cf. Modern Greek (τὸ) σύρμα.

ὁ Μῶμος αὐτὸς ἠπόρησεν ἂν ψόγου.
τί γὰρ πρὸς αὐτὴν Ἑλένης ἡ λευκότης,
ἣν μῦθος ἀνέπλασεν ἐκ Διὸς φῦναι;
γένος τὸ πρῶτον, πυριμάρμαρος θέα,
ἡ παῖς ἀπαράμιλλος, ὕψους ἀξία, 195
εὔοφρυς, εὐπρόσωπος, εὐπρεπεστάτη,
εὔοπτος, εὐπλόκαμος, εὐγενεστάτη,
τὴν ἡλικίαν ὀρθία καὶ τὴν πλάσιν
ὑπὲρ πλατάνους, ὑπὲρ ἀναδενδράδας.
οὕτως ἔχουσαν κατιδὼν καὶ θαυμάσας 200
καὶ τοῦ κρατοῦντος ἀξίαν εἶναι κρίνας
καὶ χαριτοπρόσωπον ὡς εὐχρουστάτην,
τὸν μὲν σεβαστὸν ἐπτέρουν ταῖς ἐλπίσιν,
ὡς τῶν ἐπάθλων εὐπορήσει μειζόνων
τοιόνδε δῶρον δυσπόριστον προσφέρων 205
τῷ φιλοδώρῳ βασιλεῖ γῆς Αὐσόνων·
ἐγὼ δ᾽ ὁ ταλάντατος ὠνειροσκόπουν,
ὡς τάχιον βλέψαιμι τὴν Κωνσταντίνου.
ἀλλ᾽ ἀντιπνεύσας κακίας ὁ καικίας
χειμῶνας ἐξήγειρεν ἀελλοπνόους, 210
τρικυμίας φόβητρα, ναυτίας ζάλας
καὶ βραδυτῆτας καὶ σχολὰς παραλόγους.
τί ταῦτα τλήμων εἰς μάτην καταλέγω,
τῆς Αἰσχύλου χρῄζοντα δραματουργίας
ἢ τῆς Φρυνίχου πενθικῆς στωμυλίας; 215
εἰ γὰρ τὰ πάντα κατὰ λεπτόν τις φράσει,
ὑπερβαλεῖται συγγραφὴν Θουκυδίδου.

---

[47] Momus (Blame) is mentioned by Hesiod, *Theogony*, 214, as a child of Nyx (Night): "And again the goddess murky Night, though she lay with none, bare Blame and painful Woe,..." (trans. H.G. Evelyn-White, Loeb Classical Library (Cambridge, Mass., and London, 1974)).

[48] The later poet Hermoniakos (fourteenth century), II, 194-5, stresses the unbelievable whiteness of Helen: "εἶχε γὰρ τὴν σάρκαν ὅλην / ὑπὲρ χίονα λευκόχρουν" ("her body was more white than snow"); see Aerts, "Das literarische Porträt", p. 177.

[49] The following verses bring another description of the princess, this time according to the "passport-type", such as used by Malalas, Tzetzes a.o., see Aerts, "Das literarische Porträt", pp. 165 ff.

[50] "τῷ ... βασιλεῖ γῆς Αὐσόνων", a striking use of the idea Ausonia = Italy. Here again the claim to the totality of the Roman Empire emerges. The term is only scarcely used by Byzantine historians, but the idea is more often seen in Manasses' *Σύνοψις*

Even Momus[47] himself would find nothing to blame!
For Helen's whiteness,[48] what was that with her compared,
Helen of whom in myth was told, she was Zeus' child?
From first-class stock, appearance sparkling like a fire,
the girl was just unrivalled, fully worthy of her rank:[49]   195
well-browed, well-faced, good-looking to the highest degree,
well-eyed, well-tressed, well-born in highest nobility,
her stature and her posture being straight and tall
above the plane-trees or above the climbing vines!
Such was the maiden whom I saw, whom I admired   200
and whom I thought was worthy of the emperor,
not only by her gracious face but colour too,
so that I brought His Highness to excited hopes
that in fulfilling these major tasks he would succeed
by bringing such a gift, hardly procurable,   205
to him, the generous emperor of Roman land![50]
And I, the most pitiable man, I really dreamt
I would soon see again the City of Constantine!
But the northeaster blew disastrous adverse winds
and roused furiously blowing howling winter storms   210
which caused terrible dash of waves that lashed the ship
with commensurately long delays, unlooked-for halts.
How should I, wretchèd man, sum up these miseries
which need the art of tragedy of Aeschylus
or Phrynichus's sorrowful verbosity?[51]   215
Should someone give minute descriptions of all this,
he would surpass the Story[52] of Thucydides.

ἱστορική: 2550, 3294, Αὐσονάναξ; 3212, 4110, 5589, Αὐσονάρχης; 3189, 6059, Αὐσονοκράτωρ, etc.; cf. also Trapp, *LBG*, s.v. "Αὐσονάναξ". The idea is perhaps taken from Nonnos, *Dionysiaca*, e.g. 41, 389-391: "Σκῆπτρον ὅλης Αὔγουστος ὅτε χθονὸς ἡνιοχεύσει / Ῥώμῃ μὲν ζαθέῃ δωρήσεται Αὐσόνιος Ζεὺς / κοιρανίην" ("When Augustus shall hold the sceptre of the world, Ausonian Zeus will give to divine Rome the lordship"; trans. W.H.D. Rouse, Loeb Classical Library (Cambridge, Mass., and London, 1984)).

[51] The tragic poet Phrynichus is mentioned here together with his famous younger contemporary, Aeschylus. Here Manasses undoubtedly had in mind Herodotus, 6, 21, which recounts that Phrynichus, with his tragedy Μιλήτου ἅλωσις (The Sack of Miletus), moved all the spectators in the theatre of Athens to tears, for which he was fined one thousand drachmas and forbidden to stage the tragedy again. No fragment survived.

[52] συγγραφή is the common word for "history". However, Manasses does not use the Attic form ξυγγραφή as in Thucydides, I, 98, 2.

Χρόνῳ δὲ πολλῷ καὶ μετὰ μακροὺς πόνους,
Νεαπολιτῶν τὴν πόλιν λελοιπότες,
Ἰερουσαλήμ, ὀλβιωτάτην πόλιν, 220
κατείδομεν, πλουτοῦσαν ἀσφαλῆ θέσιν
(μικροῦ γὰρ ἄνευ ἀρκτικωτέρου μέρους
κοιλὰς βαθεῖα, δυσανάβατος φάραγξ
ὅλην περιείληφε κύκλῳ τὴν πόλιν).
κατησπασάμην τὸν πολύτιμον τάφον, 225
ἐν ᾧ δι' ἡμᾶς τοὺς παρηνομηκότας
καθαπερεὶ λέοντος ὑπνώσας σκύμνος
ὁ χοῦν φυράσας εἰς Ἀδὰμ διαρτίαν
τοῖς ἐξ Ἀδὰμ ἔβλυσεν ἀειζωίαν.
τὸ Γολγοθᾶ κατεῖδον· εἶδον τὰς πέτρας 230
τὰς πρὶν ῥαγείσας καὶ λυθείσας ἐκ φόβου,
ὅταν θεός μου καὶ κεραμεὺς τοῦ γένους
τὸ κοσμοσωτήριον ὑποστὰς πάθος
ἐκ τῶν λίθων ἤγειρεν Ἀβραὰμ τέκνα,
τὴν συντριβεῖσαν ἀνακαινίζων φύσιν. 235
τὴν γῆν ἔβλεψα καὶ περιεπτυξάμην,
εἰς ἣν κατεζόφωσαν οἱ θεοκτόνοι
τὸ μακαριστὸν καὶ σεβάσμιον ξύλον.
ἐκεῖθεν ἐκβὰς εἰς Σιὼν ἀφικόμην,
ἥτις με πολλαῖς κατέθελξε χάρισιν, 240
ἐκτὸς μὲν οὖσα, πλησίον δὲ κειμένη
καὶ δὴ παραψαύουσα τῶν πυργωμάτων.
ἐκεῖ κατεῖδον τὸν τρισόλβιον τόπον,
ἐν ᾧ μαθητῶν ἀπένιψε τοὺς πόδας
ὁ τὰς θαλάσσας χαλινῶν τὰς ἀσχέτους. 245
μικρὸν μεταστὰς εἶδον οἰκίσκον βραχύν,
ὅπου μαθητῶν ἡ φάλαγξ ἀπεκρύβη
τὴν λύσσαν ἐκφεύγουσα τῶν μιαιφόνων,
καθαπερεὶ πρόβατα τὰ χλοηφάγα,

---

[53] The Palestinian town Nablus was founded as Νεάπολις in A.D. 72, and it was situated between Mount Eval and Mount Gerizim. See also the Madaba mosaic map: Michael Avi-Yonah, *The Madaba Mosaic Map* (Jerusalem, 1954), pl. 6; commentary p. 45, nr. 32.

[54] For δυσανάβατος, see LSJ (one instance) and Trapp, *LBG*, s.v., where, however, our place is not mentioned.

[55] See Matth. 27:52.

[56] καταζοφόω, a neologism < ζόφος, "darkness", "obscurity". The spot mentioned points to the (apocryphal) story of the discovery of the three crosses, among which the

Much time and also many troubles were elapsed
before we left the city with the name Nablus,⁵³
and saw the very prosperous town Jerusalem, 220
that holds a place which guarantees security
(for, with exception of a small part in the North,
it is surrounded by a great deep plain, a gorge,
which, hard to climb,⁵⁴ embraces whole the city round).
I paid my homage to the costly Holy Grave, 225
in which for us, who did transgress the divine law,
the One who rests asleep as a lion's cub, the One
who mixed the clay from which the limbs of Adam grew,
made sprout eternal life for those from Adam's seed.
I had a look at Golgotha, I saw the rocks 230
which in advance got rent and split simply from fear,⁵⁵
when He, my God, the Potter of men's family,
suffered the passion of salvation of mankind
and from the tombstones did arise Abraham's kin
and recreated nature which was at a loss. 235
I saw the ground and I embraced the sacred spot
there where the murderers of God had made obscure⁵⁶
the very blessed and venerable holy wood.
From there departed, then I went to Sion, which
enchanted me with all its charming pure delights. 240
It 's situated outside but not far away
and nearly touching the high bulwarks of the town.
I looked there at the threefold sanctifièd place
where He had washed the feet of his disciples, He⁵⁷
who bridled the infinite waters of the seas.⁵⁸ 245
A little further I saw, walking, the small house,
where took refuge the battle-line⁵⁹ of disciples
fearing the furious madness of the murderers,⁶⁰
just as would do a flock of meadow-grazing sheep

True Cross, by Helen, mother of Constantine the Great. For an analysis of this legend, see
J.W. Drijvers, *Helena Augusta: Waarheid en legende* (Groningen, 1989) (diss.); *idem*,
*Helena Augusta: The Mother of Constantine the Great and the legend of Her Finding of
the True Cross*, Brill's Studies in Intellectual History, 27 (Leiden, 1990).
⁵⁷ John 13:5 ff.
⁵⁸ Matth. 8:26.
⁵⁹ μαθητῶν ἡ φάλαγξ, a beautiful oxymoron to characterize the situation.
⁶⁰ John 20:19.

θέλω μὲν εἰπεῖν, ἀλλὰ καὶ πάλιν τρέμω 285
(ὀφθαλμὲ παντεπόπτα, μὴ θύμαινέ μοι)·
τὴν Ἰεριχὼ μηδὲ καθ᾽ ὕπνους ἴδω.
ὕδωρ Ἰορδάνειον ἀπενιψάμην·
ὕδωρ κατεῖδον παντόφυρτον ἰλύϊ,
οὐκ ἀθόλωτον οὐδὲ καλὸν εἰς πόσιν, 290
οἵα χρόα γάλακτος ἡ τούτου χρόα·
ἀργαὶ γὰρ εἰς κίνησιν αἱ τούτου ῥύσεις,
ὑπνοῦν ἂν εἴποις τοῦ ποταμοῦ τὸν δρόμον.
  Τί ταῦτα, Χριστέ, φῶς ὑπερχρόνου φάους,
πῶς μέχρι πολλοῦ πρὸς τόπους ἀνεστράφης 295
ξηρούς, πνιγηρούς, φλεκτικούς, θανασίμους;
ἂν ἐννοήσω τῆς Ναζαρὲτ τὸ πνῖγος,
ἐκπλήττομαί σου τὴν ταπείνωσιν, Λόγε.
καλῶς ἐμαρτύρησας ἀδόλως ἔχειν
τοῦ Ναθαναὴλ τὸν περὶ ταύτης λόγον· 300
«τί γὰρ ἀγαθὸν ἡ Ναζαρὲτ ἐκτρέφει;»
ἀλλ᾽ ὡς ἔοικεν, ὡς ἐπίστασαι μόνος,
ἐν πᾶσι τοῖς σοῖς σωματικοῖς ἐκλέγῃ,
εἴ τι πενιχρόν, εἴ τι τῶν ἀνωνύμων·
ἐκ μὲν ποταμῶν τὰς ῥοὰς Ἰορδάνου 305
μηδ᾽ ἐν ποταμοῖς συγκαταριθμουμένου,
ἐκ τῶν πολιχνίων δὲ τῆς Παλαιστίνης
τὰ λυπρότατα καὶ κατεσκληρυμμένα,
τὴν Καπερναοὺμ τὴν κατεστυγημένην
καὶ τὴν Ναζαρὲτ τὴν ἀπηνθρακωμένην. 310
σεπτοὶ μέν εἰσι πάντες οἱ θεῖοι τόποι,
ἐν οἷς ὁ Σωτὴρ σαρκικῶς ἀνεστράφη·
πλὴν εἴπερ ἐξέλοι τις ἀνυποστόλως
τῶν δεσποτικῶν θαυμάτων τὸ μυρίπνουν,
σκληραῖς ἀκάνθαις τοὺς τόπους παρεικάσοι. 315
τί γὰρ παρ᾽ αὐτοῖς ἐστιν ἄξιον λόγου;
ἀὴρ πονηρός, καυματώδης, πυρώδης,
ἄτακτος, ἀβέβαιος, οὐκ ἔχων στάσιν·
σφοδρὸν τὸ καῦσος, ἀνυπόστατον φέρειν.
ἄκρατος ἀὴρ ὑδάτων ἐρημίᾳ. 320
ὅπου δ᾽ ἀφ᾽ ὕψους ἐκρυήσεται δρόσος
κἀκ τῶν νεφῶν ψέκασμα μικρὸν ἐκδράμῃ,

[66] ὑπέρχρονος, "transcending time", see Lampe, s.v. 1.

I wish to say, but now again I fear to say 285
(oh, all-observing eye, don't be angry with me)
may even in my dreams I not see Jericho!
In river Jordan's water streams I took a bath
and saw the water everywhere mixed up with mud,
nowhere untroubled, nowhere being fit for drink, 290
and coloured in the same white colour as is milk.
Its currents are extremely slow of movement
so that the river could be said to be asleep.
    What's this, my Christ, You Light of super-temporal[66] Light,
that long ago You settled in a place like this, 295
so dry, so suffocating, and so deadly hot!
And when I think about the heat of Nazareth,
then I am perplexed by Your humility, oh Word!
You truly gave the evidence that what was said
about that place was well said by Nathaniel: 300
"Can any good thing come there out of Nazareth?"[67]
But as it seems, and You alone You know that best,
that always You preferred in Your somatic state
things that were poor, things that were from the anonymous:
from all the rivers in the world the Jordan stream, 305
which does not even count among the rivers, no,
and from the cities lying in Palestinian land
the most deplorable and the utmost obdurate,
such as the highly cursed and damned Capharnaum
and Nazareth which is a furnace stoked with coal. 310
Sacred, for sure, are all these places most divine,
where He, our Saviour, in the flesh did walk about,
but should a person take away without reserve
the holy odour of the wonders of the Lord,
then were these spots only compared with solid thorns. 315
For what, indeed, is in these lands worth mentioning?
The air is bad and scorching, it is full of fire,
unstable, unpredictable and without stand.
The heat is awful and is just unbearable,
and without moisture is the air where water lacks. 320
However, where some dew is falling from above
and from the clouds a little raindrop comes to earth,

[67] John 1:46.

ὡς οἶνος εὔπνους, ὡς μύρον συγκλείεται.
ἂν ὑπὸ δίψους φλεκτικοῦ φρύγοιτό τις,
δύσοσμον ὕδωρ, ἰλυῶδες ἐκπίνει, 325
ὠνούμενος καὶ τοῦτο (φεῦ λειψυδρίας).
ἀπόκροτος γῆ, κραναή, πεφρυγμένη,
ἐν ᾗ ταλαιπωροῦσιν ἀτλήτοις πόνοις
καὶ τληπαθοῦσι καμάτοις βαρυτάτοις
καὶ βοῦς ἀροτρεὺς καὶ χέρες δρεπανίται. 330
Ὦ γῆ Βυζαντίς, ὦ θεόδμητος πόλις,
ἡ καὶ τὸ φῶς δείξασα καὶ θρέψασά με,
ἐν σοὶ γενοίμην, καλλονὰς βλέψαιμί σου.
ναὶ ναί, γενοίμην ὑπὸ τὰς σὰς ἀγκάλας·
ναὶ ναί, γενοίμην ὑπὸ τὴν πτέρυγά σου 335
καὶ διατηροίης με καθὰ στρουθίον.

Λόγος δεύτερος.

Τούτων μετασχὼν τῶν καλῶν θεαμάτων,
ὑποστροφὴν ταχεῖαν εὑρεῖν ᾠόμην
καὶ τὸ προσόν μοι βάρος ἀπορραπίσαι.
ἀλλὰ φθάσασα καὶ πάλιν ταχυδρόμος
ἡ πανταχοῦ συνοῦσά μοι δυσποτμία 5
πάλιν κατέσχε, πάλιν ἐθρόησέ με.
μόλις ἀναβὰς εἰς τριήρη ταχύπλουν
εἰς τὴν στυγητὴν οὐριοδρόμουν Τύρον,
ἥτις σπανίζει καὶ κοτύλης ὑδάτων.
ὦ παγκακία, παντομίσητος Τύρος· 10
τὸν γὰρ βαρύν σου καὶ πνιγηρὸν ἀέρα
καὶ τὴν ἀποφρύγουσαν ἡλίου φλόγα
τίνων διηγήσαιντο γλῶσσαι ῥητόρων;
ἐντεῦθεν ἡμῖν ἄρχεται τὰ τῆς νόσου,
νόσου δυσαλθοῦς, βαρυσυμφορωτάτης· 15
ἀνάπτεταί μοι πυρετὸς καυματίας,
ὡς πῦρ λιπαρόν, εὐπορῆσαν φρυγάνων.
τὰ σπλάγχνα πιμπρᾷ, βόσκεται τὴν οὐσίαν.

[68] Βοῦς ἀροτρεύς: for this connection see Hesiod, "Ἔργα καὶ ἡμέραι", 406/7: "Οἶκον μὲν πρώτιστα γυναῖκά τε βοῦν τ᾽ ἀροτῆρα, / κτητήν, οὐ γαμετήν." The form ἀροτρεύς is to be found in Theocritus, 25, 1 and 51. My plural is for metrical reasons.

[69] Cf. Manasses, *Aristandros and Kallithea*, frg. III, 60,1, "Λέγεται γάρ τοι βασιλεὺς στρουθιομήτωρ ὄρνις, /..."

then is it like a fragrant wine, or fine perfume.
But when a man is shrivelled up by fiery thirst,
he finds no drink but ill-smelling and full of mire, 325
for which he has to pay much, too, (oh, lack of wet!).
The land is hard and rocky, desiccated by the heat,
in which with pains unbearable there toil and moil
and suffer from the heaviest tirednesses
both ploughing-oxen and the hands of harvesters.[68] 330
 Oh, Byzantinian land, oh City built by God,
which made me see the light and bred and fostered me,
oh, were I now in thee to see your effulgence,
yea, yea, I wish I were in your embracing arms,
yea, yea, I wish I were under your saving wing 335
while you look after me just like your little bird![69]

Second Poem

Having enjoyed the beauty of these many sights
I thought I would now find a speedy return home
and thus drive off the sorrow which I bore in me.
But there she came and in a hurry, once again,
my misfortune[70] that follows me just everywhere: 5
again she caught me and again she frightened me.
No sooner had I embarked upon a fast trireme
en route for Tyrus -before the wind- the town I hate,
where scarcely can be found a waterbowl with drink
- oh, you disastrous Tyrus, you, all-hateful place, 10
for, yes, your heavy and much suffocating air[71]
as well as this hot burning sun which dries all up,
which tongues of rhetors can these things rightly describe?-
than there began the symptoms of my being ill,
a deadly[72] illness, absolutely unbearable. 15
High fever got a hold of me and set me ablaze
just like a fire, fed by oil, consuming twigs;
it burned my heart and liver and it grazed my life,

---

[70] δυσποτμία, "ill-luck", here personified.
[71] Strabo (see n. 25) makes no remark on the climate of Tyrus; however, he censures the unpleasant living conditions due to the many dyehouses for purple (16, 2, 23).
[72] "νόσου δυσαλθοῦς". Δυσαλθής, a medical term, "incurable", "deadly", here, of course, used in an exaggerated way. The symptoms mentioned point to typhus.

ἀπηνθράκωσεν, ἐξεδαπάνησέ με·
ἐπυρπόλησεν, ἐξετηγάνισέ με. 20
ἀτμῖσι πυκναῖς τὴν κεφαλὴν ἐζόφου
καὶ τοῦ λογισμοῦ τὰς κόρας συνεζόφου.
αἱ τρίχες ἐξέπιπτον ὡς νεκροῦ τρίχες,
τῆς πυρκαϊᾶς οὐ φέρουσαι τὴν ζέσιν.
φεῦ, φεῦ, ἐγὼ δύστηνος, ἄξιος γόου, 25
ἄνθρωπος εὐμάραντος, ἐκτετηγμένος,
φορῶν κάτισχνον καὶ σκιῶδες σαρκίον,
ἢ μᾶλλον εἰπεῖν, δέρμα σαρκίου μόνον.
κοσμουργὲ Χριστὲ καὶ Θεὲ ζωοβρύτα,
οἷα μὲν ἡ κένωσις ἐκ τῶν ἐντέρων, 30
οἷα δ' ἀπὸ στόματος, ἐκτύφουσά με
καὶ τῆς παλαιᾶς ἀναμιμνήσκουσά με
τροφῆς ἐκείνης τῆς ἀπηγορευμένης,
ᾗ παρασυρεὶς καὶ κλαπεὶς ἐγὼ τάλας
τὴν πικροποιὸν κακίαν ἠλλαξάμην. 35
ἂν ἐννοήσω τῆς χολῆς τὴν πικρίαν,
θάνατον αὐτόχρημα τὸ πρᾶγμα κρίνω.
παρεῖντο χεῖρες, ἔτρεμον δὲ τὰ σκέλη,
ἃ βάσιν οὐκ ἔχοντα παγιωτέραν
εἰς γῆν με κατήρασσον ὡς ἄπνουν νέκυν. 40
ὅλας θαλάσσας ἐκροφᾶν ἠπειγόμην,
ὅλους ποταμοὺς ἐκπίνειν ἐγλιχόμην·
τὸ πῦρ γὰρ ἔνδον ἐγκαθήμενον λάβρον
ὅλην ἀπεξήραινε τὴν διαρτίαν.
αἲ αἴ, πολυστένακτον ἀνθρώπων γένος, 45
κακῶν ἄβυσσε, βυθὲ τῆς δυσποτμίας·
αἲ αἴ, πολυστρόβητε, κυκητὰ βίε,
ἀλλοπρόσαλλε, τρισκατάρατε, πλάνε,
ἄνισε, παντόφυρτε, βάσιν οὐκ ἔχων·
σκώληξ σὺ πικρός, καρδίας κατεσθίων, 50
δυσχείμερος θάλασσα μυρίων κακῶν,
ἀνήμερον πέλαγος μυρίων κακῶν.
Ὁ γοῦν σεβαστός, ἡμιθανῆ με βλέπων,
ἐσχετλίαζε, συμπαθῶς ἐδυσφόρει

---

[73] Unconsciousness or lethargy is one of the symptoms of this illness.
[74] For ζωοβρύτης, see Trapp, *LBG*, s.v.
[75] τροφῆς, literally "food". It was common belief that people were punished for their sins by illness.

it carbonized me and, what's more, exhausted me,
it baked me in the fire, and smothered me in a pan, 20
darkened my head with dense and smoky puffs
which at the same time closed the pupils of my brain.[73]
My hair fell out -just as it happens with a corpse-,
not being proof against the strain of feverish heat.
Alas, alas, unlucky me, a piteous man, 25
soon withering, emaciated to the bone,
with nothing more than very lean shadows of flesh,
or better said, no flesh at all, only the skin.
Oh, Christ, creator of the world, life-pouring[74] God,
that terrible evacuation of my paunch, 30
that vomiting out of my mouth, which scorchèd me,
and which reminded me of fruit[75] from long ago
which I enjoyed, although forbidden as it was,
by which I was seduced and cheated, I, poor wretch,
which thrust this bitter misery onto my neck! 35
Whenever I perceive the bitterness of bile
I feel this thing exactly is the same as death.
Limp were my arms, shaky my legs, and they, my legs
were powerless, not able anymore to let me walk,
only to fling me down to earth, a breathless corpse! 40
In eager haste I started gulping down whole seas,
whole rivers were my goal to drink with gluttony,
because the blazing fire, which in my entrails raged,
dried out just every bone of all my skeleton.
Ah, ah, you, human race, to be deeply deplored, 45
abyss of evils, depth of great misfortune, too!
Ah, ah, you, human life, so changeable[76] and weird,
unsteady and deceptive, thrice-accursed as well,
not very fair and all-confusing, without base,
you are the cruel worm devouring all the hearts, 50
you are the stormy sea of countless miseries,
you are the ruthless ocean of countless pains!
   In short, his Highness seeing me as almost dead,
he was alarmed, felt irritation and compassion, too,

---

[76] πολυστρόβητος < πολύς + στροβητός, again a neologism. In his poem *Aristandros and Kallithea*, Manasses repeatedly touches on this theme, e.g. frg. III, 52, 54, 55 (with an allusion to Solon's remark against Croesus in Herodotus, I, 32, 7).

καὶ φιλοτίμου τῆς προνοίας ἠξίου. 55
οὕτω κακῶς πάσχοντι συγκατηλέει
ὁ Δουκόβλαστος εὐκλεὴς Ἀλέξιος,
ὁ τηνικαῦτα κυριαρχῶν Κυπρίων,
ἀνὴρ μεγαλόδωρος, αὐτοπραότης,
ἐκ βασιλικῶν αἱμάτων κατηγμένος. 60
ἵν' οὖν τὰ πολλὰ συντεμὼν γοργῶς φράσω,
ἀμφοῖν κελεύσει καὶ θελήσει καὶ κρίσει
εἰς τὴν περιβόητον ἠνέχθην Κύπρον,
ὡς ἀέρος τύχοιμι καθαρωτέρου
καὶ τὴν προσοῦσαν ἀποκρουσαίμην νόσον. 65
οἵοις μὲν οὖν με τοῖς ἀγαθοῖς καὶ πόσοις
ἤρδευσε χειρὶ δαψιλεῖ καὶ πλουσίᾳ
Δουκῶν ὁ κλάδος, ἡ γαλήνιος φύσις,
οὐκ ἂν δυναίμην τῷ λόγῳ διαγράφειν.
πάλιν δ' ἐπῆλθεν ἡ παλαμναία νόσος, 70
ὡς ἐκ δρυμοῦ σῦς, ὡς λεαίνης σκυμνίον.
ἔβρυξε τοὺς ὀδόντας, ἤνοιξε στόμα·
καταπιεῖν ὥρμησεν ἀσχέτῳ θράσει,
τὸν φλοῦν ἀπεξήρανε τὸν τοῦ σαρκίου,
τὸν χοῦν ἀπημαύρωσε τῆς διαρτίας, 75
τὸν ῥοῦν ἐπωχέτευσε τῶν ἐντοσθίων.
ὦ σῶμα λυπρόν, ὦ γεώδης οὐσία.
κἂν μὴ σύ, πάτερ τοῦ γένους φυτηκόμε,
ὤμβρησας ἀνάψυξιν ἐμπνόου δρόσου
πεσόντι καὶ ψυγέντι καὶ ῥεύσαντί μοι, 80
τάχ' ἂν τεφρωθεὶς εἰς τὸ μηδὲν πεφθάκειν.
τέως ἀποδράς, δορκὰς ὥσπερ ἐκ βρόχων,
ἐλευθερίων ἡψάμην πετασμάτων.
καὶ νῦν παροικῶ τὴν ὑμνουμένην Κύπρον,
τὴν λιπαρὰν γῆν, τὴν πολυφόρον χθόνα, 85
ἄλλοις κύπειρον οὖσαν, ἀλλ' ἐμοὶ Κύπρον.
τί γὰρ ταπεινῶν ἀστρίων ἀμαυρότης

[77] Horna devotes an elaborate note to the question as to who this Alexios Doukas was. He was not the eldest son of Nikephoros Bryennios, but perhaps the Alexios who is mentioned in an enkolpion which came into the possession of Amalric, King of Jerusalem in 1171; the King donated it to the Grammont Monastery in 1174. This Alexios was a great-grandson of Irene, wife of Alexios Komnenos. His ἀκμή fell between 1150 and 1170 and he could be the successor of John Komnenos, grand nephew of the emperor of that name, who is mentioned as a Byzantine governor of Cyprus by Johannes Kinnamos, *Epitome* (see n. 3), IV, 17, CSHB, p. 178, 22.

and ordered an intensive and expensive care! 55
While suffering this awful fate I was indulged
with pity by the Doukas-shoot Alexios,[77]
the famous governor of Cyprus at that time,
a very generous, friendly personality,
and really descending from imperial blood. 60
 In order now to cut a verbose story short:
by will, consent, and order of both mighty men
I was transported to that famous Cyprus there,
where I should find, as it was hoped, a more fresh air
for getting rid of this disease which savaged me. 65
All kinds of healthy things, these many benefits
which has bestowed on me with rich and generous hand
the scion of Doukas family, nature serene,
impossible for me to mention these in words!
Nevertheless, again the murderous illness did 70
attack me like a boar from copse, or lioness.
It gnashed its teeth, it opened threatening its mouth
and was prepared to swallow me with brutal force.
It dehydrated all the surface of my skin,
it charred the earthen dust of all my body's shape.[78] 75
it drained away all moisture in my entrails left.
Oh wretchèd substance, oh you, creature made of earth!
And if you, Father-Planter of the human race,
hadn't rained upon me the refreshment of cool wind,
thus fallen ill, wasting away by feverish heat, 80
I would, reduced to ashes, now have passed to nil.
However, I escaped, just like a deer from snare
and clung to wings which brought me into liberty.
Therefore I live now here on Cyprus, well-renowned
for its fertility and for its fruitful land, 85
to some a land of citrus, Cyprus just for me![79]
For, what is the dull flicker of the modest stars

---

[78] διαρτία, "form", a rare word, used by Cosmas the Melodist, *Hymns* 2, 40, PG 98, 459-524, "σύμμορφος πηλίνης εὐτελοῦς διαρτίας, Χριστέ, γεγονώς"; see Lampe, s.v. Some other instances are mentioned in Trapp, *LBG*.

[79] The pun κύπειρον — Κύπρον is inimitable in English. I therefore tried the assonant juxtaposition citrus — Cyprus. The reference to κύπειρος is an allusion to Homerus, *Ilias*, φ, 351 and *Odyssey*, δ, 603. From these instances it is clear that galingale grew on fertile places and was used as horse-fodder. Manasses' pun probably means: Cyprus may be fertile as it is (for horses), as to me, it offers nothing.

πρὸς τὴν τὸ πᾶν βόσκουσαν ἡλίου φλόγα;
ἢ τί πρὸς αὐτὴν τὴν Κωνσταντίνου πόλιν
ἡ Κύπρος ἡ σύμπασα καὶ τὰ τῆς Κύπρου; 90
ὦ μόχθος, ὦ μάθησις, ὦ σοφῶν βίβλοι,
αἷς συνεσάπην ἀνοήτως ἐκ νέου·
ὦ σώματος κάκωσις, ὦ νυκτῶν δρόμοι,
ἃς ἀνάλωσα ταῖς βίβλοις ἐντυγχάνων,
ἄϋπνος, οὐ βλέφαρα κάμπτων εἰς ὕπνον, 95
ὥσπερ μονάζων στρουθὸς ἐν δωματίῳ,
ἢ μᾶλλον εἰπεῖν, ἐν σκότει νυκτικόραξ.
εἰς γῆν παροικῶ τὴν σπανίζουσαν λόγων·
ἀργὸς κάθημαι, συμπεδήσας τὸ στόμα,
ἀεργός, ἀκίνητος ὡς φυλακίτης, 100
ῥήτωρ ἄγλωσσος οὐκ ἔχων παρρησίαν,
ῥήτωρ ἄφωνος οὐκ ἔχων γυμνασίαν.
ὥσπερ δὲ παράδεισος, οὐκ ἔχων ὕδωρ,
συγκαίεται μὲν ὑπὸ τῆς λειψυδρίας,
συμφρύγεται δὲ παρὰ τῆς ἀνομβρίας 105
καὶ φυλλοριπτεῖ δενδρῖτις εὐκοσμία,
οὕτω κἀγὼ πέπονθα· καὶ διεφθάρην
καὶ κάλλος ἀπέβαλλον, οὗπερ ηὐπόρουν.
ἀργὸς διάγω, βόσκομαι ταῖς ἐλπίσιν
ἢ τὴν κίνησιν καρτερῶ τῶν ὑδάτων, 110
ὡς πρὶν ὁ παράλυτος ὑγείας χάριν.
Ὦ Ῥωμαῖς γῆ, κόσμε τῆς γῆς ἁπάσης,
ἔρρευσε τὰ βλέφαρα προσδοκῶντά σε.
αἲ αἴ, στενάζω καὶ ποθῶ σε καὶ πνέω,
κάλλιστε μητράδελφε, κόσμε συγγόνων· 115
ἀπείργομαι δὲ σῆς ἐρασμίου θέας,
ὦ κύκλε χρυσέ, τῶν μοναστῶν σεμνότης·
ἐκρυσταλλώθην, ἐξέλιπον, ἐρρύην·
ὃ τέττιγες πάσχουσιν οἱ δροσοφάγοι,
θέρους μὲν ὑπάδοντες ἔμμουσον μέλος, 120

[80] This sigh is reminiscent of the beginning of Poem III of Ptochoprodromos (ed. H. Eideneier, Neograeca Medii Aevi, V (Cologne, 1991); = Poem IV in the ed. D.C. Hesseling and H. Pernot, Verh. KNAW, afd. Letterkunde, 11,1 (Amsterdam, 1910)), whose father forced him to start a career as an intellectual, with much paperwork and little bread on the shelf.

[81] For 96 and 97 compare Psalm 101 (102):7-8, "ἐγενήθην ὡσεὶ νυκτικόραξ ἐν οἰκοπέδῳ / ἠγρύπνησα καὶ ἐγενήθην / ὡσεὶ στρουθίον μονάζον ἐπὶ δώματι".

compared with that all-feeding flame of her, the sun?
So, in comparison with the City of Constantine,
what 's Cyprus in its wholeness and particulars?   90
Oh strain, oh education, oh these learned men's books
with which from childhood I was stuffed, silly enough![80]
Oh torment of my body, oh these lengthy nights
which I spent sitting amidst my books and reading them,
awake, not letting close my eyelashes for sleep,   95
remaining like a sparrow in my room alone,
or, better said, a long-eared owl at darkness' hour.[81]
I live here in a land where literature is scarce,
I sit here idly down, hand-cuffèd at the mouth,
just unemployed, immobile like a prisoner,[82]   100
tongueless orator without liberty of speech,
voiceless orator without any exercise.
No, like a garden without any water-stream,
which suffers baking in the lack of moisture there,
which suffers withering by lasting lack of rain,   105
the splendid trees of which have dropped[83] their splendid leaves,
thus was the situation of myself: I died
and lost the beauty which I usually enjoyed;
idling away my time I feed myself with hope
or wait the movement of the waters going through   110
just as in older times the lame did for his health.[84]

Oh, Roman land, true ornament of all the earth,
my eyes and eyelashes are wet thinking of you.
Yea, yea, I groan, longing for you with every breath,
dear mother's brother, pearl of my whole family,[85]   115
because I am devoid of your so lovely look,
you, golden ring, respected in the monastery!

I froze, I fell into a swoon, wasted away.
What happened to me 's what dew-consuming crickets fare
who sing their high-melodious songs in summertime,   120

---

[82] This meaning of φυλακίτης is a new one in comparison with the meaning "police officer" (in Egypt; see LSJ). For the meaning "prisoner", see Lampe, s.v.

[83] φυλλοριπτῶ is probably a neologism which has replaced φυλλορροέω.

[84] Cf. John 5:2-7 on the pool Bethesda, around which a multitude of sick people was "waiting for the moving of the water": "whosoever then first... stepped in was made whole..."

[85] This uncle on his mother's side is further unknown. From vs. 117 one may conclude that he was an abbot of a monastery in (the neighbourhood of) Constantinople.

ἐν σοὶ γενοίμην, κατατρυφήσαιμί σου·
σὺ καὶ περιθάλποις με καὶ διεξάγοις
καὶ μητρικῶν σῶν ἀγκαλῶν μὴ χωρίσαις.

Λόγος τρίτος.

Ἔμελλον ἄρα καὶ πάλιν κινεῖν χέρα
καὶ στηλογραφεῖν τὰς ἐμὰς δυσπραγίας·
παρῆλθε καὶ γὰρ οὐδέπω τὰ δεινά μοι,
ἀεὶ δ' ἐπιρρέουσι καὶ τρύχουσί με.
κἀγὼ μὲν ᾤμην ἄχρι καὶ τοῦ τρυγίου 5
πιεῖν ἁπάσας τῆς τύχης τὰς πικρίας
καὶ συμφορῶν κύπελλα καὶ νόσων σκύφους·
τὰ δ' ἦσαν αὖθις ὡς κρατὴρ χολῆς γέμων
καὶ θλίψεων ῥοῦν ἀδάπανον βλυστάνων.
ᾤμην τὸ δένδρον τῶν ἐμῶν παθημάτων, 10
κἂν ἐν θέρει τέθηλε, χειμῶνι φθίνειν·
τὸ δ' ἦν ἀειβλάστητον, εὔκαρπον, βρύον
εἰς πάντα καιρόν, οὐ γὰρ ἐν θέρει μόνον.

Αἲ αἴ, τυφλὸν δείλαιον ἀνθρώπων γένος,
ὡς πρὸς τὸ μέλλον τὰς κόρας τυφλὰς ἔχεις. 15
ἐπεὶ γὰρ εἰς πέλαγος ἐμπεσὼν νόσων
καὶ προσραγεὶς τὸ σῶμα παντοίαις βλάβαις
εἰς νῆσον ἤχθην τὴν μεγίστην τὴν Κύπρον,
ὡς ἐκτινάξω τῶν παθῶν τὸ φορτίον,
προσέσχον αὖθις κινδύνοις παλιντρόποις 20
καὶ τραχύτης κλύδωνος ὑπέπαισέ με,
ὡσεί τις ἀρθεὶς εἰς ἀπόκρημνον λόφον
πάλιν ὀπισθόνωτος ἐξ ὕψους πέσοι.
ὡς ἀπόλοιτο κακία τῆς ἡμέρας,
ἐν ᾗ προσῆλθον ἀπὸ τῆς Βυζαντίδος· 25
μὴ συνταγείη τοῦ χρόνου ταῖς ἡμέραις,
ἡνίκα λιπὼν τὴν πόλιν τὴν ὀλβίαν,
ἐπεπλανήθην εἰς βαραθρώδεις τόπους.
ἀλλ' ὢ τί μάτην ἐγκαλῶ ταῖς ἡμέραις,
αὐτὸς καθ' αὑτοῦ κατενεγκὼν τὸ ξίφος; 30

---

[90] The basic use of κατατρυφάω + gen. is given in Psalm 36 (37):4: "κατατρύφησον τοῦ κυρίου"("delight thyself in the Lord"). See also Lampe, s.v.

[91] One of the few dubious readings of the text. Horna indicates that MS V has ὑπέβαλλέ με, but in the margin ὑπέπεσέ με, written by him as ὑπέπαισε for

I wish I were now in your arms, enjoyed[90] in you,
I wish you cherished me and gave me full support,
that never more I will be off from your embrace!

Third Poem

It was my fate that once again I moved my hand
to write my train of misfortunes on tablets down!
For these my sufferings were far from ended now,
no, they continued flooding and exhausting me!
And then I thought that I had drunk full to the dregs　　　5
the multitude of bitternesses of my fate,
the cups brimful of miseries and illnesses,
but there it was again: a bowl filled up with bile
which overflows with never-ending streams of pain!
I also thought the tree of all my sufferings,　　　10
though flourishing in summer, would in winter die.
It proved to be an evergreen, teeming with fruits
and at all seasons, not just during summertime!
　　Ah, ah, stone blind and miserable human race,
how do you have your eyes towards the future closed!　　　15
For, being tumbled in the sea of illnesses
and being physically broken by all harms
and after being brought to Cyprus, that great isle,
for shaking off the burden of my sufferings,
I was confronted with just other dangers now　　　20
and roughness of the dash of waves had hit me down,[91]
the same way as a man raised up onto a cliff
who backward falls from his position into depth!
Be cursed the badness of that miserable day
that I departed from my land, Byzantium.　　　25
Oh, wouldn't be numbered among daily time that day
when I went off to leave that City fortunate
and had to roam about the lands full of ravines!
But why to blame the days unjustifiably
where I myself let fall the sword upon myself?　　　30

---

metrical reasons from ὑποπαίω, a verb without parallel. Perhaps ὑπέπεσέ με is not more than a gloss upon the unusual meaning of ὑπέβαλλέ με, the meaning of which may be compared with Polybius, 1, 82, 2, "ὑπέβαλλε τοῖς θηρίοις (τοὺς πολεμίους sc.)".

πάλιν ἀνοίξω καὶ πλατυνῶ τὸ στόμα
καὶ τοὺς κατασχόντας με λαλήσω πόνους.
ἐγείρεταί μοι βαρυάλγητον πάθος
νεφρῶν κατ' αὐτῶν τῶν μελῶν ὀπισθίων,
καλῶς δέ, Χριστέ, καὶ μετ' ἐνδίκου νόμου· 35
οὐ γὰρ περιέσφιγξα νεφροὺς εὐφρόνως,
τὴν ὀσφὺν οὐκ ἔζωσα, σοὺς πατῶν νόμους.
αἲ αἴ, πάθος δύστλητον, ἄλγους ὀξύτης,
εἰς αὐτὸν ἐγκέφαλον ἐξικνουμένη.
κίνησις οὐκ ἦν, δυσχερὴς ἦν ἡ στάσις, 40
ἡ κατάκλισις βαρυσυμφορωτέρα.
τὸν παράλυτον ἄν τις εἴκασε βλέπειν,
ὁρῶν βεβλημένον με νεκρὸν ἐν κλίνῃ.
ἐντεῦθεν ἤλγουν, ἠθύμουν, ἐδυσφόρουν,
ὠρυόμην, ἤσχαλλον, ὤχλουν, ἠχθόμην. 45
ἥλιε, μὴ βλέψαιεν αἱ σαὶ λαμπάδες
ἄνθρωπον ὑποστάντα τοιοῦτον βάρος.
κἂν γὰρ γίγας τις, κἂν λίθινος τυγχάνῃ,
κἂν ἐξισῶται ταῖς κέδροις τοῦ Λιβάνου,
φανήσεται, φεῦ, ἰσχνότης καλαμίνη, 50
καμφθήσεται, φεῦ, ὡς ἁμάξης ἁψίδες.
ὦ πικροποιὸν καὶ χολὴν βλύσαν φυτὸν
καὶ τοῦ κακίστου σατανᾶ συμβουλία
καὶ τῶν γεναρχῶν δυστυχὴς ἀπληστία,
δι' ὧν θαλάσσας μυρίων παθημάτων 55
τὸ τληπαθὲς πέπωκεν ἀνθρώπων γένος.
    Εἶχον μὲν οὕτως, ὥσπερ ἡμίπνους νέκυς·
τοῦ <γὰρ> ποδός μοι μηδόλως κινουμένου,
ὡς δένδρον ἡμίψυχον ἀπεψυχόμην·
ἐχώλαναν γὰρ αἱ τρίβοι τῆς καρδίας· 60
οὐκοῦν δικαίως ἡ κίνησις ἐσφάλη.
ἄσιτος ἤμην, οὐ προσηγόμην ὕδωρ.
ἀπεστενώθη τὸ πλάτος τῶν ἐντέρων·
τὰ κέντρα καὶ γὰρ τῶν πικρῶν ἀλγηδόνων
ἀπερράπιζον τὴν τροφὴν καὶ τὴν πόσιν. 65
μή μοι γένοιτο, Χριστέ, μηδὲ καθ' ὕπνους

---

[92] I have followed the "neutral" wording of Manasses himself. However, I guess that νεφροί is euphemisticly used for ὄρχεις, for which use see LSJ, s.v. "νεφρός". Vs. 36 makes clear that Manasses caught some venereal disease.
[93] Cf. Ex. 12:11; Luc. 12:35.

I'll open now and once again widen my mouth
to tell the miseries which held me in their grasp.
A very painful suffering was roused in me
which struck precisely at the reins right in my back,[92]
and rightly so, my Christ, according to your law.   35
For I didn't wisely keep my reins under control
nor did I keep girded my loins,[93] breaking your laws.
Ow, ouch, untolerable pain, this knife-sharp grief,
which penetrated right away into my brain!
It was impossible to walk, hard to stand up,   40
but lying down was even more unbearable.
One would have thought, if seeing me, he saw the lame,
thus I was lying like a corpse stretched in my bed,
perished with pain, full of dejection and with wrath,
I moaned, I grudged, I felt distressed and much oppressed!   45
Oh sun, your eyes may never see again a man
who has to suffer such atrocity of pain!
For even if he should have been a giant of stone
or just as strong as cedars of the Lebanon,
it would turn out, alas, that he was weak like reed   50
and he would curve, alas, like felloes of a wheel![94]
Oh, tree[95] which richly bitterness and bile produced
and that advice given from evil Satan's side
and that disastrous gluttony of our first man,
which caused that this so very wretchèd human race   55
has drunk these oceans of innumerable pains.

   This was my situation then: as good as dead,
one of my legs was fully motionless, indeed,
just as a nearly lifeless[96] tree was I dying off:
for they, the paces of my heart went badly lame,   60
no wonder then that any move could only fail!
I could not eat, nor could I take to me some drink,
the width of my intestines grew just narrower,
for all the tortures of these painful sufferings
drove any lust for food or drink by force away.   65
I pray to you, Christ, may I even in my sleep,

---

[94] "ὡς ἁμάξης ἁψίδες". MS V reads ἀψῖδες with the correct classical accentuation. Horna changed the accent because the metre requires a short ι.

[95] This φυτόν is, of course, the tree of good and evil.

[96] For ἡμίψυχος, "semianimis", LSJ refers to glossaria.

ἰδεῖν ἐκείνου τοῦ πάθους τὰς πικρίας·
ἂν γὰρ χρονίσῃ τῶν ὀνείρων ἡ πλάνη
καὶ μὴ διαπτῇ καὶ λυθῇ παραυτίκα,
Ἅιδου με συγκλείσειε παμφάγον στόμα. 70
χρόνῳ δὲ πολλῷ προσπελάσας τῇ νόσῳ
καὶ γνοὺς τὸ λοιπὸν μηδὲ μικρὸν ἰσχύειν
Ἀσκληπιαδῶν τὴν σοφὴν τεχνουργίαν,
μόνην δὲ τριβὴν καὶ κενὴν στομαλγίαν,
ἄλλην ἀτραπὸν ἐξ ἀνάγκης ἐτράπην 75
καὶ κατ' ἐμαυτὸν εἶπον «ἐρρίφθω κύβος»
καὶ θερμολουτεῖν ἠρξάμην τὸ σαρκίον.
ὦ λουτρόν, ἀρχὴ τῆς ἐμῆς εὐρωστίας,
σὺ πολλὰ τερπνὰ τοῖς κακουμένοις φέρον
καὶ τὰς ἐμὰς ὤρθωσας εὐμενῶς τρίβους. 80
θέλω κροτῆσαι τοῖς λόγοις καὶ σαλπίσαι
τῶν σῶν ἀγαθῶν τὰς πολυρρύτους χύσεις,
ἀλλ' εἰσέτι μοι μικρόφωνον τὸ στόμα,
ἀποψυγὲν καύσωνι πειρατηρίων.
ἥλιος ἔγνω καὶ σελήνη τὴν δύσιν, 85
ὁ ποὺς δ' ὁ γοργός, ἡ ταχυπέτης πτέρυξ
τῆς συμπιεζούσης με βαρυποτμίας
οὐκ οἶδε κατάπαυσιν, οὐκ οἶδε στάσιν.
ὦ πῶς ἂν ηὐτύχησα πρὸς βραχὺν χρόνον
τοῦ συμπαθοῦς τὴν γλῶσσαν Ἰερεμίου, 90
ὡς τῶν κακῶν μου τὰς φορὰς ὠδυράμην.
αἴ αἴ, συχνῶν μου συμφορῶν καὶ κινδύνων
καὶ τῶν βελέμνων τῆς τύχης τῆς βασκάνου.
ἕως πότε στέρξω σε, τύχης πικρία;
τί πρὸς τοσοῦτον ἐκπιέζεις καὶ τρύχεις; 95
τὴν αἱματηρὰν ἐξέπιες πλημμύραν,
τὸ τῶν κρεῶν μου κατεμασσήσω λέπος,
ἦψω σχεδόν μου τοῦ βάθους τῶν ἐγκάτων.
τί γοῦν ἐπισφάττεις με; τί με συμπνίγεις;
ἥλιε καὶ φῶς καὶ χορὸς τῶν ἀστέρων, 100
ἰδὼν τὸ πρᾶγμα τοῦτο, πῶς οὐκ ἐκρύβης;

[97] See ἀνερρίφθω κύβος in Plutarchus, *Vita Caesaris*, c. 32, and Athenaeus, *Deipnosophists*, trans. C.B. Gulick, Loeb Classical Library (Cambridge, Mass., and London, 1969), XIII, 559e. See also Zonaras, x, 7: "Καῖσαρ ... τοῦτο δὴ τὸ κοινὸν ὑπειπὼν 'ἐρρίφθω κύβος' ὥρμησε, ..."

no, never see the bitter pains which I endured,
for if would last this bad deceit as caused by dreams
and not would stop and come to end inmediately,
better devours me Hades with his greedy mouth! 70
Thus being burdened with this illness a long time
and feeling that no longer would suffice the skill
of the sophisticated fellows of Asclepius
-not more than time-consuming work and hollow talk-
I took, forced by necessity, another path: 75
I uttered to myself the words: "the die be cast"[97]
and started bathing then my body in hot baths.
Oh, swimming pool and starting point for my good health,
you, that so many joyful things brings to the harmed
and that has made the paths well straight also for me, 80
I shall with words applaud and make the trumpet sound
to tell about the flooding streams of your mere goods,
though for the moment I am still a bit weak-voiced
because yet chilled by that great heat of these my trials.
The sun knows setting[98] and the same holds for the moon, 85
the fast, however, running foot, the flying wing
of my oppressive fate that really turned me down
is not aware of any rest, knows no standstill.

Oh, had I had at my disposal a short time
the tongue of sympathetic prophet Jeremiah 90
in order to bewail the blows of my bad luck
and, ouch, the many miseries and dangers, too,
and all these arrows of a fate that tortured me!
Until what time I'll have to love you, bitter fate?
Why do you sqeeze me and distress to such extent? 95
You fully drained the rich abundance of my blood,
you ate digesting all the fat which built my flesh,
and you almost attacked my body's inmost parts.
Why do you slaughter and why do you strangle me?
You, sun and moon and chorus of the many stars, 100
why didn't you disappear on seeing such event?

---

[98] Psalm 103 (104):19, "ἐποίησεν σελήνην εἰς καιρούς, ὁ ἥλιος ἔγνω τὴν δύσιν αὐτοῦ".

Ὦ χρύσεον πόλισμα τῆς Βυζαντίδος,
ἥλιε τῆς γῆς, κάλλος οὐκ ἔχον κόρον,
ἕως πότε βλέψω σε κατὰ τοὺς ὕπνους;
ἴδοιμι, παντέραστε, σὰς στιλβηδόνας· 105
βλέψαιμι, καλλίφωτε, τὰ πρόσωπά σου.

Λόγος τέταρτος.

Ὦ χεῖρες, ἰσχύσατε καὶ κινεῖσθέ μοι·
πόδες, διανάστητε καὶ σκιρτᾶτέ μοι·
ὦ γλῶσσα, ῥῆξον ὕμνον εὐχαριστίας·
χάρηθι καὶ σύ, τριτάλαινα καρδία.
ἰδοὺ γάρ, ἰδού, καθαρώτατα βλέπω 5
τὴν παντέραστον, ὀλβίαν Βυζαντίδα.
ἀλλ' ὦ τί τοῦτο; μὴ πεπλάνημαι πάλιν;
μὴ Κύπρον οἰκῶ, τὴν κάκοσμον πικρίαν,
ἢ τὴν πνιγηρὰν τοῦ Πτολεμαίου πόλιν
ἢ τὴν Ναζαρέτ, τὴν ἐμοὶ στυγητέαν; 10
φαντάζομαι ψευδῶς σε, χρυσέα πόλις;
ἐνύπνιόν μοι τοῦτο καὶ νυκτὸς γέλως,
ἢ σε τρανῶς κατεῖδον ὕπαρ, οὐκ ὄναρ;
ἀλλ' οὐχὶ Πάφος ταῦτα καὶ γῆ Κιτίου,
οὐχ ἡ πενιχρὰ Τριμιθουσίων πόλις· 15
οὐκ ἀέρος ζέουσα κακόπνους ῥύσις·
οὐχ ἀπαγωγὴ σωμάτων τεθνηκότων,
σωρηδὸν εἰς τύμβευσιν ἐκφορουμένων,
ὁποῖα πολλὰ καθορᾶν ὁσημέραι
πάρεστι τοῖς οἰκοῦσι τὴν Πτολεμαίου· 20
ἀλλ' ἡ πολυτίμητος, ἡ κλεινὴ πόλις.
ὁρῶ τὸν αἰθέριον, ἄπνουν ἱππότην·
τὸν λιμένα βλέπω δέ, τὸν μυριόναυν,
ἐκεῖνον αὐτὸν τοῦ Θεοῦ καὶ τὸν δόμον,
τὸν ἀνθρακίαν τὸν λίθον, τὸν πυρράκην, 25
τὸν ἡλιώδη τὸν φεραυγῆ, τὸν μέγαν.

[99] This passage makes clear that the composition of the poem was well-considered. The first poem starts with a dream with negative consequences; here reality looks like a dream but turns out to be a fortunate one.

[100] Though the second and third poem amply refer to Manasses' stay on Cyprus, only now do we hear about the region where he probably stayed, unless the names are to be considered geographical cliché's pointing to Cyprus. As to Trimythousians, one probably has to change Horna's text Τριμιθουσίων into Τριμυθουσίων (Trimythus was a bish-

Oh golden City in the land of Byzantines,
sun of the earth, whose beauty is inexhaustible,
how long shall I just see you only in my dreams?
Oh, may I, loved one, really see your splendours back,   105
may I, your brilliancy, see back your shining face!

Fourth poem

Oh arms, regain your strength, start moving now for me,
and legs, straighten yourselves, start dancing now for me;
oh tongue, let now burst out a hymn of gratitude.
Be happy, you too, thrice-afflicted heart of mine,
for really there I see in luminosity   5
my all-belovèd, prosperous town Byzantium!
But oh, what 's this? Am I misled here once again?
Is it not Cyprus where I stay, that bitter stench,
or Ptolemaïs, that so suffocating town
or Nazareth, which cordially I abhor?   10
You, golden town, do I see you or a mirage?
Is it a vision in my sleep, smile of the night
or am I awake and see you clearly, not a dream?[99]
But no! Not Paphos nor the land of Kition
nor that poor city of the Trimythousians![100]   15
And not the whirling draught of a big howling storm,
not the removal of a quantity of men deceased
who are by heaps for burial carried out of town,
such as can be observed in day-to-day routines
by the inhabitants of Ptolemaïs town,   20
but really this much-honoured city, famous town!
I see the horseman's lifeless statue in the air,[101]
but also the great harbour, with its countless ships,
and there that building which was built for God Himself
with stones as black as charcoal and with fiery red,   25
the sun-drenched, great illuminated holy church![102]

---

opric), though Makhairas also mentions a place Τριμιθεία either in the Paphos region or = Grimithia, south-west of Lefkosia. See Leontios Makhairas, *Recital concerning the Sweet Land of Cyprus entitled "Chronicle"*, ed. R.M. Dawkins, 2 vols (Oxford, 1932), II, §566, n. 2. I thank Prof. Metcalf for this suggestion.

[101] Probably the statue of Constantine on the Constantine Market. An inscription mentions the fact that the Emperor Manuel had the capital repaired.

[102] Doubtless a reference to the Hagia Sofia, though the description is somewhat impressionistic. Horna doubts whether the text is genuine.

τί, φεῦ, πέπονθα; ποῖ παρεπλάγχθην φρενῶν;
ὦ πῶς τὸ συχνῶν τῶν ὀνείρων τῆς πλάνης
τὸ πιστὸν ἐξέκοψε τῶν ὁρωμένων;
ἐκεῖνος ὄντως <ἔστιν> ὁ γλυκύς τόπος, 30
ἡ τῶν μακάρων νῆσος, ἡ χρυσῆ πόλις.
ἐπεὶ δὲ λοιπὸν πᾶς ἐλήλαται φόβος
καὶ τῶν ὀνείρων ἡ πλάνη τῶν νυκτέρων
καὶ φανερῶς ἔβλεψα τὴν Κωνσταντίνου,
ἐπαναλάβω τὴν διήγησιν πάλιν. 35
Ὑποστραφέντες ὑπὸ τῆς Ἰσαυρίας
καταλιπόντες τοῦ Δράκοντος τὰς δίνας,
ὃς δὴ ποταμός ἐστι τῆς Ἰσαυρίας,
ναὶ μὴν ἀφέντες καὶ Συκῆν τὴν ἀγρίαν,
τὴν παντομισῆ, τὴν κατάπτυστον πόλιν 40
(τὰ πολλὰ καὶ γὰρ βούλομαι παρατρέχειν),
εὑρήκαμεν τὴν Κύπρον ἐπτοημένην
πολλοῖς ταραγμοῖς καὶ φοβήτροις ἀγρίοις.
ὁ Τριπολίτης καὶ γὰρ ὀργῇ καχλάσας,
ὡς ἐκπεσὼν δείλαιος ἐξ ὧν ἠλπίκει, 45
(ἡ γὰρ κριθεῖσα συζυγῆναι πρὸς γάμον
τῷ βασιλεῖ μου τῷ στρατηγικωτάτῳ,
ἐκ ταυτοαίμων ἐκφυεῖσα σπερμάτων
τῷ δυσκαθέκτῳ τὸ θράσος Τριπολίτῃ,
βασιλικῶν ἥμαρτε παστοπηγίων· 50
ἡ χρυσέα γὰρ Ἀντιοχέων πόλις
τὸν τῶν Χαρίτων ὑπεμόσχευε κλάδον,
ἐπάξιον τελοῦντα τηλίκου γάμου,
κόρην χαριτόφθαλμον, εὔοπτον κόρην,
ῥηγεκγόνων βλαστῶσαν ἐκ ῥιζωμάτων), 55
ὁ Τριπολίτης τοιγαροῦν θυμῷ ζέσας,
ἀνὴρ ἐκεῖνος ἰταμός, θράσος πνέων,
(καὶ τί γὰρ ἢ Λατῖνος αὐθάδης νέος;)
στόλον κροτήσας καὶ στολάρχας ὁπλίσας,
λεηλατεῖν ὥρμητο τὴν τῶν Κυπρίων, 60
ἄνθρωπος ἀλόγιστος, ὅστις οὐκ ἔγνω,
ὡς οὐ κατισχύσειε γῆς βασιλέως·

[103] On this passage see my Introduction.
[104] "ἐκ ταυτοαίμων ἐκφυεῖσα σπερμάτων". Cf. Manasses, Σύνοψις Χρονική, 6123, "ἦσαν δ' αὐτῷ ταυτόαιμοι κἀκ τῶν αὐτῶν σπερμάτων".

But what, alas, happens to me, where erred my mind?
Is it, that the deceit produced by many dreams
has thoroughly destroyed the truth of what is seen?
Indeed, this is indubitably the sweet place, 30
the happy island of the blessed, the golden town.
However, since my fear henceforth is fully banned
and all the errors of nocturnal dreams as well
and doubtless I saw back the town of Constantine,
I shall continue now the story which I told. 35
　Returning on our journey over Isauria
and having left the eddies of the Drakon stream
- which is a river flowing in Isauria -
we left also behind us Syce in the wilderness,
a just all-hateful place, a cursed, damnable town, 40
we found (I like to skip the details, most of them)
that Cyprus was in trouble, being terrified
because of heavy turmoil and alarming scenes.[103]
　The Count of Tripolis apparently was mad,
due to the fact that what he hoped for just was gone 45
(the girl, considered worthy of a nuptial bond
with him, my very diplomatic emperor,
- for she was born out of the same seed and the blood[104]
of this audacious and unbridled Tripolite -
had been passed over for the royal nuptial tie; 50
the golden city, namely, of the Antiochenes
had generated in her midst the grace-like child,
who was the right match for a such great marriage bond,
a maiden with beautiful eyes, attractive girl,
descendant from the roots of royal families). 55
　This was the reason why the Tripolite seethèd with rage,
that reckless man, a man who glowed with courage, too,
(what 's full of stubborness more than a Latin man?)
and he called up[105] the fleet and armed the admirals
and started looting the island of the Cypriots 60
clearly not knowing, thoughtless person as he was,
that conquest of imperial land was hopeless work,

---

[105] κροτήσας = συγκροτήσας, cf. Theophanes, *Chronographia*, ed. C. De Boor (Leipzig, 1883; reprint Hildesheim, 1980), 47, 21, "σύνοδον ἐν Ἀλεξανδρείᾳ ἐκρότησε"; 484, 26: "σύνοδον ... κροτηθῆναι ἐκέλευσεν et saepius".

στρουθὸς γὰρ ἀπτέρωτος, ἐψιλωμένος,
εἰς ἀετιδοῦ καλιὰν πῶς ἐγγίσει;
νεβρὸς δὲ μικρὸς πῶς θροήσει τὸν μέγαν 65
ἐριβρύχην λέοντα, τὸν θηροκράτην;
τέως ὁ ταλαίπωρος εἶχε μὲν θράσος,
ἐπεσχέθη δὲ τῆς ῥύμης καὶ τοῦ θράσους.
ἡμεῖς δὲ πάντες ἦμεν ἠπορημένοι,
κακοῖς καταξανθέντες οἵοις καὶ πόσοις, 70
οὐκ αἰσίου δὲ τοῦ τέλους τετευχότες,
ἕως ὁ πανσέβαστος ἦλθεν εἰς Κύπρον,
πολλοὺς διαδρὰς κινδύνους καὶ θανάτους,
καὶ τηνικαῦτα τῶν λυπηρῶν ἡ ζάλη
μετῆλθεν ἡμῖν εἰς γαλήνην, εἰς ἔαρ. 75
κἂν τις ἀπιστῇ τὴν χαρὰν πολλὰ σθένειν,
ἀκουέτω μου καὶ μαθὼν πιστευέτω.
τὸ γὰρ πρὸ πολλοῦ τοῦ χρόνου με συντρίβον,
τὸ φλεκτικὸν πῦρ τοῦ τεταρταίου δρόμου,
ὡς τοῦ σεβαστοῦ τὴν παρουσίαν ἔγνω, 80
ἐδραπέτευσεν ἐξ ἐμοῦ παραυτίκα.
ὁ γοῦν σεβαστὸς πάντας εἰς ἓν ἑλκύσας,
ὡσεί τις ὄρνις τοῖς ἑαυτοῦ στρουθίοις
τὰς εὐκελάδους τῶν μελῶν συμφωνίας
ἐπισυρίζει καὶ πρὸς ἓν συναγάγῃ, 85
θήρατρα καὶ παγίδας ἐκπεφευγότα,
ἐσάλπισε ξύνθημα τῆς ἐπανόδου
καὶ πάντες ὡρμήθημεν αὐτῷ συντρέχειν.

Οὐδὲν δὲ καινὸν οὐδὲ πόρρω τῆς τέχνης
παρεισενεγκεῖν καὶ γελοῖον τοῖς λόγοις· 90
τοῖς γὰρ λυπηροῖς καὶ γέμουσι τοῦ πάθους
καὶ χαρίεντα συγκεραννύειν δέον
καὶ ταῖς σκυθρωπαῖς ἱστοριογραφίαις
γελωτοεργοὺς παιδιὰς προσαγαγεῖν.
ἡ τῆς φρικώδους ἦν ἑορτῆς ἡμέρα 95
— πεντηκοστὴν καλοῦμεν αὐτὴν ἐξ ἔθους —,
καὶ πάντες ἦμεν ἐν ναοῖς ἠθροισμένοι,

---

[106] For ἀετιδής, "eaglet", see Trapp, *LBG*, s.v. Trapp, however, does not mention this instance.
[107] θηροκράτης is a neologism, see Trapp, *LBG*, s.v.
[108] This statement is confirmed by William of Tyre, *Chronicon*, XVIII, 31, who suggests that Kontostephanos and his delegation were lucky enough to find a ship that

for how will once a wingless sparrow who's stripped bare
approach the eyrie of an eaglet, young and strong?[106]
A little fawn, how will he ever make afraid   65
a big, loud-roaring lion, king of all the beasts?[107]
The miserable man showed courage for some time,
but he was forced to stop his violence and wrath.
In the meantime we all were shocked and without plan
struck as we were by various catastrophes   70
for which we could not find a good, opportune end
until had come to Cyprus his Highness himself,[108]
who had escaped from many dangers, many deaths,
but from that moment on changed stormy miseries
for us into serenity and day in spring.   75
He, who mistrusts the power of what joy can do,
listen to me and having heard me be convinced!
The illness which had tortured me such a long time,
the burning fire of quartan fever with its heat,
as soon as it had seen his Highness's return   80
as if by magic left me alone inmediately!
His Highness concentrated us onto one spot
just as a hen which calls together all her chicks
with the sonorous[109] timbres of her cackling sounds
and thus assembles them in one and the same place   85
after their being well escaped from net and trap;
thus he let sound the horn as signal for return
and we went all together gathering with him.
 'T is not absurd, nor contrary to rules of art
inserting something laughable into my words: 90
for it is necessary with the painful, grievous things
to mix also some pleasant story to enjoy
and writing gloomy, grumbling historiography
asks for the addition of some jokes to cheer it up.
 It was the day of celebrating a big feast   95
- we name this feast traditionally Pentecost -
and all of us were gathered in our churches then

brought them to Cyprus: "inventa casu navicula in Cyprum se fecerunt deportare"; see also Horna, p. 317.

[109] εὐκέλαδος a.o. in Euripides, *Bacchae*, 160, "λωτὸς ὅταν εὐκέλαδος, ἱερὸς ἱερὰ παίγματα βρέμῃ".

τὴν ἑσπερινὴν ἐκτελοῦντες θυσίαν.
ἔτυχον ἑστὼς τῶν προθύρων πλησίον.
εἰσῆθεν ἄλλος, Κύπριος μὲν τῷ γένει,   100
πάντας δὲ νικῶν ἀφροσύνῃ Κυπρίους.
ἤγγισεν, ἦλθεν, ἐστάθη μου πλησίον·
ἀπῶζεν οἴνου, συναπῶζε σκορόδου.
κἀγὼ δὲ μιχθεὶς τὰς ῥίνας δυσοσμίᾳ
(βδελύττομαι γὰρ τήνδε τὴν κακοσμίαν,   105
ὡς τῶν κακῶν μου τὴν δυσώδη κοπρίαν,
ὡς αὐτὸν αὐτοῦ τοῦ Σατανᾶ τὸν τύπον)
ἰλιγγίασα, λειποθυμεῖν ἠρξάμην·
ὁ δὲ σκοτασμός, ἐμπεσών μου ταῖς κόραις,
μικροῦ με πρὸς γῆν ἠδάφισεν ἡμίπνουν.   110
εἶπον πρὸς αὐτόν, ἐντρανίσας ἡμέρως·
«ἄνθρωπε, πόρρω στῆθι, μὴ προσεγγίσῃς.
ὄζεις σκορόδου, τοιγαροῦν μακρὰν φύγε·
οὐκ ἰσχύω γὰρ πρὸς τὸ κακὸν ἀντέχειν.»
ἀλλ᾽ οὐ πρόσεσχεν, οὐκ ἀπέστη τοῦ τόπου.   115
πάλιν προσεῖπον ἀγριωτέρῳ λόγῳ·
«ἄνθρωπε, πόρρω στῆθι, μὴ σύμπνιγέ με·
ὡς βόρβορον γὰρ ἐκπνέει σου τὸ στόμα.»
ἀλλ᾽ ἀσπὶς ἦν ἐκεῖνος ἀκοὰς βύσας·
καὶ γὰρ τοσαύτην ἔσχε μου τὴν φροντίδα,   120
ὅσην κάπρος κώνωπος ἢ μυίας λέων.
οὐκοῦν συνιδών, ὡς περιττὸν οἱ λόγοι
καὶ χρὴ τὸν ἄνδρα σωφρονίσαι παλάμαις,
τὴν χεῖρα τείνας ἀνδρικῶς, εὐκαρδίως
παίω τὸν ἄνδρα κατὰ κόρρης καὶ γνάθων   125
πληγὴν θυμοῦ γέμουσαν ἀλκιμωτάτου·
καὶ πρὸς τοσοῦτον ἦρτο βόμβον ὁ ψόφος,
ὡς ἐντρανίσαι τῇ βοῇ τῇ τοῦ μέλους.
οὕτω μόλις πέφευγεν ὁ σκατοφάγος.
καὶ τοῦτο μὲν τοιοῦτο, κἂν μέμφοιτό τις.   130
ὁ δ᾽ εὐγενὴς τὰ πάντα καὶ καλὸς Δούκας
πάντας μεθύσας δωρεαῖς δαψιλέσι

[110] Horna interprets τῶν κακῶν as the genitiv of τὰ κακά, "die Exkremente", as in Modern Greek. I disagree for two reasons: 1. If this was Manasses' intention the reading would have been τῶν κακκῶν (for ἡ κάκκη, κακκάω, etc. see Aristophanes, *Pax*, 112, resp. *Nubes*, 1384, 1390). 2. It would be tautologic in respect to κοπρίαν, and in general contrary to his style.

[111] Psalm 57:5, "ὡσεὶ ἀσπίδος κωφῆς καὶ βυούσης τὰ ὦτα αὐτῆς".

attending there the service in the evening.
It happened that I stood quite near the portico,
when someone entered, obviously a Cypriot 100
surpassing all the Cypriots in stupidity!
He entered, came and stood just by my side,
he stank of wine and stank of garlic yet much more,
and I - my nose filled up by this mixture of stench -
(I fiercely hate this kind of evil-smelliness 105
which did remind me of my faeces, being ill,[110]
or of the type of sulphurized Satan himself)
grew dizzy and I threathened honestly to faint.
The darkness which then took possession of my eyes
did nearly throw me almost half-dead on the ground. 110
I said to him casting a friendly look his way:
"Man, please, go just a little further, don't approach.
You smell of garlic, and therefore move far away,
for I cann't stand or such a mischief tolerate!"
He did, however, not react, nor leave his spot. 115
A second time I said to him, but louder now:
"Man, please, go further just a bit, don't stifle me.
Your mouth is breathing the same breath as breathes hell!"
But he was the deaf adder that stoppeth her ear.[111]
He paid attention just as much to me as does 120
a wild boar to a gnat or lion to a fly!
Regarding any further word superfluous
and sure the man to reason should be brought by force
I clenched my fist courageously, and gave the churl
stout-heartedly a heavy box just on the ear, 125
a blow in which was concentrated all my wrath!
The noise rose up to such a high sonority
that he took note[112] of me on hearing crack his limb.
This moment finally the dung-eater pissed off!
This was what happened, though one may me blame for that. 130
But Doukas, generous and nice in all respects,
"made all of us drunk" with a plenitude of gifts[113]

---

[112] ὡς ἐντρανίσαι. For ἐντρανίζω see Trapp, *LBG*, "klar sehen", "hinsehen", "betrachten". He does not mention this place, where the meaning is rather look up, look at, take note of.
[113] I literally translated Manasses' metaphor "πάντας μεθύσας δωρεαῖς δαψιλέσι". The short (first) ι of δαψιλέσι is metrically lengthened.

χαίροντας ἐξέπεμψεν εἰς τὰς πατρίδας.
Ὦ πατρὸς υἱὲ καὶ σφραγὶς καὶ βραχίων,
παμβασιλεῦ, ἥλιε δικαιοσύνης, 135
ἔσωσας ἡμᾶς ἀπὸ τῆς Παλαιστίνης,
ὡς Ἰσραὴλ πρὶν ἐκ χερῶν Αἰγυπτίων.
οὐκ ἔστιν οὐδεὶς ἐν θεοῖς, ὡς σύ, Λόγε·
σὺ ζῶν Θεὸς κράτιστος, ὕψιστος, μόνος,
ὁ παντοποιὸς οὐρανοκράτωρ ἄναξ, 140
ἠλευθέρωσας ἐκ Λατινικοῦ θράσους,
ὡς πρὶν Δανιήλ, τὸν προφήτην τὸν μέγαν,
ἐκ τοῦ φάρυγγος τῶν λεόντων ἐρρύσω.
(τί γὰρ Λατίνων ἰταμώτερον γένος;)
ὁ ναυστολήσας εἰς Βαβυλῶνος χθόνα 145
πορθμεὺς ὁ καινὸς Ἀββακοὺμ δι᾽ ἀέρος,
ὡς τὸν Δανιὴλ τὸν προφήτην ψωμίσαι,
ὁμαλίσας μοι τὰς τρίβους παρ᾽ ἐλπίδα,
ἐναέριον ἱππότην ἀπειργάσω.
ἐξήγαγές με τοῦ πυρὸς τοῦ παμβόρου 150
Πτολεμαΐδος μυριοφονευτρίας·
ἐκ Τριπολιτῶν τῆς πολίχνης ἐρρύσω
καὶ Κυπρίων γῆς τοῦ κακίστου φρουρίου.
ναὶ γὰρ βαρὺ φρούριον ἡ νῆσος Κύπρος,
τεῖχος σιδηροῦν, γαλεάγρα πετρίνη, 155
Ἅιδης ἄφυκτος, οὐκ ἔχων διεξόδους.
ὁ δυστυχήσας συσχεθῆναι τῇ Κύπρῳ
ἐκεῖθεν οὐκ ἂν ἐκπεράσοι ῥᾳδίως·
ἄνπερ γὰρ ἐν γῇ τὰς τρίβους ποιοῖτό τις,
εἰς χεῖρας ἐγγίσειε τὰς τῶν βαρβάρων, 160
ἂν μὴ Θεὸς ῥύοιτο καὶ διεξάγοι·
ποῦ γὰρ πετασθῇ; ποῦ κρυβεὶς διαδράσῃ;
ἂν τῆς θαλάσσης τὸ πλάτος διαπλέοι,
βαβαί, πόσων ἕστηκε κινδύνων μέσον;
ἄνωθεν ἦχος πνευμάτων βαρυπνόων, 165
κάτω βρυχηθμὸς κυμάτων ἀλλοθρόων.
ῥοχθεῖ τὸ κῦμα, πνεῦμα παφλάζει μέγα.
τῶν ἐν θαλάσσῃ ληστρικῶν δὲ τοὺς φόβους

---

[114] I read βραχίων instead of ms. βραχίον. For βραχίων see LSJ.
[115] Psalm 85:8, "οὐκ ἔστιν ὅμοιός σοι ἐν θεοῖς, κύριε". Cf. also vs. 10.
[116] This version of Daniel in the lion's den and his being fed by the prophet Habakuk is told in the Supplement to Daniel, "Bel et Draco" (14:) 31-39.

and bade us a farewell and cruising speed to home.
Son of the Father, seal and strength of Your strong arm,[114]
king of the universe and sun of righteousness, 135
You granted us deliverance from Palestine
as earlier from the hands of Egypt Israel!
No one is there among the gods like You, oh Word.[115]
The living, strongest, highest God are You alone,
Creator of all things, Master of heavens, Lord, 140
You liberated us from Latin recklessness
as You saved the illustrious prophet Daniel
in older days out of the lion's den and mouth
(for what shows more brutality than Latin man?).
You, who conveyed straight to the land of Babylon, 145
You wondrous ferryman, this Habakuk by air
in order that he bring some bread to Daniel,[116]
You also straightened unexpectedly my paths[117]
and made a horseman who is riding through the air.
You carried me away from the all-devouring fire 150
of Ptolemaïs with its high mortality.
You freed me from the city of the Tripolites
and from the awful fortress of Cypriot land.
Yes, certainly, that Cyprus is a heavy fort,
a wall of iron and a mouse-trap made of stone, 155
a Hades without any exit to escape.
He, whom misfortune hits, and sits on Cyprus trapped,
he will not find an easy way to fly from there.
If one would choose to make his travelling by land
he runs the risk of being caught by barbarous hands 160
unless he will be saved by God who leads him through.
For where to fly or where to hide for coming through?
But if he likes to sail the broad back of the sea,
alas, amidst how many dangers is his stead?
The roaring of the heavy tempests from above, 165
the lapping of disastrous waves clashing beneath,
the sea is blustering, the storm roars frantically,
but on the terrors caused by pirates out at sea

---

[117] Referring to Jes. 40:3, Matth. 3:3 etc., "εὐθείας ποιεῖτε τὰς τρίβους (τοῦ θεοῦ ἡμῶν)". In the verse that follows, Kontostephanos' role is compared with Habakuk's.

ποία λαλήσει γλῶσσα καὶ ποῖον στόμα;
ὡς κρεῖσσον εἰς πῦρ ἐμπεσεῖν † ἠθαιρίων   170
ἢ πρὸς κακούργους πειρατὰς θαλασσίους.
οὐαὶ πολυστένακτος ἄνθρωπος τάλας,
ὁ συσχεθείς, φεῦ, τοῖς ἐκείνων δικτύοις.
ἄνθρωπον οὐ τιμῶσι, κἂν μάννα βρέχῃ,
κἂν πῦρ κατάγῃ, κἂν δροσίζῃ καμίνους,   175
κἂν συγκαταθλᾷ τῶν λεόντων τὰς μύλας.
ζητοῦσιν ἁδροὺς ἀποδέσμους χρυσίων.
κἂν μὴ διδῷ τις, (ποῦ γὰρ εὑρήσει τόσους;)
τῶν ὄρχεων κρεμῶσι, παίουσι ξύλοις,
δεσμοῦσιν ἱστοῖς καὶ χαλῶσιν εἰς ὕδωρ,   180
ἕως ἀπορρήξειε τὴν ψυχὴν βίᾳ.
οἶμαι τὸν ἐμπλακέντα τοῖς τούτων βρόχοις
ἄλλοις ἰταμοῖς οὐ δοθήσεσθαι τότε
ἐν τῇ φρικώδει καὶ τελευταίᾳ κρίσει,
κἂν τοὺς τελώνας ἐν κακοῖς ὑπεκδράμῃ·   185
ἀρκεῖν γὰρ αὐτῷ πειρατῶν τὰς βασάνους.
   Τὰς γοῦν τοσαύτας ἐκφυγὼν τρικυμίας
Θεοῦ κελεύσει καὶ προνοίᾳ καὶ κρίσει,
ἂν κατὰ νοῦν λάβοιμι βαδίσαι πάλιν
εἰς τοὺς ἀνίκμους τῆς Παλαιστίνης τόπους,   190
εἰ μή τις ἑλκύσει με πρὸς τούτους βίᾳ,
εἰς χεῖρας ἐμπέσοιμι τῶν ἀλλοθρόων.
Χριστῷ δὲ δόξα τῷ διεξάγοντί με
καὶ τηλικούτων κινδύνων σεσωκότι.

---

[118] I have made use of the ingenious (but doubtful) conjecture of Horna, ἡφαιστίων (better ἡφαιστείων). But perhaps one should read ἢ θηρίον, understanding "better to fall into a fire or (to meet with) a wild beast than..."). Cf. Manasses, *Aristandros and Kallithea*, frg. 1, 7, "'Αλλ' ἦν οὐδέν, ὡς ἔοικε, χεῖρον ἀνδρὸς βαρβάρου, / οὐ πῦρ, οὐχ ὕδωρ, οὐδὲ θήρ, οὐδὲ θαλάττης χάσμα". The double ἢ in different meanings could be a difficulty but also a rhetorical trick, and can have caused the corruption.

[119] Cf. Psalm 77:24, "καὶ ἔβρεξεν αὐτοῖς μαννα φαγεῖν". The other examples refer

whose tongue and mouth is able to describe these things?
Preferable the plunge into volcano fire[118]   170
to capture by the wickèd pirates of the sea.
For woe betide the miserable and poor man
who saw himself, alas, being a captive in their nets!
They don't even respect a man who manna rains,[119]
who can extinguish fire and cool a furnace down,   175
who knows to break to pieces lion's molars all.
They only do demand valises full of gold
and if one doesn't provide (for where to find that much),
they will then hang him by the balls, hit him with sticks,
tie him securely to the mast and keelhaul him,   180
until he will have lost his life, broken by force!
I think, the one who will be captured in their snares
he will be handed to no lesser hangmen than
the ones of that most fearful Judgement-Day,
even escaped as sinner from the evil ghosts:[120]   185
the torments caused by pirates are more than enough!

   Thus from these tides of miseries escaped
at the command and providence and will of God:
should I get in my head again the intention of
a travel to the dry regions of Palestine   190
- unless someone will draw me there with all his force-
then may I fall into the hands of foreigners!
But, well, glory to Christ who brought me liberty
and saved me from the dangers which thus threathened me.

---

to the story of Daniel. For συγκαταθλᾷ cf. Athenaeus, VIII, 348 f. (quoting Macho), "συγκατέθλα τὸ ποτήριον".

[120] Τοὺς τελώνας: allusion to the "publicans", who test the souls of the dead during their route to heaven. Cf. *Vita Johannis Eleemonis*, cap. 44, in Leontios de Néapolis, *Vie de Syméon le Fou et Vie de Jean de Chypre*, ed. A.J. Festugière and L. Rydén (Paris, 1974), p. 396, l. 100-1, "τί σύ, ταπεινὲ Ἰωάννη, ἔχεις εἰπεῖν ὅταν ἀπαντῶσιν εἰς πρόσωπόν σου οἱ ὠμοὶ ἐκεῖνοι καὶ ἄσπλαγχνοι τελῶναι καὶ φορολόγοι".

Conclusion

Manasses' poem is one of the few Byzantine documents which point directly to contacts between Byzantines and westerners in the Crusader States. On the one hand, we have to do with a document that is too personal to be informative about the real political relations between Constantinople and the western Middle East; on the other hand, the personal reflections of a person who did not bear political responsibility in this expedition gives a clear idea about the feelings of a Constantinopolitan intellectual with regard to regions outside the capital. In this respect his observations during the journey about the character of the places which were visited are very interesting. As a Christian, he is satisfied to have visited the Holy Places (and the manner in which he gives his report suggests that he indeed visited these places), but he reveals himself as a critical observer. At the same time it is clear that he suffered from homesickness, which became worse because of the very real diseases which afflicted him. One may assume that his negative view of Cyprus was influenced by his precarious health. Striking, however, is his outspokenness about the causes of his second illness. His attitude towards the westerners is, in a way, ambiguous. On the one hand, he is curious about and impressed by the girl who might be the prospective empress, on the other, he fiercely demonstrates the usual Byzantine arrogance towards foreigners in general and westerners in particular. As has already been remarked above, the fact that his report has been presented in the iambic trimeter suggests that Manasses wished to see his work as a classical messenger's report. He followed, of course, the Byzantine metrical rules, but proved, within these shackles, to be a very inventive linguist who succeeded in telling his story in an attractive and effective way.

Abbreviations Used in the Footnotes

Aerts, "Das literarische Porträt"
    W.J. Aerts, "Das literarische Porträt in der byzantinischen Literatur", in *Groningen Colloquia on the Novel VIII*, ed. H. Hofmann and M. Zimmerman (Groningen, 1997), pp. 151-95.
Horna   K. Horna, "Das Hodoiporikon des Konstantin Manasses", *Byzantinische Zeitschrift*, 13 (1904).
Lampe   G.W.H. Lampe, *A Patristic Greek Lexicon* (Oxford, 1991[10]).
LBG   E. Trapp, *Lexikon zur byzantinischen Gräzität* (Vienna, 1994 ff.).
LSJ   H.G. Liddell, R. Scott and H.S. Jones, *A Greek-English Lexicon* (Oxford, 1940[9]).

Manasses, *Aristandros and Kallithea*
    Manasses, *Aristandros and Kallithea*, in *Il romanzo bizantino del XII secolo*, ed. F. Conca (Torino, 1994).
Manasses, Σύνοψις ἱστορική
    Manasses, Σύνοψις ἱστορική, ed. I. Bekker, CSHB (Bonn, 1837).

EAST MEETS WEST, AND MONEY CHANGES HANDS

D. M. Metcalf

A Westphalian pilgrim in the 1330s, Ludolf of Suchem or Sudheim, visited Cyprus in the days of its greatest prosperity under the Lusignans, and in a well-known passage of his memoirs described Famagusta as a city of millionaires.

> "It is the richest of all cities, and her citizens are the richest of men. A citizen once betrothed his daughter, and the jewels of her head-dress were valued by the French knights who came with us as more precious than all the ornaments of the queen of France... In this city in one shop is more aloe wood than five carts could carry away."

That there are very rich merchants is

> "a thing not to be wondered at, for Cyprus is the furthest of Christian lands, so that all ships and all wares... must needs come first to Cyprus... And daily from the rising of the sun to its going down are heard rumours and news. And the tongues of every nation under heaven are heard and read and talked."[1]

If we move back to the twelfth century, we find William of Tyre giving a somewhat similar description of another great *entrepôt* of medieval trade:

> "Alexandria has the reputation" (he writes) "of receiving a larger supply of wares of every description than any other maritime city. Whatever our world lacks in spices, pearls, oriental treasures, and foreign wares is brought here from the two Indies, Saba, Arabia, even from both the Ethiopians and from Persia and other lands nearby. Thus masses of people from East and West flock there, making Alexandria the market-place of both worlds."[2]

Benjamin of Tudela gives a similar picture of Constantinople, and compares it with the grandeur of Baghdad.[3] All this is familiar information, and well enough known, or should be.

One aspect of pre-crusades contacts between the Italian cities and the long-distance luxury trade of the East had been that the western mer-

---

[1] C.D. Cobham, *Excerpta Cypria: Materials for a History of Cyprus* (Cambridge, 1908), pp. 19-20.
[2] Quoted in J. Prawer, *The World of the Crusaders* (Jerusalem, 1972), p. 141.
[3] *Ibid.*, p. 141.

chants could not penetrate beyond the points of exchange. The *funduqs* in the Muslim cities of the Levant coast were to go as far as they were allowed: anywhere beyond was "out of bounds". In this way the local rulers were able to control the trade, to tax it,[4] and to preserve their valuable monopoly. With the creation of the Latin states, the points of exchange fell into western hands. Muslim merchants brought their goods to ports such as Acre, Tyre, and Tripoli. In the thirteenth century the balance swung a little further, and western merchants were able to proceed as far as Alexandria, Damascus, or even Baghdad.

The interface of the *funduqs* is symbolic of the monetary problem on which I want to focus, and to put into its commercial context: the traders who travelled the long-distance routes and brought precious goods from the East to the Mediterranean seaboard had to be paid, in money (even if they then spent the money on a profitable cargo for the return journey). East met West, and money changed hands. What sort of money? How were the very different coins of the Christian and the Islamic states interchanged? The twelfth-century manual of al-Šayzārī says, in illustration of a legal point, "There are those who purchase dinars with dirhams of silver or with Frankish *qarāṭīs*...". The Muslim name *qirṭās* evidently refers here to the billon deniers of the Crusader States.[5] We know that money-changers had their tables adjacent to the bazaar, in a regular place allocated to them. The Genoese notary at Famagusta, Lamberto di Sambuceto, was in the habit of describing in each of his documents the place within the city where it was drawn up, e.g. "actum in Famaguste in banchis cambiorum Famaguste" — at the tables of the money-changers of Famagusta, or simply "ante cambia". But at the end of the day, even money-changers have to square their accounts. If the merchants from East and West both were using coins of the same metal, there would be no big problem. Silver can be recycled by the mint, from dirhams into deniers, and gold can be recycled by the mint, from dinars into bezants, but transmuting silver into gold is strictly for alchemists. If there was a persistent surplus of one metal, what were they to do about

---

[4] Similarly under the crusader rulers. An inventory from Tyre (G.L.Fr. Tafel and G.M. Thomas, *Urkunden zur älteren Handels- und Staatsgeschichte Venedigs*, 3 vols (Vienna, 1856-7), II, p. 385) shows the king taking 3,892 bezants annually by farming out the fees for the uses of balances and measures in the market.

[5] R. Irwin, "The Supply of Money and the Direction of Trade in Thirteenth-Century Syria", in *Coinage in the Latin East: The Fourth Oxford Symposium on Coinage and Monetary History*, ed. P.W. Edbury and D.M. Metcalf, British Archaeological Reports, International Series, International Series, 77 (Oxford, 1980), pp. 73-104, at p. 93 and n. 111.

it? This is the problem that we should be considering. Silver or gold may, of course, simply have accumulated in a country, as it did in Famagusta in the first half of the fourteenth century, in the hands of the middlemen whose personal profits made them so wealthy. Some of this wealth was stored in the form of money, and through taxation and other processes it was spread around the Kingdom of Cyprus. The whole island benefited from the wealth earned in Famagusta. From *ca.* 1295 the surplus stock of money was held almost entirely in silver coinage, not gold,[6] and it seems clear from what Pegolotti tells us that much of the silver originated in the West, — essentially because western merchants bought more goods than they sold. Although the money supply was only one aspect of the country's wealth, it is a conspicuous aspect, and perhaps the only quantifiable aspect. If merchants built themselves fine houses, and filled them with treasures, that is something we cannot easily assess. But an accumulating stock of coinage, e.g. in Cyprus, reflects a balance-of-payments surplus, and it offers a continuous statistical series. Indeed this may be the most secure historical evidence of the country's budget or commercial balance-sheet. The historian will be particularly interested in changes to the balance-sheet, especially large-scale changes or sudden changes.

Thus, the opening-up of Armenia, to take another example, by the chrysobulls which Levon I granted, first to Genoa and then to Venice, in 1201[7] seems to have triggered an almost immediate flooding of the country with high-value western-style silver coinage — but the coins were neither Genoese nor Venetian: they were locally-minted coins of the kings of Armenia, recycling the inflows of Italian money which created a balance-of-payments surplus.

Another vignette comes from Cyprus, again from the golden age of King Hugh IV. A merchant from Barcelona, named Joan Benet, made a trading venture to Famagusta in 1343. Because some two dozen partners had invested capital in the venture, Benet needed to be strictly accountable, and to distribute the profits correctly. He therefore kept meticulous accounts of all his receipts and expenses, and thus, most unusually, gives us as detailed a picture of all the commodities which he bought and sold, their prices and their profitability, as we could ever wish.[8] He took with

---

[6] The evidence for this statement is discussed in D.M. Metcalf, "A Hoard of Venetian Gold Ducats from the Outskirts of Nicosia", *Report of the Department of Antiquities, Cyprus* (forthcoming).

[7] V. Langlois, *Le trésor des chartes d'Arménie, ou Cartulaire de la Chancellerie royale des Roupéniens* (Venice, 1863), p. 110.

[8] J. Plana i Borràs, "The Accounts of Joan Benet's Trading Venture from Barcelona to Famagusta: 1343", *Epetiris tou Kentrou Epistemonikon Ereunon*, 19 (1992), pp. 105-68.

him to Cyprus saffron, rice, and mercury, but in no great quantities. Silver made up 88.5% of the value of what he carried. He brought with him many hundreds of pounds of the good-silver coins of Barcelona[9] (and some from Sardinia[10]), to spend on sugar and spices. The circulation of such coins in Cyprus, however, was forbidden. He had to sell them to the mint, receiving in exchange the official Cypriot silver coins of Hugh IV. This process of recycling of silver stocks was going on continuously in the context of international trade, and alas it deprives us of the evidence of where the silver was coming from. Benet's transactions with Ser Bartolo, *comprador per la secha* (the buyer for the mint) are carefully recorded in his account book. For his Catalan silver he received in total many thousands of gros of Cyprus — having paid, of course, a commission for the reminting. He bought pepper in 100-kg sacks, on which he eventually made a net profit of about 33% of the purchase price; cinnamon from Ceylon and south India, very profitable; ginger from Colombo and from Mecca; cloves from the East Indies; incense from Alexandria; borax, cotton, and brazil dye-stuff, all in quantities and at prices that are recorded in detail; and he bought large amounts of Cyprus sugar. Not all the profit came from the long-distance transit trade.

Ships from Italy and the West were docking in Famagusta week in and week out. Joan Benet's financial transactions could be multiplied many, many times; his just happens to be the venture of which records have survived. In his case he was exporting far more than he was importing into Cyprus, and settling the balance in silver. Whether that was typical of Italian merchants, we do not know; but Hugh IV was able to strike silver gros weighing 4.54g in great quantities, adding to a stock of currency which had been building up through the reign of Henry II, and which by 1380 probably totalled in excess of 20 million coins. We can know this from die-studies of Hugh's coins and of those of Henry II which allow us to say quite accurately how many dies were used; and also from hoards which, by their extended age-structure, reveal that the stock of currency was steadily growing.[11] This is the visible sign of the

---

[9] The *alfonsins d'argent*, named after Alfonso II, 1285-91, and always of the same distinctive design, weighed *ca*. 3.20 g of good silver. They were issued for many decades.

[10] Interchangeable as to quality and weight.

[11] Although the numbers of dies employed are known quite accurately, it is difficult to extrapolate to the numbers of coins struck, because we do not know the average output of a reverse die (here estimated conservatively at 10,000 coins), nor the wastage rate. For a fuller statement of the arguments on which the arithmetic rests, see D.M. Metcalf, "Die-Studies of the Lusignan Coinage: Their Potential for Historical Research", *Epetiris tou Kentrou Epistemonikon Ereunon*, 19 (1992), pp. 1-17; *idem*, *The Silver Coinage of Cyprus, 1285-1382*, Corpus of Lusignan Coinage, 2, ed. D.M. Metcalf and A.G. Pitsillides (Nicosia, 1996), esp. at p. 24.

balance of payments: not Spanish or Italian coins, but the local kind, and it is the quantity, and the changes in the accumulated quantity, that reflect the commerce.

The long-distance trade in sugar and spices and other luxury goods flowing westwards could perhaps be compared to the oil pipe-lines of today, which reach the Mediterranean coast from further east. They are delivering a valuable export commodity week in and week out, but politically they are low-profile. You will not see them mentioned in the newspapers very often. And yet this trade is important to all the parties involved, in varying degrees. Its contribution to the economic prosperity of the countries through which the trade passes, and more obviously its contribution to tax revenues, are such that one can speak of its strategic significance in underpinning national economies. This significance is perhaps greater than its monetary value would imply. It is difficult to guess even approximately what proportion of the gross national product (as we should call it today) the spice trade made up. We have a document summarizing the receipts and payments from the royal treasure in the time of King Janus, in 1412-13, which suggests that the local economy of Cyprus was thriving; but of course, that was at a time when the revenues of Famagusta were lost to the Kingdom.[12]

If a key export commodity can be so low-profile, the corresponding counter-flows of goods (or money) are even more so. In the crusader period they are virtually invisible, at least in the sense that it is very difficult for a historian to grasp their general significance. Whereas the contracts registered by Genoese notaries give us a good general idea of the activities of western merchants, we have little or no corresponding information about the personal affairs of Muslim merchants, who must also have taken their profit. That is partly because the imports were so miscellaneous, and because they were commodities that people could do without, at a pinch. Grain might be exported from Sicily to the Latin Kingdom, and perhaps onwards into Muslim Syria, but if there was a poor harvest and little grain was available, there was no point in complaining. There is plenty of anecdotal evidence, but how can one tell whether the balance of imports and exports resulted in a regional surplus or a deficit? Coinage is the nearest thing we have to systematic evidence, in the sense that the stock of currency in any of the Crusader States reflects, more or less, the bottom line of the national balance-sheet.

[12] G. Grivaud, "Un état des comptes du royaume de Chypre en 1412-1413", *Bulletin de Correspondance Hellénique* 122/1 (1998), pp. 377-401.

A chain of payments in the twelfth to fourteenth centuries stretches all the way from Spain to Ceylon and the East Indies. At half-a-dozen points the producers, shippers, and merchants had to make their profit, out of the price eventually paid by the consumer. Much of the chain is hidden from us by the lack of surviving written evidence, especially in the Muslim lands. Where exactly did East meet West in the fourteenth century? — in Famagusta (where the tongues of every nation under heaven were heard and read and talked), or in the cities of the Levant coast? Whose ships carried the commodities between the mainland and Cyprus? Even where we have excellent evidence, as in the crusader kingdoms and principalities, the resulting balance-of-payments situation is difficult to assess. It seems clear enough, however, that from *ca.* 1150 or even earlier, until *ca.* 1250 the Crusader States were a link in the chain where both gold and silver coinage were in use. In that same period the currency of the West (except for Sicily) was almost exclusively of silver, and had been since Carolingian times, whereas the Islamic states of the Near East relied on gold as their standard currency, and indeed suffered from a silver famine until *ca.* 1175 or later. Broadly speaking, silver was the sole precious-metal currency of the West, and gold was the sole precious-metal currency of the East: there was a kind of polarization across the Mediterranean. The general availability of gold or silver differed, and the use of one or the other was then reinforced by technical considerations. The polarization began to swing around from *ca.* 1216, when the Islamic states were again accumulating significant stocks of silver, and crucially from 1252, when both Genoa and Florence began to mint their famous gold coins, the *genovino d'oro* and the *fiorino d'oro*. The Italian states now had to learn how to manage a bimetallic currency. Professor Lopez celebrated the 700th anniversary of this initiative in 1952 with an article in the *Economic History Review* entitled "Back to Gold".[13] In 1967 in the same journal Professor A. M. Watson wrote a wide-ranging article of great interest about the polarization of the coinage metals in the Mediterranean world, under the title, "Back to Gold — and Silver", in which he suggested that "the European gold famine and the Islamic silver famine were two sides of the same coin", and that the Latin Kingdom was "a point of leverage around which the monetary history of both East and West turned". The mechanism or the motor which drove the polarization was, he suggested, a dif-

---

[13] R.S. Lopez, "Back to Gold, 1252", *Economic History Review*, 2nd Ser., 9 (1956-57), pp. 219-40.

ferential in the price ratio of silver and gold in East and West.[14] This is not the place to enter into any detailed criticism of Watson's handling of the numismatic evidence in his pioneering study of more than thirty years ago.[15] Almost every chapter of crusader numismatics has been radically revised in the last thirty years — Antioch, Tripoli, the Latin Kingdom, Cyprus — and numismatic expertise has been directed more towards the needs of monetary history by sharpening the focus on the detailed chronology of the coins, and by attempts to establish the quantities in which coins were minted. I will just say that the whole topic has recently been revisited by Spufford in his magisterial book, *Money and its Uses in Medieval Europe*. The broad picture of African gold reaching the southern shores of the Mediterranean, and north European silver reaching the northern shores of the same, and thus creating a gradient in relative values,[16] is fairly clear. But if we try to relate the broad trends specifically to what was happening in the Latin Kingdom of Jerusalem in the twelfth century, conviction somehow dissolves into doubt. Where there are bimetallic currencies in regions A and B, any difference in the gold: silver ration between the two will be exploited, by street-wise traders eager to make a "fast buck" — or a fast *fiorino* — whatever prohibitions governments seek to impose.[17] But up until 1252 there was not a bimetallic currency in the West; that is to say, for most of the lifetime of the mainland Crusader States (which ended, of course, in 1289-91). By 1252 the most interesting developments in crusader coinage had already taken place. Until 1252, how exactly is Andrew Watson's fulcrum or point of leverage supposed to have operated? His thesis was widely noticed, but one is not convinced that it applies to the period 1100-1250.

Something similar is true of the period following the Mongol incursions. The shock-waves of the coming storm were first felt on the Levant coast from *ca.* 1240, well before the invasions of 1259-61. Trade was dislocated far inland by the advance of the Mongols, and instead of

[14] A. M. Watson, "Back to Gold and Silver", *Economic History Review*, 20 (1967), pp. 1-34.
[15] There are various technical pitfalls, e.g. the names of moneys of account may conceal the nature of the actual coins in which payment was made; the ratio of intrinsic value between a state's gold and silver coins may be distorted by a deliberate over-valuation of one or the other (to discourage its export); exchange-rates in contracts may deliberately conceal an element of payment of interest; and one needs to have at least a rough idea of the scale on which coinages were issued, and how much wastage they suffered.
[16] P. Spufford, *Money and its Uses in Medieval Europe* (Cambridge, 1988), esp. ch. 7, "European Silver and African Gold".
[17] *Ibid.*, p.179.

reaching the Mediterranean in the ports of the Latin states, it tended to be diverted either northwards or southwards, to Cilician Armenia or to Egypt. Coastwise trade, north-south along the Levant coast, grew in relative importance. We are well informed about the context of trade in the Muslim countries from the mid-thirteenth century onwards. Irwin has written very well on "The Supply of Money and the Direction of Trade in Thirteenth-Century Syria" drawing on Islamic written sources of many kinds.[18] But again, for the century and a half from *ca.* 1100 to *ca.* 1250, that is, for most of the life-time of the Crusader States, there is relatively little information.

For the historian who is interested in change, the most promising statistical series is the balance-of-payments surplus or deficit. It is, as we have seen, only a partial measure of accumulating or wasting wealth, but it should be a reasonably reliable index. A preliminary review suggests that it may sometimes have varied significantly from decade to decade. By focussing on chronologically near-by comparisons, one may hope to discount many factors which stayed the same, and isolate those which caused the change in the regional stocks of precious metal. In a situation where each crusader state tended to have its own controlled currency, from which foreign coins were excluded, the national stock of coinage reflects the bottom line in a balance sheet, in which the profits of long-distance trade were a major item. In the Latin Kingdom, however, it is a confusing indicator of trade, because there were also considerable net receipts year in and year out from pilgrimage and from other subsidies,[19] and on the negative side (probably) expenditure on the defence of the Kingdom, and all the damage and waste caused by warfare. Because pilgrimage was heavily concentrated in the Latin Kingdom, where the Holy Places lay, it should be a useful exercise to check for differences with the monetary affairs of Antioch and Tripoli. In particular, the accumulation of a stock of gold currency in Tripoli, and the lower levels or absence of gold at Antioch, as also in Armenia, should attract historical attention. Until *ca.* 1250, the northern cities were also transfer points on long-distance trade-routes. The Genoese, for example, long had a quarter in Tripoli.

We return now to the swing in polarization in the early thirteenth century. We know that from 1216 onwards the crusaders minted large quantities of imitative silver dirhams, which are virtually indistinguishable

[18] See note 5.
[19] D.M. Metcalf, "The Templars as Bankers and Monetary Transfers between West and East in the Twelfth Century", in *Coinage in the Latin East* (see n. 5), pp. 1-17.

from the Muslim coins they copy. They seem to have been essentially an export currency destined to be spent in Damascus or Aleppo.[20] At the same time, the minting of gold dinars in Syria dwindled.[21] This should perhaps raise the general question whether the imitative gold dinars, alias crusader bezants, may not also have had a role in the twelfth century in transferring the balance of payments further eastwards. Everybody involved in using them knew perfectly well that their intrinsic value was less than that of a dinar. There was no question of deceiving the Muslims or of subverting their economy;[22] but if the bezants had a role as an export currency, their imitative design may have smoothed the path of commerce by not offending sensibilities.

During the first half of the twelfth century the Crusader States seem to have had a relatively small stock of currency of any kind. The billon denari of Lucca and the deniers of Valence were imported from the West and were allowed to circulate, in Antioch as well as in Jerusalem.[23] The gold bezants of this first phase have had such a low survival-rate[24] that it is impossible for us to work out whether that was because they were originally scarce (probably they were) or because they were drained eastwards as an export currency. From about 1140, all three mainland states (Jerusalem, Tripoli, and Antioch) instituted controlled national currencies in billon, at very much the same time. In considering whether Jerusalem enjoyed any advantage over the others because of extra revenues arising out of pilgrimage, one should take account also of the gold bezants, which were minted in very considerable quantities from *ca.* 1148, and which were certainly in use within the Latin Kingdom.

---

[20] M.L. Bates and D.M. Metcalf, "Crusader Coinage with Arabic Inscriptions", in *A History of the Crusades*, VI, ed. H.W. Hazard and N.P. Zacour (Wisconsin, 1989), pp. 421-82, where Section C, "Crusader Arabic Silver Issues", was written by Bates.

[21] Irwin, "Supply of Money" (see n. 5), p. 86 and n. 76.

[22] Cf. the pioneering work, now superseded, A.S. Ehrenkreutz, "Arabic Dinars Struck by the Crusaders: A Case of Ignorance or of Economic Subversion", *Journal of Economic and Social History of the Orient*, 7 (1964), pp. 165-82; A.A. Gordus and D.M. Metcalf, "Neutron Activation Analysis of the Gold Coinages of the Crusader States", *Metallurgy in Numismatics*, 1 (1980), pp. 119-50.

[23] At one stage it seemed not impossible that many of the denari of Lucca found in the Crusader States were local imitations. This would have had intriguing implications for inter-regional bullion flows and thus for the monetary history of the Latin East in the first half of the twelfth century, which is very much an under-documented period. The last piece of the argument has been put in place, proving that they are indeed all Italian, in M. Matzke, "Der Denar von Lucca als Kreuzfahrermünze", *Schweizer Münzblätter*, 43 (1993), pp. 36-44.

[24] On Type BY 26, see now D.M. Metcalf, "Crusader Gold Bezants of the Latin Kingdom of Jerusalem: Two Additional Sources of Information", *Numismatic Chronicle*, 160 (2000) (forthcoming).

Tripoli, too, had its own design of gold bezants, but they seem not to have been nearly so plentiful as those of Jerusalem, until the thirteenth century. Antioch, perhaps surprisingly, did not mint gold. The bezants of Antioch mentioned in the sources would seem to be based on actual coins imported from Tripoli or the Latin Kingdom; and sometimes they may be merely moneys of account.[25] Mint-output in billon, however, was particularly strong in Antioch, using up hundreds of pairs of dies, and creating an accumulating stock of currency from the 1160s onwards. The Antiochene currency weathered the shock of Ḥaṭṭin much better than that of Jerusalem, where the authorities were forced progressively to debase the "Amalricus" deniers — or, to speak more precisely, to reduce their average weight. The two or three decades after Ḥaṭṭin, when the territorial extent of the Latin Kingdom was so severely reduced, were a difficult time, but inflows of western money seem to have continued on a considerable scale, even though compulsory reminting was in abeyance. The French feudal coins which are so common as archaeological site-finds present the numismatist with some difficult technical problems of chronology,[26] but in the present context one may remark that it was in the general interest that trade should go on, in spite of hostilities. Cyprus, from the safety of its off-shore position, began to benefit financially from others' misfortunes almost immediately, that is, before the death of Guy in 1194.[27]

But it was a century later, in 1289-91, that the merchants who fled from Acre and the other cities of the Levant coast to settle in Famagusta, brought immense prosperity to Cyprus. When they came as refugees they did not bring cartloads of aloe wood with them, but they doubtless

---

[25] *Ibid.*; D.M. Metcalf, "Monetary Questions Arising out of the Role of the Templars as Guardians of the Northern Marches of the Principality of Antioch", Central European University Symposium (forthcoming).

[26] These are explained in D.M. Metcalf, *Coinage of the Crusades and the Latin East in the Ashmolean Museum* (Oxford, 1995²), ch. 16, "European Coins Imported into the Holy Land from the Time of the Third Crusade Onward". For an example of chronological revision, see L. Travaini, "Provisini di Champagne nel Regno di Sicilia: Problemi di datazione", *Revue Numismatique* (1998), pp. 211-29. Note the relative absence of the European coins in the Antioch excavations.

[27] The homespun nature of Guy's reign may be seen as part of Machairas' origin-myth of the Lusignan dynasty, and not closely in accordance with the evidence: D.M. Metcalf, "Money in the Sweet Land of Cyprus", in *Kupros apo ten proistoria stous neoterous khronous*, Cultural Foundation of the Bank of Cyprus, Annual Lectures (Nicosia, 1995), pp. 243-69. On the crowded chronology of Guy's coinage in gold, billon, and copper, see D.M. Metcalf, *The White Bezants and Deniers of Cyprus, 1192-1285*, Corpus of Lusignan Coinage, 1, ed. D.M. Metcalf and A.G. Pitsillides (Nicosia, 1998), at pp. 9 f., 28 ff., 77 ff., 107 ff., and 124.

brought pearls and precious stones, and — even more valuable in the long run — their business acumen, their network of contacts, and their ability to speak the languages.

Financial and economic strength are prerequisites of successful foreign policy, for any state. The accumulation of wealth by individual businessmen, or business families, is generally low-profile. The Cypriot economist Christodoulou, writing about the interplay of socio-political forces in the process of class formation, wisely observes that "access to wealth is everywhere wrapped up in secrecy and it is never known with any degree of accuracy even in the most open and best documented societies".[28] The processes of wealth-creation by merchants in the Levant attracted little enough written record, and such as there was has survived only patchily. Rulers granted privileges and immunities to the Genoese and the Venetians, and we can catch glimpses of their financial transactions through notarial documents. But the next link in the chain, from Acre or Tripoli into the Muslim world, is much less well known. What kind of coins did the Muslim merchants take back with them? They also were no doubt obliged to visit the mint, to convert the gold or silver of the Crusader States into the official currency of their own rulers. The evidence of monetary transfers disappears into the melting-pot.

The rulers of the Crusader States were certainly well aware of the yield from the tolls and taxes which they levied. But their economic management was, by modern standards, rather rudimentary. They often had more urgent political or military considerations to address, and there were class barriers and barriers of privilege which reduced the efficiency of their financial control. They may have judged, simply, that the decade-by-decade fluctuations in wealth-creation through commerce lay outside their ability to exercise any detailed control, and that the prosperity of their state was as heaven sent. East met West, and money changed hands, in a fruitful partnership, which helped to make the Crusader States viable.

The intentions of this paper have been to examine the monetary implications and the monetary ambiguities of long-distance trade passing through the Crusader States, and to clarify the methodology by which we may move from crusader numismatics to crusader monetary history. The historians of thirty and more years ago, who gave us the hypotheses

[28] D. Christodoulou, *Inside the Cyprus Miracle: The Labours of an Embattled Mini-Economy*, Minnesota Mediterranean and East European Monographs, 2 (1992), p. 207.

that have shaped our view of the broad trends and of the mechanisms, were not numismatists, and their enquiries were governed partly by the availability of surviving documents. One result was that they focussed on the period after *ca.* 1250, and perhaps tended to regard that as the norm. Where documentary sources are limited and insufficient to answer our questions, as they are, generally speaking, for the years 1100-1250, numismatic data are almost our only resource, and a chronological list of hoards is the student's basic text.[29] In order to create perspective, we need some idea, even if it is only a rough idea, of the quantities in which coins were minted, obtained by die-studies and statistical estimation. Such studies have been made for several of the major coinages of billon deniers,[30] and for the white bezants of Cyprus.[31] Similar projects for the gold bezants of the Latin Kingdom and of the County of Tripoli are high on the list of desiderata for future research.

---

[29] For a check-list of hoards, see the section "Hoards and Site Finds from the Latin East", in Metcalf, *Coinage of the Crusades and the Latin East* (see n. 26), pp. 308-63. For a simple exercise in using such material, see D.M. Metcalf,
"Describe the Currency of the Latin Kingdom of Jerusalem", in *Montjoie: Studies in Crusade History in Honour of Hans Eberhard Mayer*, ed. B.Z. Kedar, J. Riley-Smith, and R. Hiestand (Aldershot—Brookfield, Vermont, 1997), pp. 189-98.

[30] Summarized in Metcalf, *Coinage in the Latin East* (see n. 5), pp. 56 f., 122 ff., 162 ff., and 205. See now also M. Phillips and S. Tyler-Smith, "A Hoard of Tripoli Gros and Half Gros and French Gros Tournois", *Numismatic Chronicle*, 156 (1996), pp. 193-225.

[31] Metcalf, *White Bezants and Deniers of Cyprus* (see n. 27), pp. 27-63 and 123.

THE ICON OF THE VIRGIN *GALAKTOTROPHOUSA* IN THE COPTIC MONASTERY OF ST ANTONY THE GREAT AT THE RED SEA, EGYPT

A Preliminary Note

Zuzana Skalova[*]

Among the icons, recently re-discovered by restoration in Egypt, is a set, comprising the Nursing Virgin among four angelic guardians at the monastery of St Antony the Great — on the screen of the tiny chapel/*parecclesia* dedicated to the Four Creatures, which is, arguably, the oldest part, the *kellion,* of the Old Church (*text fig. 1* and *fig. 1*). Darkened icons in the unlit chapel gave the impression of being undistinguished recent work of Coptic *laiki techni*.[1] Yet, these misleadingly simple images — whose iconography absorbed various, even early

---

[*] Versions of this article were presented at the symposium at Hernen Castle and at the American Research Center (ARCE) in Cairo. It has benefitted from discussion at each of these places. Art works in the Old Church of the St Antony Monastery re-discovered by restoration, bear witness to Dutch achievements in research of Coptic art and its conservation. In 1988 in the framework of a small embassy project (KAP), the author and her first Egyptian trainee, Father Maximus el Antony, restored a dozen of icons in this monastery. From 1991 till 1994 the Royal Netherlands Embassy in Cairo financed another KAP (no. 3494), "Termite Control in the Coptic Monastery of St Antony", directed by the author. In cooperation with Professors Laura Sbordoni Mora and the late Paolo Mora from Rome the KAP prepared the preliminary stage for the salvation of the murals of the Old Church of the monastery — resulting in an impressive international enterprise. Between 1996 and 1999, the Italian team directed by Adriano Luzi and Luigi De Cesaris, transformed the gloomy neglected church into an Aladin's cave of mediaeval Coptic art. The Antiquities Development Project was funded by the United States Agency for International Development and managed by Michael Jones for the ARCE in collaboration with the Egyptian Supreme Council of Antiquities and the monastery of St Antony represented by Father Maximus.

My gratitude for permission to publish the icons goes to Father Maximus, who partly cleaned them in 1999. I would also like to thank the ARCE for enabling me to study their documentation, and especially Michael Jones who kindly provided the correct measurements of the panels and their settings, and Joost Hagen, Coptologist from Leiden University, for his careful reading of the draft of this article.

[1] Paul van Moorsel mentions the set as "icones récentes", see P.P.V. van Moorsel, avec contributions de P. Grossmann, K. Innemée et P.-H. Laferrière, *La peinture murale chez les Coptes*, III, *Les peintures du monastère de Saint-Antoine près de la Mer Rouge*, 2 vols, Mémoires publiés par les membres de l'Institut français d'Archéologie orientale du Caire, 112, 1-2 (Cairo, 1995 and 1997), I, p. 169. To Father Maximus the icons mattered as sacred pictures and, in 1998/99, he found time, to clean and retouch the Nursing Virgin, the Archangel Michael and, in part, the Archangel Rafael.

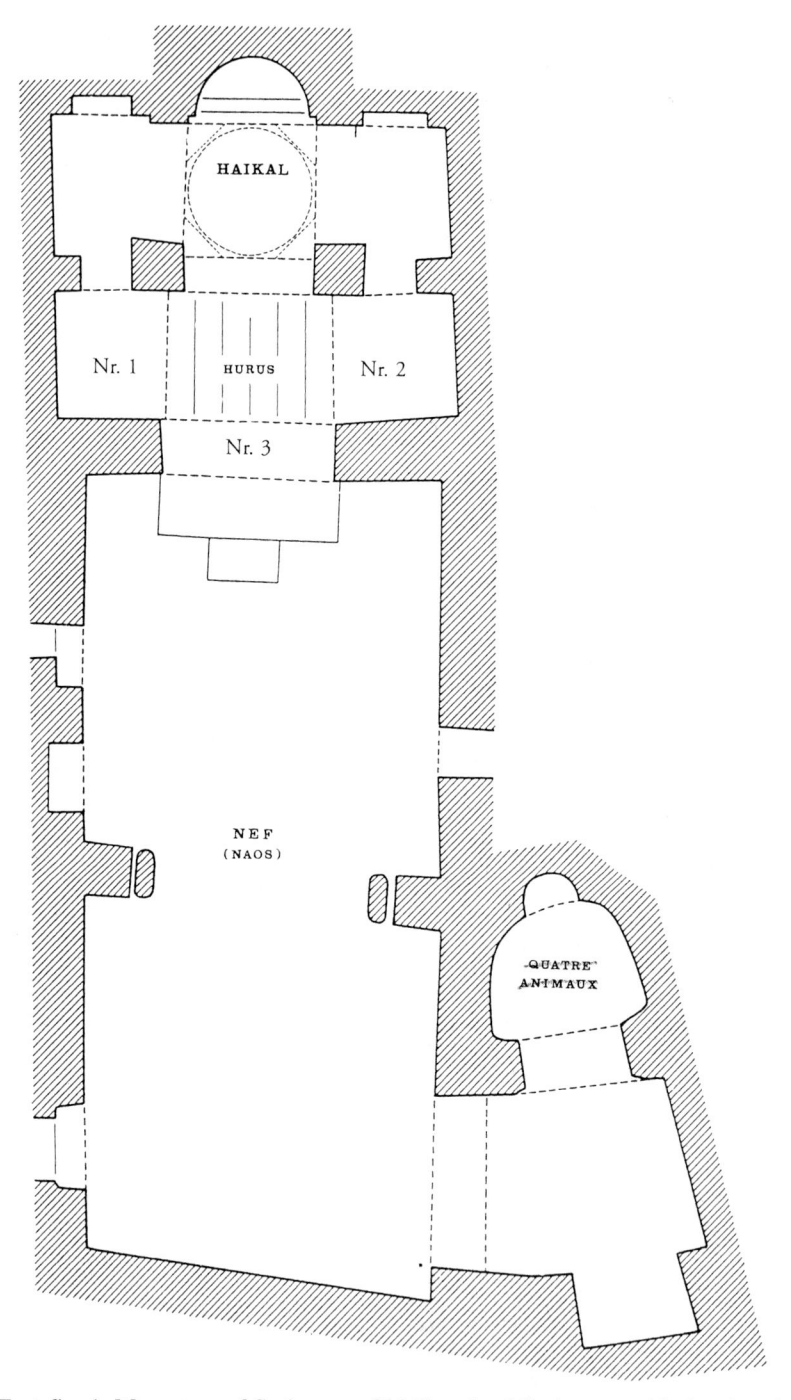

Text fig. 1. Monastery of St Antony, Old Church of St Antony with the chapel of the Four Creatures: ground plan.

Christian sources — might derive from some little known school of icon painting, more ancient.[2]

The five icons are placed in a single row at the top of a typically Coptic screen/*ḥijāb*,[3] liturgical furniture, screening the sanctuary from the beholder. It is an unassuming work, especially when compared with the mediaeval screens in the patriarchal urban churches of Cairo, exquisitely fashioned from hard wood and ivory.[4] Each icon is set into its own section within an elevated longitudinal framework.[5] The raised ochre surface of this "beam-setting"[6] is decorated in an unusual way with various elements executed in red. On the upper cornice runs a spiralled ornament, omnipresent in Egypt. The Nursing Virgin is surrounded by twelve different signs: cryptograms, ciphers, pentagrams (stars of David), diamonds and others, presumably magical.[7] A single motif is a

---

[2] The skeptical attitude towards the survival of mediaeval portable icons in Coptic collections is notorious. However, a few dozens of such panels have been re-discovered by re-restoration by the joint Egypt Netherlands Conservation of Coptic Icons Project 1989-96, directed by the author. See Zuzana Skalova's chapters "Medieval Icons in Arab and Mamluk Times" and the "Catalogue", nos 6-21, in Z. Skalova and G. Gabra, *Icons of the Nile Valley* (Cairo, 2002) (forthcoming).

[3] The screen is 2 m wide. For the earliest, seventh-century woodwork with comparable geometrical design, excavated in the desert monastery of St Epiphanius in western Thebes, see W.E. Crum, *The Coptic Monastery of St Epiphanius in Western Thebes*, I, figs 17-9, see A. Badawy, *Coptic Art and Archeology* (The Massachusetts Institute for Technology, 1978), fig. 1.2. Interestingly, the Old Church of St Antony is divided by plain wooden partitions and balusters, which demonstrate the same kind of local wood and workmanship as the chapel's *higab*. Rests of malachite-green encaustic paint, preserved on this woodwork, also occurs on the thirteenth-century commemorative crosses painted on the walls, see Van Moorsel, *Peintures du Monastère de Saint-Antoine* (see n. 1), II, fig. 100. Therefore, the woodwork may be mediaeval (see *fig 1*).

[4] L.-A. Hunt, analysing the formation of an Arab-Christian identity under Islam, pointed out that there has been a visual interplay between the Coptic patriarchal churches and the mosques of Cairo. The mediaeval carved Coptic screens were intended to mesmerise the eye of the beholder, the principle being "the same as recitation, with the design echoing the repetition of the sacred text and divine worship". The icons on these abstract screens offer a focus for the eye and for prayer, and for exegesis, see L.-A. Hunt, "Churches of Old Cairo and Mosques of Al-Qahira: A Case of Christian-Muslim Interchange", *Mediaeval Encounters*, 2/1 (1996), pp. 43-66.

[5] The measurements of each icon (without frame) is 50 cm high, 33 cm wide and *ca.* 0,34 cm thick. The technique is traditional: on the white preparation layer, applied directly on wood, egg-tempera paint layer was covered by varnish. (It was not possible to analyse these materials).

[6] In Russia such archaic setting, called *tablovyj ikonostas* (beam-setting), would be decorated with floral ornament.

[7] At the Coptic congress in Leiden, Dr D. Frankfurter informed me, that such decoration is not an unusual setting for sacred images in the Christian East. However, the choice of patterns deserves a comment of specialists. M. Mayer's "Les rituels de la magie copte", in *L'art copte en Egypte: 2000 ans de Christianisme, 15 mai - 3 septembre 2000, Institut du monde arabe* (Paris, 2000), pp. 102-4; and *idem*, *The Magical Book of Mary and Angels* (Heidelberg, 1996), suggest directions for further research.

Fatimid/Mamluk-looking heraldic bird (a pelican?) with an S-curved neck (*fig. 2a*).[8] The remaining four vertical separations bear simple geometrical designs. The bottom cornice is inscribed with a dedicatory inscription in Arabic script, damaged and not yet fully cleaned and deciphered.[9] Icons, arcane framing, its decoration[10] and the woodwork setting seem contemporary, made *in situ*, to fit the sacred space.

I. THE ICONS

The Four Archangels

In the East angels are believed to be not simply pure immaterial spirits, but to consist of a substance occasionally visible to saintly mortals "whose eyes God has opened".[11] This belief gave them bodily form on the icons, young, beautiful and androgynous. Although our painter worked with vernacular simplicity, he successfully envisioned the supernatural androgynous countenance required of angelic beings. Their pale pointed faces, framed by blond locks and orpiment-haloes have something haunting, perhaps due to a visionary gaze. Such faces can occasionally be encountered among the religious Copts, who gaze with the very same eyes: transparent pools, surrounded by equally transparent shadows, as if seeing the invisible. The four archangels flanking the Nursing Virgin witness a mystical event.

The almost identical stocky figures of the archangels and their enormous wings fill the recessed space of each panel to the utmost (this being a typically Coptic stylistic feature). They are identified with red Coptic letters in the upper corners as Michael (O ΑΓΓΕΛΟC ΜΙΧΑΙΗΛ), Rafael (O ΑΓΓΕΛΟC ΡΑΦΑΗΛ) (left) (*fig. 2b*), Gabriel (O ΑΓΓΕΛΟC ΓΑΒΡΙΗΛ) and Suriel (O ΑΓΓΕΛΟC COPHYΛ [sic])

---

[8] Although dating by comparison of different media is perilous, the design of the carved woodwork, including birds, in the ceiling of *majlis* of the Coptic Deir al-Banāt in "Babylon"/Christian Old Cairo (*ca.* 1275-1325) should be mentioned, see B. O'Kane, "Domestic and Religious Architecture in Cairo: Mutual Influences", in *The Cairo Heritage: Essays in Honor of Laila Ali Ibrahim*, ed. D. Behrens Abouseif (Cairo, 2000), fig. 4.

[9] Father Maximus argues that the name Gabriel, included in this inscription, refers to the Coptic Patriarch Gabriel VII (1525-68), who refurbished the depleted monastery after 1524. The Coptologists Dr Gawdat Gabra and Dr Nessim Youssef date the palaeography of the inscriptions to the mid-eighteenth century.

[10] The ground layer applied on the icons continues on the framework.

[11] C. Mango, *Byzantium: The Empire of New Rome* (London, 1980), pp. 154-5.

(right) *(fig. 2c)*.[12] Wearing liturgical vestments of Byzantine inspiration, all archangels hold a sceptre and a disc, marked with a cross, and the monogram IC XC. These are traditional devices symbolizing the universality of the Kingdom of Christ, evoking the presence of God Incarnate, and honouring the Virgin as the Queen of Heaven.

Representations of angels holding a circular object, usually an *oblatio*, are common in Coptic art *(figs 2a, 2b, 3a, 4a and 7c, all with an oblatio)*.[13] However, in this assembly, as shall be argued below, the Christ-Child himself presents the *oblatio,* distinguished by its central position and golden colour. Then the angelic discs could be seals or mirrors[14] — the pictorial metaphors denoting spiritual vision, as mentioned in patristic literature popular in monastic circles in Egypt, like the works of St Clement of Alexandria, St Athanasius or St Ephrem the Syrian.[15] The mirror may even convey a certain degree of "magic" used by angels, as mediators between God and the human beings, to perceive the will of God, and to receive and reflect the divine grace and light.[16] The angels' minute high-set ears are aided by ribbons, which enhance the hearing of secret harmonies.

Significantly, Gabriel is shown pointing to his ear with the index finger of his right hand.[17] This "hearing gesture" alludes to the belief expressed by St Ephrem in his verses on the "ear conception" of the Virgin Mary, that during the Annunciation the divine Word of the Father, Logos, entered Mary through her ear *(fig. 2b)*.[18]

[12] The Arabic letters in the bottom corners are not yet fully cleaned and therefore remain unreadable.

[13] O.S. Madsen, "Michael and the Oblation: Towards the Interpretation of the Circular Object in Michaels hand in Coptic Pictorial Representations", *Bulletin de la Société d'Archéologie copte*, 21 (1971/73), pp. 105-15.

[14] Z. Gavrilović, "Discs Held by Angels in the Anastasis at Dečani", in *Byzantine East, Latin West: Art Historical Studies in Honour of Kurt Weitzmann*, eds Ch. Moss and K. Kiefer (Princeton, 1995).

[15] On St Clement of Alexandria's theory concerning the symbolism of the mirror see R. Mortley, "The Mirror and I. Corr. 13.12 in Epistomology of Clement of Alexandria", *Vigiliae Christianae*, 30 (1976), pp. 109-20; on Athanasius see A. Hamilton, "Athanasius and the Simile of the Mirror", in *Vigiliae Christianae*, 34 (1980), pp. 14-8; on St Ephrem see S. Brock, *The Luminous Eye: The Spiritual World Vision of St Ephrem* (Rome, 1985), pp. 52-8, 122, as quoted by Gavrilović, "Discs" (see n. 14), p. 227.

[16] According to Z. Gavrilović, in the late Middle Ages, glass mirrors were used by pilgrims to catch the beneficial rays of the exposed relics; see H. Schwarz, "The Mirror of the Artist and the Mirror of the Devout", in *Studies in the History of Art dedicated to W.E. Suida* (London, 1959), pp. 90-105.

[17] For Coptic angelology see C.D.G. Müller, *Die Engelenlehre der Koptischen Kirche* (Wiesbaden, 1959).

[18] I am indebted to Magdalena Kuhn for the following reference: O.F.A. Meinardus, "Zur Ohrenempfangnis Mariens bei den Kopten", *Kemet*, 8/1 (1999), pp. 40-1. For the

The Nursing Virgin

The Nursing Virgin is an early Christian image, which was frequently depicted in various media in Egypt.[19] Dr Elizabeth Bolman, in her recent doctoral dissertation, proposes a new meaning for this image. Focusing on the sixth to seventh-century wall paintings found in small cells in the Coptic monasteries of Apa Apollo and Ama Rachel at Bawit, and Apa Jeremiah at Saqqara,[20] her interpretation persuasively explains why the nursing image was appropriate for a male monastic viewer:

> "Drawing from Egyptian Christian texts which equate milk with flesh, blood and the eucharist, and which explain that God is the source of the milk in the Virgin Mary's breasts, the *galaktotrophousa* reads as a metaphor for Christ's flesh and blood and for the consumption of these substances. It is the *logos*, and the Medicine of Immortality. This interpretation of the nursing image is amplified by the physical setting for these wall paintings, and the ritual practices of the Coptic baptismal eucharist."[21]

However, early-Coptic *Galaktotrophousa*-images on pages of manuscripts (*fig. 3b*), on monastic walls (*fig. 4b*) or carved in stone, all show ordinary *human* suckling as known from pre-Christian images of Isis nursing infant Horus: the seated mother lovingly offers her breast to her infant and he suckles.[22]

The Nursing Virgin in the monastery of St Antony, which is the oldest Coptic painting on panel with this subject (known to me), differs

---

hagiographic source see Ephrem the Syrian's "Hymns to Mary", in *Bride of Light: Hymns on Mary from the Syriac Churches*, trans. S. Brock (Kerala, 1994), 16:6; 27:4-6; 28:2; 45:105 and 46:18. See also K. Urbaniak-Walczak, *Die "conceptio per aurem": Untersuchungen zum Marienbild in Ägypten unter besonderer Berücksichtigung der Malerei in El-Bagawat* (Altenberge, 1992).

[19] P.P.V. van Moorsel, "Die stillende Gottesmutter und die Monophysiten", in *Kunst und Geschichte Nubiens in christlicher Zeit: Ergebnisse und Probleme auf Grund der jungsten Ausgrabungen*, ed. E. Dinkler (Recklinghausen, 1970), pp. 281-90, fig. 285; reprinted in P.P.V. van Moorsel, *Called to Egypt: Collected Studies on Painting in Christian Egypt* (Leiden, 2000), pp. 225-36; M. Blanck-Ortolan, "The Virgo Lactans", in *Coptic Encyclopedia*, I, pp. 243-4; P. van Moorsel, "Galaktotrophousa", in *Coptic Encyclopedia*, II, pp. 531-2, and bibliography.

[20] E.S. Bolman, "The Coptic 'Galaktotrophousa' as the Medicine of Immortality" (unpublished dissertation, Brynn Mawr University, 1999). I am indebted to Dr Bolman for allowing me to read her unpublished dissertation.

[21] E.S. Bolman, "The Coptic Galaktotrophousa Revisited", *Abstracts of Papers: Seventh International Congress of Coptic Studies in Leiden, 27 August-2 September 2000* (Leiden, 2000), p. 17.

[22] A. Cutler, "The Cult of Galaktotrophousa in Byzantium and Italy", *Jahrbuch der Österreichischen Byzantinistik*, 37 (1987), pp. 335-50; L. Langener, *Isis lactans, Maria lactans: Untersuchungen zur Koptischen Ikonographie* (Altenberge, 1996), pp. 5-7, 277-82, ills and bibliography.

from the earlier full-length images of the enthroned Mary suckling her son in a number of ways (*fig. 2a*). First, the Nursing Virgin is portrayed holding the young adult-like Christ-Child in half-length *Hodegetria*-like pose.[23] This close-up renders the important details more visible. Secondly, different iconographic types of icons were apparently fused to create a specific new type. Mary holds the Christ-Child with her right hand, gesturing towards Him with her left, to indicate that He is the way to salvation. This gesture would be typical for her guise as the *Hodegetria* (the guide of the faithful who shows the way), were it not that Mary's hands, which are positioned on the same level, imply that she actually assumes an *orans* stance in prayer. This iconographical twist re-charged an ancient image into a new and powerful one.[24] Third, the hybrid image addresses the beholder with unconventional gestures, manipulating the subject and object of nourishment into a multi-layered theological statement. As the icon was conceived for a monophysite monastic environment, it can be assumed that it was based on literary sources used by the monks who inhabited the monastery of St Antony the Great. They were not only Copts; Syrians, Armenians and Ethiopians resided there as well. Such a culturally miscellaneous but dogmatically united non-Chalcedon environment places the St Antony's set in a larger interpretative context: the icons must have functioned within the community as visual re-interpretations of earlier tradition(s). As will be argued below, the Nursing Virgin blends biblical, patristic and liturgical sources, which, to quote a phrase by Dr Stephen Davis, "played upon one another resulting in the layering and merging of themes".[25] Also the hybrid style of the set suggests a mixed religious environment. So, the question is raised as to

---

[23] An older, perhaps a wonder-working icon — and not necessarily eastern — might have been replicated: the rendering of this image recalls Italian half-length madonnas, placed in the centre of a dossal or a polyptych, common in Romanesque Tuscan panel painting during the thirteenth century; for general information see E.B. Garrison, *Italian Romanesque Panel Painting: An Illustrated Index* (Florence, 1949). The impression is as if an existing form or a model was put to a new use. See the contribution by Kees van der Ploeg, "On Architectural and Liturgical Aspects of Siena Cathedral in the Middle Ages", in H. van Os, *Sienese Altarpieces 1251-1460: Form, Content, Function*, I, *1215-1344* (Groningen, 1988), I, p. 134, n. 102, fig. 12.

[24] H. Belting, *Likeness and Presence* (Chicago, 1994), p. 325. This freedom from adherence to the principle that each icon must derive from a recognisable sacred archetype seems not Byzantine (or Coptic?), but western.

[25] See Dr Davis' pioneering theological contribution in the joint article by Z. Skalova and S. Davis, "A Mediaeval Icon with Scenes from the Life of Christ and the Virgin in the Church of Abu Seifein, Cairo: An Interdisciplinary Approach", *Bulletin de la Société d'Archéologie copte*, 39 (2000), part 2, pp. 230-2.

what were the references and what caused the artist/patron to combine them on this unusual *Galaktotrophousa*.

Each detail takes on a special importance. The Mother and Child are tightly composed into a window-like frame allowing a glimpse in the celestial regions, symbolised by the blue background.[26] The adult-like Christ-Child, dressed as a philosopher in a light green *chiton* with a "golden" (orpiment) *clavus* and billowing orange *himation*, is barefoot. A prominent red cross, embellished with white ornamented triangles, marks his orpiment halo. Above it is the monogram IC XC. Mary, identified as the *Theotokos* (ΜΙΘΡ ΘΕΟ],[27] wears liturgical dress: a brown-red (modelled with black lines) *maforion,* fringed with one golden dotted line, over a partly open light green robe.

An unusual feature is a visible segment of her bosom, white as an unattached breast, which the sucking Child grasps with his right hand as he might a flask. Immediately beneath this white breast, Christ's left hand appears as if holding a second breast *(fig. 2a)*. Yet, this circular object is painted — like the haloes — with the orpiment.[28] The verses of an early Syrian liturgical hymn come to mind: "The Holy Spirit opened her bosom, And mixed the milk of the two breasts of the Father ..."[29]

As this second golden breast is of the size and shape of the Coptic Eucharistic Bread, *qurbān*,[30] it can be concluded that, while being nourished Himself, the Christ-Child simultaneously offers the nourishment — the true Bread of Life, the sacrament, which comes from Heaven — to the ideal beholder, a fasting monk in the desert; this being a visual metaphor of his own words, "I am the Bread of Life" (John 6:35).[31] The Christ-Child can thus also be identified as Host and as exe-

---

[26] The Icon as a window from earth into heaven, and vice versa, is a known metaphor. For the blue background see note 45.

[27] This *nomen sacrum*, seemingly Coptic, deserves attention of a specialist. See notes 9, 12 and 43.

[28] This is most probably *orpiment,* an intense yellow pigment with sacred connotations, which was already in the Pharaonic era used to substitute or represent gold.

[29] Odes of Solomon 19.1-5 (English trans. James H. Charlesworth), as quoted by Denise Kimber Buell, *Making Christians: Clement of Alexandria and the Rhetoric of Legitimacy* (Princeton, 1999), p. 126, n. 26. For this imagery reappearance in mediaeval Christian art see Caroline Walker Bynum, *Jesus as Mother: Studies in the Spirituality of the High Middle Ages* (Berkeley and Los Angeles, 1982).

[30] On the Coptic Eucharist see A.J. Butler, *The Ancient Coptic Churches* (Oxford, 1884; reprint Norwich, 1970), II, pp. 275f, fig. 33. Butler noted that the Coptic *korban* is stamped with twelve crosses: the innermost square, consisting of four smaller squares, is called in Coptic *isbodikon*, i.e. "the body of the Lord".

[31] Hence spiritual nourishment becomes a symbol of Christ's mission of salvation. Consequently, it can be deduced that the Christ-Child is not consuming *human* milk, and that his lactation has symbolic connotations. See Kimber Buell, *Making Christians* (see n. 29), ch. 8, esp. pp. 125-30.

gesis and this is what the beholder is invited to focus on when turning to the screen his eye and supplication.

This theological hieratic representation of the Virgin and her divine Child is without any trace of a human relationship between the two figures: they both give the impression of aloofness, as if having a transcendent, awe-inspiring experience. Their ecstatic expression testifies that the depicted act of nursing must be of a spiritual nature. The icon's monophysite connotation can be glimpsed in the demonstration of Christ's humanity by Incarnation, and his ability, deriving from his divinity, to offer spiritual nourishment/salvation to others. This identification of the Child and the Host bids the focus on the screen for the eye and the supplication — and the exegesis.[32]

II

One more recent feminist study (already quoted), also astutely reinterpreting ancient teachings, may be relevant for the understanding of St Antony's *Galaktotrophousa*. Denise Kimber Buell's *Making Christians: Clement of Alexandria and the Rhetorics of Legitimacy*, especially the chapters 9 and 10, "Perfect Children: Drinking the Logos-Milk of Christ" and "The Milk of the Father: Only Those who Suckle This Breast Are Truly Blessed", speak for themselves.[33]

The icon's creator might have been knowledgeable about teachings of this influential theologian and Christian pedagogue (A.D. 150-210) that a virginal human mother could not have human milk for her divine baby. It seems that he appropriated the maternal characteristics of feeding, in an attempt to depict an abstract idea, the imaginary breasts of the divine Father. Clement's words, reinterpreted by Dr Kimber Buell, elucidate this concept: "The one who gives/inspires rebirth, nourishes us with His own milk — the Logos" and "Thus, for Christ, nourishment was the ful-

---

[32] Another possible textual source of inspiration might be the Confession of Faith preceding the Eucharist. The Copts hold the doctrine of the Real Presence (i.e. of the change of the bread and wine into the very body and blood of Christ) in its most physical literalness: "I believe and confess that this is the body of our Lord and Saviour Jesus Christ, which He received from the mother of God, the holy Virgin Mary — *and made one with His Godhead, without sundering, mingling, or confounding.*" This Coptic clause was added by Gabriel III, the 78th patriarch, see Butler, *Ancient Coptic Churches* (see n. 30), II, p. 296.

[33] Kimber Buell, *Making Christians* (see n. 29), pp. 123-7. The quotations from Clement of Alexandria in this article are all taken from her book.

filment of the paternal will, whereas for us infants who seek the Logos of heaven, Christ himself is the nourishment."[34]

Clement of Alexandria's mystical interpretation of the Logos as being everything for the infant — father, mother, pedagogue and nurse —[35] were and still are (as became clear during a discussion with some religious Copts) very vital for the Coptic monks, who live in the barren desert in continuous fasting and focus on ascetic life in pursuit of salvation. This seems to be the theme shown: it is the Father, who provides breast milk in the form of Logos to his Infant, depicted on the icon, and to the beholders of the icon, to Christians in general and to the monks in particular, whose vows of chastity are traditionally compared to rebirth. According to Clement, the manifestations of the Logos are multiple and help in understanding spiritual realities. Clement even identifies God as a mother in his homiletic piece on St Mark the Evangelist, the Apostle of the Copts, still sung in the Coptic monasteries.

The Coptic hymnography, *Psalis,* Midnight Psalmodia and *Theotokia* also resonate with these antique perceptions. A few verses will suffice: "He is feeding, He is taking his physical body/humanity and offering us Bread of Life ..." (the Midnight Psalmodia); or "They likened the golden table to the altar and the oblation bread to the Body of the Lord ..."; and "The pot, made of pure gold, wherein was hidden the true manna, the Bread of Life, which came down from heaven, and unto the world to save life ..." (the *Theotokia* for Sunday, lauding Mary).[36]

Dr Kimber Buell reminds the reader that in the Near East region, the nurses still call the first flow of milk *manna*, which is, in the case of the Christ-Child, the metaphor for the divine Logos*:* "The Lord Christ — the fruit of the Virgin — did not bless women's breast or judge them to be nourishers ..." Mary's function on the icon seems liturgical too, as she personifies the Church: "The Church as proxy mother has no milk, she is a virgin, not really a woman. Instead — it is the Logos who is the milk she feeds to her own children. It is the Father's breast and the Logos milk, which provide the true spiritual nourishment."[37]

---

[34] Christa Ihm pointed to the *Paidagogos* by Clemens of Alexandria, 1.6. as a literary source for the iconography of Maria lactans: "Für die Ikonographie der Lactans muss aber gerade in Ägypten ausserdem ein gewisser Symbolgehalt vorausgesetzt werden, wenn Clemens Alexandrinus Maria und die Kirche gleichsetzen könnte und unter der Muttermilch, mit der sie ihre Kinder nährt, den Logos verstand." See Ch. Ihm, *Die Programme der Christlichen Apsismalerei vom vierten Jahrhundert bis zum Mitte Achten Jahrhunderts* (Wiesbaden, 1960), p. 58 and n. 16.

[35] Kimber Buell, *Making Christians* (see n. 29), p. 159f.

[36] *Coptic Psalmody* (New York, undated), p. 87.

[37] I quote Kimber Buell quoting Clements of Alexandria. For the source see *Paidagogos*, 1.6., PG (Paris, 1857-67), cc. 300-1.

Finally, St Ephrem the Syrian's verse on the link between the Eucharist and Mary, when she addresses her divine Son with the prophetic words, might have been another poignant source of inspiration for an Arabophone monophysite sponsor/viewer, living in Islamic Egypt:[38]

"Your Bread, my Child,
is even more to be honoured than Your body,
For unbelievers too saw Your body,
Whereas they fail to see Your living Bread."[39]

Though divided by controversies over the nature of Christ, Christians living under Muslim rule, were nevertheless united in their belief in the Incarnation of Christ — Islam defines Jesus as a prophet, not as the Son of God.[40] It is imaginable, that the Coptic patron, wishing to assert that Jesus was the Son of God, portrayed the "adult" Christ-Child as a divinity, purposefully underplaying the humanity of a charming baby, as would be done by a Byzantine or Italian master. The retrospective hieratic quality of this icon seems typical for the traditional Coptic monastic environment.

Such concern would reflect preoccupations of the Coptic-Arabic writers, especially those of the literary revival of the twelfth to mid-fourteenth century. It has been recognised that the mediaeval Coptic-Arabic theological sources bear witness to considerable Greek, Syrian and Latin influence and further research will surely show theological tradition in Arabic to be of importance. To quote again Steven Davis, it can be assumed that other texts, contemporaneous with the icon, played upon the ancient patristic and liturgical texts.

In Roman Catholic Europe the interest in Alexandrian mystical theology led, in twelfth-century Cistercian writing, to the revival of beliefs in "the motherhood of God" and the obligation of prelates, especially abbots, "to mother" the souls in their charge.[41] As to the mystery of the

---

[38] Dr Nessim Youssef pointed out to me that the homily no. XIV, attributed to Severus of Antioch, puts the Virgin on a par with a prophet and a martyr.

[39] Brock, *Luminous Eye* (see n. 15), p. 11.

[40] S. H. Griffith, "The Kitāb Miṣbāḥ Al-ʿAql of Severus Ibn al-Muqaffaʿ: A Profile of the Christian Creed in Arabic in Tenth Century Egypt", in *Mediaeval Encounters*, 2/1 (1998), pp. 15-42; and *A Treatise on the Veneration of the Holy Icons Written in Arabic by Theodore Abu Qurah, Bishop of Harran (c. 755-c. 830 A.D.)*, trans. S. H. Griffith (Louvain, 1997).

[41] Walker Bynum, *Jesus as Mother* (see n. 29), esp. ch. 4, "Jesus as Mother and Abbot as Mother", which deals with some already familiar ideas. The author asserts that this mediaeval inverted language is not merely a repetition of patristic, particularly Clement's ideas, but that it reflects a new trend in "affective spirituality", of a lyrical, emotional piety that focussed increasingly on the humanity of Christ. Analogies, which

Eucharist, it is a typically twelfth-century Latin theological issue. By seeing the Host the beholder partook in salvation. The doctrine of transubstantiation — the notion that the Host was not just the symbol of Christ crucified but that in some mysterious way it was changed into his *true body* by the ritual of consecration — led to a change in the liturgy, approved by the Fourth Lateran Council at Rome in 1215. The growing veneration of the Host resulted in the establishment of the *Corpus Christi* as a Church feast from 1264.[42] The iconographic type of the Virgin Lactans became popular in Italy from the thirteenth century. Until now I did not find any comparable Maria Lactans image in western art. I did, however, find a miniature showing the Enthroned Virgin showing a gilded Host (*ca.* 1200-25) (*fig. 5*).

These tangents into the early Christian and mediaeval Latin mystical realms demonstrate that our icon might have been influenced by several traditions, indigenous Alexandrian/Coptic enriched with Syrian elements as well as imported European spirituality of the high Middle Ages. The latter would reach the Copts via Syria/Palestine, first transferred to the Near Eastern region by the crusaders. In the post-Byzantine era these mediaeval models would linger and merge with the Roman Catholic religious prints introduced to stagnant Ottoman Egypt by Latin missionaries and Armenian itinerant painters from a Melkite-Catholic environment.[43]

III

As it used to be a recurring practice for the artists to work in various media, there is a chance that our anonymous icon painter can be identified through dated wall paintings or manuscripts. The Latin/Syrian iconographic connection for the St Antony's icons suggested here is corroborated by their peculiar style: the facial types of Mary, Christ and the Archangels don't have parallels in Coptic or Byzantine panel painting, they are rather European of the Romanesque era, except for the far-see-

---

were inspired by human relationships, present God as caring, loving and accessible. Yet again, the ordinary mother continued to be associated with the procreation of the physicality, the flesh, of the child. It was the Father who provided the spiritual substance. I thank Dr Andrew Jotischky for this reference.

[42] Van Os, *Sienese Altarpieces* (see n. 23), p. 134, n. 102.

[43] See Z. Skalova's chapter, "Icons from the Ottoman Era (1517-1798)", in Skalova and Gabra, *Icons of the Nile Valley* (see n. 2), pp. 120-41.

ing oriental eyes, which are, nevertheless, rendered with a "Gothic" mystical touch. These features, the colouring and the linear rendering, have parallels in mediaeval manuscripts, particularly Syrian, such as the Resurrection in *the Syriac Lectionary*, in the British Library (Ad. MS 7170), written in Syriac *estrangela* script, dated 1216-20 and attributed to the monastery of Mar Mattai (St Matthew), near Mosul in Northern Iraq[44] (*fig. 6*). These features are the common handling of the faces, which are designed with dark lines on a white ground, without any additional shading, the hair accentuated with yellow strokes, giving an impression of blond locks as well as the awkward proportions of the limbs and the modelling of the draperies. The illumination is the product of a Levantine spiritual perception, familiar in Egypt.[45] Not surprisingly, some affinities in common with our *Galaktotrophousa* set of icons can be found on the thirteenth century wall paintings in the Coptic desert monasteries (*figs 4a, 7, 8*).

Thirteenth-Century Wall Paintings in the Old Church of the Monastery of St Antony at the Red Sea

The decorations of the inner walls attracted many scholars. In *Les Peintures du Monastère de Saint-Antoine près de la Mer Rouge*, Paul van Moorsel summarised all previous research.[46] He published the *secco* wall paintings in the state of preservation prior to the recent cleaning by the American Research Center in Egypt (ARCE), dividing them into two stylistically distinguished groups. Group A was firmly attributed by an inscription to a Coptic painter Theodore, son of the bishop of Iftih in Upper Egypt, and to the year 1232-33. Group B, by anonymous painters, Van Moorsel dated later, his *terminus ante quem* being the year 1436.

In 1999, when all the details and ornaments on the cleaned murals emerged from under soot and overpainting, a dating of group B to the thir-

---

[44] *Glory of Byzantium: Art and Culture of the Middle Byzantine Era, A.D. 843-1261*, eds H.C. Evans and W.D. Wixom (New York, 1997), cat. no. 254.

[45] Detailed stylistic analysis of the icons is beyond the scope of this paper. It should suffice to note that the blue background with red inscriptions and the gesture with the index finger can be found in Egypt on a group of art works, all mediaeval and some very rustic: (A) icons in the collection of the monastery of St Catherine, Mount Sinai: St Mercurius (re-attributed as Coptic by Leslie MacCoull) and the Ascension triptych with SS George and Theodore (re-attributed as Coptic by the author); (B) wall paintings in the Wadi Natrun monasteries: The Nativity in the church of the Virgin in the monastery of the Syrians (*fig. 7*) and the Archangel Michael on the pillar at the church of the Virgin in the monastery of the Syrians (*fig. 4a*).

[46] See n. 1.

teenth century also became plausible.[47] Among the traditionally Coptic Old and New Testament themes and locally venerated saints, unusual images of contemporaries — pilgrims or soldiers, wearing curious headcaps marked with crosses — recall the role pilgrimages played in the dissemination of models from *loca sancta,* which were important artistic centres.

The Arabophone itinerant masters, Copts, Armenians and Syrians, left not only inscriptions in their various languages but also stylistic and iconographic evidence, such as the gesture with one finger. Interestingly, this painted gesture has a literary source: in 1231, a Jacobite monk, Jacob bar Shakkō, abbot in the already mentioned monastery of Mar Mattai in Northern Iraq, compiled a massive theological handbook, *Book of Treasures,* in which he defends the Jacobite christological position of the "one composed nature" in Christ and the Jacobite way of making the sign of the cross, with one finger[48] (*figs 4a and 8*) As sources for art, the relationship between the mediaeval Coptic-Arabic and Syrian-Arabic hagiographical and other theological texts in the monastery of St Antony, reflect the "symphonic resonance" of the thirteenth-century international style (Middle Byzantine; western, Romanesque Italian; crusader and Islamic) in the service of Coptic visions. The question remains as to where the itinerant artists in Egypt, moving from one monophysite desert monastery to another, came from and how the workshop came into being. The wall paintings from 1225 in the church of the Virgin at the monastery of the Syrians in Wadi Natrun, studied by L.A. Hunt, testify that during the Ayyubīd period this monastery was the centre of the Syrian Jacobite community.[49]

[47] I proposed this re-dating at the Hernen Symposium, 29 September 2000. It turned out that the ARCE scholars had come to the same conclusion, informing the public on the occasion of the photographic exhibition of cleaned murals "Monastic Visions" in the ARCE Egypt headquarters, starting September 2000, that they date the second group (van Moorsel's group B) to the thirteenth century, but somewhat later than group A. Moreover, the most ancient layer of murals, newly discovered by restoration dates to the sixth/seventh century, confirming the traditional dating of the Old Church by the monks to the early period of Christianity. See the abstract by E.S. Bolman, "Monastic Visions: Thirteenth-Century Painting in the monastery of St. Antony at the Red Sea, Egypt", in *Pre-actes*, III, *Communications libres: XXe Congrès International des Etudes Byzantines* (Paris, 2001), p. 454 and *Monastic Visions: Wall Paintings from the Monastery of St. Antony*, ed. E.S. Bolman (forthcoming; to be published jointly by the ARCE Egypt and Yale University/Press). Consequently, also the chapel of the Four Creatures is now seen as the most ancient nucleus of the monastery.

[48] Herman G.B. Teule, "It Is Not Right to Call Ourselves Orthodox and the Others Heretic: Ecumenical Attitudes in the Jacobite Church in the Time of the Crusaders", in *East and West in the Crusader States*, II, pp. 11-27, esp. 19-20.

[49] L.-A. Hunt, "Christian-Muslim Relations in Painting in Egypt of the Twelfth to Mid-Thirteenth Century: Sources of Wallpainting from Deir-es-Suriani and the Illustrations of the New Testament MS Paris", Copte-Arabe 1 / Cairo, Bibl. 94, *Cahiers archéologiques*, 33 (1985), pp. 111-55.

The cleaning of the anonymous little noticed icons coincided with the final stage of the prestigious Italian/ARCE conservation mission.[50] At the very time, when the icons were (partly) revealed for stylistic research, the wall paintings — exemplarily restored to their original state — emerged devoid of all the historical overpainting, which had accumulated upon the extant thirteenth-century layer.[51] Today, neither group of the restored murals demonstrates the hand of our icon painter. However, on the archival black-and-white photos made by the Whitemore, Leroy and Van Moorsel missions, I detected, in quest of affinities between the icons in the chapel of the Four Creatures and the murals in the same sacred space, faces, which can be attributed to our icon painter: for example, the portrayals of the Enthroned Virgin with Child, local monks, the mounted martyrs St Theodore the General and St George, in the nave (*fig. 9*).[52] These extensive revitalisations painted over the obscured older images had been recognised by the French team and dated to the period between 1232-3 and the mid-sixteenth century, when Gabriel VII, the 95th patriarch (1525-68) refurbished the depleted monastery.[53]

Thirteenth-Century Wall Paintings in the Chapel of the Four Creatures of the Monastery of St Antony at the Red Sea

In my opinion, the function of the *Galaktotrophousa* set above the doorway to the sanctuary, dedicated, according to the monks of St Antony, to the Four Creatures, appears to be connected liturgically with the visionary composition dating to 1232/33 in the apse (*text fig. 2*). The four creatures of the Apocalypse (presented in a curious way and reminding of

---

[50] The cleaned murals will be presented for the first time in *Monastic Visions*, ed. Bolman (see n. 47).

[51] Again, the importance of Professor Krause's warning is valid: see M. Krause, "Die Bedeutung alter Dokumentation für die koptische Kunst", in *Coptology - Past, Present, and Future: Studies in Honour of Rodolphe Kasser*, ed. S. Giversen et al. (Leuven, 1994), pp. 17-33.

[52] Van Moorsel, *Peintures du monastère de Saint-Antoine* (see n. 1), II, the Enthroned Virgin, pls 79-80; St Theodore, pls 64, 93 and 94; and especially St George, pls 89, 90.

[53] See three articles by A. Piankoff and Thomas Whittemore: "Peintures au monastère Saint-Antoine", *Les Cahiers Coptes*, 7-8 (1954), p. 22; "Deux peintures de saints militaires au monastère Saint-Antoine", *Bulletin de la Société d'Archéologie Copte*, 10 (1956), pp. 17-25; "Peintures au monastère Saint-Antoine", *Bulletin de la Société d'Archéologie Copte*, 14 (1950-57). For the photographs see P.P.V. van Moorsel, "Les travaux de la mission de peintures coptes à Saint-Antoine", in *Called to Egypt* (see n. 19), fig. 1 (this being a repro of the photograph by B. Psiroukis, I.F.A.O, from 1975); and Van Moorsel, *Peintures du monastère de Saint-Antoine* (see n. 1), II, pls 64 and 93, to name a few.

Text fig. 2. Monastery of St Anthony, apse of the chapel of the Four Creatures: *Deesis*.

the pharaonic canopic jars) are incorporated into a basically Byzantine Deesis composition with Christ Enthroned in Glory flanked by the Interceding Virgin Mary and St John the Baptist.[54] This eclectic apsidal painting is a blend of local and imported stylistic features affirmed by an Armenian inscription of the *trisagion*.[55]

The nursing image and the vision from the Apocalypse, painted in the two-zonal composition, survived on walls of excavated desert monasteries in Saqqara and Bawit (Chapel 42).[56] It is conceivable that in the tiny and low *kellion* in the monastery of St Antony, these two themes (not necessarily from the same period) are displayed together in spatial dimension: in the apsidal sanctuary and on the screen veiling it. The connection between the Virgin *Galaktotrophousa* and the Four Creatures as suggested above is strengthened by a miniature of the *Galaktotro-*

[54] Van Moorsel attributes this wall painting to the older group A. For his emphasis on the significance of the apse in the Coptic church as the place where the Divine can manifest itself, particularly during the liturgy, see his article "The Vision of Philotheus (On apse-Decorations)", reprinted in Van Moorsel, *Called to Egypt* (see n. 19), pp. 107-15.

[55] The tenth-century Coptic *Encomium on the Four Creatures* (MS Pierpont Morgan Library, New York, MS 612), the Cherubs of the *Book of Ezekiel*, the Seraphs of the *Vision of Isaiah* and the *Zoa* of John's *Revelation,* compares the installation of these four angelic creatures to "a spiritual meal": see J. Hagen, "From the Diaries of the Apostles: Manuscript-find and manuscript-fiction in Coptic Homilies and Other Literary Texts", *Acts of the Seventh International Congress of Coptic Studies, Leiden, 27 August - 2 September 2000* (forthcoming). I am indebted to the author for allowing me to use his unpublished paper.

[56] Ihm, *Programme der Christlichen Apsismalerei* (see n. 34), Tafel xxv/2.

phousa Enthroned among angels in the frontispiece of the Codex of the Four Creatures (MS Pierpont Morgan Library, MS 612, fol. 1v), written and illuminated by the Copt Isaq (*fig. 3b*).

CONCLUSION

In anticipation of the decipherment and palaeographic expertise of the *nomina sacra* and the dedicatory inscription on the screen, which need interdisciplinary investigation, the dating of the anonymous *Galaktotrophousa* set has, at this stage of research, to remain inconclusive. A few observations, suggesting dating in the late Middle Ages or, at least, the existence of older models for these icons, can, however, be made:
- The iconography of the icons, with the typically high mediaeval emphasis on the mystical, complements the murals in the apse of the *kellion* and in the Old Church. Their synthesized style, blending the international trends — Coptic, Byzantine, Syrian, Armenian and Italian — although not crusader in the western meaning of the word, is characteristic for the Christian art of the region since the crusades. While the icons seem to be based on imported models and theological ideas, they are Coptic in derivation and fit into a longstanding Coptic tradition.
- The set may be the work of the painter who revitalised a number of faces on the thirteenth-century murals on the walls in the Old Church. To be allowed to touch these saintly figures, he must have been a resident monk, adhering to one of the non-Chalcedonian churches and — judging from his "handwriting" — a not very skilful artist. His patron advising on the iconography might have been the Coptic Patriarch himself; the answer as to whether it was Gabriel III (1268-71) or Gabriel VII (1525-68) may be found in the inaccessible manuscripts in the libraries of the monastery of St Antony or the monastery of St Paul at the Red Sea.
- The St Antony *Galaktotrophousa*'s "erudition" makes it a sacred picture "fertile with truth", representing with "theological economy"[57] a number of very old religious perceptions:

[57] These are the words of the Coptic Patriarch St Cyril of Alexandria as quoted by Herbert L. Kessler, "'Pictures Fertile with Truth': How Christians Managed to Make Images of God without Violating the Second Commandment", *Journal of the Walters Art Gallery*, 49/50 (1992), pp. 53-65, see pp. 55 and 61.

conceptio per aurem (the Archangel Gabriel's hearing gesture);
the traditional image of the Mother of God nursing her incarnated son among the angelic guard;
an abstract patristic concept of the nursing Father;
Mary as personification of the Church;
the Christ-Child as the Bread of Life and Messiah, nursing the believer;
lactation as a symbol of the Eucharist and salvation.

Both heavenly and earthly nourishment are depicted on the sacred picture, centrally placed in the screen, which is the firmament between the earthly sacred space for the monks and the sanctuary, symbolising God's heavenly dwelling.

Fig. 1. Monastery of St Antony, the chapel of the Four Creatures: sanctuary screen with the Virgin *Galaktotrophousa* guarded by the Archangels Michael, Gabriel, Rafael and Suriel.

Fig. 2a. Monastery of St Antony: the Virgin *Galaktotrophousa*.

Fig. 2b. Monastery of St Antony: the Archangels Gabriel and Suriel.

Fig. 2c. Monastery of St Antony: the Archangels Michael and Rafael.

Fig. 3a. The Archangel Michael, New York, Pierpont Morgan Library MS 603.

Fig. 3b. The *Galaktotrophousa*, tenth-century illumination in the Coptic MS in London, British Library, MS Oriental 6782, fol. 1v and New York, Pierpont Morgan Libr. MS 612, fol. 1v.

Fig. 4a. St Michael, thirteenth-century (?) mural on the south pillar in the nave of the church of the Virgin Mary, monastery of the Syrians, Wadi Natrun.

Fig. 4b. The *Galaktotrophousa*, mediaeval mural in the church of the Virgin, monastery of the Syrians, Wadi Natrun.

Fig. 5. The Enthroned Virgin holding the Child Christ and the Host, illumination from *Vitae Sanctorum*, Brussels, Bibliothèque Royale, MS II 2544, fol. 2v.

Fig. 6. The Anastasis, fol. 156v, Syriac Lectionary, 1216-20, tempera on paper, monastery of Mar Mattai (?)

Fig. 7. The Nativity, thirteenth-century mural in the church of the Virgin, monastery of the Syrians, Wadi Natrun.

Fig. 8. The Archangels Michael and Gabriel (not yet cleaned and conserved) in the Old Church of the monastery of St Antony

Fig. 9. St Theodore the Oriental, thirteenth-century mural in the nave
of the Old Church of the monastery of St Antony
(before cleaning, demonstrating an overpainting)

DIVINE CAVALRY

Mounted Saints in Middle Eastern Christian Art[*]

Mat Immerzeel

Introduction

One of the most popular subjects in the art of Eastern Christianity is that of the equestrian saint, a mounted martyr-soldier, who is often represented killing an adversary who is a symbol of evil. The most venerated are George, Theodore, Demetrius, Sergius and Bacchus. St George in particular made a deep impression on the crusaders: he was believed to have assisted them at battles, in particular during the assaults of Antioch in 1098 and Jerusalem, one year later.[1] Through the crusaders' veneration for him he became the patron saint of Venice, England (since 1222) and soldiers. In western iconography he excelled as a dragon slayer, but the transfer to the West of this particular scene has not yet been clarified. Although the iconography of St George on horseback was widespread, the killing of the monster was unknown in the Middle East in the period before the Ottoman Empire. This raises questions about the origin of the theme and the influence of the artistic tradition of the local Christian communities on that of the crusaders, and vice versa.

Wall Paintings

The Arab conquest in the seventh century inevitably resulted in the loss of Byzantine influence in the Middle East. The local Christian communities entered a period of relative isolation, which stimulated the development of local variants of the existing artistic tradition. From the end of the eleventh century onwards, the presence of the crusaders led to new impulses and brought prosperity to the native Christians. This renaissance resulted in the building and decorating of new churches, not only in the Crusader States but also in the adjacent regions under Muslim rule.

---

[*] For the abbreviations used in the footnotes see the end of this article.
[1] Cormack and Mihalarios, "A Crusader Painting", esp. pp. 132-3; for Jerusalem see Jacobus de Voragine's *Legenda aurea*, 58: *The Golden Legend: Readings of the Saints*, trans. W.G. Ryan (Princeton, 1993), p. 242.

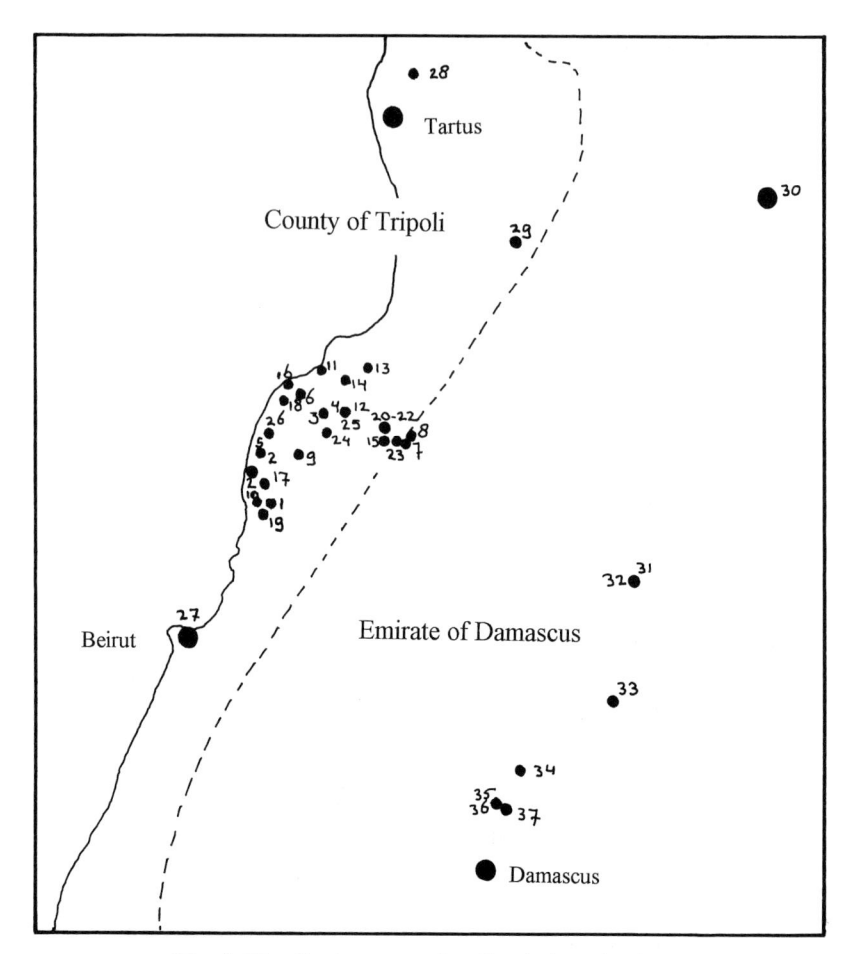

Fig. 1. Distribution map of wall paintings (author).

Although many churches and chapels in Lebanon and Syria from this period must have been decorated with wall paintings, the number of murals that have come down to us is limited. In Lebanon less than 30 sites are known, which for the greater part can be dated to the twelfth and thirteenth centuries.[2] The locations are concentrated in the area

[2] J. Sader, *Painted Churches and Rock-Cut Chapels of Lebanon* (Beirut, 1997), pp. 257-88; Cruikshank Dodd, "Christian Arab Painters"; N. Hélou, "Wall Paintings in Lebanese Churches", *ECACME*, 2 (1999), pp. 13-36; L. Nordiguian and J.-C. Voisin, *Châteaux et églises du Moyen Age au Liban* (Beirut, 1999); M. Immerzeel, "Inventory of Lebanese Wall Paintings", *ECACME*, 3 (2000), pp. 2-19; S. Westphalen, "Wandmalereien in syrischen und libanesischen Kirchen", *Antike Welt*, 31, 5 (2000), pp. 487-502.

To the Distribution Map of Wall Paintings

Lebanon

1. Bahdeidat, church of Mar Tadros
2. Ma'ad, church of Mar Charbel
3. Amioun, church of Mar Phocas
4. Qousba, monastery of Mar Mitri
5. Eddé-al-Batroun, church of Mar Saba
6. Barghoun, church of Mart Barbara
7. Hadchit, cave of Deir Salib
8. Becharreh, cave of Sayyidat Durr
9. Kafr Schleiman, cave of Saided-Naia
10. Kfour, cave of Saint Simeon
11. Qalamoun, church of Mar Marina
12. Qousba, Deir Hamatura
13. Bkeftine, Deir Sayyid
14. Kafr Qahil, church of Mar Elias
15. Monastery of Qannoubin
16. Enfé, Sayyidat al-Rih
17. Hamat, church of Mar Girgis
18. Qassouba, church of Our Lady
19. Blât, church of Mar Elias
20. Hadchit, cave of Mar Assia
21. Hadchit, cave of Mar Youhanna
22. Hadchit, cave of Mar Jirjis
23. Hadchit, monastery of Mart Chmouneh
24. Bziza, church of Mart Barbara
25. Qousba, church of the Holy Virgin
26. Rashkida, church
27. Beirut, site

Syria

28. Marqab Castle
29. Crac des Chevaliers
30. Homs, Church of Mar Elian
31. Qara, Church of SS. Sergius and Bacchus
32. Qara, Mon. of Mar Ya'qub
33. Nebk, Mon. of Mar Musa al-Habashi
34. Maalula, Mon. of SS. Sergius and Bacchus
35. Monastery of Saydnaya
36. Saydnaya, Church of Saint John
37. Ma'arrat-Saydnaya, Chapel of Saint Elijah

between Jbeil (Byblos) and Tripoli, as well as in the Qadisha Valley, that is within the borders of the former County of Tripoli (A.D. 1099-1287; *fig. 1*). Some murals are relatively well intact, in particular those in the churches of Mar Tadros in Bahdeidat, but of others only scarce fragments remain. In the north of the County, the region of Tartus in Syria, wall paintings have been found in the crusader strongholds Crac des Chevaliers and Marqab Castle (*ca.* 1200). The best-conserved scene from the Crac is that of the Presentation in the Temple in the main chapel, while in the extramural chapel the lower part of the horse of St George is still visible.[3] In Marqab Castle the vault of the chapel is decorated with the Pentecost scene.[4]

The crusaders never succeeded in extending their political influence across the Lebanese mountains, to the Emirate of Damascus, a region

---

[3] Folda, "Crusader Frescoes", pp. 181-96, figs 9-10; Cruikshank Dodd, "Monastery of Mar Musa", esp. p. 115, pl. 68; Westphalen, "Wandmalereien" (see n. 2), p. 496, fig. 27; M. Fortin, *Syrie, terre de civilisations* (Quebec, 2000), no. 322. St George: Folda, "Crusader Frescoes", pp. 192, 194, fig. 22; Hunt, "Woman's Prayer", esp. p. 84, fig. 16.

[4] Folda, "Crusader Frescoes", pp. 196-209.

with strong Christian roots. Several paintings are still to be found between Damascus and Homs, but, as has been reported by visitors, many more were visible in the past.[5] In the vicinity of Saydnaya, in a cave behind the modern Chapel of the Prophet Elijah near Ma^carrat Saydnaya there is enough left to allow a reconstruction of the scenes, of which the oldest layer was painted in the eleventh century.[6] At other locations scarce fragments are proof that murals existed here as well, in particular in the monastery of Saydnaya (one fragment of an angel in the entrance room to the Chapel of the Virgin), the church of St John the Baptist next to this monastery (on several columns), and in the church in the monastery of SS Sergius and Bacchus at Maalula.

The church in the monastery of Mar Musa al-Habashi near Nebk is covered with paintings consisting of three different layers. The nave was painted between A.D. 1058 and 1088 (layer 1), shortly before the crusader invasion, and redecorated in A.D. 1192 (layer 3). Remains of layer 2 (A.D. 1092/95) are present in the southern aisle.[7] Thirteenth-century murals in the church of SS Sergius and Bacchus in Qara show SS Theodore and Sergius on horseback (*pls 1, 2*), the Virgin with Child, and St John the Baptist.[8] In Deir Mar Ya'qub near Qara fragments have been discovered in the church[9], while the conservation and documentation of more scenes by a German-Syrian team is still in progress. Wall paintings are also present in the church of Mar Elian in Homs, but those in the apse — which cover an older mosaic — have been repainted during a restoration campaign. Only the image of St Moses on the south wall has

---

[5] J. Nasrallah, "La peinture monumentale des patriarcats melkites", in *Icônes melkites: Exposition organisée par le Musée Nicholas Sursock*, ed. V. Cândea (Beirut, 1969), pp. 67-84, esp. pp. 79-80.

[6] K.C. Innemée, "The Chapel of Saint Elijah near Ma^carrat Saydnaya and its Mural Paintings", *ECACME*, 1 (1998), pp. 73-82; K.C. Innemée and M. Immerzeel, "The Chapel of the Prophet Elijah near Ma^carrat Saydnaya (Syria) and its Mural Paintings", *Al-Masaq*, 12 (2000), pp. 69-79.

[7] Cruikshank Dodd, "Monastery of Mar Musa"; *idem, Frescoes*, pp. 14-7, 72; *Il restauro del monastero di San Mose' l'abissino, Nebek, Syria* (Damascus, 1998); Westphalen, 'Wandmalereien' (see n. 2), pp. 493-6, figs 16-25.

[8] J. Leroy, "Découvertes de peintures chrétiennes en Syrie", *Les Annales archéologiques arabes syriennes*, 25, 1-2 (1975), pp. 95-104, esp. pp. 96-9, figs 1-3; Cruikshank Dodd, "Monastery of Mar Musa", p. 118, pls 64, 65; *idem, Frescoes*, pp. 110-1, pls 89-91; Hunt, "Woman's Prayer", p. 80 ff., figs 4, 5.

[9] Now in the Archeological Museums of Damascus and Deir Attiyya; *Ebla to Damascus: Art and Archaeology of Ancient Syria*, ed. H. Weiss (Washington, D.C., 1985), nos 230, 231, pls on p. 430; *The Glory of Byzantium: Art and Culture of the Middle Byzantine Era, A.D. 843-1261*, ed. H.C. Evans and W.D. Wixom (New York, 1997), nos 257A, B; Cruikshank Dodd, "Monastery of Mar Musa", p. 119, pls 66, 67; *idem, Frescoes*, pp. 111-2, pls 92-3.

remained in its original state, and has allowed a dating in the thirteenth century.[10]

Local and "foreign" artists

The artists who were responsible for these wall paintings were active during a period of more than two centuries. Nevertheless, there are many common points allowing us to relate the different murals on former crusader territory in Lebanon to those in the Emirate of Damascus. In most of the cases the same typical stylistic elements can be observed. Prominent examples of this particular local or "Syrian" style are the paintings of layer 3 in Deir Mar Musa. While those of layer 1 bring contemporary murals in Cappadocia and Cyprus in mind, on layer 3 the modelling is flat while the persons have strong outlines and the use of colours is limited (*pl. 3*). This style is closely related to that of Fatimid Islamic art, and variants can be found as far as in the Palatine Chapel in Palermo (*ca.* 1143).[11] Similar features are present at both locations in Qara, and in several Lebanese churches (e.g. Bahdeidat and Ma'ad).

In a few cases the style is fully Byzantine, of which the Dormition on the north wall in the church of Mar Saba at Eddé (Lebanon) is the most typical example. Erica Cruikshank Dodd has dated it to A.D. 1261 on the basis of a Syrian inscription next to the scene mentioning the Seleucid year 1573.[12] According to this author, the Byzantine contribution might reflect the ameliorated relations between the Syrian Orthodox and Byzantine Orthodox Churches in this period.

The iconography in Lebanon and Syria is largely similar to that in the Byzantine context, which is not astonishing as both share the same centuries-old iconographic tradition. A frequently occurring theme is that of the *Deesis*, which is commonly located in the apses.[13] Other scenes

---

[10] Only the image of St Moses on the south wall has remained in its original state, and has allowed a dating to the thirteenth century. Leroy, "Découvertes" (see n. 8), pp. 99-106, figs 4-13; Cruikshank Dodd, "Monastery of Mar Musa", p. 1, n. 1.

[11] *Ibid.*, pp. 112-22; Cruikshank Dodd, *Frescoes*, pp. 109-24.

[12] At present the inscription can hardly be read; it was recorded by Patriarch Stephen ad-Dwaihi (seventeenth century); Cruikshank Dodd, "Christian Arab Painters", p. 271.

[13] Lebanon: church of Mar Tadros (Bahdeidat), monastery of Mar Mitri (Qousba), Cave of Saided-Naia (Kafr Schleiman), Cave of Mar Sema'an (Kfour), monastery of Qannoubin, church of Our Lady (Qassouba), the church of Mar Marina (Qalamoun), the church of Rashkida; see N. Hélou, "La représentation de la Déisis-vision dans deux églises du Liban", *Parole de l'Orient*, 23 (1998), pp. 33-59. church of Mar Elian, Homs; Leroy, "Découvertes" (see n. 8), pp. 99-106.

demonstrate that the local painters were well informed about recent developments in the Byzantine Empire, such as the Last Judgment of Deir Mar Musa. Both the subject and its location on the west wall of the church reflect the eleventh-century mosaics in the Dome of Torcello.[14]

As far as the compositions are concerned, a difference with Byzantine murals is the absence of hierarchy. The paintings are often concentrated in the eastern part of the church buildings while those in Byzantine churches cover the entire interior. In Syria this is only the case in Deir Mar Musa.[15]

The contribution of the crusaders to the decorative programmes was limited, even in a typical crusader construction such as Crac des Chevaliers. The depicted theme of the Presentation in the Temple is common in Byzantine art, while its style is local. Yet the presence of a supplicator with his name written in Latin, points at a western origin of the person who had commissioned the painting. Similar supplicators are also represented in Bahdeidat, Ma'ad and Amioun, as well as on several crusader icons in the monastery of St Catherine at Sinai (see below).[16] Their presence does not necessarily prove that these works of art were made on behalf of westerners, as suchlike representations were also common in Byzantine art. Nevertheless, it is likely that crusaders have encouraged or commissioned several decoration projects, which were executed by local painters according to their own tradition. This might have been the case in the church of Mar Charbel in Ma'ad. Cruikshank Dodd has suggested a relation between the painting of the Dormition in the south chapel, the reported burial of "Hanna al-Frangiye, Bint el-Khabbaz" in this church in A.D. 1243, and the rebuilding of its front section by Hanna's father on the occasion of her death.[17] Whether the paintings were made to commemorate a certain French lady "Anne Boulanger" or not, the artists were without any doubt local.

Only the murals in the church of Mar Marina near Qalamoun (Lebanon) can be written on the account of a western artist. The first layer, showing St Marina, the Annunciation, the *Deesis*, and St Demetrius — with Greek inscriptions —, has been painted over with a new programme, very likely in the thirteenth century, consisting of com-

---

[14] E. Cruikshank Dodd, "The Three Patriarchs of Mar Musa al-Habashi: Syrian Painting and its Relationship with the West", *Al-Masaq*, 12 (2000), pp. 99-139; idem, *Frescoes*, pp. 77-99, 140- 4, figs 8A-E.

[15] Westphalen, "Wandmalereien" (see n. 2), p. 500.

[16] For this subject see Hunt, "Woman's Prayer".

[17] Reported by Patriarch Stephan ad-Dwaihi (seventeenth century); Cruikshank Dodd, "Christian Arab Painters", p. 267.

Fig. 2. Qalamoun, church of Mar Marina: Saint Demetrius and scenes from the life of Saint Marina (Sader, *Painted Churches*, fig. 123).

partmentalized scenes from the life of St Marina with inscriptions in Latin (*fig. 2*).[18]

Icons

In spite of the absence in Lebanon and Syria of icons earlier than the sixteenth century, there are reasons to suppose an involvement of local artists in icon painting as well. The only exception known is a two-sided icon in the monastery of Our Lady of Kaftoun near Batroun.[19] On one side the Virgin *Hodegetria* is depicted between the busts of two angels. The subject on the reverse is the Baptism of Christ (*pls 4, 5*). In the centre, Christ is standing in the Jordan, with St John represented to the left and six angels to the right. In the top left corner King David is holding an opened scroll with Psalm 114 and 77 written in Arabic. Opposite to him the Prophet Isaia has a similar scroll, but the text is here in Syrian (Isaiah 1:16; 12:3), while Greek is used for their names and the title of the scene ("Baptism").

The formal similarities in the faces of the angels as well as the identical shapes and the use of colours in their dress and wings indicate that the same artist has painted both sides. This icon can be dated to the sec-

[18] Sader, *Painted Churches* (see n. 2), pp. 146-64, figs 116-23, with further references.
[19] A. Lammens, "Notices", in the catalogue *Icônes du Liban* (Paris, 1996), pp. 21-7.

ond half of the thirteenth century, as in details the Virgin reveals a strong resemblance with another Virgin on a two-sided icon from this period in St Catherine's Monastery. The reverse of this icon deserves our particular interest, because it shows SS Sergius and Bacchus on horseback (*pl. 6*).[20] They have a typical beaded coronet and a thin necklace, and are dressed in a short chlamys, a coat of mail and trousers. Both are holding a lance in their right hand. To the lance of St Sergius a white banner with a red cross has been fixed.

In his study on the paintings in the church of SS Sergius and Bacchus in Qara, Jules Leroy has emphasized the striking stylistic and iconographic similarities between the equestrian saints in the church (*pls 1, 2*), and those on the icon.[21] In Qara the characteristic crowns, the coat of mail and the banner, which, in this case too, is fixed to Sergius' lance, are present too. The icon has been classified amongst the crusader icons in St Catherine's Monastery. It has been suggested that its painter originally came from southern Italy (Weitzmann), or from a Syrian community at Cyprus (Mouriki), but in view of the similarities with the paintings in Qara an origin from present Lebanon, or Syria, is more likely. According to Lucy-Anne Hunt, the icon was painted in the County of Tripoli. At least one more example in the collection of St Catherine's Monastery can be attributed to a "Syrian" painter: that of St Sergius on horseback holding a lance with the red-crossed banner, with a supplicating veiled woman at the feet of his horse.[22]

The typical banner can also be found in Deir Mar Musa. Six equestrian saints are painted at the upper zone of the north and south walls (on layer 1 as well as on layer 3), amongst whom Sergius, Theodore, and George.[23] Two saints on the upper layer, Sergius on the western part of the south wall (*pl. 3*) and probably Bacchus at his opposite, carry this attribute on their lance, respectively a white banner with a red cross and a red banner with a white cross. This flag has been subject to discussion concerning

[20] G. Soteriou and M. Soteriou, *Icônes du Mont Sinaï*, 2 vols (Athens 1956/1958) [in Greek], I, figs 185-6; II, pp. 170-1; K. Weitzmann, "Icon Painting in the Crusader Kingdom", *DOP*, 20 (1966), pp. 49-83, esp. pp. 71-2, fig. 49; D. Mouriki, "Icons from the 12th to the 15th Century", in *Sinai: Treasures of the Monastery of Saint Catherine*, ed. K.A. Manafis (Athens, 1990), pp. 102-24, esp. p. 119, fig. 66 (Sergius and Bacchus); Hunt, "Woman's Prayer", p. 79 ff., figs 2, 3; Cruikshank Dodd, *Frescoes*, p. 116.

[21] Leroy, "Découvertes" (see n. 8), p. 104.

[22] Soteriou and Soteriou, *Icônes* (see n. 20), fig. 187; Weitzmann, "Icon Painting" (see n. 20), pp. 71-2, fig. 49; Cormack and Mihalarios, "A Crusader Painting", p. 133, fig. 3; Hunt, "Woman's Prayer", pp. 78 ff., fig. 1; Cruikshank Dodd, *Frescoes*, pp. 51-3, 133-4.

[23] Cruikshank Dodd, "Monastery of Mar Musa", pp. 84-9, pls 28, 29, 32, 33.

the contribution of the crusaders to Christian art in the Middle East. To Weitzmann, its presence was a reason to relate icons such as that of Sergius and Bacchus to the Order of the Knights Templar,[24] but Cruikshank Dodd rejects any direct influence by the crusaders, as "... this motif must have been adopted in the fresco, as in the icons, as a sign of militant Christianity in a hostile environment".[25] Supposedly, also to the Christians who lived within a predominantly Muslim society, the banner might have symbolized their struggle for survival of their religion.

The crusader icons reflect the interest of the crusaders in the monastery of St Catherine[26] but they certainly do not form a coherent group. Some can be attributed to artists from Venice, Cyprus, or the Kingdom of Jerusalem, while others seem to have been painted in Lebanon or Syria. It has been suggested that the icons came to the monastery from Latin territory, but in view of the similarities with the murals in Syria this is questionable in the case of the icon of Sergius and Bacchus. It can better be considered as a "Syrian" icon, leaving the matter of its origin and that of the patrons open.

St George and his fellow combatants

Equestrian saints were common in Eastern Christian art, in particular in the Middle East, but also on Cyprus, the Byzantine mainland and in Eastern Europe. The motif of the horseman has a long history. Although in the early Christian period the equestrian saints must have had a wider distribution in the area, the oldest surviving examples have been found in Egypt only.[27] A mounted saint who is killing an adversary from Chapel XVII in the monastery of St Apollo at Bawit has only survived in a copy.[28] He has been identified as St Sisinnios, who is defeating a half-naked woman called Alabasdria. Sisinnios is surrounded by several

---

[24] K. Weitzmann, *Studies in the Art of Sinai* (Princeton, 1982), pp. 354, 435.

[25] Cruikshank Dodd, "Monastery of Mar Musa", p. 87; idem, *Frescoes*, p. 52; see also Cormack and Mihalarios, "A Crusader Painting", pp. 134-7; and Westphalen, "Wandmalereien" (see n. 2), p. 496.

[26] J. Lafontaine-Dosogne, "Le monastère du Sinaï: Creuset de culture chrétienne (Xe-XIIIe siècle)", in *East and West in the Crusader States*, I, pp. 103-29, esp. pp. 116-7.

[27] For this subject see K.-H. Brune, *Der koptische Reiter — Jäger, König, Heiliger: Ikonographische und stilistische Untersuchung zu den Reiterdarstellungen im spätantiken Ägypten und die Frage ihres "Volkskunstcharakters"* (Altenberge, 1999).

[28] J. Clédat, *Le monastère et la nécropole de Baouit*, MIFAO, 111 (Cairo, 1904), I, part 2, pl. LVI; M. Meyers, "Les rituels de la magie copte", in *L'art copte en Egypte: Catalogue de l'exposition* (Paris, 2000), pp. 102-4, esp. pp. 103, 104; Brune, *Der koptische Reiter* (see n. 27), p. 233, fig. II. 5.

Fig. 3. Mosaic from Olynthos: Bellerophon.

symbols of evil, such as a winged female demon with a snake's tail ("Daughter of Alabasdria"), a centaur, a crocodile, and a scorpion. The message of this representation speaks for itself: the Saint, who is reputed for his role in the theological discussions with the Manicheans, represents the good defeating the bad.

A similar example in sculpture from Bawit shows an equestrian saint piercing an adversary between the feet of his horse, but the identity of the victim cannot be determined because of the damage to the stone.[29] In Egypt, horsemen killing animals or human adversaries were also very

---

[29] Musée du Louvre, inv. no. 17075; Clédat, *Le monastère et la nécropole de Baouit* (see n. 28), fig. 208.

popular in minor arts, e.g. in textile decorations,[30] but there is often no evidence for any Christian content, or they show common hunting scenes.

The horseman motif was not a Christian invention, but belonged to the artistic repertory of horse-riding cultures in general. In Greek and Roman art, hunting and battle scenes were widespread, and even the layout of the common composition was used centuries before its introduction into Christian art. An example from the fourth century B.C. is a mosaic from Olynthos, showing Bellerophon mounted on Pegasus and threatening the monster Chimaera with his lance (*fig. 3*).[31] A "translation" into Egyptian mythology is the equestrian Horus killing a crocodile (Seth), of which a limestone relief in the Louvre, probably from the fourth century A.D., is the best-known representative.[32] This subject has often been considered the prototype of the equestrian saint, but it makes more sense to suppose that both variants were based on the traditional blueprint of the victorious horseman-hunter.[33]

The recent discovery of three mounted saints in the *khurus* of the church of al- ᶜAdra in Deir al-Surian (Wadi al-Natrun), most likely from the early eighth century,[34] shows the continuity in the pictorial tradition of the theme after the Arab conquest. The side panels of a triptych in St Catherine's Monastery (ninth-tenth century) show St Theodore killing a snakelike dragon (left) and St George injuring a man, likely his persecutor who is known as the Persian King Dadianus (right; see below). A contemporary icon in the monastery represents St Mercurius killing his particular adversary, the Emperor Julian.[35] Several manuscripts from the

---

[30] Meyers, "Les rituels" (see n. 28), p. 104, cat. nos 175-8.

[31] J.G. Pedley, *Griekse kunst en archeologie* (Cologne, 1999), p. 309, pl. 9.43; a useful contribution to the discussion about the antique tradition is L. Török, "Zur Ikonographie der koptischen Kunst im 6. bis 7. Jahrhundert", *Wissenschaftliche Zeitschrift der Humboldt- Universität zu Berlin*, Ges.-Sprachw. R., 20 (1971), pp. 295-306.

[32] Inv. no. E4850; A. Badawi, *Coptic Art and Archaeology* (Cambridge, Mass., and London, 1978), p. 152, pl. 3.71.

[33] L. Toorians, "Is Isis Mary and Osiris the Crucified?", *ECACME*, 3 (2000), pp. 29-39, esp. pp. 31-2.

[34] K.C. Innemée, L. Van Rompay and E. Sobczynski, "Deir al-Surian (Egypt): Its Wall- Paintings, Wall-texts and Manuscripts", *Hugoye*, 2, 2 (July 1999), pp. 5-6, ill. 6, 7 (Internet).

[35] George and Theodore: Soteriou and Soteriou, *Icônes* (see n. 20), figs 30-1; K. Weitzmann, *The Monastery of Saint Catherine at Mount Sinai: The Icons*, I (Princeton, 1967), B43-4, pls XXIX, XCVII-XCVIII; St Mercurius: G. Galavaris, "Early Icons (from the 6th to the 11th Century)", in, *Sinai: Treasures of the Monastery of Saint Catherine*, ed. K.A. Manafis (Athens, 1990), pp. 91- 101, fig. 11; Weitzmann, *The Monastery*, B49, pls XXXI, CIV. The dating of these icons has recently been called into question by Hunt, who proposes a dating in the thirteenth century and a Coptic origin (Hunt, "Christian Art", figs 1, 4, 11).

same period have been illuminated with mounted saints, for example St Theodore in a manuscript from Fayyum (*ca.* 900).[36] The holy horseman was popular as far as in Nubia; about A.D. 1000 five equestrian saints were painted in the church of Abdallah Nirqi near Abu Simbel.[37]

During the flourishing period of wall painting in the Middle East, between the eleventh and thirteenth century, equestrian saints had a dominant place in many churches. In that of Mar Tadros at Bahdeidat St Theodore is represented killing the dragon, while St George is rescuing the boy from Mytilene (see below). To the examples which have already been mentioned (Qalamoun, Crac des Chevaliers, Qara, Deir Mar Musa) murals in the churches of Mar Saba (Eddé al-Batroun), Sayyidat al-Rih (Enfé), and St Elijah (Blāt),[38] and in Egypt in Deir Malak Gabriil (Fayyum)[39], Deir al-Chohada (Esna)[40], Deir Anba Antonius,[41] Deir Maymun[42], and the church of Abu Sefein in Old Cairo can be added.[43] Suchlike representations also appear in Coptic illuminations and in woodcarvings in Coptic churches.[44]

---

[36] From the monastery of St Michael, Hamouli; Pierpont Morgan Library, New York, M 613; L. Depuydt, *Catalogue of Coptic Manuscripts in the Pierpont Morgan Library*, 2 vols (Leuven, 1993), no. 144/411, pl. 19; see also Cruikshank Dodd, *Frescoes*, p. 54, n. 158.

[37] P. van Moorsel, J. Jacquet and H. Schneider, *The Central Church of Abdallah Nirqi* (Leiden, 1975), pp. 109-24, pls 63, 67, 83, 92-8; on the horseman in Islamic art see Cruikshank Dodd, *Frescoes*, pp. 54-5.

[38] Eddé al-Batroun: Sader, *Painted Churches* (see n. 2), pp. 120-34, pl. 103; Qalamoun: pp. 146- 64, fig. 123, pl. 118; Enfé: pp. 143-44, pl. 115; Blāt: pp. 57-9, pl. 19; see also Immerzeel, "Inventory" (see n. 2).

[39] Traces of seven equestrian saints, very likely to be dated between A.D. 1022-32; G. van Loon and M. Immerzeel, "Inventory of Coptic Wall-Paintings", *ECACME*, 1 (1998), pp. 6-55, on pp. 39-40, fig. 22 (with further references); W. Godlewski, "Naqlun 1993-1996", in *Ägypten und Nubien in spätantiker und christlicher Zeit: Akten des 6. Internationalen Koptologenkongresses Münster, 20.-26. Juli 1996*, ed. S. Emmel a.o., I (Wiesbaden, 1999), pp. 157-62.

[40] Dated A.D. 1129/30 or 1179/80; St Claudius, Theodore Stratelates and unidentified saint, J. Leroy, *Les peintures des couvents du Désert d'Esna*, MIFAO, 94 (Cairo, 1975), pp. 1-16.

[41] See P. van Moorsel, *Les peintures du monastère de Saint-Antoine près de la Mer Rouge*, MIFAO, 112 (Cairo, 1995/97), pp. 89-95, 151-65; *khurus*: Mercurius, pls 39, 42; George, pls 45, 46; nave: George, two anonymous saints, Sisinnios; Theodore Stratelates, Menas, Victor, Claude, and Theodore the Oriental (pls 89-98).

[42] Very fainted traces; Van Loon and Immerzeel, "Inventory" (see n. 39), p. 38, no. 11.

[43] See *ibid.*, pp. 23-5, no. 5, with further references; Hunt, "Christian Art", pp. 21 ff., figs 9, 10.

[44] St Theodore: MS Vatican Copt. 66, fol. 210v (J. Leroy, *Les manuscrits coptes et coptes-arabes illustrés* (Paris, 1974), pp. 184-5; Hunt, "Christian Art", p. 21, fig. 7); St Mercurius: *idem*, fol. 287v (Leroy, *Les manuscrits*, pl. 105, 2; Hunt, "Christian Art", p. 22, fig. 8). Dated by Leroy in the ninth-tenth century, by Hunt in the thirteenth century; wooden panel in the iconostasis of the church of Abu Sarga, Old Cairo: Hunt, "Christian Art", p. 18, fig. 6, with further references (mid-thirteenth century).

The difficulty in determining direct crusader influences in the discussed icon of Sergius and Bacchus is the lack of indications for the origin of its patrons. This problem does not exist with another thirteenth-century icon in the monastery of St Catherine. It shows George and Theodore, both with the red cross on a white banner, while a small bearded man is supplicating to the first one.[45] A Greek inscription identifies him as "George de Paris". This George might have been a pilgrim who visited the monastery and left his icon as a gift. It was probably painted by a western artist in one of the crusader states, who was influenced by the Byzantine style.[46] The similarity between this icon and a thirteenth-century illustration on a parchment folium in the Augustinermuseum in Freiburg, showing two equestrian saints, "Theodore" and "Constantine" (a confusion with George; *fig. 4*), is remarkable.[47] Obviously, a western artist has copied an icon during his stay somewhere in the eastern Mediterranean.

The special attention that the crusaders paid to equestrian saints requires an explanation. An important factor was the predominance of chivalry in medieval warfare, and it is imaginable that, at the sight of those well-armed defenders of their own faith, the crusaders had the impression as if they were looking in a mirror. No wonder that amongst others St George had the reputation of having offered a helping hand during important battles (see Introduction). Evidently, the veneration of holy horsemen was encouraged by the fact that the crusaders were fighting against anti-Christian forces as well. At their return to their homelands, they carried these saints with them in their hearts and in images, but these "exported" saints never rooted well in Western Europe. The only exception is St George.

The origin of St George's veneration is Lydda, where his relics were buried. The Saint's fame had already spread over Western Europe in the early medieval period; from the fifth century onwards several churches and chapels were dedicated to him.[48] The oldest written account in the West is Adamnan's *De Locis Sanctis* from about A.D. 683-6, but Adamnan had recorded what had been told to him by Bishop Arculf, who

---

[45] Weitzmann, "Icon Painting" (see n. 20), pp. 79-80, fig. 64; Cormack and Mihalarios, "A Crusader Painting", pp. 134 ff., fig. 5; Hunt, "Woman's Prayer", p. 88, fig. 12; *idem*, "Christian Art", pp. 17-8, fig. 5.

[46] Cormack and Mihalarios, "A Crusader Painting", p. 137.

[47] Weitzmann, "Icon Painting" (see n. 20), pp. 71, 78-81, fig. 62; Hunt, "Woman's Prayer", p. 113, fig. 17, with further references.

[48] E.A. Wallis Budge, *George of Lydda — The Patron Saint of England: A study of the Cultus of St. George in Ethiopia* (London, 1930), pp. 22-4.

Fig. 4. Parchment leaf, Augustinermuseum, Freiburg.

had shipwrecked on the English shore after his return from a voyage to the Middle East (presumably between 679 and 782).[49] *De Locis Sanctis* contains elements from eastern hagiography, and as in other early accounts one particular story which is inextricably bound up with St George is lacking: that of the slaying of the dragon. Since this legend is also absent in the iconography of Lebanon, Syria and Egypt from before the Ottoman period, the question of its origin requires further consideration.

The oldest reference to the slaying of the dragon is a short passage in a twelfth-century *Codex Monacensis*.[50] This manuscript is the only source from an earlier period than the version that became popular in the West: the Saint's hagiography in Jacobus de Voragine's *Legenda*

---

[49] Adamnan's *De Locis Sanctis*, ed. D. Meehan (Dublin, 1958), pp. 111-8.
[50] Staatsbibliothek München, Clm. 14473; see Brune, *Der koptische Reiter* (see n. 27), p. 247.

aurea from about 1260.[51] In Voragine's work St George acts as the rescuer of the king's daughter from the monster, a story that is located in Silene in Lybia. Supposedly de Voragine had written down what was known at that time about George's life in the eastern Mediterranean, and we now have to look for an explanation for the dragon's appearance in the story.

It has been suggested that Coptic versions were at the origin of his role as a dragon slayer, because these refer to his persecutor, King Dadianus, as "the dragon".[52] Another proposal is that the acts of St George have been mixed up with those of Theodore Stratelates. In the oldest written tradition Theodore is the dragon slayer,[53] and he is represented as such on, for example, the afore-mentioned triptych wing from St Catherine's Monastery. Theodore is always recognizable by his pointed black beard while George is always beardless. This suggestion might be close to the truth, but as the earlier *Codex Monacensis* mentions St George as the dragon killer, the mixing up of both horsemen can certainly not be written on the account of the author of the *Legenda aurea*. It is a fact that the theme was already known in the pictorial tradition of the Byzantine Empire and Eastern Europe. Especially in Cappadocia, Greece and Russia several murals anticipate the *Legenda aurea*. In Cappadocia, George and Theodore killing snakelike dragons are depicted in Chapel 28 in Göreme (eleventh/twelfth century),[54] while in the church of the Forty Martyrs near Suves George and the dragon are represented on a layer dated A.D. 1216-17.[55] They can also be found in the church of Geraki (Greece; twelfth century)[56] and in that of St George in Staraja Ladoga (Russia; *ca*. A.D. 1167).[57] Undoubtedly, the crusaders knew similar representations. However, they did not see them in the Crusader States of the Holy Land, but on former Byzantine territory, very likely in Cappadocia. A highlight in their veneration of the Saint was the rebuilding of the church over his tomb in Lydda after its destruction in A.D.

---

[51] *Legenda aurea*, 58: Ryan, *Golden Legend* (see n. 1), pp. 238-40.

[52] Wallis Budge, *George of Lydda* (see n. 48), pp. 34-5; D. O'Leary, *The Saints of Egypt* (New York, 1937), p. 141.

[53] *Ibid.*, p. 141; St Theodore: p. 264; Brune, *Der koptische Reiter* (see n. 27), p. 247.

[54] J. Myslivec, "Saint-George dans l'art chrétien oriental", *Byzantinoslavica* (1934), pl. xv, fig. 2; M. Restle, *Die byzantinische Wandmalerei in Kleinasien* (Recklinghausen, 1967), I, p. 52; II, p. 129-30, pls 246-7.

[55] *Ibid.*, I, pp. 157-8; T. Velmans, *La peinture murale byzantine à la fin du Moyen Age* (Lille, 1983) (diss.), pp. 156-7.

[56] Cruikshank Dodd, "Monastery of Mar Musa", p. 115; *idem*, *Frescoes*, pp. 97, 115.

[57] W.F. Volbach and J. Lafontaine-Dosogne, *Byzanz und der christliche Osten* (Berlin, 1968), p. 308, pl. 308.

1010. The western presence in the city lasted until 1292, when the church was ruined again.[58]

Supposedly, the story of George the dragon slayer originated in the Byzantine tradition, and strangely enough not in that of the Christian communities in the Middle East. It was unknown in the iconography in Lebanon, Syria and Egypt at least until the fourteenth century. It is also remarkable that another story, the miraculous rescue by St George of the young slave from Mytilene (Lesbos) at the moment when the boy was pouring out wine for his Muslim master, was popular in the Middle East, but never made it to the West.[59] The little cupbearer is depicted sitting behind the Saint, while between the feet of the horse the sea rich in fish, which separates the island from the mainland, is visible. This miracle is represented in Bahdeidat and it was also found in Enfé, Deir Mar Musa, and Crac des Chevaliers, where fragments show the sea and the fish. The Copts, on the contrary, showed preference for the killing of George's royal adversary, Dadianus, or the conversion of a Jew, themes they knew from their own literary sources.[60]

The popularity of the dragon theme in the Christian world from after the crusader period was great, both in Western Europe and in the East. St George became the widely venerated personification of the struggle with evil forces symbolized by a monster.[61] In the Middle East, this story was the central motif of the scenes from the Saint's life from the fifteenth century onwards. Later accounts have situated this event in the Bay of Jounieh near Beirut.[62] The possibility that the influence of its mentioning in the *Legenda aurea* had reached the Middle East through the growing contacts with Western Europe during the Ottoman period must not be overestimated. The many representations on icons combining the killing of the dragon and the rescuing of the boy from Myti-

---

[58] Wallis Budge, *George of Lydda* (see n. 48), pp. 21-2; Cormack and Mihalarios, "A Crusader Painting", p. 138.

[59] Cormack and Mihalarios, "A Crusader Painting", p. 137. See also O. Meinardus, "The Equestrian Deliverer in Eastern Iconography", *Or. Chr.*, 5 (1973), pp. 142-55.

[60] O'Leary, *The Saints* (see n. 52), p. 141; for the conversion of the Jew in Deir Anba Antonius see Van Moorsel, *Les peintures* (see n. 41), pp. 153-5, pls 89, 90.

[61] In this context a recent publication by Svetlana Luchitskaya can be referred to, in which she points at the symbolic meaning of heraldry on the shields of the fighting parties in medieval illuminations. The Muslim knights can be distinguished by heraldry with a negative connotation, and in some cases a dragon is represented on a shield: S. Luchitskaya, "Muslims in Christian Imagery of the Thirteenth Century: The Visual Code of Otherness", *Al-Masaq*, 12 (2000), pp. 37-67, esp. pp. 45-51, fig. VIII (Paris MS fr. 22495, fol. 154v).

[62] Cormack and Mihalarios, "A Crusader Painting", p. 137.

lene, which is unknown in the West, plead against this.[63] Already in the crusader period, the contacts between the Melkite communities from Crete, Cyprus and the Greek mainland, and those in the Middle East were re-established, and they were extended from the time when all were living within the borders of the Ottoman Empire. This relatively favourable situation must have played a role in the transition of iconographic elements.

ABBREVIATIONS USED IN THE FOOTNOTES

ECACME   *Essays on Christian Art and Culture in the Middle East.*
MIFAO   Mélanges de l'Institut Français d'Archéologie Orientale au Caire.
Cormack and Mihalarios, "A Crusader Painting"
   R. Cormack and S. Mihalarios, "A Crusader Painting of St George: 'Maniera greca' or 'lingua franca'?", *The Burlington Magazine*, 126 (1984), pp. 132-41.
Cruikshank Dodd, "Christian Arab Painters"
   E. Cruikshank Dodd, "Christian Arab Painters under the Mamluks", *Aram*, 9-10 (1997-98), pp. 257-88.
Cruikshank Dodd, *Frescoes*
   E. Cruikshank Dodd, *The Frescoes of Mar Musa al-Habashi: A Study in Medieval Painting in Syria* (Toronto, 2001).
Cruikshank Dodd, "Monastery of Mar Musa"
   E. Cruikshank, "The Monastery of Mar Musa al- Habashi near Nebek, Syria", *Arte Medievale*, 2nd ser., 6, n. 1 (1992), pp. 61-144.
Folda, "Crusader Frescoes"
   J. Folda, "Crusader Frescoes at Crac des Chevaliers and Marqab Castle", *DOP*, 36 (1982), pp. 177-210.
Hunt, "Christian Art"
   L.-A. Hunt, "Christian Art in Greater Syria and Egypt: A Triptych of the Ascension with Military Saints reattributed", *Al-Masaq*, 12 (2000), pp. 1-29
Hunt, "Woman's Prayer"
   L.-A. Hunt, "A Woman's Prayer to Saint Sergius: Interpreting a Thirteenth-Century Icon at Mount Sinai", in *Byzantium, Eastern Christendom and Islam: Art at the Crossroads of the Medieval Mediterranean*, II (London, 2000), pp. 78- 126; reprint from *Byzantine and Modern Greek Studies*, 15 (1991), pp. 96-145.

---

[63] M. Chatzidakis, "Les icônes grecques post-byzantines au Liban", in *Icônes melkites*, ed. Cândea (see n. 5), pp. 223-33, esp. pp. 228-9.

Pl. 1. Qara, church of SS Sergius and Bacchus: Saint Theodore.

Pl. 2. Qara, church of SS Sergius and Bacchus: Saint Sergius.

Pl. 3. Deir Mar Musa al-Habashi: Saint Sergius
(after Westphalen, "Wandmalereien"(see n. 2), p. 499).

Pl. 4. Monastery of Our Lady, Kaftoun: Virgin with Child (*Icônes du Liban* (see n. 19), p. 21).

Pl. 5. Monastery of Our Lady, Kaftoun: Baptism (*Icônes du Liban* (see n. 19), p. 27).

Pl. 6. Monastery of Saint Catherine: the Saints Sergius and Bacchus.

SELECTIVE INDEX

A

Abaqa, son of Hülagu: 120
ʿAbdīšoʿ III, Nestorian patriarch: 103
ʿAbdīšoʿ b. Brikā, *Book of the Pearl*: 111, 112
ʿAbdīšoʿ of Nisibis: *Book of Canon Law*: 105, 109, 117, 119
Abraham of Tripoli: 105, 106
Abu l-Barakāt, see Zayn
ʿAbud: 15, 16
Abū Saʿd: 71
Abū Simbel, church of Abdallah Nirqi near: 276
Achilles Tatius: 166, 171
Acre: 14, 17, 18, 46, 53, 56, 106, 139, 141, 143, 144, 147-149, 152-158, 160-162, 166, 177-179, 209, 217, 224, 232, 233
Adam of Bremen: 12
Adamnan: 277, 278
Addai and Mari, Apostles of the East: 69, 117
Adhémar, bishop of Le Puy, papal legate: 1
al-ʿAdil, brother of Saladin: 56, 157
Adrianopel: 143
Agathangelos, *History of the Armenians*: 79-99
Agathon, Saint: 86
Agnes, mother of Baldwin IV: 160
Aidhab: 154
Aimery the Monk, Latin patriarch of Jerusalem: 17, 18
ʿAin Karim, church of: 15, 16
Alabasdria: 273, 274
Albert of Vercelli: 17
Aleppo: 231
Alexandrette: 56
Alexandria: 38, 45, 84, 87, 123-136, 153, 223, 224, 226, 245
Alexandrian Crusade: 123-136
Alexios Doukas, governor of Cyprus: 167, 196, 197, 201, 215

Alexius I, Byzantine emperor: 143
Alfonso of Toulouse: 27, 28
Aljijidai, Mongol representative in Iran: 119
aloe: 223, 232
Amalfitans: 143
Amalric I, king of Jerusalem: 148, 168, 196, 232
Amalricus of Floreffe, abbot: 30
Amid: 65, 71, 101, 120
Amioun: 270
André de Longjumeau, Dominican friar: 108, 120
Andronikos II, Byzantine emperor: 42, 43, 45, 49
Anna Comnena: 168, 170, 171
Anne Boulanger, see Hanna
Anonymi auctoris chronicon ad annum Christi 1234 pertinens: 53-76
Ansellus, cantor: 36
Antalya, see Attalia
Antioch: 3, 23, 25, 53, 62, 67, 75, 84, 87, 107, 143, 148, 149, 165-220 esp. 177 and 211, 229-232, 265
Antonius, Saint: 83, see also Red Sea, monastery of
Apocalypse: 249
Arabic language: passim, esp. 3, 5, 7, 68, 238, 239, 245, 248, 271
Arculf: 277
Argun: 104
Aristotle, see *Commentary on Aristotle's Categories*
Armenia, Armenians: 3-19, 49, 64, 70, 72, 73, 79-99, 225, 230, 246, 248
Armenian Church: 49, 79-99
— Union with Rome: 79-99
Armenian language: 79-99, 250
Arshakuni: 81, 86
Ascalon: 56, 145

Athanasios II, Greek Orthodox patriarch of Jerusalem: 39, 40
Athanasios III, Greek Orthodox patriarch of Jerusalem: 48, 49
Athanasios VII, Syriac Orthodox patriarch of Jerusalem: 65
Athanasius, Saint: 239
Athos, Great Lavra: 39
Attalia: 66
auricular conception: 239, 252
auricular confession: 6
al-ʿAynī: 43-45, 50, 51, 127-129, 131-134, 136
Ayyubids: 38, 129, 248
azymes: 14, 119

B
Babylon: 217
Bacchus, Saint: 265-281; see also Maalula
Badr ad-Dīn al-ʿAynī, see al-ʿAynī
Baghdad: 108, 152, 223, 224
Bahā' ad-Dīn ibn Šaddād: 37, 38
Bahdeidat, church of Mar Tadros: 267, 269, 270, 276, 280
Baḥr as-Silsila, port of Alexandria: 125, 129, 133
Baldwin II, king of Jerusalem: 24, 27, 30, 58, 64
Baldwin III, king of Jerusalem: 27, 28, 32, 169, 170
Baldwin IV, king of Jerusalem: 37, 160
Bar ʿEbrōyō, Gregory, *Chronicle*: 54-76, 106, 113
Bar Yaʿqūb Wagih, Ṣalībā: 106
Barakāt, see Zayn
Barcelona: 225, 226
Barsauma, monastery, see Mōr Barṣawmō
Barṣawmō, guardian: 73
Bar Šūmōnō family: 75; see also Basilius
Bartolo, Ser: 226
Basil I, Byzantine emperor: 81
Basileios Kamateros: 170
Basilius bar Šūmōnō: 71, 72
Bawit: 250

— monastery of Ama Rachel: 240
— monastery of Apa Apollo: 240, 273, 274
Baybars al-Manṣūrī, sultan: 40-45, 47, 50
Bedouins: 127, 129, 153
Beirut: 148, 166, 177
Bejaia: 154
Benē KMRA: 65
Benē QRYA: 65
Benedict IX, Pope: 113, 114
Benjamin of Tudela: 223
Berke, leader of the Golden Horde: 40
Bernard of Clairvaux, Saint: 12, 29, 55
Bertha of Sulzbach, see Irene
bezants: 231, 232
Bethlehem: 15, 167, 189
— church of the Nativity: 16
Bithynia: 168
Blāt, church of St Elijah: 276
Blemmyan tribes: 92
Bohemund of Tarent: 183
Bonfilius of Foligno: 150
Boniface VIII, Pope: 113
Book of the Tower, East Syrian Patriarchal Chronicle: 103, 104, 107; see also Ṣalībā b. Yuḥannā
borax: 226
Burchard of Mount Sion: 5 s., 105, 106
Byblos: 267

C
Cairo: 127, 128, 154, 156, 237
Cairo, Old
— church of Abu Sarga: 276
— church of Abu Sefein: 241, 276
— Deir al-Banāt: 238
— Deir Maymun: 276
— Synagogue: 45
Capharnaum: 191
Cappadocia: 70, 269, 279
Capuchine Fathers: 120
Catalans: 49; see also Barcelona
Celestine I, Saint, Pope: 96
Ceylon: 226, 228
Chalcedon, Council of: 96, 119

SELECTIVE INDEX

China: 109
Chortuanel Tornikian: 88
Chronicle ad a. 1234, see Anonymi *Chronicon Universale Laudunense*: 23, 26, 31
Cicero: 11
Cilicia: 64, 67, 75, 79, 82, 84, 85, 97, 98, 166, 168, 170, 177, 230
cinnamon: 226
circumcision: 6
Cistercians: 245
Claudius, Saint: 276
Clement I, Saint, Pope: 96
Clement IV, Pope: 114
Clement of Alexandria, Saint: 239, 243, 244
cloves: 226
Cocquelines, Charles: 93
coinage: 223-234
Commentary on Aristotle's Categories: 80, 98, 99
Conrad III of Hohenstaufen, king of Germany: 27 n. 21, 165
Conrad of Montferrat: 149, 157
Constance, wife of Raymond de Poitiers: 166
Constantine, fictional name for Christian rulers: 102
Constantine, Armenian catholicos: 66
Constantine, regent of the Armenian Kingdom: 67
Constantine the Great, Byzantine emperor: 79-99, 102, 120, 209, 211, 277; see also *Donatio Constantini*
Constantine: see also Konstantinos
Constantinople: 4, 168-170, 185, 193, 199, 201, 203, 209, 211, 223
— conquest of 1204: 87
— hospice S. Maria Alemannorum: 143
— See of: passim, esp. 48, 87
Continuatio Praemonstratensis: 21-33
Copts, Coptic Church: 45, 64, 67, 68, 102, 235-252
cotton: 226
Council, see Chalcedon, Fourth Lateran, Hromkla, Lyons, Nicaea

Crac des Chevaliers: 267, 270, 276, 280
Cross, Holy, see True Cross
Crown of Thorns: 120
Crusade, Second: 25, 143, 165
Crusade, Third: 17, 143, 157
Crusade, Seventh: 101
Crusade, Eighth: 101
Cyprus: 1, 18, 66, 107, 120, 123-136, 167-170, 197-220, 223, 225-229, 232, 234, 269, 272, 273
Cyril, Coptic patriarch of Alexandria, 5th c.: 251
Cyril Ibn Laqlaq, Coptic Patriarch of Alexandria: 67

D

Dadianus, Persian King: 275, 279, 280
dair alamāna, see Jerusalem
Damanhūr: 126, 130
Damascus: 45, 46, 56, 64, 105, 107, 128, 139, 151, 152, 154, 156, 157, 159-161, 224, 231, 267, 269
— church of Maria: 160
Damasus, Saint, Pope: 96
Damietta: 56
Daniel, Old Testament: 216, 217, 219
Daniel, Russian pilgrim: 141, 145-147, 149
Daphne: 177
David the Invincible: 80
David IV, king of Georgia: 36, 37
De Propaganda Fide: 82
Deesis: 250, 269, 270
Demetrius, Saint: 265-281
Diarbakır, see Amid
Dimitri II, king of Georgia: 41
dinars: 224, 231
Dionysius, Syrian Orthodox bishop: 68
dirhams: 224, 230
Dominicans: 68, 69, 75, 106, 108, 113, 114, 120
Donatio Constantini: 79, 83, 88, 94
Doquz Khatun, wife of Hülagu: 102
Doukas, see Alexios Doukas
dye-stuff: 226, 235-252

E

ear conception, see auricular conception
ear confession, see auricular confession
East Syrians: 101-120
Eddé al-Batroun, church of Mar Saba: 269, 276
Edessa, County of: 53, 57, 64, 65, 70-72, 75, 83, 107, 143, 152
Egypt: 45, 49, 123-136, 217, 230, 235-252, 265-281
Eleanore, wife of Louis VII: 27, 148
Eliah, guardian: 73
Elias, author: 80
Elias, Nestorian bishop of Damascus: 107
Elias of Nisibis: 115
Enfé, church of Sayyidat al-Rih: 276, 280
Ensoaib, see Išoʻyahb b. Malkon
Ephesus, See of: 87
Ephrem the Syrian, Saint: 83, 239, 245
Epiphanius, St, monastery of, in Egypt: 237
equestrian saints: 265-281
Esna, Deir al-Chohada: 276
Ethiopia, Ethiopians: 92, 223, 241
— the Church of: 67
Eugenius IV, Pope: 107
Eusebius, Pope: 90
Eusebius of Caesarea, *Ecclesiastical History*: 91, 92

F

Famagusta: 103, 107, 124, 223-228, 232
Fayyum, church of Deir Malak Gabriil: 276
Florence: 228
Fontevrault: 27, 29
forgeries: 79-99
Fourth Lateran Council: 246
France: 21-33, 81, 232
Franks, see Latins
Fredegar: 9
Frederick II, German emperor: 108
frēr, see loan words
Friedrich von Schwaben: 148
Frotmund: 146, 147
Fulcher of Chartres: 8
Fulk of Anjou: 24, 27, 31, 32, 156

G

Gabriel III, Coptic patriarch: 251
Gabriel VII, Coptic patriarch: 238, 249, 251
Gabriel, Archangel: 238, 239
Gabriel Broulas, Greek patriarch of Jerusalem: 48
Gaiane, Saint: 92
Galaktotrophousa, see Virgin
Ǧanġarā, Amir: 126, 130
Gargar: 73
Gaza: 153
al-Ǧazīra: 125
Genoa, Genoese: 125, 129, 154, 224, 225, 227, 228, 230, 233
George, Saint: 247, 249, 265-281
George of Antioch: 25, 26
George de Paris: 277
Georgia, Georgians: 3-19, 35-51, 152
Geraki, church of: 279
Gerald of Wales: 12, 13
Gerard, Latin bishop of Laodicea: 18
Gibelin, patriarch of Jerusalem: 36
ginger: 226
gold, coins: 224-234
Golden Horde: 40, 49
Göreme: 279
grain: 227
Great Lavra, see Athos
Greek Orthodox (Byzantines): 3, 4, 6, 7 (and passim)
Gregorios II, Greek patriarch of Jerusalem: 46
Gregorius Bar ʻEbrōyō, see Bar ʻEbrōyō
Gregory III, Armenian catholicos: 98, 148
Gregory IV, Armenian catholicos: 98
Gregory IX, Pope: 107, 108
Gregory, Armenian bishop: 98
Gregory, Saint, Vita: 96
Gregory the Illuminator, Saint: 79-99

SELECTIVE INDEX

Guillaume de Machaut: 131-135
Guillaume de Nangis: 23, 26-28, 30, 31
Guillaume de Tyr, see William of Tyre
Guy de Lusignan, king of Jerusalem, later king of Cyprus: 232

H
Habakuk: 216, 217
Ḥadir Ibn Abī Bakr al-Mihrānī, Šayk: 41, 43-45
Hanna, Frankish woman: 270
al-Harawī: 155
Ḥarīm, battle of: 56
Ḥaṭṭin, battle of: 38, 56, 57, 152, 160, 232
Helena, mother of Constantine I: 102, 187
Helena (of Troy): 184, 185
Heliodorus: 166
Henry II, king of Cyprus: 226
Henry VI, German emperor: 17
Hodegetria, see Virgin
Homs, church of Mar Elian: 268, 269
Hospitallers, Order of St John: 54-76, 135, 140, 145, 148, 160
Hromkla, Synod of: 71, 97, 98
Hugh IV, king of Cyprus: 107, 118, 225, 226
Hugh de Payen: 58
Hülagu, ilkhan of Persia: 40, 102
Ḥusam ad-Dīn, head of Mardin: 71

I
Ibn 'Iyās al-Ḥanafī, see Zayn
Ibn Jubayr: 139, 153-156, 158-163
Ibn Katīr: 43
Ibn Šaddād, see Bahā'
Ibn Taġrībirdī: 128
Ibn al-Ṭayyib: 109, 117
Ibrahim, Ayyubid: 148
Iconium: 166, 177
Ignatius III David, Syriac Orthodox patriarch: 66-69
Ilkhanids: 40, 41
incense: 226
India, Indians, Indies: 92, 109, 223, 226
Innocent III, Pope: 17, 18, 48

Innocent IV, Pope: 105, 106, 108, 109, 120
Irene, wife of Alexius I, emperor: 196
Irene, first wife of Manuel I: 165
Isabel, queen of Armenia: 66, 67
Isaq: 251
Isauria: 168, 170, 211
Išoʿyahb b. Malkon, metropolitan of Nisibis: 109-112, 116, 118
— *Book of Proof*: 111
Ivane, Georgian prince: 38
Iveta, abbess of Bethany: 27, 29

J
Jacob, bishop of Edessa: 69
Jacob, Nestorian *rhêtor*: 106
Jacob, Saint, bishop of Nisibis: 83
Jacob bar Shakkō, Jacobite monk: 248
Jacobites, see also West Syrians: 6-8
Jacobus de Voragine: 278-280
Jacques d'Arles-sur-Tech, Dominican friar: 114
Jacques de Vitry: 1-19, 37, 39, 105, 106
James of Vitry, see Jacques de Vitry
Janus, king of Cyprus: 227
Jbeil, see Byblos
Jean d'Ibelin: 148
Jericho: 167, 189, 191
Jerusalem
— sees: passim
— churches, monasteries, Holy places:
— Anastasis: 37, 47, 91
— Calvary, see Golgotha
— Cross, Holy, monastery: 37, 39, 41-45, 49, 50
— David, Tower of: 148
— Gethsemane: 167, 189
— Golgotha, Calvary: 49, 91, 167, 187
— James, St: 91
— John, St, Hospital of: 144
— Mary, St, monastery *Alamana* (Alemannorum): 46, 47
— Mary, St, Tomb: 189
— Olives, Mount of: 189
— Sabas, St (Mar Saba), Metochion, near Jerusalem: 17, 37, 39

— Sepulchre complex, Holy: 15, 36, 38, 109, 160, 167, 187
— Sion: 167, 187
— Templum Domini: 158
— Templum Salomonis: 58, 157
Jews: 8, 280
Joachim of Fiore: 150, 151
Joan Benet, merchant from Barcelona: 225, 226
Jocelyn II, count of Edessa: 63-66, 71
Johannes Comnenus, Byzantine emperor: 23-25, 27, 32
Johannes Comnenus, Byzantine governor of Cyprus: 196
Johannes Kinnamos: 165, 196
Johannes Kontostephanos, cousin of Manuel I: 165, 167, 170-173, 212
Johannes Malalas: 171, 184
Johannes Oxeites, patriarch of Antioch: 4
Johannes Phokas, pilgrim: 177
Johannes von Quedlinburg: 161
Johannes von Würzburg: 105 s, 141, 144, 158
John, see also Johannes
John, Prester, see Prester John
John, St, knights of, see Hospitallers
John VIII, Greek Orthodox bishop of Tyre: 4
John XII, Pope: 107, 111, 118
John Bekkos, unionist: 47
John of Salisbury: 12
Jordan: 145, 152, 191, 271
Joseph II, Chaldean patriarch, *Book of the Magnet*: 101, 102, 119, 120
Joseph and Habacuc, Saints, abbey of: 30
Joseph of Telkepe, Chaldean Syriac priest, *On Revealed Truth*: 102
Jounieh, bay of, near Beirut: 280
Julian, Byzantine emperor: 275
Julius I, Pope: 96
Justinian, Byzantine emperor: 179

K

Kaftoun, monastery of Our Lady: 271
Kerak: 152, 153, 155, 160
Khwarizmians: 35
Kirakos of Ganjak: 38, 40, 90, 108

Kition: 168, 209
Knights Templar, see Templars
Konstantinos Manasses: 165-220
Kontostephanos, see Johannes Kontostephanos
KSWS castle: 71
Kurds: 70, 72, 73

L

Lamberto di Sambuceto, Genoese notary: 224
Laodicea: 18
Laon: 21, 24
— church of St Martin: 21
Latin Kingdom of Jerusalem: passim
Latins: passim
Laurence, Saint: 31
Lefkosia: 209
Leonard, Saint: 31
Leontios Makhairas: 131-134, 169, 232
Letter of Love and Concord: 79-99
Levon I, king of Armenia: 225
Limassol, see Trimythous
Litani, river, battle on: 56
literary forgeries: 79-99
loan words: 57-76, 85 s, 226 (*Ser*)
long-distance trade: 223 s
Louis VII, king of France: 25, 27, 32, 148
Louis IX, Saint, king of France: 101-120, 148
Lucan: 42
Lucas, abbot of the monastery of the Holy Cross in Jerusalem: 41
Lucas of Cosenza: 150
Lucca: 231
Lucius III, Pope: 98
Ludolf of Suchem: 223
Ludolf of Sudheim, see Ludolf of Suchem
Lydda: 17, 145, 277, 279
Lyons, First Council of: 108
Lyons, Second Council of: 7, 47

M

Ma'ad: 269, 270
Maalula, monastery of SS Sergius and Bacchus: 268

SELECTIVE INDEX

Ma'arrat Saydnaya: 268, see also Saydnaya
Macarius, Saint: 83
Makharebeli, abbot: 37
Malik al-'Ādil: see Al-'Adil
al-Malik al-Ašraf: 38
Mamluks: 35, 40, 41, 43, 46, 48, 49, 123-136, 238
Manasses, see Konstantinos Manasses
Manicheans: 274
al-Manṣūr Ibrahim of Ḥomṣ: 157
Manuel I Comnenus, Byzantine emperor: 24, 25, 27, 97, 98, 165-220, esp. 166, 181
al-Maqrīzī: 13, 44, 45, 51, 128-136
Mar Ḥnānišo', Synod of: 109
Mar Yahbalāhā, catholicos of the East, see Yahbalāhā
Mar Yahbalāhā and Rabban Ṣawmā, *History* of, see Yahbalāhā
Mardin: 70, 72
Maria, daughter of Manuel I Comnenus: 180
Maria, daughter of Raymond de Poitiers: 165, 166, 211
Marina, Saint: 270, 271
Mark, Evangelist: 244
Maronites: 102
Marqab Castle: 267
Martin, Saint: 31
Matrona, Greek nun: 46
Matthew Paris: 108
Mecca: 142, 154-157, 160, 226
Melisende, daughter of Baldwin II: 24, 27-32
Melisende of Tripoli: 165-220, esp. 171, 181 s
Melitene: 70, 72, 73
Menas, Saint: 276
Mendicants: 64
Mercurius, Saint: 247, 275, 276
mercury: 226
Methodius, Saint: 86
Metsop'eci, Step'anos and Nerses, *History of the First Invasion by Lank-T'amur*: 89
Michael, Archangel: 235, 238
Michael Palaiologos, Byzantine emperor: 49, 114

Michael bar Šūmōnō: 65, 71
Michael Syrus, Jacobite patriarch of Antioch (Michael the Great), *Chronicle*: 53-76, 148
military orders, see also Hospitallers, Templars, Teutonic Order: 30, 53-76,
monetary history: 223-234
money-changers: 224
Mongols: 35, 40, 41, 46, 47, 104 s, 107, 108, 120, 229
Montgisard, battle of: 56, 62
Montréal Shobak: see Shobak
Mōr Barṣawmō, monastery of: 65, 72-74
Morphia, wife of Baldwin II: 24
Mosul: 154
— monastery of Mar Mattai, near: 73, 247, 248
Mount Hermon: 201
Movses, Armenian catholicos: 89
Movses Khorenac'i, *History of the Armenians*: 96
al-Mu'aẓẓam, Ayyubid lord of Jerusalem: 38
Mufaḍḍal Ibn Abī Faḍā'il, chronicler: 42-46, 50
Mu'in ad-Dīn: 156
Mu'izz: 156
Mytilene: 276, 280-281

N

Nablus: 28, 30, 156, 161, 167, 178, 186, 187
an-Nāṣir Muḥammad, sultan: 45, 46, 49
Nathaniel: 191
Nazareth: 167, 191, 209
Neapolis, see Nablus
Nebk, monastery of Mar Musa al-Habashi near: 268-270, 272, 276, 280
Nero, Roman emperor: 91
Nerses, Saint: 84, 86
Nestorians, see East Syrians
Nestorius: 113
Nicaea: 143, 166, 176, 177
— Council of: 96
Nicene Creed: 96
Nicetas Choniates: 26

Nicolas IV, Pope: 112, 113
Nicolas, Saint: 83
Nicolas, Saint, Georgian: 46
Nikolaos, *hegoumenos* of Mar Saba: 39
Nisibis: 83, 94, 104, 109
Norbert of Xanten, *Life* of: 21, 22, 30, 32
Normans: 24, 25, 27, 165
Nursing Father, the concept of: 242-246, 254
an-Nuwayrī al-Iskandarānī: 123-136

O

Oliver von Paderborn: 105, 107
Öljeitü, ilkhan: 46
origines gentium: 8 s
Otto IV, German emperor: 148
Otto of Freising: 86

P

Palermo, Palatine Chapel: 269
Paphos: 168, 209
Paris, Sainte Chapelle: 120
Paul, Apostle, Saint: 83, 109, 151
pearls: 223, 233
Pentecost: 267
pepper: 226
Peter I of Lusignan, king of Cyprus and Jerusalem: 123-136
Peter, Apostle, Saint: 83, 116, 189
Peter of Beth Garmai: 105
Peter of Lucedio: 17
Philadelphus, king: 98
Philip, Dominican prior: 108
Philip, king of Armenia: 67
Photius, patriarch, *Genealogy*: 81, 86
Prémontré, abbey and Order of: 21-33
Presentation in the Temple: 267, 270
Prester John: 106
Procession of the Holy Spirit: 14
Procopius: 168, 178
Psellos: 171
Pseudo-Aristotelian: 80
Pseudo-Isidore, *The Decrees*: 80
Pseudo-Nicean canones: 109
Pseudo-Pythagorean: 80
Ptolemaïs, see Acre

Ptolemy: 98
Pythagoras, Pythagoreans: 98, see also Pseudo-Phythagorean

Q

Qadisha Valley: 267
Qalamoun, church of Mar Marina, near: 269, 270, 276
Qara
— church of SS Sergius and Bacchus: 268, 269, 272, 276
— Deir Mar Ya'qub, near Qara: 268, 269
Qlaudia: 70, 72
qnomē: 110, 112, 118, 119
Quarantena: 144, 145

R

Rabban Ata, see also Simeon, monk: 105-107, 109, 119
Rabban Ṣawmā, visitor general: 104, 112, 113, 119, 120
Rafael, Archangel: 235, 238
Rainerius Pisanus: 147, 149
Raymond III, count of Tripoli: 165
Raymond Bequin, Latin patriarch of Jerusalem: 107
Raymond of Poitiers, ruler of Antioch: 23, 32, 33, 166
Red Sea
— monastery of St Antony: 235-264 passim
— monastery of St Paul: 251
Reformation: 81
Reynald of Châtillon: 56
Rhipsime, Saint: 93
Rhodes, island of: 123, 125, 129
Riccoldo da Monte Croce: 113
rice: 226
Richard of Cornwall: 148
Richard Lionheart: 56, 106, 157, 161
Roger II, king of Sicily: 24, 25, 27, 33
Roman Church, Rome: passim, esp. 69, 79-99, 245, 246
— supremacy of: 15, 48, 79-99, 109, 116
Romanesque: 246
Rorgo Fretellus: 140
Rusudan, Georgian queen: 40

S

Sabas, St, monastery of, in Palestine: 149, see also Jerusalem
Sabrišoʿ V, East Syrian Catholicos: 105, 108, 109
Saewulf: 141
saffron: 226
Sahak, Saint, vision of: 86
Saint-Denis (France): 120
Sala, priest: 18
Saladin: 13, 16, 17, 35, 37-39, 57, 155, 157, 161
Ṣalībā bar Yuḥannā al-Mawṣilī
— *Book of Dates*: 103
— *Book of History*: 103
— *Books of the Mysteries*: 103, 105, 107, 110, 111, 117, 118
— *Treatise of Demonstration and Guidance*: 103, 117
Samaria, see Sichum
Samosata: 70
Samuel, St, church of: 30
Samuel Kamrjadzorec'i, *Apologetic Epistle*: 96
Saqqara: 250
— monastery of Apa Jeremiah: 240
Saracens: passim
Sardinia: 226
Sava of Serbia, Saint: 39
Ṣawmā, monk, see Rabban Ṣawmā
Saydnaya: 151, 152, 268
al-Šayzārī: 224
Schildberger, Hans: 93
Sebaste: 143, 178
Segestan, bishop of: 63, 74
Seleucia: 67
Ser Bartolo, see Bartolo
Sergius, Saint: 265-281
Severus of Antioch: 245
Severus bar al-Muqaffaʿ, Coptic theologian: 111
Shobak (Montréal): 152, 153, 160
Sichem: 160, 166, 178, 179, 181
Sicily, see also Roger II: 2, 32, 165, 173, 227, 228
Sidon: 30, 167, 177
Sigebert de Gembloux: 21, 32
silver, coins: 224-234
Silvester, Saint, and *Vita*: 79-99
Simeon, monk, also called Rabban Ata: 108-110
Sinai, monastery of St Catherine: 38, 145, 146, 152, 153, 247, 270, 271, 275, 277, 279
Sisinnios, Saint: 273, 276
Socrates, *Ecclesiastical History*: 95
Sophronios III, Greek patriarch of Jerusalem: 46
Sozomenos: 94
spices: 223, 225-227
Staraja Ladoga, church of St George: 279
Sufi convents: 41, 45
sugar: 226, 227
Suriani, see Syrians
Suriel, Archangel: 238
Suves, church of the Forty Martyrs: 279
Syce: 168, 170
Sylvester, see Silvester
Symeon II, patriarch of Jerusalem: 1, 4
Synaxar, Georgian: 41, 46
Syria, Syrians, Syrian Orthodox: passim, esp. 3-5, 53-76, 241, 246-248, 269; see also East Syrians, West Syrians
Syriac language: passim, esp. 7, 16, 53-76, 95, 269, 271

T

Tabriz: 108
Tʿamar, queen of Georgia: 37-39
Tankiz, governor of Syria: 46
Tarsus: 107
Tartus (Tortosa): 267
Tell Basher: 143
Templars: 54-76, 145, 148, 157, 160, 273
Teutonic Order: 46, 143
Theodericus, German pilgrim: 141, 143-145
Theodor bar Wahbūn: 64
Theodore, Coptic painter: 247
Theodore the Oriental, Saint: 276
Theodoros Prodromos: 183, 198
Theodoros Stratelates, Saint (the General): 247, 249, 265-281
Theophanes: 170

Theophanes Continuatus: 86
Theophrastes: 99
Thietmar, magister: 141, 152, 153, 155, 159, 161
Thoros, prince of Armenia: 56
Timothy I, patriarch: 109
Timothy, metropolitan of Tarsus: 107, 148
Torcello, Dome: 270
Torgomians (Armenians): 85
Tortosa: see Tartus
Tractatus de locis et statu sancte terre: 4-19
Trdat I, Armenian king: 79-99
Trimythous: 168, 208, 209
Tripoli, County of: 27, 28, 105, 106, 143, 148, 165, 166, 168-170, 211, 217, 224, 229-234, 267, 272: see also Raymond III
Trojans: 9
True Cross, relic of the: 24, 36, 38, 83, 187
Turbessel, see Tell Basher
Tyre: 4, 10, 147, 154, 158-161, 163, 166, 167, 177, 193, 224
Tzetzes: 184

U
Union: passim, esp. 79-99
unitas et concordia: 79-99
unleavened bread, see azymes
Urban II, Pope: 1, 12
Urban VIII, Pope: 89
Uriel, Archangel: 238
Usāma ibn Munqid: 3, 155-158, 160

V
Valence: 231

Venice, Venetians: 125, 129, 131, 147, 225, 233, 265, 273
Victor, Saint: 276
Vincent de Beauvais: 26, 31, 33, 108
Virgin Enthroned: 249
Virgin Hodegetria: 241, 271
Virgin Lactans (Nursing Virgin, Virgin Galaktotrophousa): 235-252

W
Wadi Natrun, Deir al-Surian: 247, 248
— Church of al-ʿAdra: 275
Wernigerode: 161
West Syrians: passim, esp. 4, 6, 102; see also Syrians and Jacobites
Wilbrand von Oldenburg: 141, 148
William of Malmesbury: 12
William de Monteferrato O.P., Dominican friar: 108
William of Tyre, Latin archbishop of Tyre: 5, 6, 8-10, 23, 28-30, 32, 64, 165, 212, 223

Y
Yahbalāhā III, Mongol patriarch-catholicos of the Church of the East: 104, 105, 112, 113-117
Yalbuġa l-Ḫāṣṣakī, Egyptian commander of the army: 127, 130

Z
zāwiya, see Sufi convents
Zayn ad-Dīn Abu l-Barakāt Muḥammad b. Aḥmad Ibn Iyās al-Ḥanafī: 130-131

INDEX OF MANUSCRIPTS

BERLIN, Deutsche Staatsbibliothek, Phillipps 1880: 23

BIRMINGHAM, Mingana Syriac 491: 101

BRUSSELS, Bibliothèque Royale, II 2544: 260

CAIRO, National Library, 1584: 127

JERUSALEM, Greek Orthodox Patriarchate, Sabas 144: 46

LONDON, British Library
— Add. 2889: 103
— Oriental 6782: 257
— 7170, Syriac Lectionary: 247, 261

MUNICH, Clm. 14473: 278

NEW YORK, Pierpont Morgan Library
— 603: 256
— 612: 251, 257
— 613: 276

PARIS, Bibliothèque Nationale
— Ar. 204: 103
— Ar. 6744: 112, 118
— Copte-Arabe 1 / Cairo, Bibl. 94: 248
— Fr. 22495: 280
— Lat. 5011: 23

VATICAN CITY
— Ar. 110 (olim MS scand 41): 110
— Ar. 180 (olim 49): 111
— Copt. 66: 276
— Gr. 1881: 166

VENICE, Marcianus 524: 166

YEREVAN, Mashtots' Matenadaran
— Arm. 516: 79
— Arm. 1520: 79
— Arm. 1920: 79
— Arm. 1930: 80
— Arm. 2272: 79 s.
— Arm. 3078: 79

ORIENTALIA LOVANIENSIA
ANALECTA

1. E. Lipiński, Studies in Aramaic Inscriptions and Onomastics I.
2. J. Quaegebeur, Le dieu égyptien Shaï dans la religion et l'onomastique.
3. P.H.L. Eggermont, Alexander's Campaigns in Sind and Baluchistan and the Siege of the Brahmin Town of Harmatelia.
4. W.M. Callewaert, The Sarvāṅgī of the Dādūpanthī Rajab.
5. E. Lipiński (ed.), State and Temple Economy in the Ancient Near East I.
6. E. Lipiński (ed.), State and Temple Economy in the Ancient Near East II.
7. M.-C. De Graeve, The Ships of the Ancient Near East (c. 2000-500 B.C.).
8. W.M. Callewaert (ed.), Early Hindī Devotional Literature in Current Research.
9. F.L. Damen, Crisis and Religious Renewal in the Brahmo Samaj Movement (1860-1884).
10. R.Y. Ebied - A. Van Roey - L.R. Wickham, Peter of Callinicum, Anti-Tritheist Dossier.
11. A. Rammant-Peeters, Les pyramidions égyptiens du Nouvel Empire.
12. S. Scheers (ed.), Studia Paulo Naster Oblata I. Numismatica Antiqua.
13. J. Quaegebeur (ed.), Studia Paulo Naster Oblata II. Orientalia Antiqua.
14. E. Platti, Yaḥyā ibn ʿAdī, théologien chrétien et philosophe arabe.
15. E. Gubel - E. Lipiński - B. Servais-Soyez (eds.), Studia Phoenicia I-II.
16. W. Skalmowski - A. Van Tongerloo (ed.), Middle Iranian Studies.
17. M. van Mol, Handboek Modern Arabisch.
18. C. Laga - J.A. Munitiz - L. Van Rompay (eds.), After Chalcedon. Studies in Theology and Church History.
19. E. Lipiński (ed.), The Land of Israel: Cross-Roads of Civilizations.
20. S. Wachsmann, Aegeans in the Theban Tombs.
21. K. Van Lerberghe, Old Babylonian Legal and Administrative Texts from Philadelphia.
22. E. Lipiński (ed.), Phoenicia and the East Mediterranean in the First Millennium B.C.
23. M. Heltzer - E. Lipiński (eds.), Society and Economy in the Eastern Mediterranean (1500-1000 B.C.).
24. M. Van De Mieroop, Crafts in the Early Isin Period.
25. G. Pollet (ed.), India and the Ancient World.
26. E. Lipiński (ed.), Carthago.
27. E. Verreet, Modi Ugaritici.
28. R. Zadok, The Pre-Hellenistic Israelite Anthroponomy and Prosopography.
29. W. Callewaert - M. Lath, The Hindī Songs of Nāmdev.
30. A. Shisha-Halevy, Coptic Grammatical Chrestomathy.
31. N. Baum, Arbres et arbustes de l'Égypte ancienne.
32. J.-M. Kruchten, Les Annales des prêtres de Karnak.
33. H. Devijver - E. Lipiński (eds.), Punic Wars.
34. E. Vassilika, Ptolemaic Philae.
35. A. Ghaith, La Pensée Religieuse chez Ǧubrân Ḫalil Ǧubrân et Miḫâʾîl Nuʿayma.
36. N. Beaux, Le Cabinet de curiosités de Thoutmosis III.
37. G. Pollet - P. Eggermont - G. Van Damme, Archaeological Sites of Ancient India.
38. S.-A. Naguib, Le Clergé féminin d'Amon thébain à la 21e dynastie.
39. U. Verhoeven - E. Graefe (eds.), Religion und Philosophie im Alten Ägypten.
40. A.R. George, Babylonian Topographical Texts.
41. A. Schoors, The Preacher Sought to Find Pleasing Words.
42. G. Reinink - H.E.J. Van Stiphout (eds.), Dispute Poems and Dialogues in the Ancient and Mediaeval Near East.

43. C. Traunecker, Coptos. Hommes et dieux sur le parvis de Geb.
44. E. Lipiński (ed.), Phoenicia and the Bible.
45. L. Isebaert (ed.), Studia Etymologica Indoeuropaea Memoriae A.J. Van Windekens dicata.
46. F. Briquel-Chatonnet, Les relations entre les cités de la côte phénicienne et les royaumes d'Israël et de Juda.
47. W.J. van Bekkum, A Hebrew Alexander Romance according to MS London, Jews' College no. 145.
48. W. Skalmowski - A. Van Tongerloo (eds.), Medioiranica.
49. L. Lauwers, Igor'-Severjanin, His Life and Work — The Formal Aspects of His Poetry.
50. R.L. Vos, The Apis Embalming Ritual. P. Vindob. 3873.
51. Fr. Labrique, Stylistique et Théologie à Edfou. Le rituel de l'offrande de la campagne: étude de la composition.
52. F. De Jong (ed.), Miscellanea Arabica et Islamica.
53. G. Breyer, Etruskisches Sprachgut im Lateinischen unter Ausschluß des spezifisch onomastischen Bereiches.
54. P.H.L. Eggermont, Alexander's Campaign in Southern Punjab.
55. J. Quaegebeur (ed.), Ritual and Sacrifice in the Ancient Near East.
56. A. Van Roey - P. Allen, Monophysite Texts of the Sixth Century.
57. E. Lipiński, Studies in Aramaic Inscriptions and Onomastics II.
58. F.R. Herbin, Le livre de parcourir l'éternité.
59. K. Geus, Prosopographie der literarisch bezeugten Karthager.
60. A. Schoors - P. Van Deun (eds.), Philohistor. Miscellanea in honorem Caroli Laga septuagenarii.
61. M. Krause - S. Giversen - P. Nagel (eds.), Coptology. Past, Present and Future. Studies in Honour of R. Kasser.
62. C. Leitz, Altägyptische Sternuhren.
63. J.J. Clère, Les Chauves d'Hathor.
64. E. Lipiński, Dieux et déesses de l'univers phénicien et punique.
65. K. Van Lerberghe - A. Schoors (eds.), Immigration and Emigration within the Ancient Near East. Festschrift E. Lipiński.
66. G. Pollet (ed.), Indian Epic Values. *Rāmāyaṇa* and its impact.
67. D. De Smet, La quiétude de l'Intellect. Néoplatonisme et gnose ismaélienne dans l'œuvre de Ḥamîd ad-Dîn al-Kirmânî (X[e]-XIe s.).
68. M.L. Folmer, The Aramaic Language in the Achaemenid Period. A Study in Linguistic Variation.
69. S. Ikram, Choice Cuts: Meat Production in Ancient Egypt.
70. H. Willems, The Coffin of Heqata (Cairo JdE 36418). A Case Study of Egyptian Funerary Culture of the Early Middle Kingdom.
71. C. Eder, Die Ägyptischen Motive in der Glyptik des Östlichen Mittelmeerraumes zu Anfang des 2. Jts. v. Chr.
72. J. Thiry, Le Sahara libyen dans l'Afrique du Nord médiévale.
73. U. Vermeulen - D. De Smet (eds.), Egypt and Syria in the Fatimid, Ayyubid and Mamluk Eras. Proceedings of the 1st, 2nd and 3rd International Colloquium organized at the Katholieke Universiteit Leuven in May 1992, 1993 and 1994.
74. P. Arènes, La déesse Sgrol-Ma (Tara). Recherches sur la nature et le statut d'une divinité du bouddhisme tibétain.
75. K. Ciggaar - A. Davids - H. Teule (eds.), East and West in the Crusader States. Context - Contacts - Confrontations. Acta of the Congress Held at Hernen Castle in May 1993.
76. M. Broze, Mythe et Roman en Egypte ancienne. Les Aventures d'Horus et Seth dans le papyrus Chester Beatty I.
77. L. Depuydt, Civil Calendar and Lunar Calendar in Ancient Egypt.
78. P. Wilson, A Ptolemaic Lexikon. A Lexicographical Study of the Texts in the Temple of Edfu.
79. A. Hasnawi - A. Elamrani - M. Jamal - M. Aouad (eds.), Perspectives arabes et médiévales sur le tradition scientifique et philosophique grecque.

80. E. Lipiński, Semitic Languages: Outline of a Comparative Grammar.
81. S. Cauville, Dendara I. Traduction.
82. C. Eyre (ed.), Proceedings of the Seventh International Congress of Egyptologists.
83. U. Vermeulen - D. De Smet (eds.), Egypt and Syria in the Fatimid, Ayyubid and Mamluk Eras II.
84-85. W. Clarysse - A. Schoors - H. Willems (eds.), Egyptian Religion. The Last Thousand Years.
86. U. Vermeulen - J.M. Van Reeth (eds.), Law, Christianity and Modernism in Islamic Society.
87. D. De Smet - U. Vermeulen (eds.), Philosophy and Acts in the Islamic World Proceedings of the Eighteenth Congress of the Union européenne des Arabisants et Islamisants held at the Katholieke Universiteit Leuven.
88. S. Cauville, Dendara II. Traduction.
89. G.J. Reinink - A.C. Klugkist (eds.), After Bardaisan. Studies on Continuity and Change in Syriac Christianity in Honour of Professor Han J.W. Drijvers.
90. C.R. Krahmalkov, Phoenician-Punic Dictionary.
91. M. Tahtah, Entre pragmatisme, réformisme et modernisme. Le rôle politico-religieux des Khattabi dans le Rif (Maroc) jusqu'à 1926.
92. K. Ciggaar - H. Teule (eds.), East and West in the Crusader States. Context — Contact — Confrontations II. Acta of the Congress held at Hernen Castle, the Netherlands, in May 1997.
93. A.C.J. Verheij, Bits, Bytes, and Binyanim. A Quantitative Study of Verbal Lexeme Formations in the Hebrew Bible.
94. W.M. Callewaert - D. Taillieu - F. Laleman, A Descriptive Bibliography of Allama Muhammad Iqbal (1877-1938).
95. S. Cauville, Dendara III. Traduction.
96. K. Van Lerberghe - G. Voet (eds.), Languages and Cultures in Contact: At the Crossroads of Civilizations in the Syro-Mesopotamian Realm.
97. A. Cabrol, Les voies processionnelles de Thèbes.
98. J. Patrich, The Sabaite Heritage in the Orthodox Church from the Fifth Century to the Present. Monastic Life, Liturgy, Theology, Literature, Art, Archaeology.
99. U. Verhoeven, Untersuchungen zur Späthieratischen Buchschrift.
100. E. Lipiński, The Aramaeans: Their Ancient History, Culture, Religion.
101. S. Cauville, Dendara IV. Traduction.
102. U. Vermeulen - J. Van Steenbergen (eds.), Egypt and Syria in the Fatimid, Ayyubid and Mamluk Eras.
103. H. Willems (ed.), Social Aspects of Funerary Culture in the Egyptian Old and Middle Kingdoms.
104. K. Geus - K. Zimmermann (eds.), Punica — Libyca — Ptolemaica. Festschrift für Werner Huß, zum 65. Geburtstag dargebracht von Schülern, Freunden und Kollegen.
105. S. Cauville, Dendara. Les fêtes d'Hathor.
106. R. Preys, Les complexes de la demeure du sistre et du trône de Rê. Théologie et décoration dans le temple d'Hathor à Dendera.
107. A. Blasius - B.U. Schipper (eds.), Apokalyptik und Ägypten. Eine kritische Analyse der relevanten Texte aus dem griechisch-römischen Ägypten.
108. S. Leder (ed.), Studies in Arabic and Islam.
109. A. Goddeeris, Economy and Society in Northern Babylonia in the Early Old Babylonian Period (ca. 2000-1800 BC).
110. C. Leitz (Ed.), Lexikon der ägyptischen Götter und Götterbezeichnungen, Band I.
111. C. Leitz (Ed.), Lexikon der ägyptischen Götter und Götterbezeichnungen, Band II.
112. C. Leitz (Ed.), Lexikon der ägyptischen Götter und Götterbezeichnungen, Band III.

113. C. Leitz (Ed.), Lexikon der ägyptischen Götter und Götterbezeichnungen, Band IV.
114. C. Leitz (Ed.), Lexikon der ägyptischen Götter und Götterbezeichnungen, Band V.
115. C. Leitz (Ed.), Lexikon der ägyptischen Götter und Götterbezeichnungen, Band VI.
116. C. Leitz (Ed.), Lexikon der ägyptischen Götter und Götterbezeichnungen, Band VII.
117. M. Van Mol, Variation in Modern Standard Arabic in Radio News Broadcasts.
118. M.F.J. Baasten - W.Th Van Peursen (Eds.), Hamlet on a Hill. Semitic and Greek Studies Presented to Professor T. Muraoka on the Occasion of his Sixty-Fifth Birthday.
119. O.E. Kaper, The Egyptian God Tutu. A Study of the Sphinx-God and Master of Demons with a Corpus of Monuments.
120. E. Wardini, Lebanese Place-Names (Mount Lebanon and North Lebanon).
121. J. Van der Vliet, Catalogue of the Coptic Inscriptions in the Sudan National Museum at Khartoum (I. Khartoum Copt).
122. A. Łajtar, Catalogue of the Greek Inscriptions in the Sudan National Museum at Khartoum (I. Khartoum Greek).
123. H. Niehr, Ba'alšamem. Studien zu Herkunft, Geschichte und Rezeptionsgeschichte eines phönizischen Gottes.
124. H. Willems - F. Coppens - M. De Meyer - P. Dils (Eds.), The Temple of Shanûr. Volume I : The Sanctuary, The *Wabet*, and the Gates of the Central Hall and the Great Vestibule (1-98).
125. K. Ciggaar - H.G.B. Teule (Eds.), East and West in the Crusader States. Context – Contacts – Confrontations III.